The theory of accommodation is concerned with motivations underlying and consequences arising from ways in which we adapt our language and communication patterns toward others. Since accomodation theory's emergence in the early 1970s, it has attracted empirical attention across many disciplines and had been elaborated and expanded many times.

In *Contexts of Accommodation,* accommodation theory is presented as a basis for sociolinguistic explanation, and it is the applied perspective that predominates this edited collection. The book seeks to demonstrate how the core concepts and relationships invoked by accommodation theory are available for addressing altogether pragmatic concerns. Accommodative processes can, for example, facilitate or impede language learners' proficiency in a second language as well as immigrants' acceptance into certain host communities, affect audience ratings and thereby the life of a television program, affect reaction to defendants in court and hence the nature of the judicial outcome, and be an enabling or detrimental force in allowing handicapped people to fulfill their communicative potential.

Contexts of Accommodation will appeal to researchers and advanced students in language and communication sciences, as well as to sociolinguists, anthropologists, and sociologists.

Howard Giles was Chair of Social Psychology at the University of Bristol before taking up a Professorship in Communication at the University of California, Santa Barbara. He has to his credit fifteen books and over two hundred articles and book chapters in the areas of social psychology of language, intercultural communication, and language attitudes, among other topics. His research has earned him a number of Paper Awards at Communication Association Meetings in the United States, as well as the British Psychological Society's Spearman Medal (1978) and the 1989 President's Award. He is the founding editor of the *Journal of Language and Social Psychology* and the *Journal of Asian Pacific Communication,* and he edits four book series in the social psychology of language, social psychology and society, and interdisciplinary communication studies.

Justine Coupland is lecturer in sociolinguistics at the University of Wales College of Cardiff, where she was Research Associate from 1985 to 1989. She has coauthored *Language Society and the Elderly* and coedited a journal special issue on *Sociolinguistic Issues in Ageing.* She has published articles in numerous journals, including *Language in Society, Language and Communication, Text, Discourse Processes, Textual Practice,* and the *Journal of Language and Social Psychology.*

Nikolas Coupland is Director of the Centre for Applied English Language Studies at the University of Wales College of Cardiff. For the session 1989/90 he was Fulbright Scholar and Visiting Associate Professor at the University of California, Santa Barbara. He is author of *Dialect in Use* and coauthor of *Language: Contexts and Consequences.* With colleagues he has edited four further books in sociolinguistics, dialectology, and communication.

Studies in Emotion and Social Interaction

Paul Ekman
University of California, San Francisco

Klaus R. Scherer
Université de Genève

General Editors

Contexts of accommodation

Studies in Emotion and Social Interaction

This series is jointly published by the Cambridge University Press and the Editions de la Maison des Sciences de l'Homme, as part of the joint publishing agreement established in 1977 between the Fondation de la Maison des Sciences de l'Homme and the Syndics of the Cambridge University Press.

Cette collection est publiée co-édition par Cambridge University Press et les Editions de la Maison des Sciences de l'Homme. Elle s'intègre dans le programme de co-édition établi en 1977 par la Fondation de la Maison des Sciences de l'Homme et les Syndics de Cambridge University Press.

Contexts of Accommodation
Developments in applied sociolinguistics

Edited by

Howard Giles
University of California, Santa Barbara

Justine Coupland
University of Wales College of Cardiff

Nikolas Coupland
University of Wales College of Cardiff

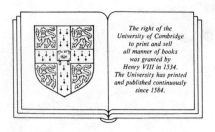

The right of the
University of Cambridge
to print and sell
all manner of books
was granted by
Henry VIII in 1534.
The University has printed
and published continuously
since 1584.

Cambridge University Press

Cambridge
New York   Port Chester   Melbourne   Sydney

Editions de la Maison des Sciences de l'Homme
Paris

Published by the Press Syndicate of the University of Cambridge
The Pitt Building, Trumpington Street, Cambridge CB2 1RP
40 West 20th Street, New York, NY 10011, USA
10 Stamford Road, Oakleigh, Melbourne 3166, Australia
and
Editions de la Maison des Sciences de l'Homme
54 Boulevard Raspail, 75270 Paris, Cedex 06

First published 1991

Printed in the United States of America

Library of Congress Cataloging-in-Publication Data
Contexts of accommodation : developments in applied sociolinguistics /
edited by Howard Giles, Justine Coupland, Nikolas Coupland.
p.   cm. – (Studies in emotion and social interaction)
Includes bibliographical references and index.
ISBN 0-521-36151-6
1. Sociolinguistics.   2. Adjustment (Psychology).   I. Giles,
Howard.   II. Coupland, Justine.   III. Coupland, Nikolas, 1950–   .
IV. Series.
P40.C57   1991
306.4'4 – dc20   91-24695
                                                                       CIP

British Library Cataloguing in Publication Data
Contexts of accommodation : developments in applied
sociolinguistics. – (Studies in emotion and social
interaction).
1. Sociolinguistics
I. Giles, Howard   II. Coupland, Justine   III. Coupland,
Nikolas   IV. Series
306.44

ISBN-0-521-36151-6 hardback
ISBN-2-7351-0409-5 hardback (France only)

Contents

vi   Contents

Contributors

Allan Bell
  Department of Linguistics
  Victoria University of Wellington, New Zealand

Richard Y. Bourhis
  Département de Psychologie
  Université du Québec à Montréal, Canada

Victor J. Callan
  Department of Psychology
  University of Queensland, St. Lucia, Australia

Justine Coupland
  Centre for Applied English Language Studies
  University of Wales College of Cardiff, UK

Nikolas Coupland
  Centre for Applied English Language Studies
  University of Wales College of Cardiff, UK

Kathleen Ferrara
  Department of English
  Texas A&M University, College Station, Texas, U.S.A.

Cynthia Gallois
  Department of Psychology
  University of Queensland, St. Lucia, Australia

Howard Giles
     Department of Communication
     University of California, Santa Barbara, California, U.S.A.

Heidi E. Hamilton
     Department of Linguistics
     Georgetown University, Washington, DC, U.S.A.

Per Linell
     Department of Communications Studies
     Linköping University, Linköping, Sweden

Richard L. Street, Jr.
     Department of Speech Communication
     Texas A&M University, College Station, Texas, U.S.A.

Jane Zuengler
     Department of English
     University of Wisconsin–Madison, Wisconsin, U.S.A.

1. Accommodation theory: Communication, context, and consequence

HOWARD GILES, NIKOLAS COUPLAND, AND JUSTINE COUPLAND

1.1. Introduction

When academic theorizing addresses everyday communication phenomena, there are losses as well as gains. Research may, selectively or otherwise, partially represent the full subtlety of contextualized interaction. Methodological constraints may impose their own selectivity, so that we tend to access the accessible and learn what is most readily learnable. The real-time nature of programmatic research will reflect epistemological shifts and disciplinary development. It is altogether likely that academic and lay versions of the phenomena themselves and their boundaries will not perfectly mirror each other at any one point.

On the other hand, research can discover regularities within communicative interchanges and identify, and perhaps even predict, contextual configurations that relate systematically to them. If it is amenable to methodological triangulation upon data and research questions, and if it incorporates within its own activities a mechanism for building cumulatively on empirical insights, communication research can begin to impose order on the uncertainty that interaction presents to us. More particularly, research that addresses the contexts as much as the behaviors of talk can tease out the ordering – motivational, strategic, behavioral, attributional, and evaluative – that interactants themselves impose upon their own communication experiences, and the ways in which the social practices of talk both are constrained by and themselves constrain goals, identities, and social structures.

In the case of "accommodation theory," the focus of the present collection, we have a research program that has developed over more than a dozen years, undergoing many extensions and elaborations, as an account of contextual processes impinging on sociolinguistic code, style,

1

and strategy selections. Our primary goal in this introductory chapter is in fact to trace the growth of accommodation theory from its origins as a strictly sociopsychological model of speech-style modifications to its current status as an integrated, interdisciplinary statement of relational processes in communicative interaction. Indeed, in the view of some commentators, it may even be considered the predominant theory at the interface between language, communication, and social psychology (Bradac, Hopper, and Wiemann 1989; Messick and Mackie 1989).

At one level, accommodation is to be seen as a multiply organized and contextually complex set of alternatives, ubiquitously available to communicators in face-to-face talk. It can function to index and achieve solidarity with or dissociation from a conversational partner reciprocally and dynamically. At another level, accommodation strategies can characterize wholesale realignments of patterns of code or language selection, although again related to constellations of underlying beliefs, attitudes, and sociostructural conditions. A noteworthy, and perhaps unique, characteristic of accommodation is precisely this openness to micro and macro contextual communicative concerns within a single theoretical and interpretive frame.

But there is necessarily some slippage between lay and academic formulations, and, indeed, variation across academic treatments of "accommodation" and related concepts. For some, the notion of cooperativity in talk is the defining essence of all communicative acts (cf. Grice 1975; Heritage 1987). Similarly, "interactional synchrony" (e.g., Erickson and Schulz 1982; Jasnow et al. 1988) is held to be universal, even in early life (Lieberman 1967; Street 1983). Terms that overlap with those we shall introduce in this chapter (accommodation, convergence, divergence) have likewise surfaced in other academic arenas (see, e.g., Abrahamson 1966; Bormann 1985; Kincaid 1988; Piaget 1955; Thibaut and Kelley 1959). A variety of related constructs can also be identified (e.g., Bauer 1964; Chapple 1939; Durkheim 1964; Flavell et al. 1968; Krauss and Glucksberg 1969; Le Page 1968; Mead 1934; Peng, 1974; Sacks 1987), as well as many contemporaries who examine some overlapping interpersonal influences in communication under one or other of the following rubrics: "listener adaptedness," "person-centered or other-related/directed speech," taking the role/perspective of another (e.g., Applegate and Delia 1980; Burleson 1987; Graumann and Hermann 1988; Isaacs and Clark 1987; McCann and Higgins 1990), and positive politeness (Brown and Levinson 1987).

All of these approaches have made inroads into what "being accommodative" may constitute and implicate linguistically and interactionally, though the single theoretical frame offered in the accommodation model is necessary to integrate and indeed distinguish different traditions.[1] There are many ways of performing acts we could deem to be accommodative, many reasons for doing or not doing so, and a wide range of specifiable outcomes. Sometimes there are beneficial outcomes to one or the other participant in talk, or both; the effects of accommodation can be altogether unexceptional and routine or, on the other hand, critical. For instance, speakers' ability to adapt their messages to take account of listeners' characteristics can induce good health habits among patients in health care establishments (Kline and Ceropski 1984), peer acceptance (Burleson 1986), and willingness in sharing (Burleson and Fennelly 1981) in childhood. But again, a more qualitative perspective exploring degrees and modes of accommodation will, as we shall see, permit more differentiated, and ultimately more deeply explanatory, interpretations in particular social contexts.

It is in fact the *applied* perspective that predominates in the following chapters and in accommodation theory as a whole. As the title of the volume implies, we present accommodation theory here less as a theoretical edifice and more as a basis for sociolinguistic explanation. The book as a whole seeks to demonstrate how the core concepts and relationships invoked by accommodation theory are available for addressing altogether pragmatic concerns – in particular, understanding relational alternatives, development, difficulties, and outcomes in medical, clinical, and caring settings; strategic options in legal discourse; the alignment of radio broadcasters with their audiences; processes of second-language learning and of acculturation in an interethnic context; and language switching in organizational settings in a bilingual community. We will see that accommodative processes can, for example, facilitate or impede language learners' proficiency in a second language, as well as immigrants' acceptance by certain host communities; affect audience ratings and thereby the life of a program and its contributors' viability; influence job satisfaction and hence productivity; affect reactions to defendants in court and hence the nature of the judicial outcome; affect

[1] A thorough critical comparison of past and contemporary theoretics is not yet available, although Street and Giles (1982) provide a critical comparison of some earlier models [namely, Webb's (1972) adaptation of the activation-level model, Natale's (1975a) communication model, and Cappella's (1981) adaptation of discrepancy arousal (see also Cappella and Greene 1982)]. Such a task is beyond the limits of the present chapter, and in any case, we would now construe other positions as holding, in the main, complementary accounts of *some* phenomena.

satisfaction with medical encounters and thereafter compliance with certain crucial regimens; and be an enabling or a detrimental force in allowing handicapped people to fulfill their communicative and life potentials. Although many subdisciplines of the language and communication sciences have, of course, paid sustained attention to these and similar social environments of talk, the accommodation model holds out the possibility of inferring underlying similarities in the relational options and tensions that render them researchable as key dimensions of our social lives.

In the primarily historical overview that follows in this chapter, it will be apparent that accommodation research has spanned several radically different methodological designs. Consistent with its sociopsychological origins and interests in motivational and evaluative trends, much of the earliest work was laboratory based and relatively insensitive to the descriptive linguistic dimensions of the varieties and speech styles it researched. In fact (see later), it was precisely to redress an insensitivity to social contextual variables in early (linguistically sophisticated) sociolinguistic research that the basic tenets of accommodation theory were developed. Today, however, we can point to an established history of fine-grained sociolinguistic and discourse analytic research explicitly within the model's limits, and the counterbalancing of experimentally controlled empirical efforts with observational studies in wide-ranging naturally occurring settings.

Our overview presents accommodation theory as a robust paradigm in the particular sense that it is, perhaps uniquely, able to attend to (1) social consequences (attitudinal, attributional, behavioral, and communicative), (2) ideological and macro-societal factors, (3) intergroup variables and processes, (4) discursive practices in naturalistic settings, and (5) individual life span and group-language shifts. As we shall see, the theory has attracted researchers from a wide range of disciplines and hence very broad levels of communicative and linguistic analysis, and has the potential for future application across a very wide range of media (see Bell, this volume), including writing [cf. the social and listener-oriented approaches of Fish (1980), Nystrand (1986), and Rafoth and Rubin (1987)], song (Prince, 1988; Trudgil 1983; Yaeger-Dror 1988), human–computer interaction (Leiser 1988), and doubtless many other media (e.g., telephonic, teleconferencing, electronic mail).

In the remainder of this chapter, then, we aim to update developments and ideas, as well as to lay out the parameters of "communication accommodation theory (CAT), "alluding to contributions made by authors in this volume as appropriate. This is an important quest not only in its own right but because the background is fundamental to appreciating the content of the chapters that follow. A reading of the chapters relies on a shared review of CAT that is provided here. Hence, we will review the origins of CAT together with its fundamental strategies and important conceptual distinctions. Then we will examine the motives underlying convergence and divergence as well as their social consequences, discussing the complexities and caveats necessary for considering these when grounded in particular contexts. Next, we will introduce a recent sociolinguistic elaboration of the theory, considering its implications for the health context. Finally, we will conclude with a brief overview of the significance of the subsequent chapters, assembling, as they do for the first time in this volume, analyses of communication accommodation in an array of crucial applied settings.

1.2. Basic concepts and strategies

Convergence and divergence

The first publications concerning "speech accommodation theory (SAT)" emerged in 1973. Giles (1973) demonstrated the phenomenon of interpersonal accent convergence in an interview situation and introduced his "accent mobility" model in the context of a critique of some aspects of the Labovian (1966) paradigm (see also Bell 1984). It was argued that the presumed role of formality-informality of context and the criterion of "attention to speech" that was seminally associated with the prestigiousness of speech styles by Labov could be reinterpreted, at least in part, as having been mediated by interpersonal accommodation processes. For example, casual speech may have been produced not so much because of the informality of the context but perhaps because the interviewer (equally prone to sociolinguistic forces) had shifted to less standard speech forms when the interview was supposedly over (i.e., the tape recorder was supposedly turned off) and when he introduced certain topics (e.g., being close to death, nursery rhymes). In other words, the supposition was that context formality-informality determining the prestigiousness of phonological variants could be supplanted by an interpretation in terms of interpersonal influence – the interviewee's convergence with the interviewer. At that time, "context" was the zeitgeist of sociolinguistic theory, and we wished to redirect theoretical attention to more focused contextual dimensions, including language itself (Smith,

Giles, and Hewstone 1980), and to argue the primacy of receiver characteristics over other considerations (Giles and Powesland 1975). More recently, and more elegantly, Krauss (1987: 96) argued that

> the addressee is a full participant in the formulation of the message – that is, the vehicle by which meaning is conveyed – and, indeed, may be regarded in a very real sense as the cause of the message. Without the addressee that particular message would not exist. But the message, in the concrete and particular form it takes, is as much attributable to the existence of the addressee as it is to the existence of the speaker.

This then was the legacy and blueprint for subsequent formulations addressing a wide variety of speech variables (Giles and Powesland 1975). To this end, Giles, Taylor, and Bourhis (1973) confirmed empirically some fundamental ideas inherent in what subsequently became labeled as SAT. In the bilingual context of Montreal at that time, they found that the more effort at convergence a speaker was perceived to have made (e.g., the more French that English Canadians used when sending a message to French Canadians), the more favorably that person was evaluated and the more listeners converged in return. Moreover, a plethora of convergent strategies was discovered even in what, for some, would be described as a socially sterile laboratory setting (see Bourhis, this volume, for further details). Since then, theoretical refinements have come in profusion (see Coupland and Giles 1988a for a catalog of these), particularly in the 1980s (namely Ball, Giles, and Hewstone 1985; Coupland et al. 1988; Gallois et al. 1988), and have intermeshed with significant empirical developments as well (e.g., Coupland and Giles 1988b; Giles 1984).

SAT focused in the pioneering years upon the social cognitive processes mediating individuals' perceptions of the environment and their speech styles as a foil to the omnipresent and determining role ascribed to norms in molding sociolinguistic behaviors. Its theoretical framework developed out of a wish, in those days, to demonstrate the value and potential of social psychological concepts and processes for understanding the dynamics of speech diversity in social settings. SAT therefore aimed to clarify the motivations underlying speech and intermeshed in it, as well as the constraints operating upon it and their social consequences. Specifically, it originated in order to elucidate the cognitive and affective processes underlying speech convergence and divergence, although other speech strategies (complementarity, over- and underaccommodation – see later) have more recently been recognized theoret-

Table 1. *Convergent features and selected source*

Features converged	Selected sources
Utterance length	Matarazzo et al. (1968)
Speech rate	Street (1983)
Information density	Aronsson et al. (1987)
Vocal intensity	Natale (1975a)
Pausing frequencies and lengths	Jaffe and Feldstein (1970)
Response latency	Cappella and Planalp (1981)
Self-disclosure	Ehrlich and Graeven (1971)
Jokes, expressing solidarity–opinions–orientations	Bales (1950)
Gesture	Mauer and Tindall (1983)
Head nodding and facial affect	Hale and Burgoon (1984)
Posture	Condon and Ogston (1967)

ically. As we shall see later in this chapter, SAT has been moving in a more interdisciplinary direction and the focus has broadened from exploring specific linguistic variables to encompass nonverbal (see von Raffler-Engel 1980; also Goodwin 1981; Grabowski-Gellert and Winterhoff-Spurk 1987) and discursive dimensions of social interaction; hence the wider notion of CAT (*communication* accommodation theory; Giles et al. 1987).

"Convergence" has been defined as a strategy whereby individuals adapt to each other's communicative behaviors in terms of a wide range of linguistic-prosodic-nonverbal features including speech rate, pausal phenomena and utterance length, phonological variants, smiling, gaze, and so on [cf. the notions of "congruence," "synchrony," and "reciprocity" in the work of Feldstein (1972), Argyle (1969), and Webb (1972), respectively]. Table 1 provides a sample of studies showing how widespread convergence has been shown to be, although not all studies listed were conceived and interpreted explicitly in a CAT perspective. Most of these studies were laboratory-controlled investigations, but many studies have also emerged showing convergence in naturally occurring contexts (Ray and Webb 1966), such as the demonstration of John Dean's convergence of median word frequencies (a measure of formality) to his different Senate interrogators in the Watergate trials (Levin and Lin 1988) and Coupland's (1984) fine-grained phonological analysis of a travel agent's convergence to her many clients of varying socioeconomic status and education. Although most studies have been conducted in the West and in English-language settings, convergence on temporal, phonological, or language-switching dimensions has been noted in many different languages, including Hungarian (Kontra and Gosy 1988), Frisian and Dutch (Gorter 1987; Ytsma 1988), Hebrew (Yaeger-Dror 1988), Taiwanese Mandarin (van den Berg 1986), Japanese (Welkowitz, Bond, and Feldstein 1984), Cantonese (Feldstein and Crown 1990), and Thai (Beebe 1981). Pertinently, Yum (1988) argues that East Asian communication is far more receiver centered than the more sender-oriented communications of the West, and Gudykunst, Yoon, and Nishida (1987) observe that members of collectivistic cultures (e.g., Japan and Korea) perceive their ingroup relationships to be more synchronized than those of individualistic societies (e.g., Australia and the United States). Hence future research may show more of the ubiquity of CAT phenomena and processes in the East (see, however, Bond 1985 for an implied cultural caveat) and perhaps elsewhere.

Although convergent communicative acts reduce interpersonal differences, interindividual variability in extent and frequency of convergence is, perhaps not surprisingly, also apparent, corresponding to sociodemographic variables such as age (Delia and Clark 1977; Garvey and BenDebba 1974; Welkowitz, Cariffe, and Feldstein 1976). (There is, however, some contradictory evidence in some of the relationships characterized later). Hence, it has been found that field dependents (individuals who found it difficult to disembed core perceptual features from their field) and those with strong interpersonal orientations converge on noncontent features of speech more than their opposite-trait partners [Welkowitz et al. (1972) and Murphy and Street (1987), respectively]; high self-monitors match the emotionality, intimacy, and content of their interactants' initial self-disclosure more than low self-monitors (Schaffer, Smith, and Tomarelli 1982); and extroverts as well as cognitively more complex communicators who are high on construct differentiation are more listener adaptive than introverts and low differentiators (Burleson 1984a; Hecht, Boster, and LaMer 1989; Kline in press). Obviously, other measures of cognitive and perceptual functioning, as well as those of social sensitivity [e.g., Paulhus and Martin's (1988) construct of functional flexibility], should provide positive relationships with convergence.

"Divergence" was the term used to refer to the way in which speakers accentuate speech and nonverbal differences between themselves and others. Bourhis and Giles (1977) designed an experiment to demonstrate the use of accent divergence among Welsh people in an interethnic context (as well as the conditions that would facilitate its occurrence). The study was conducted in a language laboratory where people who placed a strong value on their national group membership and its language were learning the Welsh language (only about 26 percent of Welsh persons at that time, as now, could speak their national tongue). During one of their weekly sessions, Welsh people were asked to help in a survey concerned with second-language learning techniques. The questions in the survey were presented verbally to them in English in their individual booths by a very English-sounding speaker, who at one point arrogantly challenged their reasons for learning what he called a "dying language with a dismal future." Such a question was assumed to threaten their feeling of ethnic identity, and the informants broadened their Welsh accents in their replies, compared with their answers to a previously asked emotionally neutral question. In addition, some informants introduced Welsh words and phrases into their answers, and one Welsh woman did not reply for a while and then was heard to conjugate a less than socially acceptable verb gently into the microphone. Interestingly, even when asked a neutral question beforehand, the informants emphasized their Welsh group membership to the speaker in terms of the content of their replies (so-called content differentiation). Indeed, it may well be that there is a hierarchy of divergent strategies available to speakers ranging from indexical and symbolic dissociation to explicit propositional nonalignment to physical absence (e.g., emphasis of a few ingroup stereotyped phonological features versus language switches, to abrasive humor, to verbal abuse and interactional dissolution; see also Segalowitz and Gatbonton 1977).

Language divergence was investigated by Bourhis et al. (1979). The study involved different groups of trilingual Flemish students (Flemish-English-French) being recorded in "neutral" and "ethnically threatening" encounters with a Francophone (Walloon) outgroup speaker. As in the previous study, the context of the interaction was a language laboratory where participants were attending classes to improve their English skills. Many Flemish and Francophone students converse together in English, as an emotionally neutral compromise (cf. Scotton 1979) between maintaining rigid differentiation and acquiescing to pressures to converse by using the other's language. In this experiment, the speaker spoke to students in English, although revealing himself as a Walloon by means of distinctive Francophone pronunciation. It was found that when the speaker demeaned the Flemish in his ethnically threatening question, listeners rated him as sounding more Francophone (a process termed "perceptual divergence") and themselves as feeling more Flemish. This cognitive dissociation was manifested behaviorally at a covert level by means of muttered or whispered disapproval while the Walloon was speaking (which was being tape-recorded, unknown to the informants) and at an overt level through divergent shifts to own-group language. However, this divergence occurred only under certain specific experimental conditions, and then for only 50 percent of the sample. It was found that these listeners diverged only when their own group membership and that of the speaker was emphasized by the investigator and when the speaker had been known from the outset to be hostile to Flemish ethnolinguistic goals. In a follow-up study, however, language divergence into Flemish did occur for nearly 100 percent of the informants under these same conditions, but only when the Walloon speaker himself diverged into French in his threatening question. Interestingly, the form of the language divergence in the first of these Belgian studies differed from that in the second. It was found that in the first setting, the ingroup initially replied to the outgroup threat in English – and then switched to Flemish. In the second (more threatening) setting, listeners replied in a directly divergent manner by an immediate shift to Flemish.

Linguistic divergence, like convergence, can take many forms, both verbal and nonverbal (LaFrance 1985). Scotton (1985) introduced the term "disaccommodation" to refer to those occasions when people switch registers in repeating something uttered by their partners – not in the sense of a "formulation" proferred as a comprehension check (Heritage and Watson (1980), but rather as a tactic to maintain integrity, distance, or identity when misunderstanding is not even conceivably an issue. For example, a young speaker might say, "Okay, mate, lets get it together at my place around 3:30 tomorrow," and receive the reply from a disdainful elder, "Fine, young man, we'll meet again, at 15:30, at your house tomorrow." Although keeping one's speech style and nonverbal behaviors congruent across situations may be construed as a communicative *nonevent* sociopsycholinguistically – and, indeed, there is a fair amount of stability in our speech and nonverbal patterns across many encounters (Cappella and Planalp 1981; Jaffe and Feldstein 1970; Patterson 1983) – Bourhis (1979) has pointed out how, in many interethnic contexts, "speech maintenance" is a valued (and possibly conscious and even effortful) act of maintaining one's group identity. Similarly at the level of personal identity, those individuals Hart, Carlson, and Eadie (1980) take to embody "Noble Selves" would be predicted to maintain their idiosyncratic speech and nonverbal characteristics across many situations. No-

Table 2. *Distinctions in characterizing convergence and divergence*

Upward versus downward
Full versus partial versus hyper-/crossover
Large versus moderate
Unimodal versus multimodal
Symmetrical versus asymmetrical
Subjective versus objective

ble Selves are those straightforward, spontaneous persons who see deviation from their assumed "real" selves as being against their principles and, thus, intolerable.

Some important distinctions

These basic convergent-divergent shifts are, of course, not as descriptively simple as they might at first appear. Table 2 outlines several of the principal distinctions that have been made at varying times in the accommodation literature; others will emerge later in the chapter.

Both convergence and divergence may be either upward or downward [see Giles and Powesland (1975) for schematizations of these in terms of accent shifts], where the former refers to a shift toward a consensually prestigious variety and the latter refers to modifications toward more stigmatized or less socially valued forms in context [e.g., nonstandard accent, low lexical diversity; see James (1989) for illustrations of native and nonnative speakers' use of these accommodative tactics in the language-learning context]. Adopting the prestigious dialect of an interviewer is an example of upward convergence, and shifting to street language in certain minority communities is an example of downward convergence (see Baugh 1983; Edwards 1986).

   Convergence on some features of language does not mean that speakers will converge all available variables and levels, and (see Ferrara this volume) Giles et al. (1987) made the distinction between unimodal and multimodal convergent-divergent shifts, where the latter term, of course, implies shifting in several dimensions. Beyond this, we should not conceive of convergence and divergence as necessarily mutually exclusive phenomena, since SAT does acknowledge the possibility that convergence of some features will be matched by simultaneous divergence of others. In this vein, Bilous and Krauss (1988), in their study of same- and mixed-sex interactions, showed that females converged to males on some dimensions (including total number of words uttered and interruptions) but diverged on others, such as laughter. Informal observations of bilingual switching in Montreal in the 1970s on occasion exemplified "mixed-accommodations" apparently motivated, such that French Canadian shoppers were known to address Anglophone store assistants in fluent English while requesting the services of a Francophone assistant instead; convergence was in code, but propositionally the message was one of dissociation.

The distinction between partial and full convergence has proved valuable for some methodological designs too (Street 1982). Thus, for example, a speaker initially exhibiting a rate of 50 words per minute can move to match exactly another speaker's rate of 100 words per minute (total) or can move to a rate of 75 words per minute (partial; and see the notion of "underaccommodation" later). In their study of lexical diversity accommodation, Bradac, Mulac, and House (1988) distinguish between full shifts (upward or downward) that are moderate or large (lexical diversity indexed shifts in this case of .92 to either .82 or .72, respectively).

Additionally, in any interaction, convergence and divergence can be symmetrical or asymmetrical. An example of mutual convergence can be found in an investigation by Mulac et al. (1988: 331), who reported that "in mixed-sex dyads, it appears that both genders adopted a linguistic style more like that of their out-group partner than they would have maintained with an in-group partner." Similarly, in Booth-Butterfield and Jordan's (1989) study of intra- and intercultural encounters between female students, blacks were rated as far more expressive in within-group encounters than whites when talking with their peers. However, blacks were rated as less expressive when conversing with whites than when talking with other black women, whereas whites became more communicatively expressive in mixed-racial than in same-racial encounters – both thereby converging, presumably, to outgroup norms.

An example of asymmetrical convergence can be found in White's (1989) study of American–Japanese interactions where convergence by one party was not reciprocated by the other. When speaking with other members of their culture, Japanese informants in this study produced far more backchannels of certain kinds (e.g., *mmhm, uh-huh*) than their American

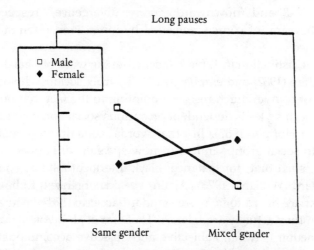

Figure 1. Frequency of long pauses by males and females in same- and mixed-gender dyads (from Bilous and Krauss, 1988, p. 188).

counterparts in within-culture situations. When it came to cross-cultural encounters, however, Americans used significantly more backchannels when speaking with Japanese (that is, they converged) who themselves did not significantly change but maintained their high level of backchanneling.

The possibility was raised (Giles 1971) that speakers can "overshoot" even in full convergence and "hyperconverge" [see Bradac et al. (1988) for social evaluations of hyperconvergence in lexical diversity]. Again, this can be accomplished asymmetrically (and see the later discussion of the notion of "overaccommodation") or symmetrically when both parties overshoot, with the latter being well illustrated by Bilous and Krauss (1988) in their analysis of (long) pauses in mixed-sex interactions (see Fig. 1); once again, presumably such hyperconvergences can be moderate or very large overshoots.

Relatedly, divergence of a sort may occur not only by simple dissociation away from the interlocutor toward an opposing reference group, but also by expressing sociolinguistically a greater identification with that other's reference group than others can display themselves. For example, when talking to an old school friend who is using a less prestigious code than you while chiding your apparent aloofness, you might adopt an even more basilectal code than he or she in order to show your greater identification with local values. Giles (1980) termed these strategies "upward" and "downward *crossover* divergence," respectively, although they are, of course, achieved by initial (and often substantial) convergence.

The final distinction in Table 2 arises from the work of Thakerar, Giles, and Cheshire (1982) and emphasizes CAT's truly sociopsychological core. There is, of course, much research pointing to the fact that our perception of speech styles is dependent on various social and cognitive biases (Street and Hopper 1982). In other words, sometimes stereotyped responses to social groups influence how speakers are apparently heard to sound, such that, for instance, black interlocutors may sound more nonstandard (Williams 1976). Again, speakers believed to be relatively competent are heard to be more standard-accented (Thakerar and Giles 1981) than they actually are. Hence, Thakerar et al. invoked the conceptual distinction between subjective and objective accommodation. The objective dimension refers to speakers' shifts in speech *independently measured* as moving toward (convergence) or away from (divergence) others, whereas the subjective dimension refers to speakers' *beliefs* regarding whether they or others are converging or diverging (see the discussion of Bell's New Zealand newscasters in this volume). Thakerar et al. found in a couple of studies that interlocutors shifted their speech styles (speech rate and segmental phonology, e.g., glottal stop in place of word-final /t/) toward where they believed their partners to be, irrespective of how they actually sounded. Hence, for instance, initially similar-sounding low- and high-status interactants were measured objectively as diverging from each other, although the low-status speaker was subjectively converging (toward the interlocutor's faster speech and more standard accent, stereotypically associated with a higher-status speaker) and the higher-status speaker was accomplishing precisely the converse (see also Zuengler this volume).

These processes may be responsible in part for the kinds of "behavioral confirmation" demonstrated by Snyder (1981). For instance, he showed that if males believed they were interacting with attractive (rather than unattractive) females over an intercom link, the latter sounded lively and outgoing (the known social stereotype of attractive women). Although no data on the sociolinguistics of behavioral confirmation apparently exist, it could well be that the males in this condition provided the vocal environment facilitating and even constructing these women's expressed affableness by converging to their presumed speech style in the first place; put another way, the women may have converged on objectively linguistic criteria to the males' stereotype-based conver-

Table 3. *Subjective and objective dimensions of speech accommodation*

		Subjective accommodation	
		Convergence	Divergence
Objective accommodation	Convergence	A	B
	Divergence	C	D

Source: After Thakerer et al. (1982).

gence. Interestingly, Cohen and Cooper (1986) described situations where sojourners in foreign climes actively converge over time toward the (often ill-conceived) convergent attempts of individuals from the host community toward them! Relatedly, Giles et al. (1987) argued that speakers not only converge to where they believe others to be, but also in some (as yet unspecified) conditions to where they believe others expect them to be. The notion of prototypicality (see later) is relevant here and in some role-relevant situations, people may gain kudos for "acting their age," using a professional line, and so forth. But we should be wary of considering prototypical sociolinguistic styles as unidimensional givens, as illustrated in Johnson's (1980) observation that physicians' adoption of "doctorspeak" not only involves highly specialized medical jargon but can also be intermeshed with very abstract, vague statements (which can increase patients' uncertainty levels about their medical status and consequently the physicians' social control). Finally here, speakers who might converge psychologically toward their interlocutors or audience may not have the sociolinguistic experience or repertoire to enable them to achieve their desired convergent effect, and they may compensate by converging linguistically and nonverbally along some alternative dimension. Seltig (1985) provided a compelling instance of this with respect to a radio interviewer with an Aachen dialect interviewing standard dialect German speakers with a Ruhr dialect audience. When the interviewer wished to dissociate from her expert interviewee and side with her local audience, the only linguistic resource available to her to signal this was to converge on her colloquial Aachen-like features.

But to return full circle, and as Table 3 indicates in Cells A and D, speakers' beliefs about where they are shifting are often enough in accord with objective sociolinguistic realities; in other words, they get it right. However, even when speakers are actually "on target," misattributions can still be potentially rife, as in Cell C. Giles and Bourhis (1976) found evidence that black West Indian immigrants in a British city thought they were converging toward white local speech norms – actually the working-class variety of the neighborhood – and did in fact (as an evaluative phase of the study showed) sound indistinguishable from local whites. Yet, whites did not interpret blacks as sounding convergent, but rather dissociatively heard them as moving toward a speech style – the same nonstandard urban dialect – from which the whites were trying to rid themselves. In a very different cultural setting, Beebe (1981) found that Chinese Thai bilingual children used Chinese phonological features when being interviewed by an (objectively) standard Thai speaker who looked ethnically Chinese – another instance arguably of miscarried convergence that amounted to actual divergence. Similarly, some Singaporeans' and Australian immigrants' attempts – lexically, grammatically, and prosodically – to match "upwardly" the speech of native English speakers may miscarry; and in other cases, native English speakers mismanage their downward convergent attempts toward what they believe Singaporeans and aborigines sound like (Platt and Weber 1984).

From these examples (we have no empirical illustrations as yet of the kind of feasible mismatches implied in Cell B), it can be argued that accommodation is often cognitively mediated by our stereotypes of how socially categorized others will speak (Hewstone and Giles 1986). Moreover, foreigners' talk (see Zuengler this volume) and talk to young children (Greenbaum and Cooper 1988) can be construed as exemplars of this (see DePaulo and Coleman 1986). A gerontological demonstration of the same general phenomena (albeit not discussed in accommodation terms) is reported by Caporael and associates (e.g., Caporael 1981; Caporael, Lukaszewski, and Culbertson 1983), who found that some nurses used baby talk to some groups of institutionalized elderly, irrespective of the latter's actual capabilities. In some cases, this was obviously mismatched, as elderly recipients who had functional autonomy resented, of course, the social meanings implied in the nature of the discourse and found it demeaning and irritating [see also Coupland, Giles, and Benn (1986) for a discussion of similar processes operating with the visually impaired]. The chapter in this volume by Hamilton vividly illustrates how such mismatched, stereotyped-based accommodation can create dysfunctional communicative environments for the handicapped, constraining successful adaptation. Returning to the Caporeal et al. (1983) study, it is significant, however, that other elderly recipients, whose competencies were far lower, found the baby talk strategy nurturant and reacted to it favorably (see also Ryan and Cole 1990). Hence such linguistic devices can sometimes be "hits" in both senses of the term. Interestingly, we have data that show not only Cell C behavior (since divergence can be achieved through hyperconvergence, as discussed earlier) with respect to the socially mobile, cognitively active, noninstitutionalized elderly (Coupland et al. 1988), but also strategically different (but evaluatively equivalent) forms of it occurring. This overaccommodation to elderly communicators can, moreover, be witnessed even when *avoidance* of such tactics has been vigorously and normatively prescribed, for example, in the training regimes of home-care assistants (Atkinson and Coupland 1988).

Gallois and Callan (1988) developed the notion of stereotypically driven accommodation further by invoking Turner's (1987) notion of prototypicality. These scholars developed an index for measuring the extent to which Australians (including recent immigrants) accommodated the nonverbal prototype of what it was to be an Anglo-Australian. Indeed, they found that prototypicality indexes were much better predictors of raters' social evaluations of these individuals than their actual or even perceived behaviors. Interestingly, those who accommodated the prototype well received moderately favorable ratings on a solidarity factor (i.e., nonaggressive, good, kind, and friendly) by listener-judges, whereas those further away from the prototype were downgraded. That said, those who were different from the prototype but in a socially desirable manner (i.e., smiled and gazed more and had softer voices) were judged most positively. It is as if new members to a community get first-base support for their movement toward the group prototype as an indication of their willingness to adopt group attributes, but there is additional room for positive evaluation if the person can assume other societally valued speech habits. In sum, then, people use whatever resources are available to them in terms of accommodating to another (see Prince 1988), and the actual focus of such movements may not be the addressees' communicative styles themselves. We believe that prototypicality is likely to be just as important an issue in the process of (linguistic) self-stereotyping in the context of *divergent* acts as it is in convergent acts.

1.3. Accommodative motives and consequences

In this section, we discuss the basic motives that have been demonstrated or inferred to hold for convergence and (the lesser studied) divergence, and the complex ways they function psychologically.

Convergence and integration

CAT proposes that speech convergence reflects, in the unmarked case, a speakers' or a group's need (often unconscious) for social integration or identification with another. In the early days of its development, the theory relied heavily on notions of similarity attraction (Byrne 1971), which, in its simplest form, suggests that as one person becomes more similar to another, this increases the likelihood that the second will like the first. Thus, convergence through speech and nonverbal behaviors is one of the many strategies that may be adopted to become more similar to another, involving the reduction of linguistic dissimilarities. Thus, for example, Welkowitz and Feldstein (1969, 1970) reported that dyadic participants who perceived themselves to be similar in terms of attitudes and personality converged pause duration patterns more than those who perceived dissimilarities. Also, Welkowitz et al. (1972) found that dyadic participants who perceived themselves to be similar converged vocal intensity more than informants who were randomly paired. Hence, those who believed themselves to be similar coordinated and influenced one another's speech patterns and timing more than other dyads, presumably because perceived similarity induces a more positive orientation and a relatively high level of interpersonal certainty.

Increasing behavioral similarity along a dimension as salient as speech is likely to increase a speaker's attractiveness (Dabbs 1969; Feldstein and Welkowitz 1978), predictability and perceived supportiveness (Berger and Bradac 1982), intelligibility (Triandis 1960), and interpersonal involvement (LaFrance 1979) in the eyes of the recipient. Moreover, Buller and Aune (1988) found that slow- and fast-speaking informants who were addressed at their own rates of talking by a target male rated him as more "immediate" [i.e., as having nonverbal patterns indicative of closeness; see Weiner and Mehrabian (1968)] and as more intimate; they were also more likely to comply with his request for volunteered assistance than when appealed to by speakers with nonaccommodated rates. From these findings, then, although largely by inference from studies of adjudged effects, convergence may plausibly be considered a reflection of an individuals' desire for social approval: If people are cognizant of (and/or have experienced in the past) positive cognitive, affective, and behavioral outcomes from convergence, then this is sufficient grounds for us to consider that an approval motive may often trigger it (see Sunnafrank 1986). In this way, Purcell (1984) observed that Hawaiian children's convergent shifts in prosodic and lexicogrammatical features depended on the likeability of the particular peers present when talking together in small groups; and Putman and Street (1984) reported shifts in interviewees' speech rate and turn duration when intending to sound likeable to an interviewer.

As we noted earlier in the Montreal bilingual study, a variety of studies on impression formation have shown speech convergence (over speech maintenance) to have been positively evaluated (Bourhis, Giles, and Lambert 1975). Putman and Street (1984 and just cited) found that interviewees who converge toward their interviewers in terms of speech rate and response latency are reacted to favorably by the latter in terms of perceived social attractiveness. Other research too indicates that relative similarity in speech rates, response latencies, language, and accent are viewed more positively than relative dissimilarity on the dimensions of social attractiveness (Street, Brady, and Putman 1983), comunicative effectiveness (Giles and Smith 1979), perceived warmth (Welkowitz and Kuc 1973), and cooperativeness (Feldman 1968; Harris and Baudin 1973). Furthermore, professional interviewers' perceptions of student interviewees' competence also has been shown to be positively related to the latter's convergence on speech rate and response latency (Street 1984), with Bradac et al. (1988) showing *downward* convergence in lexical diversity to be very favorably perceived (see, however, Bradac and Mulac 1984).

It appears to follow from this that the greater the speakers' need to gain another's social approval, the greater the degree of convergence there will be. Factors that influence the intensity of this particular need include the probability of future interactions with an unfamiliar other, an addressee's high social status, and interpersonal variability in the need for social approval itself. In the last respect, Natale (1975a,b) found that speakers scoring higher on a trait measure of need for social approval converged more to their partner's vocal intensity and pause length than speakers who scored lower. Furthermore, Larsen, Martin, and Giles (1977) showed that the greater one's desire for specified others' approval, the more similar overall their voices will sound subjectively to one's own (even if the latter contain a stigmatized speech feature such as a lisp). This cognition of a reduced linguistic barrier between oneself and another, termed "perceptual convergence," no doubt facilitates the convergence process, since the latter will appear a more attainable target toward which to converge (see Summerfield 1975).

The power variable is one that often emerges in the accommodation literatures and in ways that support the model's central predictions. Josiane Hamers (pers. comm.), using role-taking procedures in a bilingual industrial setting in Quebec, has shown greater convergence to the language of another who was an occupational superior than to the language of one who was a subordinate; foremen converged more to managers than to workers, and managers converged more to higher managers than to foremen (see also Taylor, Simard, and Papineau 1978). Van den Berg (1985), studying code switching in commercial settings in Taiwan, found that salespersons converged more to customers than vice versa, as the customers in these settings hold more of the economic power (Cooper and Carpenter 1969). Interestingly, Cohen and Cooper (1986), drawing upon data in Thailand, showed that many tourists to the Third World do not expend the effort to acquire much, if any, competence in the language of the country visited, whereas locals in the service industries whose economic destiny is in many ways tied to tourism often become proficient in the foreigners' languages.

It is evident just from the previous studies that the mechanics of everyday interpersonal convergences in important social networks are the breeding ground for longer-term shifts in individual as well as group-level language usage (see Giles and Johnson 1987; Trudgill 1986). The potentially different trajectories of long-term accommodations in different situations are certainly worthy of longitudinal study, as are the different clusters of motives driving diverse accommodative acts. CAT has had much recourse to approval motives as the main trigger of convergence. However, it is clear from the last study cited that *instrumental* goals represent the antecedent conditions for convergence under some conditions more adequately than any motives of social approval, which in any case could be largely situationally irrelevant. Moreover, integration and approval are not necessarily coterminous, so future analyses of CAT processes need to reflect explicitly on the nesting of perceived task, identity, and relational goals (Argyle, Furnham, and Graham 1981; Clark and Delia 1979), both global and local (see also Scotton 1988).

Much of the literature on long- and mid-term language and dialect acculturation can also be interpreted in convergence terms whereby immigrants may seek the economic advantages and social rewards (although there are clearly also costs) that linguistic assimilation sometimes brings. In other words, group accommodation here may often be asymmetrical and unilateral toward the power source. Hence, Wolfram (1973) reported that in New York City, where both Puerto Ricans and blacks agree that the latter hold more power and prestige, Puerto Ricans adopted the dialect of blacks far more often than vice versa. Stanback and Pearce

(1981) contended that blacks adapt communicatively to whites more than the converse due to the socioeconomic muscle of whites in the United States. Moving to the gender context, Mulac et al. (1987) found that women but not men converged toward their partners' gaze in mixed-sex dyadic acquaintanceship settings (see Bradac, O'Donnell, and Tardy (1984). The foregoing notwithstanding, Genesee and Bourhis (1988) made a telling point about the role of sociostructural conditions mediating accommodative evaluations (see also Stieblich 1986). In their study contrasting bilingual shifts in Montreal with Quebec City, they showed that convergent shifts toward a less prestigious minority group can sometimes bring considerable social accolades.

We see at least four set of interrelated caveats to the overriding social benefits that are claimed to accrue from convergence (and what will later be extended to attuning strategies). These relate to multiple meanings and social costs; social and societal norms; causal attributions and intentions; and optimal levels.

Caveats

Multiple meanings and social costs. In the same way that interactions usually have multiple goals (O'Keefe 1988; Tracy 1991; Tracy and Coupland 1990), language behaviors often have multiple social meanings for hearers (Ryan and Giles 1982). For instance, in some settings, use of the standard dialect is associated with high status and competence, yet, at the same time, low trustworthiness and friendliness (Ryan and Giles 1982). Following social exchange principles (Chadwick-Jones 1976), convergence may entail rewards as well as costs. As we have seen, rewards may include gains in listeners' approval and cooperativeness, with specific rewards being dependent on the particular speech and nonverbal features being converged in specific situations [see, e.g., Giles and Smith (1979), where speech rate convergence was evaluatively appreciated by audiences more than accent or even content convergences; see the later discussion]. Potential costs, on the other hand, may include possible loss of personal and social identity (see Turner 1987) and expended effort, the last especially so if the accommodations in context are widespread, not reciprocated, and long-term.

An illustration of the multiple meanings of convergence was demonstrated by Bourhis, Giles, and Lambert (1975). Six groups of Welsh respondents were told that a Welsh athlete had recently been placed seventh in a Commonwealth Games diving competition and that they were to hear him in two consecutive radio interviews, purportedly taped after the competition. In one of these, the athlete's interviewer was a standard English speaker; in the other, the interviewer had a mild Welsh accent. With the latter interviewer, the athlete too consistently employed a mild Welsh accent, but with the standard interviewer his speech style varied from condition to condition. In one condition he maintained his Welsh accent, in another he modified it toward that of the interviewer (i.e., more standard and less Welsh-like), and in yet another he diverged away from the interviewer toward broad Welsh. The order of the interviews was counterbalanced, and the different texts were matched for duration, information content, vocabulary, and grammar. It was found that the athlete was perceived as more intelligent when he shifted to the standard than when he did not shift at all, and more intelligent in the latter case than when he broadened his Welsh accent. That said, convergence also involved a decrease in perceived trustworthiness and kindheartedness relative to the no-shift condition. The divergent shift to broad Welsh (although associated with diminished intelligence) resulted in the athlete's being rated as more trustworthy and kindhearted than in the other conditions [see Bourhis et al. (1975) for a near replication in the Francophone setting of Quebec].

Social norms. Genesee and Bourhis (1982, 1988) have shown how situational norms may well override accommodative tendencies at certain sequential junctures during an interaction. For instance, they found that the act of salesmen converging to customers does not necessarily result in positive evaluations because of the established situational norm that "the customer is always right." That said, we should acknowledge the additional or confounding attributed motive of ingratiation in the context of this particular norm, which makes us somewhat wary of its (as well as perhaps other norms') autonomy and purity. Further complexities abound and, as such, underscore the need for research on the relationships between the management of social identities and the dilemmas of appropriately sequencing interpersonal accommodations in context. Having converged toward each other, interlocutors may feel less socially constrained and may thereby feel free to adopt the speech patterns of their own choosing. Alternatively, some persons may feel the need to establish their own identities through talk at the outset and then may feel more comfortable about adopting accommodative behavior. In addition, what can be parsimoniously interpreted as accommodation may in actuality be an artifact on occasion. For instance, an interviewee who sounded more like his or her prestigious interviewer may not have so shifted strategically in the latter's direction sociolinguistically. Rather, the interviewee may simply have been attempting a so-called assertive self-presentation (Tedeschi, Lindskold, and Rosenfeld (1985) via language, thereby portraying a competent persona (Coupland, 1984). Put another way, whatever speech patterns the interviewer may have encoded at the time would have had little impact on the interviewer's face intents (see Ball et al. 1984); any "addressee focus" here (see the generalized model in Fig. 4 later) would have been very limited. As Gallois and Callan (this volume) articulate and illustrate, the area of conversational rules and social norms in relation to CAT (as well as their sociopsycholinguistic reality; see McKirnan and Hamayan 1984) requires further empirical exploration.

Causal attributions, awareness, and intentions. Attributional principles suggest that very often we evaluate behavior directed toward us in the light of the motives that we assume gave rise to it (Heider 1958). This analysis has been applied to linguistic and communicative behaviors as well (e.g., Detweiler 1986; Hewstone 1983) in sociopsychologically oriented research, and paradigmatically so in the work of Grice (1971) and Brown and Levinson (1987). It has been proposed that a perceiver takes into account three factors when attributing motives to an act: the other's ability, effort, and external pressures impelling the person to act in a particular way. Simard, Taylor, and Giles (1976) examined the implications of attribution principles for the evaluation of convergence and nonconvergence. They found that listeners in an interethnic laboratory task who attributed another's convergence toward them as a desire to break down cultural barriers perceived this act very favorably. When this same shift was attributed externally to situational pressures forcing the speaker to converge, then the act was perceived less favorably. Similarly, when a nonconvergent act was attributed externally to situational pressures, the negative reactions were not as pronounced as when the maintenance of speech was attributed internally to the speaker's lack of effort (see Giles 1980).

The discussion thus far has linked accommodative acts implicitly to strategic communication (see Cody and McLaughlin 1989) and intentions. In this respect, Giles et al. (1973) suggested that different forms of convergence (e.g., complete language shifts, slowing of the speech rate) may be placed along a continuum of perceived effort whereby both speaker and listener might construe a given linguistic strategy as involving high, medium, or low social concessions. Indeed, it was suggested that apologizing for a lack of ability to converge toward another language may be emotionally more "giving" than simply switching to the other's language. Needless to say, the relationship between perceptions of accommodation and attending social consequences is one in which misattribution is rife, as sometimes partners' perceptions of each others' behaviors are decidedly at odds. For instance, Canadian patients report converging to medical language when interacting with their physicians, who in turn self-report moving more to everyday language with them (Bourhis, Roth, and MacQueen 1988). Unfortunately, neither side acknowledges perceiving such moves from the other, with nurses acting as linguistic brokers (see also Cohen and Cooper 1986) by functioning as intermediaries and claiming to converge to both parties.

Adopting a self-regulation perspective (Gilbert, Krull, and Pelham 1988) would lead us to predict that when convergence is deliberate and mindful, encoders of it will be less able to process accurately the intentions of their accommodating or nonaccommodating partners. This will be so because regulating certain personal behaviors (e.g., bilingual convergence when nonfluent in a second language, feigning involvement, deceiving another, creative accounting) can be so cognitively involving that insufficient resources are left for detailed decoding processing, to the extent that the listeners' responses are more likely to be taken at face value. It should be noted, however, that seemingly purposive designs are not necessarily either enacted or evaluated with full awareness; indeed, even accommodative bilingual and dialectal code switching can occur without the sender's knowledge or memory of it. Berger and Roloff (1980) suggest that much communication is produced and received at low levels of awareness, and that in many instances speech accommodation may be scripted behavior (see Schank and Abelson 1977). Factors such as a discrepancy between expectations and what is encountered, or encountering a novel situation (Langer 1978), may, however, intervene and bring speech and nonverbal behaviors to a state of greater awareness. Certainly, evidence attests to the fact that certain accommodated features are more consciously self-perceived under some conditions than others. In Street's (1982) study, subjects were unaware of response latency and speech rate convergence but were highly aware of divergence of these behaviors, whereas in Bradac et al.'s (1988) study, decoders were more accurate with respect to perceiving downward (than upward) accommodative movements in lexical diversity. Interestingly, and in complete contrast, Bourhis et al. (1975) found a distinct tendency for listeners to claim that they perceived interviewees' upward shift in accent, with prestigious-sounding interviewers even though mainte- nance was actually in evidence, an effect due perhaps to the social ex- pectation that convergence here would virtually be a conversational rule [see Higgins's (1980) "communication game" theory]. In other words, awareness is not commensurate with perceptual accuracy.

It seems then that a speaker's goals may be more or less overtly rep- resented and that speech adjustments cannot uniformly be taken as in- dicative of wholly intentional orientations. An interesting study with regard to both scripted and overtly intentionalized behavior is Bourhis's (1983) study in Quebec. The results of this social survey showed that speakers can be consciously aware of convergence and divergence in language switches on occasion, as well as the probable reasons for them (Taylor and Royer 1980). Thus, for example, English Canadians reported being more likely to converge to French in Montreal today than in the past, and they also reported that French Canadians were less likely to converge to them in English today than in the past. The converse was true for the French Canadians' reports. However, in a follow-up set of field studies designed to test how these reports matched actual accom- modative behavior, Bourhis (1984) found little overlap. French Cana- dians were more likely than English Canadians to reciprocate conver- gence in intergroup encounters, and English Canadians were more likely than French Canadians to maintain their own language. Bourhis sug- gested that in spite of sociopolitical changes favoring the ethnolinguistic ideals of French Canadians in Montreal, English Canadians are still in the habit of maintaining English when interacting with French Cana- dians, and French Canadians are still in the habit of converging to En- glish with English Canadians. That is, it may be that, contrary to their avowed intentions, old habits for intergroup communication die hard.

Optimal levels. As discussed thus far, CAT suggests that full conver- gences would be more positively evaluated than partial convergences. This was the empirical concern of a study by Giles and Smith (1979), who intuited that such a linear relationship would not hold (Jones and Jones 1964). They presented eight versions of a taped message to an English audience. The taped voice was that of a Canadian exhibiting various combinations of convergence-nonconvergence on three linguis- tic dimensions (pronunciation, speech rate, and message content) in a factorial design. Listeners appreciated convergence on each level separately but found that convergence on all three levels was perceived negatively as patronizing; content plus speech rate convergences was the interpersonally effective optimum. Although recipients may find nonconvergence a blow to their esteem, as it implicitly indicates that the speaker finds them unworthy of seeking their approval, it could well be that recipients of multimodal accommodation feel extremely uncomfortable with those who can demonstrate that their own idiolectal features are so easily matched. Hence, and in the same way that listeners have ranges of acceptable or preferred linguistic and nonverbal behaviors (Argyle and Dean 1965; Cappella and Greene 1982; Street 1982), Giles (1980) contended that listeners may have a *tolerance* for certain amounts of convergence, and hence a move beyond a certain threshold (which may vary situationally) may be negatively perceived by them (see Sherif, Sherif, and Nebergall 1965).

Besides optimal magnitudes of convergence, Giles and Smith (1979) speculated that there might also be optimal *rates* of convergence (and divergence). Aronson and Linder's (1965) gain-loss theory of attraction proposed that we like more those people whose respect we are acquiring rather than those whose admiration we already possess. It could be, then, that convergence is more effective when it takes place slowly enough so that the change is perceived by degrees rather than all at once (see Altman and Taylor 1973). The latter might be costly to speakers, making them vulnerable to the inference that their respect was transparent and secure from the outset. Interestingly, there are data showing that unfamiliar others converge toward each other gradually across subsequent occasions (Lennard and Bernstein 1960; Welkowitz and Feldstein 1969; see also Ferrara this volume), thereby appearing to conserve some convergent acts as bargaining tools or "aces in the hole," as gain-loss theory would predict. In this way, the structure and process of mutual convergences can be quite negotiative and can be precursors to communicative innovations at the lexical, grammatical, prosodic, and nonverbal levels (see Bell, Buerkel-Rothfuss, and Gore 1987; Hymes 1972; Knapp 1984). The meanings of these mutual convergences are very likely relationally unique and serve to enhance shared couple (Giles and Fitzpatrick 1984) and family identities (Bossard 1955; Read 1962), as well as emergent small-group identities (Gregory 1986). Gain-loss theory also claims that individuals will most dislike someone else *not* when they have never been shown respect by that person but when it appears that the other's respect is gradually being eroded. In accommodation terms, then, disapproval would be levied against those who diverge sequentially away rather than against those who diverged fully on the initial meeting. Interestingly, the frequent use of what Ragan and Hopper (1984) called the "suspension of the let-it-pass rule" (e.g., "I don't know what you mean") with longstanding intimates – be it contrived strategically or not – can be interpreted as a significant diverging set of acts that ultimately signals lack of intersubjectivity and can, if used often enough, be one of the precursors of (as well as an excuse for) relational dissolution.

Divergence and intergroup processes

Giles and Powesland (1975) argued that both speech convergence and divergence may be seen as representing strategies of conformity and identification. Convergence is a strategy of identification with the communication patterns of an individual internal to the interaction, whereas divergence is a strategy of identification with linguistic communicative norms of some reference group external to the immediate situation. To the extent that divergent strategies are probably adopted more often in dyads where the participants derive from different social backgrounds, the incorporation of ideas from Tajfel's theory of intergroup relations and social change (Tajfel 1978; Tajfel and Turner 1979) provides an appropriate context in which to consider divergent shifts more generally (Giles, Bourhis, and Taylor 1977).

Tajfel (1974) has suggested that when members of one group interact with members of another, they compare themselves on dimensions that are important to them, such as personal attributes, abilities, material possessions, and so forth. He suggested that these "intergroup social comparisons" lead individuals to search for, or even to create, dimensions on which they may be seen to be positively distinct from a relevant outgroup. The perception of such a positive distinctiveness contributes to individuals' feeling of an adequate social identity, which enhances their feeling of self-worth. In other words, people experience satisfaction in the knowledge that they belong to a group that enjoys some superiority over others. Given that speech style is for many people an important subjective dimension of, and objective cue to, social and particularly ethnic group membership (Fishman 1977; Taylor, Bassili, and Aboud 1973; although see Giles and Franklyn-Stokes 1989 for a discussion of the complexities herein), it has been proposed that in certain encounters, individuals might search for a positively valued distinctiveness from an outgroup member on communicative dimensions they value highly – a process formerly termed "psycholinguistic distinctiveness"

(Giles et al. 1977) but now more broadly labeled "group communicative distinctiveness." This process would operate in intergroup (rather than interindividual) encounters where participants construe themselves in terms of, and hence communicate in accord with, their social category memberships rather than engage each other in terms of their idiosyncratic moods, temperaments, and personalities (Giles and Hewstone 1982; Tajfel and Turner 1979). Hence, interlocutors will not only stereotype and depersonalize their interlocutor(s) but also will take on the communicative patterns believed to be prototypical of their group (see Gallois and Callan 1988). From this perspective, a dyadic encounter could well be acted and/or described as intergroup, and it is our belief that many situations classified as interpersonal are actually of this nature (see Gallois et al. 1988; Gudykunst 1986; Gudykunst and Ting-Toomey 1990).

In sum, then, divergence can be a tactic of intergroup distinctiveness of individuals in search of a positive social identity and is well exemplified in the studies reported earlier by Bourhis and others (Bourhis and Giles 1977; Bourhis et al. 1979). By diverging and by emphasizing one's own social (and sometimes idiosyncratic) communicative style, members of an ingroup accentuate the differences between themselves and the outgroup members present (Ros and Giles 1979) on a salient and valued dimension of their group identity. Taylor and Royer (1980) found in Quebec that French Canadian students who expected in due course to meet personally an Anglophone speaker they heard on an audiotape anticipated speaking more French with a target who completely agreed than with one who disagreed with their ethnolinguistic ideals. Furthermore, their anticipated divergence was accentuated after they had discussed together their probable language strategies toward the target. This "linguistic polarization" (see Myers and Lamm 1976) was attributed explicitly by the French Canadians themselves on postexperimental questionnaires to their feeling of ingroup belongingness and the need to assert their ethnic identity.

A number of other studies of impression formation have shown that maintenance of divergence is often seen by its recipients as insulting, impolite, or downright hostile (Deprez and Persoons 1984; Sandilands and Fleury 1979), that is, unless it is attributed situationally to extenuating circumstances (Simard, Taylor, and Giles, 1976) and/or to adherence to valued norms (Ball et al. 1984; Bradac 1990). Such negative reactions make perfect evaluative and attributional sense in light of the social implications of the absence of convergence discussed earlier. Although some social situations value divergent over convergent speech patterns in certain competitive contexts, as shown in Switzerland by Doise, Sinclair, and Bourhis (1976), social norms in many other kinds of situations (see Genesee and Bourhis 1988) make divergent patterns costly. As an example, Gorter (1987) discusses the general norm of convergence in Dutch society where two bilingual Frisian speakers may converse together in Dutch. And so in the context of Wales, it was found that situations had to be very intergroup in nature for bilingual Welsh persons to even anticipate diverging into Welsh with an English person (Giles and Johnson 1986). Indeed, the latter had to threaten directly core elements of the Welsh persons' ethnic identity to which they were strongly committed. Hence, the dimensions of intergroup salience, the nature of communicative norms, and the degree of commitment to social identification are all crucial interacting variables, not only in determining whether or not divergence occurs but also the form it takes.

One of the factors associated with the degree of social identification communicators have with one or another of their social group memberships has been termed "perceived vitality" (see, e.g., Giles, Rosenthal, and Young 1985; Sachdev et al. 1990). This global concept refers to the extent to which members of a social group consider certain sociostructural factors to be operating in their favor or not. Hence, a group that considered itself to have relatively low vitality (e.g., many immigrant minority groups) vis-à-vis a relevant outgroup (e.g., the host community) might well, for example, construe itself to be low in status factors (economic, political, and social), demography (defined territory, absolute numbers, emigrating members), and institutional support for its language in many everyday contexts (e.g., school, media, government), and cultural institutions. Giles and Johnson (1987), again in Wales, found that the degree of anticipated divergence from a culturally threatening English person by the use of Welsh words, phrases, and the language itself was an interactive function of the Welsh persons' degrees of cultural identification and perceived ingroup vitality. More specifically, when Welsh persons strongly identified with their group, a low sense of ingroup vitality was associated with divergent code switching. However, when Welsh persons only moderately identified with their group, a high level of ingroup vitality was required for divergence to be envisaged. In the first case, it was as though decreasing vitality was perceived to be mobilizing to those already committed to the group, and communicative distinctiveness emerged as a compensating consequence to the threatened identity; but equally, those committed but feeling that their group had enough "going for it" were secure enough not to feel the need to dissociate face-to-face. On the other hand, those not entirely committed to the group (and who in any case have other valued social group memberships on which to call) needed to feel that the group had sufficient sociostructural strength for it be worthwhile investing an effort, and being seen to so do, in thereafter being the butt of derisory feelings from the diverged recipients.

Invoking constructs such as vitality grounds CAT as a model that recognizes the role of macrofactors – not always available for analysis in the ongoing situation but nonetheless part of the historical, sociopolitical backdrop – in molding the communicative dynamics of the situated here and now.[2] A number of intergroup factors have been posited as being theoretically linked to the extent of divergence operating (Giles and Jonnson 1981, 1987). These include the *perceived hardness-softness* of the group boundaries – for example, whether or not an ingroup language defies acquisition by outsiders (see Giles, 1979; Hall and Gudykunst 1986; Hildebrandt and Giles 1984; Huffines 1986); the *perceived legitimacy–illegitimacy* of the prevailing intergroup hierarchy (e.g., the extent to which low power groups believe their social position is just and fair or not; see Turner and Brown 1978), and the extent of the communicator's *multiple group memberships* (see Gudykunst 1988 for an empirically grounded consideration of these variables in terms of uncertainty reduction theory). Obviously, age is an important variable here. We know from language attitude studies that even three-year olds are surprisingly sophisticated about some of the social meanings of group membership (Day 1982), and bilingual convergence in intergroup settings has been shown at six years of age (Aboud 1976). That said, more complete knowledge of Western sociostructural norms relating to language usage is usually acquired slowly throughout childhood and adolescence (see Genesee 1984).

In formulating and revising the intergroup model of second-language learning (Giles and Byrne 1982; Garrett, Giles, and Coupland 1989; see also Hall; and Gudykunst 1986), we have suggested that the same factors leading individuals to diverge in an intergroup encounter also contribute to many immigrant minorities' resistance to acquiring a host language with anything resembling native proficiency. In different contexts, of course, these factors are also enabling forces contributing to ingroup

---

[2]Indeed, CAT can quite easily be extended to account for a more transactional perspective in which others' communications in temporally and spatially distant contexts may have unforeseen and profound implications for our accommodative behaviors elsewhere [see Bronfenbrenner's (1979) analysis of contexts, as well as Fisher and Todd (1986)].

members' motivation to acquire their ethnic group's tongue, which they may never have been taught (Giles, Garrett, and Coupland 1988). Furthermore, and in line with Trudgill's (1986) theory that interpersonal accommodative forces are an integral element in long-term language and dialect shifts, we have argued that intergroup processes, along the lines discussed earlier, are part of the psychological climate of long-term language maintenance and survival (Giles, Leets, and Coupland 1990). Interestingly, Yaeger-Dror (1988), in an Israeli study, reported data showing that an increasing accentuation of ethnic speech markers in the recorded Hebrew singing of certain Arab-speaking Jews maps directly the increased ingroup vitality of this group over the same period.

Intergroup divergence can be appreciated by those overhearing it when they belong to the same ingroup as a speaker who is linguistically dissociating from an outgroup member. In a very interesting unpublished study using the Prisoner's Dilemma Game (see Eiser 1975), Bourhis (1977) had Anglo-Welsh listeners rate a dialogue sequence involving two Welsh-accented suspects who were supposedly being interrogated by a standard-accented English policeman on audiotape. The same two Welsh-accented actors played the role of two suspects in different guises by either converging to the received pronunciation (RP) accent of the English policeman or by diverging and accentuating their Welsh accent in English. Although the content of the interviews was kept the same across the different experimental conditions, Anglo-Welsh listeners' evaluations of the suspects differed depending on which accent strategy was adopted. Results showed that the suspects were rated more favorably on social attractiveness traits and were considered more nationalistic when they diverged away from rather than converged toward the (English) policeman. (However, and in line with the previous section on multiple meanings of accommodation, these suspects were rated unfavorably on competence-related scales.) Moreover they were rated as less guilty and as worthy of a milder sentence when they diverged than when they converged during the interrogation. Taken in the intergroup setting of the day, these findings suggest that listeners were ready to punish the suspects for having betrayed ingroup solidarity (by converging) and to reward them for upholding their Welsh identity and integrity (by diverging) even in this threatening encounter.

We are not claiming that all divergences are intergroup in nature. Certainly, divergence to another communicative form may signal individual disdain regarding another's dress, mannerisms, habits, language style, and so forth. For example, when Putman and Street (1984) required interviewees to act out being dislikable in an interview setting, they were found, predictably, to diverge in noncontent speech features away from their interviewers. Indeed, sometimes it is virtually impossible to disentangle the intergroup from the inter-individual dimension, as in Seltig's (1985) analysis of a German radio program (see earlier), where an interviewer diverged from purported experts as a signal of identification with other views, including those of the interactive audience. To add one further complexity here, we would like to attend to Giles and Wiemann's (1987) notion that people construe encounters not only in terms of their individual and group identities but also in terms of their relational and/or couple identities. Indeed, it is possible to conceive of a romantic heterosexual relationship, for instance, as on some occasions being simultaneously high on all three dimensions: that is, "I'm me, but I'm a feminist, although I am us." Hence, when it suits desired needs, an individual could diverge from another by adopting couple talk (Giles and Fitzpatrick 1984), even with his or her partner not present, perhaps through proliferating couple disclosures and invoking a privately constructed code. Further contemplation about couple divergence opens up a plethora of complexities and situational caveats, the exciting exploration of which would be better suited to a relational discussion elsewhere.

1.4. Further distinctions

Thus far, we have considered divergence as a dissociative communicative tactic. In this section, we consider further complexities, such as the notion that some divergent acts can occur for seemingly convergent motives and even some convergent acts accomplished toward divergent ends (as noted in the section on "Some Important Distinctions"). In this way, we introduce the distinction between psychological and communicative accommodation, as well as the need to consider the function of accommodative strategies.

Psychological versus linguistic accommodation

Thakerar et al. (1982) defined psychological convergence and divergence as "individuals' *beliefs* that they are integrating with and differentiating from others respectively, while [objective] linguistic convergence and divergence can be defined as individuals' speech shifts towards and away from others respectively" (p. 222). Accepting now the need to invoke communicative levels other than speech, very often psychological and communicative accommodations will be perfectly isomorphic. Psychological convergence attending communicative divergence may be vividly evident in role-discrepant situations where dissimilarities are not only acceptable but even expected (Grush, Clore, and Costin 1975). For instance, a sociolinguistically sensitive interviewee is hardly likely to be evaluated favorably if he or she assumes communicatively the directive, interrogative language and nonverbal controlling stances of the interviewer; complementarity on certain levels, then, is expected by both parties (Matarazzo and Weins 1972; Putman and Street 1984).

A complementary relationship obtains when one participant is acknowledged to have a subordinate role to the other (Watzlawick, Beavin, and Jackson 1967). There are many examples of a status or power discrepancy in a dyad, including employer–employee, teacher–pupil, veteran–novice, and so forth. However, not all relationships can be classified in such power terms, and talk in many stable, intimate relationships veers in a status-equivalent and then in a status-unequal direction, depending on the nature of the topic discussed or the situation involved. It is important to emphasize that complementary relationships do not abound without the consensus of the participants involved. Indeed, we would argue that complementarity increases mutual predictability (Berger and Bradac 1982), as proposed earlier in this chapter with respect to convergence. Miller and Steinberg (1975: 235) commented:

> Many people do indeed seem to choose to be one-down in their relationships with others; they consistently adopt subservient, deferential or even totally dependent positions. In doing so, they are able to achieve some measure of certainty in their communication transactions. Their consistently one-down behavior tends to elicit predictably one-up kinds of responses from their companions. In this sense, any role is preferable to a variable one, or to no role at all.

Classic examples of speech complementarity may occur when two young people are out on a date. Even though laboratory problem-related tasks have shown mutual convergences by males and females in situations where gender identity was probably lacking in salience (Mulac et al. 1987, 1988) – and, arguably, male divergence in the direction of masculine-sounding voices when it was (Hogg 1985) – males and females with initial romantic inclinations are likely to diverge toward prototypically strong and soft communicative patterns, respectively, in many communities where traditional sex-role ideologies abound. Montepare and Vega (1988) found that women sounded more "feminine" (e.g., higher and more variable pitch) when talking to an intimate as opposed to an unknown male other by telephone. We would take this to be an instance of complementarity rather than descriptive divergence as the authors themselves described it. This does not, however preclude the possibility of convergence occurring simultaneously on other linguistic dimensions. For instance, a woman may adopt a soft voice and certain paralinguistic and prosodic features with an eligible bachelor lawyer, yet may wish to gain his attraction, approval, and respect not only by fulfilling her feminine role requirements but also by converging to his more prestigious dialect. As noted earlier, Bilous and Krauss (1988) showed that women converged toward men's utterance length, interruptions, and pausing but diverged on backchannels and laughter. Notwithstanding the different forms and functions of laughing, they could be instances of speech complementarity, signaling as they do traditionally role-related involvement and functioning as compliments to the entertainment value of male discourse. Again, it is likely that there are optimal levels of speech complementarity, with Miller and Steinberg (1975: 239–40) providing an illustration:

> When the scene shifts to social activities with the husband's professional associates, the wife assumes the submissive one-down position. He, in turn, refrains from exploiting the situation: he does not become unduly dominant or unreasonable in his demands, for he knows that at a certain point his wife will be forced to defect from her one-down position.

Speech convergence, then, is often accompanied by speech complementarity of other linguistic features. Naturally, the optimal degree and rate of convergence, together with the optimal balance of complementarity is difficult to encode from situation to situation. Relatedly, Goffman's (1967) view of a speaker was that of a juggler and synthesizer, an accommodator and appeaser, who achieved one goal while apparently playing out another. Seen in this light, and also by Tracy (1990) in her analysis of the encoding of multiple aspects of face, it is no wonder that interpersonal communication is often fraught with difficulties and misunderstandings. Street (this volume) provides a compelling analysis of doctor–patient relationships in which he argues that a fine meshing of physician convergence and complementarity is essential for patient satisfaction and compliance with health regimens.

The other "incongruent" combination remaining is psychological divergence allied to linguistic convergence, as for instance in the reciprocation of both verbal abuse (Mosher, Mortimer, and Grebel 1968) and interruptive behavior (Argyle and Kendon 1967), referred to by Giles and Powesland (1975) as "negative response matching." Drawing once again on observational experience from Montreal in the 1970s, many English Canadian students reported effortful instances of accommodating to presumed French Canadians in what was to them nonfluent French, and then being replied to, and often interrupted by, fast, fluent English by French Canadians in what was interpreted as a prosodically denigrating manner. Woolard (1989: 69) has reported similar patterns in Catalonia, where the linguistic etiquette of an "accommodation norm" is that "Catalan should be spoken only between Catalans." Hence, Castillian individuals who accommodate Catalan speakers with their language will be responded to in Castillian. Similarly, Miller (1982) has claimed that a common strategy adopted by Japanese to show their displeasure to a Caucasian who is speaking Japanese is to adopt a foreign talk register or refuse to carry on a conversation in Japanese and instead diverge in the direction of English. Such patterns of response have been shown experimentally to be highly favored by the Japanese (especially women) even in response to highly proficient Japanese-speaking Westerners, although the reasons for it are self-presentationally complex and not as divergent as perhaps Miller assumed (Ross and Shortreed 1990). Somewhat similarly, and highlighting the implicit variability in this process, Ellingsworth (1988: 265) has reported:

> In sojourns in Latin America and Southeast Asia, the author's use of inelegant but workable host-country language or expressions often was countered with requests to proceed in English, even when the host's competence in it was severely limited. Some people perceived the visitor's initiative as a pejorative reflection on their English ability; still others appeared pleased at the effort, but indicated that they preferred to practice their English.

Other instances of linguistic convergence and psychological divergence are available in the mimicking sphere (see, however, Bavelas et al. 1988). Up to this point, CAT has, perhaps naively, focused mainly on accommodations occurring only when speakers have the repertoire to accomplish this. However, this restriction may have turned out to be theoretically limiting given the relationship between accent mimicry, everyday humor, and media humor. However, Coupland (1985) has shown in a case study how a Cardiff disk jockey frequently shifted pronunciation in a consciously mimicked but nonetheless comfortable convergent manner across a whole range of British and American dialects

Table 4. *Some linguistic and psychological parameters of accommodation*

	Linguistic			
	Convergence		Divergence	
	Objective	Subjective	Objective	Subjective
Psychological				
Convergence	A	B	C	D
Divergence	E	F	G	H

in seeming solidarity with particular listeners, singers, and figureheads. Nevertheless, mimicking can often be accomplished with divergent aims, as shown in Basso's (1979) study, where Amerindians mocked whites by mimicking their communicative behavior. Such negative mocking, but with more critical intent, has been observed by Kathryn Sheils (pers. comm.) among Jamaican schoolteachers (who usually adopt a standardized form in the classroom) converging and mimicking their pupils' creolized forms when the latter are deemed disruptive, inattentive, or lacking in academic effort. Indeed, the sender's motives and recipient's attributions of mimicking and mocking are an intriguing dynamic that, if interpersonally incongruent, can lead to acute misunderstandings.

The conceptual picture becomes even more complex when we distinguish between objective and subjective levels. Following Thakerar et al. (1982), we have then the following 2 × 2 × 2 design where logically eight combinations of communicative and psychological accommodations emerge from Table 4. These are A + B, C + B, A + D, C + D, G + H, E + H, G + F, and E + F. Note here that A + B was our original "pure" convergence, G + H was our original "pure" divergence, C + D encapsulates our notion of communicative complementarity (see also later), and E + F shows our examples of on-target convergence with divergent intent. Although it is possible to contrive would-be illustrations of the remaining combinations (which doubtless actually occur), as well as to introduce additional dimensions, such as partners' perceptions, attributions, and evaluations of these sender-focused tactics, we will note only B + C (given that hyperconvergence can be taken as a case of divergence), which captures conceptually the notion of hyperconverging to such an extent that the act is seen as derisory (e.g., baby talk to the functionally competent elderly).

Cognitive organization versus identity maintenance functions

Thus far, convergence and divergence have been treated essentially as affective phenomena. Thakerar et al. (1982), however, suggested that such shifts may function psychologically for two main reasons: cognitive organization and identity maintenance (Giles, Scherer, and Taylor 1979; see also Brown 1977). The cognitive organization function involves communicative features used by interlocutors to organize events into meaningful social categories, thereby allowing a complex social situation to be reduced to manageable proportions. In this way, speakers may organize their outputs to take into account the requirements of their listeners (Applegate and Delia 1980; Blakar 1985; Higgins 1980), and listeners may select from this and organize it according to the cognitive structures most easily available for comprehension (Brown and Dell 1987; Mangold and Pobel 1988). As mentioned earlier, increased intelligibility is a valued by-product of convergent acts and may on occasion be the principal motive for accommodating (see later). Indeed, Greenbaum and Cooper (1988) have argued that baby talk, which undoubtedly fulfills a cognitive organization function in providing simplified input, could usefully be considered in CAT terms (see also Zuengler this volume). Similarly, Pierson and Bond (1982: 136), investigating American–Cantonese bilingual interviews, reported:

> During the interview itself, Cantonese bilinguals broke up their speech units with filled pauses more when working in Cantonese with Americans. They also slowed down their speed of speaking Cantonese by 8.4%, even though this reduction was not statistically significant. Both changes functioned to assist the interviewer in decoding their meaning by giving him more time.

On other occasions, interlocutors may wish to communicate in a manner that will allow them to present themselves most favorably, and listeners may, in turn, wish to select creatively from among the multiple messages coming their way in a manner that maintains or even enhances their own self- or group esteem. Thus the identity maintenance function of communication serves to fulfill the emotional needs of participants as they attend to speech markers and nonverbal features that positively reinforce their egos and fail to process any information that may have a negative effect on their images (see Snyder and Swann 1978). As Fig. 2 suggests, these two dimensions may be considered orthogonal, allowing for the likelihood that virtually every social episode has a modicum of both functions, and often multiple other goals as well

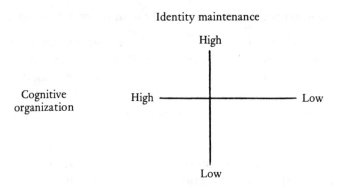

Figure 2. Accommodative functions according to two-dimensional space.

(O'Keefe 1988). In other words, those whose approval we desire may come to be those with whom we wish to, or want to be seen to wish to, establish clarity. Relatedly – and some British migrants to certain areas in the United States may identify with this example – interlocutors may desire speedy and effective service interactions and accordingly converge, not in any sense to gain approval but as a tactic to reduce their cultural distinctiveness and so avoid the routinized (often well-disposed) metalinguistic commenting that nonconvergence would predictably elicit. In addition, such convergence would circumvent the predictable request for repetition that would ensue by recipients who anticipate hearing there local dialect.

In the Thakerar et al. studies outlined earlier, it was suggested that the low-status speakers were converging toward where they *believed* the standard speakers to be as an act of identity maintenance; that is, they wished to be seen as more competent than they had been believed to be thus far. The high-status speakers converged, it was argued, toward where they believed the low-status speakers to be as an act of cognitive organization in order to assist the latter's comprehension and grasp of the situation. Hence, the same accommodative acts may emerge to fulfill different and complex functions. That said, we should be alert to the fact that locating speakers' goals and accommodative acts, as in Fig. 2, is a conceptual convenience that does little justice to the frequent occasions when convergence and divergence are collaborative acts somewhat unsuited to individualistic schematic depictions. Nevertheless, we believe the distinction modeled by Gallois et al. (1988) of (stable) preinteractional versus (jointly constructed) interactional goals, the former sometimes assuming irrelevance in light of the emergent latter, is a useful way of breaching the seemingly irreconcilable objectivist and subjectivist traditions in social and communicative studies (see Burrell and Morgan 1979; Gudykunst and Nishida 1989; Tracy and Coupland 1990).

Divergence too may function not only to express attitudes but also to give order and meaning to the interaction and to provide a mutually understood basis for communication, that is, to fulfill a cognitive organizational function. For example, the accentuation of accent, as well as content differentiation in certain contexts or other forms of divergence, may serve to indicate that interlocutors are not members of the host community or familiar with the current situation in which they find themselves. This self-handicapping tactic (Weary and Arkin 1981) thereby increases the probability that norms inadvertently broken can be attributed externally and that a greater latitude of acceptance will be made available for the speaker; divergence here has some real social utility (Ellen Ryan pers. comm.), perhaps particularly in intercultural environments. This divergence, moreover, acts as a form of self-disclosure to indicate that certain spheres of knowledge and behavior may not be shared and that intersubjectivity, as a consequence, is at a premium (see also Rommetveit 1979).

In other situations, speech divergence may be employed to bring another's behavior to an acceptable level or to facilitate the coordination of speech patterns. Two studies have indicated that sometimes interactants (e.g., therapists and adults) may diverge in the amount of talking they do in order to encourage their partners (i.e., clients and children) to talk more (Matarazzo et al. 1968; Street, Street, and Van Kleeck 1983). Anecdotally, it is not uncommon for people to slow their speech rate when speaking with extremely fast-talking and or excited others in order to "cool them down" to a more comfortable communicative and cognitive level [see Cappella (1981) and Hale and Burgoon (1984) with respect to proximity and body orientations, respectively, in terms of the notion of "compensation"]. In a different theoretical context, Ickes et al. (1982) showed that when males were expecting to talk via intercom to a "cold" rather than a "warm" interlocutor, they sounded far more warm in the former than in the latter condition, presumably to enhance the projected warmth of their partners.

1.5. Discourse attuning

The essential structure of the accommodation model, as we have introduced it in the foregoing discussion, is shown schematically in Fig. 3.

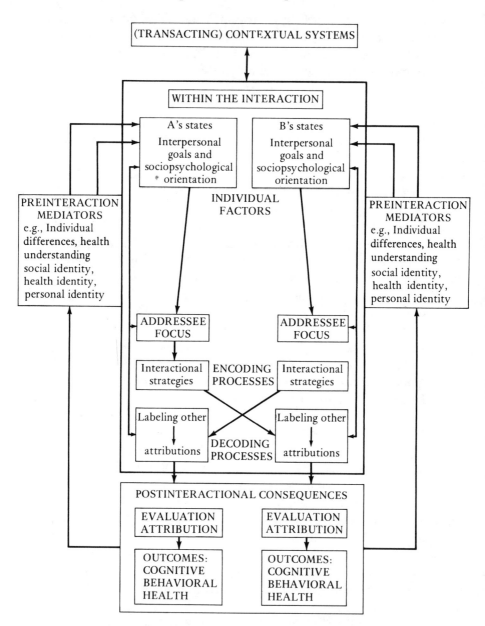

Figure 3. An accommodation model of communication, health, and aging.

Here CAT processes are linked explicitly to social support, health concerns, and health outcomes – an area to which we turn shortly. For the moment, however, we note that the *addressee focus* in the previous discussion has centered on the other's communicative patterns, or, rather, on perceptions or expectations of the other's communicative performance. From this perspective, convergence, divergence, and complementarity as we have discussed them may be labeled "approximation strategies." Coupland et al. (1988) elaborated CAT so as to include a broader range of addressee foci, and hence *attuning* strategies, than the approximation ones, and so to open the door to the reconceptualizing of accommodation in terms of discursive and sequential acts. One alternative addressee focus involves attending to the other's interpretive competence, which we often assess through his or her social category memberships (by such cues as accent, lexical diversity, skin color, and so forth) and the inferences we derive from these (Clark and Marshall 1981). Sometimes, as with the generic elderly, such competences are stereotyped negatively as an impaired ability to understand (Ryan and Cole 1990). This then leads to a set of *interpretability* strategies that can be used to modify the complexity of speech (e.g., by decreasing the diversity of vocabulary or simplifying the syntax), increase clarity (by changing pitch, loudness, and/or tempo by incorporating repetition, clarification checks, explicit boundarying devices, and so on), and/or influence the selection of conversational topics (by staying in areas that are familiar, safe, and unthreatening for the other; see Hamilton this volume).

Two other addressee foci involve attending to the addressee's conversational needs and role relationships that lead to sets of *discourse management* and *control strategies*, respectively. The first of these is to be seen as a highly diverse set of discursive options whereby a speaker may facilitate a partner's contribution to ongoing talk, for example by offering turns, eliciting disclosable information, repairing problematical sequences, and generally working to redress positive or negative face threats to a recipient (Brown and Levinson 1987; Penman 1990). Alternatively, attuned discourse management involves supportive recipiency strategies (Coupland et al. 1990) whereby a speaker's contribution can be endorsed and accredited through backchanneling or more explicit approbatory moves. Control strategies likewise embody degrees of attuning, reflecting the disposition of role options in talk, as for example when a young speaker may suppress her own disclosure and offer "the floor" to an elderly partner (Coupland et al. 1988).

The explanatory value of this more propositionally and functionally based specification of CAT is only now beginning to be demonstrated, with the chapters (in this volume) by Ferrara, Hamilton, and Linell being important instances. The *theoretical* necessity for this expanded perspective is, however, already clear. Accommodative or attuned talk is frequently achieved strategically when behavior matching, participant to participant, is either not the evaluatively salient criterion or is highly inappropriate. One interesting case emerges from the conversation analysis literature on troubles telling (Jefferson 1980, 1984a,b). Although "laughing together is a valued occurrence which can be the product of methodic, coordinate activities" (Jefferson 1984b: 348), the established pattern in troubles telling is that "the troubles-teller laughs, and the troubles-recipient declines to laugh by talking to the prior utterance and thus by talking to the trouble" (ibid.: 350). So, laughter by teller and recipient enter quite polarized strategies and evaluative frames during troubles talk vis-à-vis the "laughability" of circumstances from one or another perspective. A possible objective similarity between teller's and recipient's behavior – laughter – is here not in itself the interpersonally meaningful concern; rather, it is the contextual and sequential organization of laughter, and its highly attuned *absence*, that signify.

More generally, psychological and subjective convergence along these dimensions (i.e., approximation, interpretability, discourse, and control strategies) – a phenomenon we have termed "high *attuning*" – can then attenuate sociolinguistic distance, bring the other person psychologically closer, and enhance conversational effectiveness and smoothness; in other words, it can fulfill both cognitive organization and identity maintenance functions. Of course, the converse can occur by means of *contra*-attuning. The exposition of Coupland et al. (1988) outlines further possibilities of *under*- and *over*attuning when interactional strategies deemed appropriate by one or the other party (e.g., an elderly recipient) are perceived to have been under- or overplayed. Thus, for example, "overattuning" (or overaccommodation; see Hamilton and Linell this volume) can be specified to characterize demeaning or patronizing talk – often well intentioned in its own terms – when excessive concern is paid to vocal clarity or amplitude, message simplification, or repetition (see Caporael 1981), as well as "over-accounting" when excuses, justifications, and apologies proliferate when recipients do not feel they are really warranted. Similarly, Fanon (1961) has discussed the patronizing speech whites sometimes adopt with blacks, making them feel that they are considered childlike or even subhuman. Alternatively, excessively authoritarian and dismissive styles may, for example, be characterized as underattuned (or underaccommodative) along the dimensions of control and discourse management, respectively. Moving toward a life span perspective on accommodation, recent data show that in intergenerational encounters the elderly are perceived – as a consequence, for instance, of generating many painful self-disclosures – by the young as underaccommodating the young's communicative position and identity (Coupland et al. 1991). Although there are many ways to construe such seemingly egocentric disclosures in functionally valuable ways for the elderly (see Coupland et al. 1988), there are nonetheless data to suggest that the elderly's linguistic habits change in later life as a proposed consequence of their grounded lack of interest in matters of social prestige – for instance, increased use by immigrants of an ethnic tongue not much utilized for many years (Clyne 1977).

Interpretive competences are, of course, more dynamic than discussed thus far and can change according to topic change. In other words, and particularly with unfamiliar others, we constantly need to assess – and reassess – the amount of shared knowledge we have on particular issues, events, and people as these are sequentially focused upon during the course of a conversation; sometimes this is necessary not simply to accommodate their lack of expertise but, more strategically, to ensure that our own discourse does not appear naive or ill-fated given our addressees' competences, dispositions, and evaluative tendencies. Commenting on research on (mainly referential) perspective taking, Krauss and Fussell (1988) have outlined the kinds of appraisals (and social comparisons) individuals need to make if they are, in our terms, to estimate their partner's interpretive competences. These are the extent to which interlocutors share the same (1) background knowledge on topic-relevant areas and affective orientations to these; (2) situational definitions, goals, plans, and task orientations; (3) definition of the relationship (e.g., intimacy); and (4) physical context (e.g., norms of appropriate behaviors). Processing such social data is often achieved swiftly and in a conversationally implicit manner, as reported by Anderson and Garrod (1987). They observed misunderstanding occurring between pairs of speakers cooperating to solve a problem involving the movement of pieces in a maze graphically displayed. Even so, as the dialogue continued, the speakers gradually began to adopt the same terms to describe and refer to items in the maze without any discussion of this strategy or any apparent need for it. Similarly, Isaacs and Clark (1987) found that subjects in their experiment swiftly appraised whether or not their interlocutors were experts on New York City without any apparent explicit indication and often within their first exchange of utterances. That said, it is a *collaborative* and dynamic venture that requires that individuals negotiate what is conversationally necessary to ensure that ongoing interpretive competences are optimal (Clark and Shaefer 1987). Indeed, Clark and Wilkes-Gibbs (1986) claim that conversationalists take for granted this process and use their so-called principle of mutual responsibility. This is described thus: "The participants in a conversation try to establish, roughly by the initiation of each new contribution, the mutual belief that the listeners have understood what the speaker meant in the last utterance to a criterion sufficient for current purposes" (33). Schober and Clark (1989) argue that a significant portion of this collaborative process is rather *opportunistic* – termed "grounding" – to the extent that participants in novel communicative contexts try out various referential (and presumably affective as well) shortcuts that are either accepted by the other(s) that are acted upon or else rejected and alternatives negotiated instead (see also Clark and Schaefer 1989).

Attuning to others' interpretive competences would seem essential when we wish to persuade them, attempt to regulate their behavior, or induce them to comply with a request. The extensive work of Delia and his associates (e.g., O'Keefe and Delia 1985) has examined the kinds of listener-adapted messages respondents claim they would utilize to persuade [and to comfort; see Burleson (1985)] another in an imaginary situation. The strategies reported as indicative of cognitively complex individuals give us guidelines as to the interpretability strategies accommodating persuaders might adopt in regulative disputes. Based on this research tradition, and specifically the work of Clark (1984) and Kline (in press), sophisticated social influencers would attempt to use language so as to coordinate their recipients' beliefs and actions with their own. More specifically, this attuning process would include the following strategies: (1) expressing mutually held values; (2) outlining the problem and arguing so as to induce the other to reflect on it in a way that is presumed to be different from the perspective originally held by the other; (3) and creating a resolution that is appealing to the other, does not damage, and even promotes his or her positive identity and face needs. It is interesting that this constructivist school of listener-adaptive communication and the cognitivist, referential school of perspective taking rarely cite each other and would doubtless profit from each others' insights; in addition, they rarely make recourse to CAT formulations. Obviously, the time is ripe for theoretical as well as empirical rapprochments; the recently elaborated format of CAT allows cross-fertilizations to occur to mutual benefit in understanding the negotiative character of interpersonal, small group, and intergroup relations and communication.

1.6. Attuning and health care

In the course of our CAT work in gerontology, it became clear to us that accommodative discourse and dilemmas were intricately related to psychological well-being as well as physical health (see, e.g., Coupland et al. 1988; Giles and Coupland 1991). Moreover, we have adduced that socially supportive activities so conducive to life satisfaction for many people are necessarily grounded in accommodative discourse. Figure 3 offers a generalized template for construing communication, health, and aging dimensions in these terms. The area of social support is a zeitgeist in the health care literatures, albeit not without controversy (e.g., Ganster and Victor 1988). The general notion here is that being provided with informational, social, and emotional support can be a prevailing resource as well as a ready-made buffer against specific stresses and illnesses (e.g., Cohen and Syme 1985). Although there are many complexities and caveats to this in the literature, it is claimed that those who believe they can access supportive networks, as well as the feeling that they contribute reciprocally to them, have greater psychological and physical well-being then those who do not consider such resources to be available to them (Heller, Swindle, and Dusenbury, 1986; Ingersoll-Dayton and Antonucci 1988). It has been argued recently (Giles, Williams, and Coupland 1990) that CAT can be important to health in the sense that high attuning may be a core component of many supportive encounters, not only productively but also receptively in terms of active listening (see McGregor and White 1990). Indeed, feeling supported may be a function, to a greater or lesser extent, of the degree of attuning one receives, and so those who are known or perceived to possess high attuning skills (Burleson 1984b) may be preferentially sought out as supporters (see also Albrecht and Adelman 1984).

Nevertheless, high attuning and supportiveness are not intrinsically positive correlates, and attuning may not always be a sufficient criterion for support. Giles, Williams, and Coupland (1990), then, distinguish not only between attuning and support (high and low on each) but also, as shown in Table 5, between positive and negative *long-term* outcomes. There may be occasions when encounters designed to be supportive are

Table 5. *A three-dimensional model of the interrelationships among attuning, support, and health outcomes*

	Support			
	High		Low	
	Attuning			
	High	Low	High	Low
Long-term health outcomes				
Positive	A	B	C	D
Negative	E	F	G	H

discursively managed by supporters employing low attuning strategies (e.g., Cell B in Table 5). Supporters, for example, may challenge recipients' assumptions and identities, predictably through interruptions, repeated clarification requests, subverting discourse, and generally contra-attuning in pursuit of positive support. In this vein, it is worthwhile noting that Arntson and Droge (1987) have shown, by observing epileptic support groups, that positive self-images, healthier attitudes, and healthier life styles are fostered when the group discourages indulgent "victim narratives." This is not to argue that support is a property of a single interaction itself – although it can be – as low support from any one localized interaction can be instrumental in the design of long-term support programs. Moreover, high attuning can in fact comprise nonsupportive behavior (Cell G in Table 5) where familial security, empathy, and understanding shown (with perhaps the best of motives) can encourage dependence, use of a sick role, and so forth (Rook and Pietromonaco 1987). In this way, recipients' negatively valenced perceptions can be validated that may not boost their own psychosocial resourcefulness and capacity to adapt (e.g., Eggert 1987; Kobasa and Puccetti 1983), for instance, to some conditions of aging and ill health.

Lehman, Ellard, and Wortman (1986) point to some supposedly emphatic comments made by supporters in a bereavement context (e.g., *I know exactly how you feel*) that can actually be evaluated by the recipient, in terms of CAT, as exceedingly underaccommodative. Thus it is suggested that failed support attempts, rather than reflecting misunderstandings or upsets, may be related to intense anxiety of supporters caused by extreme sensitivity to the listener's vulnerability and heightened awareness that a negative outcome may result from saying the wrong thing (see also Dunkel-Schetter and Wortman 1982). In Brown and Levinson's (1987) terms, support providers may be anxious about the possibility of intruding upon their recipients' *negative* face – their valued privacies and identities. Space precludes attention to each cell in Table 5, but a couple of further exemplars can be aired. First, we conceptualize the feasibility of high social support and high attuning leading to poor health outcomes in the long term, as, for instance, when two close friends depend on each other to promote their mutual alcohol or drug abuse (Cell E). Second, contra-attuning and low (or ultimately withdrawn) support could in some circumstances (e.g., airing interpersonal grievances in the context of a loving relationship) eventuate in significant cognitive reappraisals and positive health outcomes (Cell D).

1.7. Epilogue

CAT has, then, developed extensively since its inception. We now consider that accommodative processes can, over the long term, affect even issues of life and death. For instance, an aging person who is the recipient of over-attuning across different contexts and different interactional partners (among the array of agist social representations freely available in many societies) is likely to induce many people to feel that others believe him to have lost his competence. And in a very short time, given that many Western societies socialize us (and even our having colluded in the past with respect to others) into accepting the links between aging, ill health, and incompetence, we are susceptible to accepting others' definition of us in the same terms. As a consequence, we are then prone to the linguistic self-categorization (Turner 1987) introduced earlier and take on the attributes we prototypically associate with being elderly. In short, we constrain our own possibilities and life spans (Giles and Coupland 1991).

As we noted at the outset, it is in this same generally *applied* spirit that the following chapters have been compiled. In them, accommodation theory is invoked to model sometimes very small-scale, local interactional happenings, sometimes wholesale shifts of alignment between social groups. In *all* cases, the authors invoke key components of the accommodation framework, in the social and particularly institutional contexts that bound their chapters, to explore the complex interrelations of communication strategies and styles, the multiple social and psychological dimensions that contextualize them, and their social implications.

Chapters 2 and 3 show how accommodation concepts can explain adaptive processes in radio broadcasting (Bell) and courtroom (Linell) settings. The dislocation of speaker and audience in mass communication, Bell argues, limits the interpersonal dynamic of local convergence and divergence. On the other hand, broadcaster styles are no less strategically accommodative, since mismatches between broadcasters and their audiences carry heavy penalties. Bell thus shows, using Labov's sociolinguistic variable methodology, New Zealand newscasters' speech being designed to match audience characteristics, but also reflecting the prescriptions of corporate styles.

Linell's courtroom data, on the other hand, demonstrate how face-to-face talk needs to be characterized as "a multilayered and multimodal phenomenon" whereby accommodation processes, even in the same sequence of talk, can similarly show different and even contradictory trends. Patterns emerge, however, showing, for example, that legal professionals do attune their discourse to defendants' characteristics, and that judges and lawyers do modify their styles of talk – more or less interrogative, more or less conversational – in relation to the severity of the offenders' offense. Linell's chapter makes thus an important contribution to our understanding of language and interaction as factors relevant to, indeed as the achievement of, judicial outcomes.

The chapters by Street, Hamilton, and Ferrara show CAT at work in medical, caring, and clinical domains respectively. Street gives us an authoritative, critical review of communication research in doctor–patient consultations and a reinterpretation in terms of the accommodation framework. Given that the relevant literatures show some important inconsistencies, the chapter works toward a clear statement of priorities for future research. Suggesting that particular configurations of accommodation and nonaccommodation can severely impair practitioner–patient relations, and hence potentially health-care delivery and acceptance, Street concludes that more theoretically integrated, relational, and process-focused research is urgently needed.

Hamilton's analysis of interaction between normal and mentally disabled speakers, and in particular her longitudinal case study of her own interaction with Elsie, an Alzheimer's disease patient, is therefore a timely contribution. In these often problematic exchanges, Hamilton outlines the functioning of accommodation strategies, for example to buoy up social interaction or forestall interactional difficulties. More generally,

CAT can clarify the constraints on role-taking abilities that characterize several disability syndromes.

Ferrara's chapter, based on data from psychotherapeutic encounters, highlights methodological alternatives for CAT, showing the wide range of accommodative phenomena available for quantification. Her data show progressive, real-time convergence at syntactic, morphosyntactic, and phonological levels – primarily by lower-status clients to therapists. These findings are then set against analyses of discursive attuning variables – collaborative, echoing, and mirroring moves – that have specific salience as means of achieving rapport, and therefore, by implication, potentially successful intervention, during therapy.

The book's final three chapters deal, in various ways, with multilingual and interethnic concerns. In the second-language learning area, Zuengler again emphasizes the paucity of integrated theory and assesses what CAT can offer as a theory of second-language sociolinguistic variation. Accommodation, for example, provides appropriate conceptual apparatus for the (re)interpretation of Ferguson's notion of "foreigner talk" in a contextually richer and more differentiated manner. Once again, here we see the potential for CAT to model more or less problematical intergroup and interpersonal orientations, and the positive and negative potential consequences for language learning itself.

Gallois and Callan discuss situations where immigrants are expected to accommodate host communicative norms. They point out that an analysis of subjective norms in terms of their content, range, and clarity is crucial to understanding when accommodative acts are situationally appropriate or inappropriate. In an interesting study on the multiethnic context of Australia, these authors examine what males and females construe as acceptable and unacceptable verbal and nonverbal behaviors in response to compliments and criticism from Anglos and Italians of different statuses. Finding highly interpretable, yet complex, patterns of response that are dependent on subjects' sex, target ethnicity, and status, as well as whether the response was to a compliment or a criticism, Gallois and Callan make some telling points regarding the need to develop CAT further so as to take into account norm-following and norm-violating situations – particularly as they relate to perceived threats to personal and group identities. Putting into practice these empirical and theoretical ideas as inputs into intercultural training programs would likely enhance their efficacy significantly.

Bourhis argues for the value of CAT in providing a fuller understanding of formal and informal channels of organizational communication and in four theoretical traditions in this area of inquiry. For example, he points to the fact that accommodation has great potential for exploring the constituents of a so-called open organizational climate that is believed to be important for job satisfaction and effective performance. While highlighting the lack of attention to bilinguality in organizational research and theory, Bourhis describes a large-scale Canadian study on bilingual civil servants in New Brunswick. There he shows how Francophone employees converge more to the first language of their coworkers than do their Anglophone counterparts. Moreover, he shows how this phenomenon is a function of the employees' level of bilinguality, as well as the organizational status of the potential accommodative target; and importantly, by means of his innovative "linguistic work environment" indexes, he shows the ethnic and language background of employees' immediate occupational networks. Like the other authors, Bourhis cogently opens up exciting new areas for the viability of CAT in crucial – and hitherto unexplored – applied domains.

These chapters, which often introduce new data, richly demonstrate CAT in action as a resource for applied sociolinguistics. Still, we are, of course, not blind to the further issues and exciting challenges that lie ahead. An important prospectus for us has already been introduced (Section 1.5) in terms of building real links with cognitivist and constructivist traditions so as to effect a clear understanding of the collaborative aspects of talk and the manner in which relationships, identities, situations, and their goals are negotiated and emerge through talk. Relatedly, future research needs to address, explicitly, sequential concerns, in line with our earlier observation that addressee foci (as specified in Fig. 3) are themselves interactionally *variable*, rarely holding for the duration of an entire episode of talk. In this connection, participants' own involvement in forms of protocol analysis, to chart the contingent nature of accommodation strategies in relation to prior conversational moves, may contribute new insights. By these means, more qualitative and interpretive designs should allow us to refine claims and findings relating to accommodation across groups or situations and temper the idealization implicit in the somewhat mechanistic conceptualizations of accommodative options as specified in the model's early life.

As discursive concerns come more to the fore in social psychological theory and analysis generally (see Potter and Wetherell 1987), there will indeed be value in reexamining quantitative research – for example, the accent-based studies of convergence and divergence with which speech accommodation theory began – *in relation to* the functional organization of talk (see the modest beginnings of such an approach in Coupland 1988). For example, Maynard (1988) has argued that there are clear limits to the kinds of sociolinguistic markers that are amenable to quantative, contrastive analysis and that have relatively stable social significance independent of their local positioning in rhetorical structures. A way to begin, then, is to focus on the "interaction order" as the locus for interpersonal accommodation, and then to explore the specific contribution of indexical sociolinguistic variables, such as segmental phonology, rate, or information density, to locally grounded accommodative moves. [This prescription is in fact very similar to that of Hymes (1977) for "socially constituted linguistics" generally.]

We began this chapter by placing accommodation theory among other traditions of research concerned with adaptive interpersonal processes in language and communication. Another task for the future is to impose further conceptual and taxonomic order on the range of sociolinguistic processes that may be implicated in interpersonal attuning. One intriguing area of overlap will be with Brown and Levinson's (1987) specification of "positive politeness" strategies, construed as diverse moves to claim common ground with an interlocutor, portraying interactants as cooperators generally fulfilling interlocutors' wants. Although these authors discuss such strategies exclusively in terms of moves made to redress face threats, their strategic currency is presumably broader, fulfilling face *promotion* and *maintenance* goals (see Penman 1990). They would appear to fall well in the context of traditionally invoked accommodative motives (to gain approval and increase communication efficiency). Correspondingly, CAT seems well suited to supplying the contextual elaboration that Brown and Levinson themselves suggest (in the introduction to their 1987 volume) their framework requires, and that has apparently limited its predictive power to date.

Theoretical models, perhaps particularly those seeking to capture generalizations about communication and relational processes, are unlikely to achieve stasis. As this chapter has amply demonstrated, CAT has seen major shifts of emphasis and, we would argue, has incorporated their new insights into its explanatory compass. Further changes (along the lines sketched earlier or otherwise) will doubtless follow. However, the rationale for the present volume is that a sociolinguistics that incorporates and articulates social psychological premises in its considerations of the practices and contexts of talk – and this fusion is the essence of the accommodation perspective – is already delivering insight into

52   H. Giles, N. Coupland, and J. Coupland

the routine and exceptional relational experiences that comprise our social lives.

References

Aboud, F. E. 1976. Social developmental aspects of language. *Papers in Linguistics*, 9: 15–37.

Abrahamson, M. 1966. *Interpersonal Accommodation*. Princeton, NJ: Van Nostrand.

Albrecht, T. L., and Adelman, M. B. 1984. Social support and life stress: New directions for communication research. *Human Communication Research*, 11: 3–32.

Albrecht, T. L., Adelman, M. B., and Associates (eds.). 1987. *Communicating Social Support*. London: Sage.

Alloway, R., and Bebbington, P. 1987. The buffer theory of social support – review of the literature. *Psychological Medicine*, 17: 91–108.

Altman, I., and Taylor, D. A. 1973. *Social Penetration: The Development of Interpersonal Relationships*. New York: Holt, Rinehart and Winston.

Anderson, A., and Garrod, S. C. 1987. The dynamics of referential meaning in spontaneous conversation: Some preliminary studies. *In* R. G. Reilly (ed.), *Communication Failure in Dialogue and Discourse: Detection and Repair Processes*, pp. 161–87. Amsterdam: North Holland.

Appelgate, J. L., and Delia, J. G. 1980. Person-centered speech, psychological development and the contexts of language usage. *in* R. St. Clair and H. Giles (eds.), *The Social and Psychological Contexts of Language*, pp. 245–82. Hillsdale, NJ: Erlbaum.

Argyle, M. 1969. *Social Interaction*. London: Methuen.

Argyle, M., and Dean J. 1965. Eye-contact, distance and affiliation. *Sociometry*, 28: 289–304.

Argyle, M., Furnham, A., and Graham, J. A. (eds.). 1981. *Social Situations*. Cambridge: Cambridge University Press.

Argyle, M., and Kendon, A. 1967. The experimental analysis of social performance. *In* L. Berkowitz (ed.), *Advances in Experimental Social Psychology*, Vol. 3, pp. 55–98. New York: Academic Press.

Arntson, P., and Droge, D. 1987. Social support in self-help groups: The role of communication in enabling perceptions of control. *In* T. L. Albrecht and M. B. Adelman (eds.), *Communicating Social Support*, pp. 148–70. Newbury Park, CA: Sage.

Aronson, E., and Linder, D. 1965. Gain and loss of esteem as determinants of interpersonal attractiveness. *Journal of Experimental Social Psychology*, 1: 156–71.

Aronsson, K., Jonsson, L., and Linell, P. 1987. The courtroom hearing as middle ground: Speech accommodation by lawyers and defendants. *Journal of Language and Social Psychology*, 6: 99–116.

Atkinson, K., and Coupland, N. 1988. Accommodation as ideology. *Language and Communication*, 8: 321–8.

Bales, R. F. 1950. *Interaction Process Analysis*. Cambridge, MA: Addison-Wesley.

Ball, P., Giles, H., Byrne, J. L., and Berechree, P. 1984. Situational constraints on the evaluative significance of speech accommodation: Some Australian data. *International Journal of the Sociology of Language*, 46: 115–30.

Ball, P., Giles, H., and Hewstone, M. 1985. Interpersonal accommodation and situational construals: An integrative formalisation *In* H. Giles and R. St. Clair (eds.), *Recent Advances in Language, Communication and Social Psychology*, pp. 263–86. London: Erlbaum.

Basso, K. H. 1979. *Portraits of "The Whiteman."* Cambridge: Cambridge University Press.

Bauer, R. A. 1964. The communicator and his audience. *In* L. A. Dexter and D. M. White (eds), *People, Society and Mass Communications*, pp. 125–39. Glencoe, IL: Free Press.

Baugh, J. 1983. *Black Street Speech*. Austin: University of Texas Press.

Bavelas, J. B., Black, A., Chovil, N., Lemery, C. R., and Mullett, J. 1988. Form and function in motor mimicry: Topographic evidence that the primary function is communicative. *Human Communication Research*, 14: 275–99.

Beebe, L. 1981. Social and situational factors affecting communicative strategy of dialect code-switching. *International Journal of the Sociology of Language*, 32: 139–49.

Bell, A. 1984. Language style as audience design. *Language in Society*, 13: 145–204.

Bell, R. A., Buerkel-Rothfuss, N. L., and Gore, K. E. 1987. "Did you bring the yarmulke for the cabbage patch kid?" The idiomatic communication of young lovers. *Human Communication Research*, 14: 47–67.

Berg, M. E., van den. 1985. *Language Planning and Language Use in Taiwan*. Dordrecht: ICG Printing.

Berg, M. E., van den. 1986. Language planning and language use in Taiwan: Social identity, language accommodation, and language choice behaviour. *International Journal of the Sociology of Language*, 59: 97–115.

Berg, M. E., van den. 1988. Long term accommodation of (ethno) linguistic groups toward a societal language norm. *Language and Communication*, 8: 251–70.

Berger, C. R. 1979. Beyond initial interaction: Uncertainty, understanding, and the development of interpersonal relationships. *In* H. Giles and R. St. Clair (eds.), *Language and Social Psychology*, pp. 122–44. Oxford: Blackwell.

Berger, C. R., and Bradac, J. J. 1982. *Language and Social Knowledge*. London: Edward Arnold.

Berger, C. R., and Roloff, M. E. 1980. Social cognition, self-awareness and interpersonal communication. *In* B. Dervin and M. J. Wright (eds.), *Progress in Communication Science*, Vol. 2, pp. 1–50. Norwood, NJ: Ablex.

Bilous, F. R., and Krauss, R. M. 1988. Dominance and accommodation in the conversational behaviours of same- and mixed-gender dyads. *Language and Communication*, 8: 183–94.

Blakar, R. M. 1985. Towards a theory of communication in terms of preconditions: A conceptual framework and some empirical explorations. *In* H. Giles and R. St. Clair (eds.), *Recent Advances in Language, Communication and Social Psychology*, pp. 10–40. London: Erlbaum.

Bond, M. H. 1985. Language as a carrier of ethnic stereotypes in Hong Kong. *Journal of Social Psychology*, 125: 53–62.

Booth-Butterfield, M., and Jordan, F. 1989. Communication adaptation among racially homogeneous and heterogeneous groups. *The Southern Communication Journal*, 54: 253–72.

Bormann, E. G. 1985. Symbolic convergence theory: A communication formulation. *Journal of Communication*, 35: 128–38.

Bossard, J. H. S. 1955. Family modes of expression. *American Sociological Review*, 10: 226–37.

54   H. Giles, N. Coupland, and J. Coupland

Bourhis, R. Y. 1977. Language and social evaluation in Wales. Unpublished Ph.D. thesis, University of Bristol.

Bourhis, R. Y. 1979. Language in ethnic interaction: A social psychological approach. *In* H. Giles and B. Saint-Jacques (eds.), *Language and Ethnic Relations*, pp. 117–41. Oxford: Pergamon.

Bourhis, R. Y. 1983. Language attitudes and self-reports of French-English usage in Quebec. *Journal of Multilingual and Multicultural Development*, 4: 163–79.

Bourhis, R. Y. 1984. Cross-cultural communication in Montreal: Two field studies since Bill 101. *International Journal of the Sociology of Language*, 46: 33–47.

Bourhis, R. Y., and Giles, H. 1977. The language of intergroup distinctiveness. *In* H. Giles (ed.), *Language, Ethnicity and Intergroup Relations*, pp. 119–35. London: Academic Press.

Bourhis, R. Y., Giles, H., and Lambert, W. E. 1975. Social consequences of accommodating one's style of speech: A cross-national investigation. *International Journal of the Sociology of Language*, 6: 55–72.

Bourhis, R. Y., Giles, H., Leyens, J. P., and Tajfel, H. 1979. Psycholinguistic distinctiveness: Language divergence in Belgium. *In* H. Giles and R. St. Clair (eds.), *Language and Social Psychology*, pp. 158–85. Oxford: Blackwell.

Bourhis, R. Y., Roth, S., and MacQueen, G. 1988. Communication in the hospital setting: A survey of medical and everyday language use amongst patients, nurses and doctors. *Social Science and Medicine*, 24: 1–8.

Bourhis, R. Y., and Sachdev, I. 1984. Vitality perceptions and language attitudes. *Journal of Language and Social Psychology*, 3: 97–126.

Bradac, J. J. 1990. Language attitudes and impression formation. *In* H. Giles and W. P. Robinson (eds.), *Handbook of Language and Social Psychology*, pp. 387–412. Chichester: Wiley.

Bradac, J. J., Hopper, R., and Wiemann, J. M. 1989. Message effects: Retrospect and prospect. *In* J. J. Bradac (ed.), *Message Effects in Communication Science*, pp. 294–317. Newbury Park, CA: Sage.

Bradac, J. J., and Mulac, A. 1984. Attributional consequences of powerful and powerless speech styles in a crisis-intervention context. *Journal of Language and Social Psychology*, 3: 1–19.

Bradac, J. J., Mulac, A., and House, A. 1988. Lexical diversity and magnitude of convergent versus divergent style-shifting: Perceptual and evaluative consequences. *Language and Communication*, 8: 213–28.

Bradac, J. J., O'Donnell, M., and Tardy, C. H. 1984. Another stab at a touchy subject: Affective meaning of touch. *Women's Studies in Communication*, 7: 38–50.

Bronfenbrenner, U. 1979. *The Ecology of Human Development: Experiments by Nature and Design*. Cambridge, MA: Harvard University Press.

Brown, P., and Levinson, S. 1987. *Politeness: Some Universals in Language Usage*. Cambridge: Cambridge University Press.

Brown, P. M., and Dell, G. S. 1987. Adapting production to comprehension: The explicit mention of instruments. *Cognitive Psychology*, 19: 441–72.

Brown, R. 1977. Introduction. *In* C. E. Snow and C. A. Ferguson (eds.), *Talking to Children: Language Input and Acquisition*. Cambridge, MA: MIT Press.

Buller, D. B., and Aune, R. K. 1988. The effects of vocalics and nonverbal sensitivity on compliance: A speech accommodation theory explanation. *Human Communication Research*, 14: 301–32.

Burleson, B. R. 1984a. Age, social-cognitive development, and the use of comforting strategies. *Communication Monographs*, 51: 140–53.

Burleson, B. R. 1984b. Comforting communication. *In* H. E. Sypher and J. L. Applegate (eds.), *Communication by Children and Adults: Social Cognitive and Strategic Processing*, pp. 63–104. Beverly Hills, CA: Sage.

Burleson, B. R. 1985. The production of comforting messages: Social-cognitive foundations. *Journal of Language and Social Psychology*, 5: 253–74.

Burleson, B. R. 1986. Communication skills and childhood peer relationships: An overview. *In* M. McLaughlin (ed.), *Communication Yearbook 9*, pp. 143–80. Beverly Hills, CA: Sage.

Burleson, B. R. 1987. Cognitive complexity. *In* J. C. McCroskey and J.A. Daly (eds.), *Personality and Interpersonal Communication*, pp. 305–49. Beverly Hills, CA: Sage.

Burleson, B. R., and Fennelly, D. A. 1981. The effects of persuasive appeal form and cognitive complexity on children's sharing behavior. *Child Study Journal*, 11: 75–90.

Burrell, G., and Morgan, G. 1979. *Sociological Paradigms and Organisational Analysis*. London: Heinemann.

Byrne, D. 1971. *The Attraction Paradigm*. New York: Academic Press.

Caporael, L. R. 1981. The paralanguage of caregiving: Baby talk to the institutionalized elderly. *Journal of Personality and Social Psychology*, 40: 876–84.

Caporael, L. R., Lukaszewski, M. P., and Culbertson, G. H. 1983. Secondary baby talk: Judgments by institutionalized elderly and their caregivers. *Journal of Personality and Social Psychology*, 44: 746–54.

Cappella, J. N. 1981. Mutual influence in expressive behavior: Adult–adult and infant–adult dyadic interaction. *Psychological Bulletin*, 89: 101–32.

Cappella, J. N., and Greene, J. 1982. A discrepancy-arousal explanation of mutual influence in expressive behavior for adult–adult and infant–adult interaction. *Communication Monographs*, 49: 89–114.

Cappella, J. N., and Planalp, S. 1981. Talk and silence sequences in informal conversations III: Interspeaker influence. *Human Communication Research*, 7: 117–32.

Chadwick-Jones, J. 1976. *Social Exchange Theory*. London: Academic Press.

Chapple, E. D. 1939. Quantitative analysis of the interaction of individuals. *Proceedings of the National Academy of Sciences*, 25: 58–67.

Clark, H. H., and Marshall, C. 1981. Definite reference and mutual knowledge. *In* A. Joshi, I. Sag, and B. Webber (eds.), *Elements of Discourse Understanding*. Cambridge: Cambridge University Press.

Clark, H. H., and Schaefer, E. F. 1987. Collaborating on contributions to conversations. *Language and Cognitive Processes*, 2: 19–41.

Clark, H. H., and Schaefer, E. F. 1989. Contributing to discourse. *Cognitive Science*, 13: 259–94.

Clark, H. H., and Wilkes-Gibbs, D. 1986. Referring as a collaborative process. *Cognition*, 22: 1–39.

Clark, R. A. 1984. *Persuasive Messages*. New York: Harper & Row.

Clark, R. A., and Delia, J. G. 1979. Topoi and rhetorical competence. *Quarterly Journal of Speech*, 65: 165–206.

Clyne, M. 1977. Bilingualism of the elderly. *Talanya*, 4: 45–65.

Cody, M., and McLaughlin, M. (eds.). 1989. *The Psychology of Tactical Communication*. Clevedon: Multilingual Matters.

Cohen, E., and Cooper, R. L. 1986. Language and tourism. *Annals of Tourism Research*, 13: 535–63.

Cohen, S., and Syme, S. L. (eds.). 1985. *Social Support and Health*. New York: Academic Press.

Condon, W. S., and Ogston, W. D. 1967. A segmentation of behaviour. *Journal of Psychiatric Research*, 5: 221–35.

Cooper, R. L., and Carpenter, S. 1969. Linguistic diversity in the Ethiopian market. *Journal of African Languages*, 8: 160–8.

Coupland, N. 1984. Accommodation at work: Some phonological data and their implications. *International Journal of the Sociology of Language*, 46: 49–70.

Coupland, N. 1985. "Hark, hark the lark": Social motivations for phonological style shifting. *Language and Communication*, 5: 153–71.

Coupland, N. 1988. *Dialect in Use*. Cardiff: University of Wales Press.

Coupland, N., Coupland, J., Giles, H., and Henwood, K. 1988. Accommodating the elderly: Invoking and extending a theory. *Language in Society*, 17: 1–41.

Coupland, N., Coupland, J., Giles, H., and Henwood, K. 1991. Intergenerational talk: Goal consonance and intergroup dissonance. In K. Tracy (ed.) *Understanding Face-to-Face Interaction: Issues Linking Goals and Discourse*, pp. 79–100. Hillsdale, NJ: Erlbaum.

Coupland, N., Coupland, J., Giles, H., Henwood, K., and Wiemann, J. 1988. Elderly self-disclosure: Interactional and intergroup issues. *Language and Communication*, 8: 109–33.

Coupland, N., and Giles, H. 1988a. Communicative accommodation: Recent developments. Special issue of *Language and Communication*, 8 (3/4): 175–327.

Coupland, N., and Giles, H. 1988b. Introduction: The communicative contexts of accommodation. *Language and Communication*, 8: 175–82.

Coupland, N., Giles, H., and Benn, W. 1986. Language, communication and the blind. *Journal of Language and Social Psychology*, 5, 63–70.

Coupland, N., Henwood, K., Coupland, J., and Giles, H. 1990. Accommodating troubles-talk: The young's management of elderly self-disclosure. In G. M. McGregor and R. White (eds.), *Reception and Response: Hearer Creativity and the Analysis of Spoken and Written Texts*, pp. 112–44. London: Croom Helm.

Dabbs, J. M., Jr. 1969. Similarity of gestures and interpersonal influence. *Proceedings of the 77th Annual Convention of the American Psychological Association*, 4: 337–8.

Day, R. R. 1982. Children's attitudes toward language. In E. B. Ryan and H. Giles (eds.), *Attitudes towards Language Variation: Social and Applied Contexts*, pp. 116–31. London: Arnold.

Delia, J. G., and Clark, R. A. 1977. Cognitive complexity, social perception, and the development of listener-adapted communication in six-, eight-, ten-, and twelve-year old boys. *Communication Monographs*, 44: 326–45.

DePaulo, B. M., and Coleman, L. M. 1986. Talking to children, foreigners, and retarded adults. *Journal of Personality and Social Psychology*, 51: 945–59.

Deprez, K., and Persoons, K. (1984). On the identity of Flemish high school students in Brussels. *Journal of Language and Social Psychology*, 3: 273–96.

Detweiler, R. 1986. Categorisation, attribution and intergroup communication. In W. B. Gudykunst (ed.), *Intergroup Communication*, pp. 74–85. London: Arnold.

Doise, W., Sinclair, A., and Bourhis, R. Y. 1976. Evaluation of accent convergence and divergence in cooperative and competitive intergroup situations. *British Journal of Social and Clinical Psychology*, 15: 247–52.

Dunkel-Schetter, C., and Wortman, C. B. 1982. The interpersonal dynamics of cancer: Problems in social relationships and their impact on the patient. In H. S. Friedman and M. R. DiMatteo (eds.), *Interpersonal Issues in Health Care*, pp. 68–100. New York: Academic Press.

Durkheim, E. 1964. *The Division of Labour in Society*. New York: Free Press.

Edwards, V. 1986. *Language in a Black Community*. Clevedon: Multilingual Matters.

Eggert, L. L. 1987. Support in family ties: Stress, coping, and adaptation. *In* T. L. Albrecht and M. B. Adelman (eds.), *Communicating Social Support*, pp. 80–104. Newbury Park, CA: Sage.

Ehrlich, H. J., and Graeven, D. B., 1971. Reciprocal self-disclosure in a dyad. *Journal of Experimental Social Psychology*, 7: 389–400.

Eiser, J. R. 1975. Attitudes and the use of evaluative language: A two-way process. *Journal for the Theory of Social Behaviour*, 5: 235–48.

Ellingsworth, H. W. 1988. A theory of adaptation in intercultural dyads. *In* Y. Y. Kim and W. B. Gudykunst (eds.), *Theories in Intercultural Communication*, pp. 259–79. Newbury Park, CA: Sage.

Erickson, F., and Schulz, J. 1982. *The Counselor as Gatekeeper*. New York: Free Press.

Fanon, F. 1961. *Black Skin, White Masks*. New York: Grove Press.

Feldman, R. E. 1968. Response to compatriots and foreigners who seek assistance. *Journal of Personality and Social Psychology*, 10: 202–14.

Feldstein, S. 1972. Temporal patterns of dialogue: Basic research and reconsiderations. *In* A. W. Siegman and B. Pope (eds.), *Studies in Dyadic Communication*, pp. 91–113. New York: Pergamon.

Feldstein, S., and Crown, C. L. 1990. Oriental and Canadian conversational interactions: Chronographic structure and interpersonal perception. *Journal of Asian Pacific Communication*, 1: 247–66.

Feldstein, S., and Welkowitz, S. 1978. A chronography of conversation: In defense of an objective approach. *In* A. W. Siegman and S. Feldstein (eds.), *Nonverbal Behavior and Communication*, pp. 329–78. Hillsdale, NJ: Erlbaum.

Fish, S. 1980. *Is There a Text in This Class? The Authority of Interpretive Communities*. Cambridge, MA: Harvard University Press.

Fisher, S., and Todd, A. 1986. Introduction: Communication in institutional contexts: Social interaction and social structure. *In* S. Fisher and A. Todd (eds.), *Discourse and Institutional Authority: Medicine, Education and Law*, pp. ix–xvii. Norwood, NJ: Ablex.

Fishman, J. A. 1977. Language and ethnicity. *In* H. Giles (ed.), *Language, Ethnicity and Intergroup Relations*, pp. 15–58. London: Academic Press.

Flavell, J. H., Botkin, P. T., Fry, C. L., Jr., Wright, J. W., and Jarvis, P. E. 1968. *The Development of Role-Taking and Communication Skills in Children*. New York: Wiley.

Gallois, C., and Callan, V. J. 1988. Communication accommodation and the prototypical speaker: Predicting evaluations of status and solidarity. *Language and Communication*, 8: 271–84.

Gallois, C., Franklyn-Stokes, A., Giles, H., and Coupland, N. 1988. Communication accommodation in intercultural encounters. *In* Y. Y. Kim and W. B. Gudykunst (eds.), *Theories in Intercultural Communication*, pp. 157–85. Newbury Park, CA: Sage.

Ganster, D. C., and Victor, B., 1988. The impact of social support on mental and physical health. *British Journal of Medical Psychology*, 61: 17–36.

Garrett, P., Giles, H., and Coupland, N. 1989. The contexts of language learning: Extending the intergroup model of second language acquisition. *In* S. Ting-Toomey and F. Korzenny (eds.), *Language, Communication, and Culture: Current Directions*, pp. 201–21. Newbury Park, CA: Sage.

Garvey, C., and BenDebba, M. 1974. Effects of age, sex, and partner on children's dyadic speech. *Child Development*, 45: 1159–61.

Genesee, F. 1984. The social-psychological significance of code-switching for children. *Applied Psycholinguistics*, 5: 3–20.

Genesee, F., and Bourhis, R. Y. 1982. The social psychological significance of code switching in cross-cultural communication. *Journal of Language and Social Psychology*, 1: 1–28.

Genessee, F., and Bourhis, R. Y. 1988. Evaluative reactions to language choice strategies: The role of sociostructural factors. *Language and Communication*, 8: 229–50.

Gilbert, D. T., Krull, D. S., and Pelham, B. W. 1988. Of thoughts unspoken: Social influence and the self-regulation of behavior. *Journal of Personality and Social Psychology*, 55: 685–694.

Giles, H. 1971. A study of speech patterns in social interaction: Accent evaluation and accent change. Unpublished Ph.D. thesis, University of Bristol.

Giles, H. 1973. Accent mobility: A model and some data. *Anthropological Linguistics*, 15: 87–105.

Giles, H. 1977. Social psychology and applied linguistics. *ITL: Review of Applied Linguistics*, 33: 27–42.

Giles, H. 1979. Ethnicity markers in speech. In K. R. Scherer and H. Giles (eds.), *Social Markers in Speech*, pp. 251–90. Cambridge: Cambridge University Press.

Giles, H. 1980. Accommodation theory: Some new directions. *York Papers in Linguistics*, 9: 105–36.

Giles, H. (ed.). 1984. The dynamics of speech accommodation (Special issue). *International Journal of the Sociology of Language*, 46.

Giles, H., and Bourhis, R. Y. 1976. Black speakers with white speech – a real problem? In G. Nickel (ed.), *Proceedings of the 4th. International Congress on Applied Linguistics*, Vol. 1., pp. 575–84. Stuttgart: Hochschul Verlag.

Giles, H., Bourhis, R. Y., and Taylor, D. M. 1977. Towards a theory of language in ethnic group relations. In H. Giles (ed.), *Language, Ethnicity, and Intergroup Relations*, pp. 307–48. London: Academic Press.

Giles, H., and Byrne, J. L. 1982. An intergroup model of second language acquisition. *Journal of Multilingual and Multicultural Development*, 3: 17–40.

Giles, H., and Coupland, N. 1991. Language attitudes: Discursive, contextual, and gerontological considerations. In A. G. Reynolds (ed.), *Bilingualism, Multiculturalism, and Second Language Learning: The McGill Conference in Honor of Wallace E. Lambert*, pp. 21–42. Hillsdale, NJ: Erlbaum.

Giles, H., and Fitzpatrick, M. A. 1984. Personal, group and couple identities: Towards a relational context for the study of language attitudes and linguistic forms. In D. Schiffrin (ed.), *Meaning, Form and Use in Context: Linguistic Applications*, pp. 253–77. Washington, DC: Georgetown University Press.

Giles, H., and Franklyn-Stokes, A. 1989. Communicator characteristics. In M. K. Asante and W. B. Gudykunst (eds.), *Handbook of International and Intercultural Communication*, pp. 117–44. Newbury Park, CA: Sage.

Giles, H., Garrett, P., and Coupland, N. 1988. Language acquisition in the Basque country: Invoking and extending the Intergroup Model. In *Proceedings of the Conference on the Basque Language*, Vol. 2, pp. 297–310. San Sebastian: Central Publishing Services of the Basque Government, Spain.

Giles, H., and Hewstone, M. 1982. Cognitive structures, speech and social situations: Two integrative models. *Language Sciences*, 5: 187–219.

Giles, H., and Johnson, P. 1981. The role of language in ethnic group relations. In J. C. Turner and H. Giles (eds.), *Intergroup Behaviour*, pp. 199–243. Oxford: Blackwell.

Giles, H., and Johnson, P. 1986. Perceived threat, ethnic commitment, and interethnic language behavior. *In* Y. Y. Kim (ed.), *Interethnic Communication: Recent Research*, pp. 91–116. Beverly Hills, CA: Sage.

Giles, H., and Johnson, P. 1987. Ethnolinguistic identity theory: A social psychological approach to language maintenance. *International Journal of the Sociology of Language*, 68: 66–99.

Giles, H., Leets, L., and Coupland, N. 1990. Minority language group status: A theoretical conspexus. *Journal of Multilingual and Multicultural Development*, 11, 37–55.

Giles, H., Mulac, A. Bradac, J. J., and Johnson, P. (1987). Speech accommodation theory: The next decade and beyond. *In* M. McLaughlin (ed.), *Communication Yearbook 10*, pp. 13–48. Newbury Park, CA: Sage.

Giles, H., and Powesland, P. F. 1975. *Speech Style and Social Evaluation*. London: Academic Press.

Giles, H., Rosenthal, D., and Young, L. 1985. Perceived ethnolinguistic vitality: The Anglo- and Greek-Australian setting. *Journal of Multilingual and Multicultural Development*, 3: 253–69.

Giles, H., Scherer, K. R., and Taylor, D. M. 1979. Speech markers in social interaction. *In* K. R. Scherer and H. Giles (eds.), *Social Markers in Speech*, pp. 343–81. Cambridge: Cambridge University Press.

Giles, H., and Smith, P. M. 1979. Accommodation theory: Optimal levels of convergence. *In* H. Giles and R. St. Clair (eds.), *Language and Social Psychology*, pp. 45–65. Oxford: Blackwell.

Giles, H., and Street, R. 1985. Communicator characteristics and behavior. In M. L. Knapp and G. R. Miller (eds.), *Handbook of Interpersonal Communication*, pp. 205–61. Beverly Hills, CA: Sage.

Giles, H., Taylor, D. M., and Bourhis, R. Y. (1973). Towards a theory of interpersonal accommodation through language: Some Canadian data. *Language in Society*, 2: 177–92.

Giles, H., and Wiemann, J. 1987. Language, social comparison, and power. *In* S. Chaffee and C. R. Berger (eds.), *Handbook of Communication Science*, pp. 350–84. Newbury Park, CA: Sage.

Giles, H., Williams, A., and Coupland, N. 1990. Communication, health and the elderly: Frameworks, agenda and a model. *In* H. Giles, N. Coupland, and J. Wiemann (eds.), *Communication, Health and the Elderly: Fulbright International Colloquium 8*, pp. 1–28. Manchester: Manchester University Press.

Goffman, E. 1967. *The Presentation of Self in Everyday Life*. Harmondsworth: Penguin.

Goodwin, C. 1981. *Conversational Organization: Interaction between Speakers and Hearers*. New York: Academic Press.

Gorter, D. 1987. Aspects of language choice in the Frisian-Dutch bilingual context: Neutrality and asymmetry. *Journal of Multilingual and Multicultural Development*, 8: 121–32.

Grabowski-Gellert, J., and Winterhoff-Spurk, P. 1988. Your smile is my command: Interaction between verbal and nonverbal components of requesting specific to situational characteristics. *Journal of Language and Social Psychology*, 7: 229–42.

Graumann, C. F., and Hermann, Th. (eds.) 1987. Other-relatedness in language processing. Special issue of *Journal of Language and Social Psychology*, 7 (3/4): 159–279.

Greenbaum, C. W., and Cooper, R. L. 1988. Speech accommodation: Model for effects on language learning and interpersonal attraction. Mimeo. Jerusalem: Psychology Dept., Hebrew University.

Gregory, S. W., Jr. 1986. A sociolinguistic indicator of group membership. *Journal of Psycholinguistic Research*, 15: 189–207.

Grice, H. P. 1971. Meaning. In D. D. Steinberg and L. A. Jakobovitz (eds.), *Semantics: An Interdisciplinary Reader*, pp. 53–59. Cambridge: Cambridge University Press.

Grice, J. 1975. Logic and conversations. In P. Cole and J. Morgan (eds.), *Syntax and Semantics*, Vol. 3, *Speech Acts*, pp. 41–58. New York: Academic Press.

Grush, J. E., Clore, G. L., and Costin, F. 1975. Dissimilarity and attraction: When difference makes a difference. *Journal of Personality and Social Psychology*, 32: 783–9.

Gudykunst, W. B. (ed.). 1986. *Intergroup Communication*. London: Edward Arnold.

Gudykunst, W. B. 1988. Uncertainty and anxiety. In Y. Y. Kim and W. B. Gudykunst (eds.), *Theories in Intercultural Communication*, pp. 123–56. Newbury Park, CA: Sage.

Gudykunst, W. B., and Nishida, T. 1989. Theoretical perspectives for studying intercultural communication. In M. K. Asante and W. B. Gudykunst (eds.), *Handbook of International and Intercultural Communication*, pp. 17–46. Newbury Park, CA: Sage.

Gudykunst, W. B., and Ting-Toomey, S. 1990. Ethnic identity, language and communication breakdown. In H. Giles and W. P. Robinson (eds.), *Handbook of Language and Social Psychology*, pp. 309–29. Chichester: Wiley.

Gudykunst, W. B., Yoon, Y. C., and Nishida, T. 1987. The influence of individualism-collectivism on perceptions of communication in ingroup and outgroup relationships. *Communication Monographs*, 54: 295–306.

Hale, J. L., and Burgoon, J. K. 1984. Models of reactions to changes in nonverbal immediacy. *Journal of Nonverbal Behavior*, 8: 287–314.

Hall, B. J., and Gudykunst, W. B. 1986. The intergroup theory of second language ability. *Journal of Language and Social Psychology*, 5: 91–302.

Harris, M. B., and Baudin, H. 1973 The language of altruism: The effects of language, dress and ethnic group. *Journal of Social Psychology*, 97: 37–41.

Hart, R. P., Carlson, R.E., and Eadie, W. F. 1980. Attitudes toward communication and the assessment of rhetorical sensitivity. *Communication Monographs*, 47: 1–22.

Hecht, M. L., Boster, F. J., and LaMer, S. 1989. The effect of extroversion and differentiation on listener-adapted communication. *Communication Reports*, 2: 1–8.

Heider, F. 1958 *The Psychology of Interpersonal Relations*. New York: Wiley.

Heller, K., Swindle, R. W., and Dusenbury, L. 1986. Component social support processes: Comment and integration. *Journal of Consulting and Clinical Psychology*, 54: 466–70.

Heritage, J. C. 1987. Ethnomethodology. In A. Giddens and J. Turner (eds.), *Social Theory Today*, pp. 224–72. Cambridge: Polity Press.

Heritage, J. C., and Watson, D. R. 1980. Aspects of the properties of formulations in natural conversations: Some instances analyzed. *Semiotica*, 30: 245–62.

Hewstone, M. 1983. The role of language in attribution processes. In J. Jaspars, F. D. Fincham, and M. Hewstone (eds.), *Attribution Theory and Research: Conceptual, Developmental and Social Dimensions*, pp. 241–60. London: Academic Press.

Hewstone, M. 1989. *Causal Attribution*. Oxford: Blackwell.

Hewstone, M., and Giles, H. 1986. Social groups and social stereotypes in intergroup communication: Review and model of intergroup communication breakdown. *In* W. B. Gudykunst (ed.), *Intergroup Communication*, pp. 10–26. London: Edward Arnold.

Higgins, E. T. 1980. The "communication game": Implications for social cognition and persuasion. *In* E. T. Higgins, C. P. Herman, and M. P. Zanna (eds.), *Social Cognition: The Ontario Symposium*, pp. 343–92. Hillsdale, NJ: Lawrence Erlbaum.

Hildebrandt, N., and Giles, H. 1984. The Japanese as subordinate group: Ethnolinguistic identity theory in a foreign language context. *Anthropological Linguistics*, 25: 436–66.

Hogg, M. 1985. Masculine and feminine speech in dyads and groups: A study of speech style and gender salience. *Journal of Language and Social Psychology*, 4: 99–112.

Huffines, L. M. 1986. Strategies of language maintenance and ethnic marking among the Pennsylvanian Germans. *Language Sciences*, 8: 1–16.

Hymes, D. 1972. Models of the interaction of language and social life. *In* J. J. Gumperz and D. Hymes (eds.), *Directions in Sociolinguistics*, pp. 35–71. New York: Holt, Rinehart and Winston.

Hymes, D. 1977. *Foundations in Sociolinguistics: An Ethnographic Approach*. London: Tavistock.

Ickes, W., Patterson, M. L., Rajecki, D. W., and Tanford, S. 1982. Behavioral and cognitive consequences of reciprocal and compensatory responses to preinteraction expectancies. *Social Cognition*, 1: 160–90.

Ingersoll-Dayton, B., and Antonucci, T. 1988. Reciprocal and nonreciprocal social support: Contrasting sides of intimate relationships. *Journal of Gerontology: Social Sciences*, 43: S65–S73.

Isaacs, E. A., and Clark, H. H. 1987. References in conversation between experts and novices. *Journal of Experimental Psychology: General*, 116: 26–37.

Jaffe, J., and Feldstein, S. 1970. *Rhythms of Dialogue*. New York: Academic Press.

James, C. 1989. Accommodation in crosslanguage encounters. Mimeo: Linguistics. Bangor, North Wales: University College.

Jasnow, M. D., Crown, C. L., Feldstein, S., Taylor, L., Beebe, B., and Jaffe, J. 1988. Coordinated interpersonal timing of Down-syndrome and nondelayed infants with their mothers: Evidence for a buffered mechanism of social interaction. *Biological Bulletin*, 175: 355–60.

Jefferson, G. 1980. On "trouble-premonitory" response to inquiry. *Sociological Inquiry*, 50: 153–5.

Jefferson, G. 1984a. On "stepwise transition" from talk about a "trouble" to inappropriately next-positioned matters. *In* J. Atkinson and J. Heritage (eds.), *Structures of Social Action*, pp. 191–222. Cambridge: Cambridge University Press.

Jefferson, G. 1984b. On the organisation of laughter in talk about troubles. *In* J. Atkinson and J. Heritage (eds.), *Structures of Social Action*, pp. 346–69. Cambridge: Cambridge University Press.

Johnson, D. 1980. Doctor talk. *In* G. Goshgarian (ed.), *Exploring Language*. Boston: Little, Brown.

Jones, R. G., and Jones, E. E. 1964. Optimum conformity as an ingratiation tactic. *Journal of Personality*, 32: 4–36.

Kincaid, D. L. 1988. The convergence theory and intercultural communication. *In* Y. Y. Kim and W. B. Gudykunst (eds.), *Theories in Intercultural Communication*, pp. 280–98. Newbury Park, CA: Sage.

Klemz, A. 1977. *Blindness and Partial Sight*. Cambridge: Woodhead-Faulkner.

Kline, S. L. In press. Construct differentiation, legitimate authority, and features of regulative messages. *Journal of Language and Social Psychology*.

Kline, S. L., and Ceropski, J. M. 1984. Person-centered communication in medical practice. *In* J. T. Wood and G. M. Phillips (eds.), *Human Decision-Making*, pp. 120–41. Carbondale, IL: Southern Illinois University Press.

Knapp, M. L. 1984. *Interpersonal Communication and Human Relationships*. Boston: Allyn and Bacon.

Kobasa, S. C. O., and Puccetti, M. C. 1983. Personality and social resources in stress resistance. *Journal of Personality and Social Psychology*, 45: 839–50.

Kontra, M., and Gosy, M. 1988. Approximation of the standard: A form of variability in bilingual speech. *In* A. R. Thomas (ed.), *Methods in Dialectology*, pp. 442–55. Clevedon: Multilingual Matters.

Kraus, R. M. 1987. The role of the listener: Addressee influences on message formulation. *Journal of Language and Social Psychology*, 6: 81–97.

Krauss, R. M., and Fussell, S. R. 1988. Other-relatedness in language processing: Discussion and comments. *Journal of Language and Social Psychology*, 7: 263–79.

Krauss, R. M., and Glucksberg, S. 1969. The development of communicative competence as a function of age. *Child Development*, 40: 255–66.

Labov, W. 1966. *The Social Stratification of English in New York City*. Washington, DC: Center for Applied Linguistics.

LaFrance, M. 1979. Nonverbal synchrony and rapport: Analysis by the cross-lag panel technique. *Social Psychology Quarterly*, 42: 66–70.

LaFrance, M. 1985. Postural mirroring and intergroup relations. *Personality and Social Psychology Bulletin*, 11: 207–17.

Langer, E. J. 1978. Rethinking the role of thought in social interaction. *In* J. H. Harvey, W. J. Ickes, and R. F. Kidd (eds.), *New Directions in Attribution Research*, Vol. 2, pp. 36–58. Hillsdale, NJ: Erlbaum.

Larsen, K., Martin, H. J., and Giles, H. 1977. Anticipated social cost and interpersonal accommodation. *Human Communication Research*, 3: 303–8.

Lehmann, D. R., Ellard, J. H., and Wortman, C. B. 1986. Social support for the bereaved: Recipients' and providers' perspectives on what is helpful. *Journal of Counseling and Clinical Psychology*, 54: 438–46.

Leiser, R. G. 1988. Improving natural language understanding by modelling human dialogue. *Proceedings of the 5th. Annual ESPIT Conference, Brussels: Putting the Technology to Use*, pp. 649–58. Amsterdam: North Holland.

Lennard, H. L., and Bernstein, A. 1960. Interdependence of therapist and patient verbal behaviour. *In* J. A. Fishman (ed.), *Readings in the Sociology of Language*, pp. 170–9. The Hague: Mouton.

Le Page, R. B. 1968. Problems of description in multilingual communities. *Transactions of the Philological Society*, pp. 189–221. Oxford: Blackwell.

Levin, H., and Lin, T. 1988. An accommodating witness. *Language and Communication*, 8: 195–8.

Lieberman, P. 1967. *Intonation, Perception and Language*. Cambridge, MA: MIT Press.

Mangold, R., and Pobel, R. 1988. Informativeness and instrumentality in referential communication. *Journal of Language and Social Psychology*, 7: 181–92.

Matarazzo, J. D., and Weins, A. W. 1972. *The Interview: Research on Its Anatomy and Structure*. Chicago: Aldine-Atherton.

Matarazzo, J. D., Weins, A. N., Matarazzo, R. G., and Saslow, G. 1968. Speech and silence behaviour in clinical psychotherapy and its laboratory correlates. *In* J. Schlier, H. Hunt, J. D. Matarazzo, and C. Savage (eds.), *Research in Psychotherapy*, Vol. 3, pp. 347–94. Washington, DC: American Psychological Association.

Mauer, R. E., and Tindall, J. H. 1983. Effects of postural congruence on client's perceptions of counselor empathy. *Journal of Counseling Psychology*, 30: 158–63.

Maynard, D. W. 1988. Language, interaction and social problems. *Social Problems*, 35: 311–34.

McCann, C. D., and Higgins, E. T. 1990. Social cognition and communication. *In* H. Giles and W. P. Robinson (eds.), *Handbook of Language and Social Psychology*, pp. 13–32. Chichester: Wiley.

McGregor, G., and White, R. (eds.). 1990. *Reception and Response: Hearer Creativity and the Analysis of Spoken and Written Texts*. London: Croom Helm.

McKirnan, D. J., and Hamayan, E. V. 1984. Speech norms and attitudes towards outgroup members: A test of a model in a bicultural context. *Journal of Language and Social Psychology*, 3: 21–38.

Mead, G. H. 1934. *Mind, Self and Society*. Chicago: Chicago University Press.

Messick, D. M., and Mackie, D. M. 1989. Intergroup relations. *Annual Review of Psychology*, 40: 45–81.

Miller, G. R., and Steinberg, M. 1975. *Between People: A New Analysis of Interpersonal Communication*. Chicago: Science Research Associate.

Miller, R. A. 1982. *The Japanese Language: The Myth and Beyond*. Tokyo: Weatherhill, Inc.

Montepare, J. M., and Vega, C. 1988. Women's vocal reactions to intimate and casual male friends. *Personality and Social Psychology Bulletin*, 14: 103–12.

Mosher, D. L., Mortimer, R. L., and Grebel, M. 1968. Verbal aggressive behavior in delinquent boys. *Journal of Abnormal Psychology*, 73: 454–60.

Mulac, A., Studley, L. B., Wiemann, J., and Bradac, J. J. 1987. Male/female gaze in same-sex and mixed-sex dyads: Gender-linked differences and mutual influence. *Human Communication Research*, 13: 323–43.

Mulac, A., Wiemann, J. M., Widenmann, S., and Gibson, T. W. 1988. Male/female language differences and effects in same-sex and mixed-sex dyads: The gender-linked language effect. *Communication Monographs*, 55: 315–35.

Murphy, T. M., and Street, R. L., Jr. 1987. Interpersonal orientation and speech behaviour. *Communication Monographs*, 54: 42–62.

Myers, D. G., and Lamm, H. 1976. The group polarization phenomenon. *Psychological Bulletin*, 83: 606–27.

Natale, M. 1975a. Convergence of mean vocal intensity in dyadic communications as a function of social desirability. *Journal of Personality and Social Psychology*, 32: 790–804.

Natale, M. 1975b. Social desirability as related to convergence of temporal speech patterns. *Perceptual and Motor Skills*, 40: 827–30.

Nystrand, M. 1986. *The Structure of Written Communication: Studies in Reciprocity between Writers and Readers*. Orlando: FL: Academic Press.

O'Keefe, B. J. 1988. The logic of message design: Individual differences in reasoning about communication. *Communication Monographs*, 55: 80–103.

O'Keefe, B. J., and Delia, J. G. 1985. Psychological and Interactional dimensions of communicative development. *In* H. Giles and R. St. Clair (eds.), *Recent Advances in Language, Communication and Social Psychology*, pp. 41–85. London: Erlbaum.

Patterson, M. 1983. *Nonverbal Behaviour: A Functional Perspective*. New York: Springer-Verlag.

Paulhus, D. L., and Martin, C. L. 1988. Functional flexibility: A new conception of interpersonal flexibility. *Journal of Personality and Social Psychology*, 55: 88–101.

Peng, F. C. C. 1974. Communicative distance. *Language Sciences*, 31: 32–5.

Penman, R. 1990. Facework and politeness: Multiple goals in courtroom discourse. *Journal of Language and Social Psychology*, 9: 15–38.

Piaget, J. 1955. *The Language and Thought of the Child*. New York: World.

Pierson, H. D., and Bond, M. H. 1982. How do Chinese bilinguals respond to variations of interviewer language and ethnicity? *Journal of Language and Social Psychology*, 1: 123–40.

Platt, J., and Weber, H. 1984. Speech convergence miscarried: An investigation into inappropriate accommodation strategies. *International Journal of the Sociology of Language*, 46: 131–46.

Potter, J., and Wetherell, M. 1987. *Discourse and Social Psychology*. London: Sage.

Prince, E. F. 1988. Accommodation theory and dialect shift: A case study from Yiddish. *Language and Communication*, 8: 307–20.

Purcell, A. K. 1984. Code shifting in Hawaiian style: Children's accommodation along a decreolising continuum. *International Journal of the Sociology of Language*, 46: 71–86.

Putman, W., and Street, R. 1984. The conception and perception of noncontent speech performance: Implications for speech accommodation theory. *International Journal of the Sociology of Language*, 46: 97–114.

Rafoth, B. A., and Rubin, D. L. (eds.) 1987. *The Social Construction of Written Communication*. Norwood, NJ: Ablex.

Ragan, S. L, and Hopper, R. 1984. Ways to leave your lover: A conversational analysis of literature. *Communication Quarterly*, 32: 318–27.

Ray, M. L., and Webb, E. J. 1966. Speech duration effects in the Kennedy news conference. *Science*, 153: 899–901.

Read, A. W. 1962. Family words in English. *American Speech*, 37: 5–12.

Roloff, M., and Berger, C. R. (eds.). 1982. *Social Cognition and Communication*. Beverly Hills, CA: Sage.

Rommetveit, R. 1979. On the architecture of intersubjectivity. *In* R. Rommetveit and R. M. Blakar (eds.), *Studies of Language, Thought, and Communication*, pp. 93–107. London: Academic Press.

Rook, K. S., and Pietromonaco, P. 1987. Close relationships: Ties that heal or ties that bind? In W. H. Jones and D. Perlman (eds.), *Advances in Personal Relationships*, pp. 1–35. Greenwich, CT: JAI Press.

Ros, M., and Giles, H. 1979. The language situation in Valencia: An accommodation framework. *ITL: Review of Applied Linguistics*, 44: 3–24.

Ross, S., and Shortreed, I. 1990. Japanese foreigner talk: Convergence or divergence? *Journal of Asian Pacific Communication*, 1: 135–46.

Ryan, E. B., and Cole, R. 1990. Perceptions of interpersonal communication with elders: Implications for health professionals. *In* H. Giles, N. Coupland, and J. Wiemann (eds.), *Communication, Health and the Elderly: Fulbright International Colloquium 8*, pp. 172–91. Manchester: Manchester University Press.

Ryan, E. B., and Giles, H. (eds.). 1982. *Attitudes towards Language Variation: Social and Applied Contexts*. London: Arnold.

Sachdev, I., Bourhis, R. Y., D'Eye, and Phang, S.-W. 9190. Chinese vitality in London (UK). *Journal of Asian Pacific Communication*, 1: 209–28.

Sacks, H. 1987. On the references for agreement and contiguity in sequences in conversation. *In* G. Button and J. R. Lee (eds.), *Talk and Social Organisation*, pp. 54–69. Clevedon: Multilingual Matters, Ltd.

Sandilands, M. L., and Fleury, N. C. 1979. Unilinguals in des milieux bilingues:

One analyse of attributions. *Canadian Journal of Behavioural Science*, 11: 164–8.

Schaffer, D. R., Smith, J. E., and Tomarelli, M. 1982. Self-monitoring as a deter-minant of self-disclosure reciprocity during the acquaintance process. *Journal of Personality and Social Psychology*, 43: 163–75.

Schank, R., and Abelson, R. P. 1977. *Scripts, Plans, Goals, and Understanding*. Hillsdale, NJ: Erlbaum.

Schober, M. F., and Clark, H. H. 1989. Understanding by addressees and ov-erhearers. *Cognitive Psychology*, 21: 211–32.

Scollon, R., and Scollon, S. B. 1979. *Linguistic Convergence: An Ethnography of Speaking at Fort Chipewyon, Alberta*. New York: Academic Press.

Scotton, C. M. 1979. Codeswitching as a "safe choice" in choosing a lingua franca. *In* W. C. McCormack and S. Wurm (eds.), *Language and Society: Anthropo-logical Issues*, pp. 71–83. The Hague: Mouton.

Scotton, C. M. 1985. What the heck, sir: Style shifting and lexical colouring as features of powerful language. In R. L. Street, Jr., and J. N. Cappella (eds.), *Sequence and Pattern in Communicative Behaviour*, pp. 103–19. London: Ed-ward Arnold.

Scotton, C. M. 1988. Self-enhancing codeswitching as interactional power. *Lan-guage and Communication*, 8: 199–212.

Segalowitz, N., and Gatbonton, E. 1977. Studies of the non-fluent bilingual. *In* P. Hornby (ed.), *Bilingualism: Psychological and Social Implications*, pp. 77–91. New York: Academic Press.

Seltig, M. 1985. Levels of style-shifting exemplified in the interaction strategies of a moderator in a listener participation programme. *Journal of Pragmatics*, 9: 179–97.

Sherif, C. W., Sherif, M., and Nebergall, R. E. 1965. *Attitude and Attitude Change*. Philadelphia: Saunders.

Simard, L., Taylor, D. M., and Giles, H. 1976. Attribution processes and inter-personal accommodation in a bilingual setting. *Language and Speech*, 19: 374–87.

Smith, P. M., Giles, H., and Hewstone, M. 1980. Sociolinguistics: A social psy-chological perspective. *In* R. St. Clair and H. Giles (eds.), *The Social and Psychological Contexts of Language*, pp. 283–98. Hillsdale, NJ: Erlbaum.

Snyder, M. 1981. On the self-perpetuating nature of social stereotypes. *In* D. L. Hamilton (ed.), *Cognitive Processes in Stereotyping and Intergroup Behavior*. Hillsdale, NJ: Erlbaum.

Snyder, M., and Swann, W. B., Jr. 1979. Hypothesis-testing processes in social interaction. *Journal of Personality and Social Psychology*, 36: 1202–12.

Stanback, M., and Pearce, W. B. 1981. Talking to "The Man": Some commu-nication strategies used by members of "subordinate" social groups. *Quar-terly Journal of Speech*, 67: 21–30.

Stieblich, C. 1986. Interpersonal accommodation in a bilingual setting. *Language Planning and Language Policy*, 10: 158–76.

Street, R. L., Jr. 1982. Evaluation of noncontent speech accommodation. *Lan-guage and Communication*, 2: 13–31.

Street, R. L., Jr. 1983. Noncontent speech convergence in adult – child interac-tions. *In* R. N. Bostrom (ed.), *Communication Yearbook 7*, pp. 369–95. Beverly Hills, CA: Sage.

Street, R. L., Jr. 1984. Speech convergence and speech evaluation in fact-finding interviews. *Human Communication Research*, 11: 139–69.

Street, R. L., Jr., Brady, R. M., and Putman, W. B. 1983. The influence of speech rate stereotypes and rate similarity on listeners' evaluations of speakers. *Journal of Language and Social Psychology*, 2: 37–56.

Street, R. L., Jr., and Giles, H. 1982. Speech accommodation theory: A social cognitive approach to language and speech behavior. *In* M. Roloff and C. R. Berger (eds.), *Social Cognition and Communication*, pp. 193–226. Beverly Hills, CA: Sage.

Street, R. L., Jr., and Hopper, R. 1982. A model of speech style evaluation. *In* E. B. Ryan and H. Giles (eds.), *Attitudes towards Language Variation: Social and Applied Contexts*, pp. 175–88. London: Edward Arnold.

Street, R. L., Jr., Street, N. J., and Van Kleeck, A. 1983. Speech convergence among talkative and reticent three-year-olds. *Language Sciences*, 5: 79–86.

Summerfield, A. B. 1975. Errors in decoding tone of voice during dyadic interaction. *British Journal of Social and Clinical Psychology*, 14: 11–18.

Sunnafrank, M. 1986. Predicted outcome value during initial interactions: A reformulation of uncertainty reduction theory. *Human Communication Research*, 13: 3–33.

Tajfel, H. 1974. Social identity and intergroup behaviour. *Social Science Information*, 13: 65–93.

Tajfel, H. (ed.). 1978. *Differentiation between Social Groups*. London: Academic Press.

Tajfel, H., and Turner, J. C. 1979. An integrative theory of intergroup conflict. *In* W. G. Austin and S. Worchel (eds.), *The Social Psychology of Intergroup Relations*, pp. 33–47. Monterey, CA: Brooks/ Cole.

Taylor, D. M., Bassili, J., and Aboud, F. 1973. Dimensions of ethnic identity: An example from Quebec. *Journal of Social Psychology*, 89: 185–92.

Taylor, D. M., and Royer, E. 1980. Group processes affecting anticipated language choice in intergroup relations. *In* H. Giles, W. P. Robinson, and P. M. Smith (eds.), *Language: Social Psychological Perspectives*, pp. 185–92. Oxford: Pergamon.

Taylor, D. M., Simard, L., and Papineau, D. 1978. Perceptions of cultural differences and language use: A field study in a bilingual environment. *Canadian Journal of Behavioural Science*, 10: 181–91.

Tedeschi, J. T., Lindskold, S., and Rosenfeld, P. 1985. *Introduction to Social Psychology*, pp. 65–96. New York: West.

Thakerar, J. N., and Giles, H. 1981. They are – so they speak: Noncontent speech stereotypes. *Language and Communication*, 1: 251–6.

Thakerar, J. N., Giles, H., and Cheshire, J. 1982. Psychological and linguistic parameters of speech accommodation theory. *In* C. Fraser and K. R. Scherer (eds.), *Advances in the Social Psychology of Language*, pp. 205–55. Cambridge: Cambridge University Press.

Thibaut, J. W., and Kelley, H. H. 1959. *The Social Psychology of Groups*. New York: Wiley.

Tracy, K. 1990. The many faces of facework. *In* H. Giles and W. P. Robinson (eds.), *Handbook of Language and Social Psychology*, pp. 209–26. Chichester: New York.

Tracy, K. (ed.). 1991. *Understanding Face-to-Face Interaction: Issues Linking Goals and Discourse*. Hillsdale, NJ: Erlbaum.

Tracy, K., and Coupland, N. (eds.). 1990. Multiple goals in discourse. Special issue of *Journal of Language and Social Psychology*, 1–170.

Triandis, H. C. 1960. Cognitive similarity and communication in a dyad. *Human Relations*, 13: 175–83.

Trudgill, P. 1983. Acts of conflicting identity. *In On Dialect*, pp. 141–60. Oxford: Blackwell.

Trudgill, P. 1986. *Dialects in Contact*. Oxford: Blackwell.

Turner, J. C. 1987. *Rediscovering the Social Group: A Self-Categorization Theory*. Oxford: Blackwell.

Turner, J. C., and Brown, R. J. 1978. Interpersonal and intergroup behaviour. *In* J. C. Turner and H. Giles (eds.), *Intergroup Behaviour*, pp. 33–65. Oxford: Blackwell.

von Raffler-Engel, W. 1980. The unconscious element in inter-cultural communication. *In* R. St. Clair and H. Giles (eds.), *The Social and Psychological Contexts of Language*, pp. 101–30. Hillsdale, NJ: Erlbaum.

Watzlawick, P., Beavin, J. H., and Jackson, D. 1967. *Pragmatics of Human Communication*. New York: Norton.

Weary, G., and Arkin, R. M. 1981. Attributional self-presentation. *In* J. H. Harvey, M. J. Ickes, and R. Kidd (eds.), *New Directions in Attribution Theory and Research*, Vol. 3, pp. 223–46. Hillsdale, NJ: Erlbaum.

Webb, J. T. 1972. Interview synchrony. *In* A. W. Siegman and B. Pope (eds.), *Studies in Dyadic Communication*, pp. 115–33. Oxford: Pergamon.

Weiner, M., and Mehrabian, A. 1968. *Language within Language: Immediacy, a Channel in Verbal Communication*. New York: Appleton-Century-Crofts.

Welkowitz, J., Bond, R. N., and Feldstein, S. 1984. Gender and conversational time patterns as Japanese-American adults and children in same- and mixed-gender dyads. *Journal of Language and Social Psychology*, 3: 127–38.

Welkowitz, J. G., Cariffe, G., and Feldstein, S. 1976. Conversational congruence as a criterion of socialization in children. *Child Development* 47: 269–72.

Welkowitz, J., and Feldstein, S. 1969. Dyadic interaction and induced differences in perceived similarity. *Proceedings of the 77th Annual Convention of the American Psychological Association*, 4: 343–44.

Welkowitz, J., and Feldstein, S. 1970. Relation of experimentally-manipulated interpersonal perception and psychological differentiation to the temporal patterning of conversation. *Proceedings of the 78th Annual Convention of the American Psychological Association*, 5: 387–8.

Welkowitz, J., Feldstein, S., Finkelstein, M., and Aylesworth, L. 1972. Changes in vocal intensity as a function of interspeaker influence. *Perceptual and Motor Skills*, 35: 715–18.

Welkowitz, J., and Kuc, M. 1973. Inter-relationships among warmth, genuineness, empathy and temporal speech patterns in interpersonal attraction. *Journal of Consulting and Clinical Psychology*, 41: 472–3.

White, S. 1989. Backchannels across cultures: A study of Americans and Japanese. *Language in Society*, 18: 59–76.

Williams, F. 1976. *Explorations in the Linguistic Attitudes of Teachers*. Rowley, MA: Newbury House.

Wolfram, W. 1973. Sociolinguistic aspects of assimilation: Puerto Rican English in East Harlem. *In* R. W. Shuy and R. W. Fasold (eds.), *Language Attitudes: Current Trends and Prospects*. Washington, DC: Georgetown University Press.

Woolard, K. A. 1989. *Double Talk: Bilingualism and the Politics of Ethnicity in Catalonia*. Stanford, CA: Stanford University Press.

Yaeger-Dror, M. 1988. The influence of changing vitality on convergence toward a dominant linguistic norm: An Israeli example. *Language and Communication*, 8: 285–306.

Ytsma, J. 1988. Bilingual classroom interaction in Friesland. *In* A. Holman, E.

Hansen, J. Gimbel, and J. N. Jorgensen (eds), *Bilingualism and the Individual*, pp. 53–68. Clevedon: Multilingual Matters.

Yum, J. O. 1988. The impact of Confucianism on interpersonal relationships and communication patterns in East Asia. *Communication Monographs*, 55: 374–88.

2. Audience accommodation in the mass media

ALLAN BELL

Mass media offer an illuminating site to examine the processes and effects of linguistic accommodation. This chapter first addresses general questions of mass communication and its relation to speech accommodation theory. It then examines one particular set of language data drawn from radio news broadcasts and its implications for the theory.

2.1. Mass communicators and their audience

Mass communication research shares with speech accommodation theory (SAT) an interest in the relation of communicators and their audiences.[1] Much early media research had a disciplinary base in social psychology and was concerned with the effects of mass communication: What do media do to people? After decades of contradictory and inconclusive studies (see Howitt 1982), this question was turned around: What do people do with media? The "uses and gratifications" approach (e.g., Klapper 1960) waned, and interest in the communicator and communication content – always present but often overshadowed by the popular and political focus on media effects – has predominated in research. The many current approaches include the sociology of knowledge (e.g., Tuchman 1978), organizational sociology (Burns 1977), and textual and cultural studies (Glasgow University Media Group 1980).

The data portions of this chapter have had a long history, and I am grateful to the Center for Applied Linguistics, Washington, D.C., for its hospitality during one phase of its development (1981). Thanks to Janet Holmes, Nik Coupland, Justine Coupland, and Howard Giles for the many perceptive editorial comments, which have influenced this final version; to William Labov for encouragement and critique at different times; and to Peter Clare for the graphs. And I record my debt to the late Colin Bowley, who supervised the Ph.D. thesis where the work began.

[1] In 1957, fifteen years before the first formulations of SAT, Bauer (1964: 132) wrote of speakers' "accommodation . . . to the values and expectations of the intended audience."

Mass communication is structurally different from face-to-face communication. It involves a disjunction of place, and often also of time, between communicator and audience. This fracture in the communication process has significant consequences for language production. Centrally, the feedback that is an integral factor in individual spoken communication is delayed, impoverished, or lacking altogether in mass communication. Audiences are deprived of the usual means of inducing communicators to modify their production. Mass communicators are deprived of the usual access to recipients' reactions (McQuail 1969).

This structural divide has radical effects, particularly on broadcast media. Broadcasters operate from moment to moment, with no assurance that they even have an audience. Their production is a continuing act of technological faith, since even without mechanical problems, the broadcaster may doubt that an audience exists: Witness the late-night disk jockey (DJ) whom I heard end his show with the words "Good night, you three."

Feedback and isolation

Although feedback is not absent from the mass communication process, in few cases is the audience member on equal terms with the communicators. Apart from the phone-in radio program, direct feedback by the audience is subject either to delay – influencing subsequent but not immediate production – or to reduction: The audience member's response remains under the editorial control of the communicators. Although media organizations do tend to pay disproportionate attention to letters or telephone calls, actual working communicators dismiss such respondents as cranks (Schlesinger 1987: 107).

The second form of feedback is audience or circulation figures. The audience exercises its main influence on the media just by being the audience. Media managers are riveted by the feedback of audience ratings or paid circulations, because it is this that keeps their organization alive. However, such figures generally come to hand somewhat after the time they refer to. Both types of feedback, therefore, are available only as input to future, not present, communication.

Even these limited sources are often ignored by mass communicators, and the more directly a person is involved in production, the less notice he or she takes of the figures produced by audience research. Broadcasters follow their program's ratings – the size of the audience – especially where this is a factor in the continuation of their output and employment. But they take little note of even the gross demographic data offered by an ordinary audience survey. The focus of ratings or circulations is audience size, not audience kind. Such figures are little concerned with the composition of the audience. So, although they may give communicators some idea of how many are in their audience, they offer little information on the sort of person to whom communicators should be attuning their production.

In my experience as both journalist and researcher, mass communicators have only the haziest concept of what kind of people comprise their audience. Isolation from the audience is a characteristic of mass communicators. Ironically, the more "mass" the medium, the greater the isolation, so that one (radio) broadcaster speaks of "the degree of self-absorption, amounting almost to autism, which is one of the most pronounced traits of television" (McIntyre 1988:8). Burns's (1977) study of the BBC reflects this phenomenon in its title, *Public Institution and Private World*. His finding has been echoed by others (e.g., Donsbach 1983; Schlesinger 1987): Communicators are not just ignorant of the nature of their audience, they are uninterested. Their attitude ranges between "cultivated indifference and contemptuous dismissal" (Burns 1977: 133).

Professionalism and stereotyping

Such conclusions are surprising to the researcher and the media consumer, and one begins to wonder on what basis mass communicators manage to operate. The missing link between media producers and consumers is professionalism (Schlesinger 1987: 106). Mass communicators are interested in their peers, not their public. Fellow communicators and coprofessionals are their salient audience. Donsbach (1983) found that British and German journalists held a very low opinion of their readers, which legitimated journalists' serving as their own imaginary audience, despite the fact that they were clearly unrepresentative of the public. But although communicators in a real sense talk *for* other communicators, this does not mean they are talking *to* each other. Professionalism involves a consensus among communicators about how they should address different kinds of audiences.

Regardless of how inadequately based their conceptions may be, communicators do work with an idea both of the audience they are speaking to and of what it wants. Pool and Shulman (1959) questioned journalists on who they had in mind while writing a particular news story. The journalists claimed to think of "imaginary interlocutors," but those images were formulated only in the most general terms. Although mass communicators do not usually volunteer descriptions of their target audience, they respond with (often derogatory) stereotypes of audience members: "Mum sitting in the best armchair drinking cocoa with a teenage son on the sofa trying to get his hand up his girl's skirts" (quoted in Burns 1977: 133). Such stereotypes are evoked as reasons for specific editorial choices, and some journalists speak of writing for family members or friends (Schlesinger 1987: 119).

Ignorance of the audience is thus no barrier to formation of a stereotyped image. We may suppose that it is even an aid. The mass audience is so large and diverse that conscious attempts to cater to it could be counterproductive. McQuail (1969: 79) writes: "No 'imaginary interlocutor' is likely to approximate to the realities of the undifferentiated mass audience, and whatever assumptions the communicator makes are bound to be of an imprecise and limited kind."

2.2. Mass communication and accommodation theory

SAT was developed, tested, and elaborated largely to analyze and account for how speakers modify their speech in the complex dynamics of interpersonal encounters where one moment's speaker becomes hearer the next moment. We have seen that mass communication is very different from a situation where speakers are continuously adjusting their language production as they monitor their interlocutors' reactions and production and evaluate their own production. Most media content is also not ad lib speech, but is scripted in whole or in part. It might be better, then, discussed in terms of *communication* accommodation, a broader label suggested by Giles et al. (1987) and elaborated in Coupland and Giles (1988).

Accommodative processes

Coupland et al.'s elaborate, generalized model of SAT processes (1988: 8) becomes greatly simplified in mass communication. That model presents two individuals, A and B, who are constantly exchanging roles as speaker and hearer in an interaction. As hearer, B evaluates A's performance as speaker, and A takes account of feedback from B. Then, taking a turn as speaker, B applies the evaluation of A and adds self-monitoring of his or her own language performance.

In mass communication, however, no language is produced by speaker B (the audience). Speaking rights belong solely to A – the mass communicator. Nor is there feedback from B to A during the communication. Speaker A can take no account of B's actual or even perceived language production. But although the essentially interactive components of an SAT model are inapplicable, the factors that remain redress the balance and become more important.

First, as we have seen, beliefs and stereotypes about recipients and their speech patterns are the sole practical input to mass communicators' accommodative processes. The fact that speakers often accommodate not to an interlocutor's actual speech but to what they believe to be the interlocutor's speech has long been recognized in SAT (Thakerar, Giles, and Cheshire 1982). The mass communicator cannot "attend to other's actual or perceived performance," only to a stereotype of that language, a possibility that Coupland et al. (1988: 28) encompass in their model. The delayed feedback of audience research or direct response contributes to the communicator's stereotype for future, but not present, communication.

Second, in the absence of any direct audience language performance that can be sampled, communicators become more reliant on monitoring their own production [which Coupland et al. (1988) also model]. This involves more than just individuals critiquing their own output. Media language is rarely a solo performance. It is the composite product of multiple professional communicators – writers, editors, producers, technicians, and so on. Many of these are employed for the exact purpose of monitoring and modifying other communicators' production (Bell 1984a, 1991). Thus, professional practices operate directly to mold the language output of the mass media. We find then that mass communication research and SAT both suggest independently that the twin factors of audience stereotyping and professional self-monitoring operate significantly in molding the language of mass communication.

Strategies and motivations

Many of the communicative strategies identified by SAT (e.g., Giles et al. 1987: 14) are inapplicable in mass communication. There is no mutual convergence because the audience does not (generally) talk back. Recipients do not show divergence, maintenance, or style matching relative to the mass communicator.[2] Nevertheless, the linguistic behavior of mass communicators can be characterized by SAT-related concepts. As the data presented subsequently will show, strategies of convergence and divergence, of a shift toward national or local norms, or in relation to actual and stereotyped audiences are all operative.

SAT also attempts to specify the motivations that lie behind the use of particular accommodative strategies. From the earliest formulations of SAT (e.g., Giles 1973; Giles and Powesland 1975), approval seeking has been recognized as a prime motive in accommodation. This is very powerful in mass communication, where we can assume that communicators are always in some sense trying to win the approval of their audience (McQuail 1969). There is no contradiction here between communicators' bids for approval and their ignorance and disdain of the audience cited earlier. Communicators need the audience, whose approval must be won. But the audience is at the same time denigrated precisely for being thus persuaded. To us as media audience members, such a contradiction is disagreeable and sounds impossible to live with. It is nevertheless evident both to perceptive insiders and to casual observers in media organizations. Similar paradoxical attitudes occur among stage performers and service personnel such as waiters and salespeople. Burns (1977: 133) notes the "countervailing, and ordinarily concealed, posture of invidious hostility" that such occupations show when the served public is absent.

More recently, SAT has taken account of the simple factor of communicative efficiency – the need to be heard and understood, to allow for recipients' physical situation and abilities (e.g., Coupland et al. 1988). Such a concern for receipt of a clear signal has always been a prime motivation in mass communication. Aside from keeping the channel open and noise free, the communicator must take account of the range of situations in which the message will be received. The broadcaster repeats certain information on a regular cycle in the knowledge that radio is rarely the sole object of a listener's attention, that the audience comes and goes.

---

[2] This is not to deny that features of media language are adopted by members of media audiences, but such adoptions take place over time, not in the immediate situation. They are in the realm of long-term language change rather than short-term accommodation, although the two processes are unquestionably related (see Trudgill 1986). It is also notoriously difficult to prove that any given linguistic change is caused by media influence.

The audience accommodates

Mass communication also offers an intriguing reverse form of accommodation that is impossible in one-to-one interaction but can also operate in public speaking situations. SAT recognizes that a speaker's belief about an interlocutor's style may not coincide with reality. Beebe (1981) noted how Chinese Thai bilinguals used Chinese phonological variants when speaking to an ethnic Chinese despite the fact she spoke standard Thai. In face-to-face communication, direct feedback from a recipient may persuade the speaker to modify an unsuitable style. In extreme cases, failure to adjust may lead the audience to break off the interaction. But in mass communication the weight of the two types of feedback is reversed. The audience has the power of choice. The second, supposedly extreme method becomes the norm; dissatisfied audience members switch off or tune in elsewhere. And the usual means of face-to-face feedback becomes the extreme: Only a small minority of the mass audience ever directly contacts the media with complaints or suggestions.

Assuming that audience membership usually signifies approval of the communicator's style, it follows that media attract the audiences that suit them. If the communicator is unsuccessful in accommodating to the audience, the audience will do the accommodating – by voting with their feet. The communicator will then have an audience that was unintended but whose composition in fact suits his or her style. In mass communication the actual audience will generally coincide with the communicator's stereotype, assuming that a mismatch between communicator style and audience will be short-lived. The data presented in this chapter therefore are based on an actual audience survey rather than communicator perceptions. But to what extent the stereotype and the actual coincide, and if so, which better predicts the communicator's accommodative strategies, remain empirical questions.

2.3. Audience design

Two phenomena perhaps more evident in mass communication than face to face were identified in the audience design framework proposed by Bell (1984b). That framework originated in an attempt to account for the language style differences found in the data set to be presented. Audience design has parallels to SAT but arose from a disciplinary background in sociolinguistics rather than social psychology. It looks at style shifting and other linguistic processes in a wide range of situations. Reacting – as SAT also had done – to the mechanistic view that style is simply the result of degrees of attention paid to speech (Labov 1972), audience design proposes that the audience is the primary factor in influencing speakers to shift their style.

The differentiated audience

Two features of audience design are relevant to this discussion. First, there is a differentiation of roles within the audience:

addressees, who are directly addressed;
auditors, who are ratified as part of an interaction but not addressed;
overhearers, known to be present but neither ratified nor addressed;
eavesdroppers, whose presence is not even known.

Bell (1984b) presents a range of evidence on how speakers are able to design aspects of their language production to accommodate these different audience members. Despite the generally vague concept that mass communicators have of their audience, they are capable of adjusting to different audience segments such as their own managers, owners, pressure groups, and politicians. Montgomery (1988) shows how a BBC Radio 1 DJ on occasion selects individuals for direct address, briefly reclassifying the rest of the audience as auditors, not addressees. A listener who has written in may be addressed with a vocative – "hi to Bob Sproat" – creating the fiction that a specific individual is the sole if temporary addressee. Fill (1986) notes the complex maneuvers that politicians may have to accomplish in a single media speech in order to satisfy diverse constituents. A speech delivered in an international forum when a politician is abroad may in fact be primarily directed to the absent audience of the politician's constituency back home.

We must expand the notion of audience roles to recognize that the audience for mass communication is (at least) two-layered, each containing its own potential set of the four roles. There is, for example, an inner, physically present audience to a television interviewer's speech – interviewee (addressee), producers, technicians, camera operators, and sometimes a studio audience (all auditors). These are the immediate, "embedded audience" (see Bell 1991; Leech and Short 1981). And there is the outer, mass audience – separated in space and often in time from the embedded communication situation.

Accommodating one's speech to both inner and outer audiences can strain the abilities of a communicator, particularly a nonprofessional. Solomon (1978) analyzes the notorious 1976 *Playboy* interview with U.S. presidential candidate Jimmy Carter. She interprets Carter's use of terms such as "screw" and "shack up with" as appropriate to the immediate addressee, the journalist, but unsuitable for the wider mass audience. Carter also had problems with different segments of the public audience. He may arguably have catered adequately to his mass addressees, the regular readership of *Playboy*, as well as to the journalist. But he certainly did not cope with the mass auditors and overhearers – in an election year, effectively the rest of the American public.

Response and initiative

A second dimension of audience design suggests that communicators' accommodative strategies will sometimes be "responsive" and sometimes "initiative" (Bell 1984b: 182). That is, speakers often respond to their audience primarily in the language they produce (see Linell's use of the scripts, this volume). But they also, on occasion, take more initiative and use language to redefine their relationship to their audience. A typical example of initiative strategies can be found in Selting's (1983) analysis of an audience participation radio program. Here the presenter defies the social expectation by her use of colloquial German to redefine a media situation as informal.

Response and initiative are poles of a continuum rather than a dichotomy. Response always has an element of speaker initiative, and initiative is invariably in part a response to one's audience. Initiative strategies are regarded as usually instances of "referee design." They focus on an absent reference group, for example by adopting a nonnative accent, rather than on the present addressee. They are therefore always directed toward a stereotyped rather than an actual recipient.

Within the media, some genres are more prone to response and others to initiative. The more formal formats, such as newscasting, are toward the responsive end. National newscasts still retain the depersonalized, status-oriented flavor advocated in a 1936 BBC memorandum: "The BBC . . has many voices but one mouth. . . . It is a commonplace that 'announcers sound all alike.' That is a tribute to their training" (quoted in Kumar 1975: 77). Other formats, such as advertising, DJ patter, and on-air discussions, are more prone to communicator initiative. This "hierarchy" of program types has more often been assumed than demonstrated. There is, however, supporting evidence in Lipski's (1985) collation of data from Spanish-language radio in the Americas. It shows a clear grading in all countries from news, the most "responsive" format with the lowest frequency of local phonological variants, through DJ patter, to sports commentary with the highest frequency of local, initiative variants.

This chapter concentrates on data from radio news, indicating how newscasting styles largely respond to their audiences' expectations. But there is considerable research on more initiative formats, especially on radio, where talk is the presenter's main instrument in reaching the audience. Montgomery (1988) characterizes a DJ's talk as "foregrounding the personal" – using talk to create a relationship with his audience. The DJ makes frequent use of first- and second-person pronouns, vocatives, deictics, imperatives, questions, and other devices of face-to-face conversation – all features that are notable for their absence from news language.

But initiative audience design can reach beyond the speech community's normal repertoire in order to achieve certain effects. Bell (1986, 1991) found that New Zealand television commercials use foreign accents of English to associate certain products with certain images. In some cases, only a few occurrences of marked phonological variants were enough to represent an accent such as "Cockney." Coupland (1985) describes a Cardiff music show presenter who shifted from a solidarity-oriented, stigmatized local dialect (in itself an initiative style) to American phonological features in announcing certain kinds of songs. Arguably, the more initiative formats of broadcast media offer a greater invitation to exploit linguistic resources than does everyday speech (Coupland pers. comm.).[3]

Initiative strategies are of different kinds (see Bell 1984b: 187). The Cardiff presenter's are "hyperaddressee" oriented – converging to a sometimes exaggerated local ingroup stereotype. His occasional adoption of American phonology is divergent – directed to an outgroup stereotype – and short-term. Long-term accommodation to an outgroup stereotype is also possible, as in the regular imitation of American ac-

---

[3] It is no accident that radio has been the medium researched in most of these studies. The sound-only nature of radio makes it attractive to linguistic analysis. The medium also requires the least technology. It is the most immediate and flexible of all media, and the one that has the most potential for communicator–audience feedback and interaction. Radio is thus most open to the "audience-as-communicator" formats researched in West Germany by Selting (1985) and in Jamaica by Mody (1986). The breakout of format in both of these cases is accompanied by an initiative language shift. In the Jamaican experiment, local news was broadcast in basilectal creole in an "on-air simulation of the casual everyday exchange of news" (Mody 1986: 156).

cents by British pop singers (Trudgill 1983). Because of ignorance of out-group accents, the linguistic consequences of accommodation to them may be very different from the consequences of adoption of accents with which the speaker has greater contact.

2.4. Radio in Auckland

The data that will be used here to illustrate accommodation in media language are drawn from extensive research undertaken since the 1970s on radio news in New Zealand (Bell 1977). The research sought to specify and account for differences between news styles on different radio stations. A number of phonological and syntactic variables were analyzed as representative of those styles, in the manner of Labov (1966), Trudgill (1974), and many other studies of sociolinguistic variation.

Auckland is New Zealand's largest city, with a population of some 750,000. At the time of my original 1974 study,[4] five radio stations (all AM) broadcast news from and to Auckland, three of them operated by the public corporation, Radio New Zealand. The corporation's head office is in the capital, Wellington, which remains the principal center of news gathering and distribution, as well as the source of nationally networked news and other programming.

Table 1 charts a number of characteristics of these five stations. Although news is the focus of this study, it is only one ingredient of a station's programming. Music is radio's main content. It filled most broadcast hours on stations 1ZM and 1XA, and was the staple of all otherwise unprogrammed time on other stations. Music on the five stations is largely age-graded, ranking the audience accordingly: 1YA older, 1ZB and 1XI middle, 1ZM and 1XA young. Other programming, announcer language, and advertising are also important elements of a station's content and indicators of its style – perhaps more so than news. Broadcasters and audiences alike recognize news as significant far be-

[4] I describe the situation as it was at the time of the main language sample used in this research (1974) while updating some labels that have changed in the interim. The same data set was introduced in Bell (1982a) and is here presented in more detail and reinterpreted in an explicit accommodation framework. Much of the basic programming and character of the stations remain remarkably unchanged despite several reorganizations of public broadcasting and the addition of several more stations (mostly FM). New programming, formats, sources, and networking have altered more, yet the accommodative patterns are largely constant. Several resamplings of specific linguistic variables at intervals since the original sample indicate that the basic patterns to be described here have remained very stable. In tables and lists, the stations are always given in the order of their medium wave frequencies: 1YA, 1ZB, 1ZM, 1XA, 1XI.

Table 1. *Characteristics of five radio stations in Auckland*

Station	Ownership	Audience	Community involvement	Programming
1YA carries National Programme network from Wellington	Radio New Zealand (public corporation)	Older, higher education, professionals	Nil	Highly scheduled: news, current affairs, concerts, drama
1ZB local Community Network station	Radio New Zealand	Age thirties and forties, family, mid-status	Very high; main local service and information station; local sponsorships, interviews, advertising	Community information, sport, horse racing news, shopping tips, household advice, local news
1ZM	Radio New Zealand	Young, largely male	Low	Continuous music
1XA Radio Hauraki	Private	Young, low status, largely male	Some community information and sponsorship	Music
1XI Radio i	Private	Mid-age and status, largely female	High involvement, especially through talkback, interviews	Telephone talk-back (especially in daytime), interviews, music

yond the rather small amount of air time it occupies – an average of less than 7 percent of broadcast hours across all these stations.

Here is the news

The five stations in fact broadcast eight distinct sets of news (Table 1, last column). National Radio is the prestigious service of public corpora-

Music	Advertising	Announcer Style	News
Light, often from 1940s and 1950s	Nil	Detached, measured: prestige radio, prestige speech	YA: National Radio news, live from Wellington YAR: Regional news from 1YA Auckland BBC: Overseas Service relayed live from London
Popular, middle-of-the-road, established hits	A lot of advertising, much of it read in a chatty fashion by the announcer	Homely, familiar: program "hosts" – especially in breakfast session – are local notables	ZB: Community Network news relayed live from Wellington ZBR: Regional news from Auckland (coded jointly as ZB/R for audience survey)
Rock: recent and often specialist	Some advertising, often music related	Archetypal DJ: dramatic, suave, frequent talk over music	ZM: Own news
Rock: softer than that of ZM	Much advertising, aimed at teenage and twenties audience	A little quieter than that of ZM	XA: Own news
Popular, some rock	Household oriented	Familiar	XI: Own news

tion radio, with almost all programs originating in Wellington and networked to repeater stations throughout the country. At this time it carried three separate sets of news. Its own news (coded YA) was edited and broadcast from Radio New Zealand's head office in Wellington. The local Auckland repeater station, 1YA, broke out of the network once daily for a bulletin of regional news (YAR). In addition, three to four bulletins (coded BBC) were carried live from the BBC Overseas Service in London (now transmitted via the highbrow Concert Programme network).

Station 1ZB carried two distinct types of news. Radio New Zealand's head office broadcast bulletins to be carried live on the network of more than 20 local community stations throughout New Zealand. 1ZB carried most of the Wellington-originated bulletins (coded ZB), broadcast on the hour and every half hour at peak periods. In addition, 1ZB's own Auckland newsroom compiled bulletins of regional and local news (coded ZBR) that were broadcast immediately after many of the network bulletins. These five sets of news – YA, YAR, BBC, ZB, and ZBR – were treated as separate and distinct populations for the language analysis. The situation on the other three stations, ZM, XA, and ZI, was more straightforward. Each compiled and presented its own bulletins, usually every hour, but with additional bulletins at peak (meal) times and fewer ones in the evenings.

The multiple stations of New Zealand's public broadcasting system provided an unforeseen bonus for the linguistic analysis. YA and ZB news originate in the same suite of studios in Wellington, and the same individual newscasters are heard on both networks. YAR, ZBR, and ZM all broadcast from Radio New Zealand's Auckland studios and also share a common pool of newscasters. Comparing the styles of a single newscaster recorded on two different stations yields crucial evidence on the nature of style differences. We will see how individual mass communicators accommodate their language production to suit their different audiences.

The language sample

Since Labov's New York City study (1966), sociolinguistic research has recognized a sufficiently large random sample as the main data base for the study of linguistic variation across a speech community. Drawing on sampling methods developed in media content analysis (e.g., Budd, Thorp, and Donohew 1967), I defined the universe to be sampled as all scheduled, general-topic, hard news bulletins[5] broadcast on Auckland radio stations between 6 A.M. and midnight from Monday to Friday.

The sample followed the "constructed week" design first developed by Jones and Carter (1959) and used in many subsequent studies of news

---

[5]"Hard" news is the staple news product: immediate announcements, events, accidents, political activity, and so on. It contrasts with "soft" news, which is less time-bound and more discursive – human interest, background, and commentary.

content. It is a stratified random sample in which a week is constructed of days selected from several separate weeks. All news was recorded on all five stations on the five chosen days. Content such as headlines, repeated items, speech by reporters and interviewees, and nonnews matter (e.g., station identification) was excluded, leaving about 17 hours of newscaster speech available for linguistic analysis. This provided adequate (80–200) tokens of phonological variables for between four and nine newscasters on each station except YAR. Only two of the fifty-two newscasters were women. Because they read so few bulletins, their speech was not analyzed, eliminating potential variation according to gender.[6]

An additional nonrandom sample was collected in the months following the main sampling period. It recorded additional speech from two separate groups of Radio New Zealand newscasters: those from Wellington who broadcast on both YA and ZB, and those from Auckland heard on all three stations, YAR, ZBR, and ZM. Data from this additional sample are used only for comparison and are not combined with data from the main random sample.

Characterizing the audience

This study argues that differences that may be identified between the news styles of Auckland's radio stations are the result of differences in audiences and their values. It assumes that membership in a station's audience evinces general approval of that medium, its content, and its communicators' style.

For this study, random surveys of the Auckland urban area at the time of the language sample provided some characterization of the audience. Each survey questioned 586 respondents in two areas: media reception habits and demographic characteristics (gender, age, education, occupation). The survey distinguished five age groups and five divisions of the education variable. The occupation scale had four ranked groups, plus a residual category for nonworkers (omitted from rankings for social status).

These surveys enable us to construct a demographic profile of each station's audience, focusing on the proportion of that audience that comes from each age, education, or occupation level. Although there are no great education differences among the five stations' audiences, the age and occupation variables show a clear stratification. The audience data

[6]New Zealand broadcast journalism is now considerably less male dominated.

rank the stations in three distinct groups. YA has the older listeners (average age, forty-seven years) and the highest education and occupation levels. ZB/R and XI rank in the middle for occupation and age. ZM and XA have the young male audience (average age, twenty-six years) and low occupation level [Bell (1982a) presents further detail on audience profiles].

A second axis of audience characterization intersects with the one just presented. These two dimensions have been identified under a range of labels, including "power and solidarity" (Brown and Gilman 1960), "overt and covert prestige" (Trudgill 1972), "standard and local prestige" (Bell 1982a), and "status and solidarity" (Coupland 1985; Milroy 1980). The first term in each pair is associated with overtly and often nationally acknowledged speech norms used by groups whose social status is evidenced in high occupations, education levels, and incomes. The second term is associated with more covert norms oriented to family, peer group, local community, and often working-class values. Many studies have shown how such covert local values influence language, modifying or replacing linguistic variants widely regarded as prestigious with those that mark local, ingroup solidarity.

The local solidarity dimension was not directly surveyed for this research. Program content was used to infer the degree to which stations and their audiences are locally oriented. The description in Table 1 indicates the relative strength of local commitment by the different stations. The national stations YA and ZB clearly have little or no local identity. ZM and XA show a little local identity, and ZBR is the most locally oriented station, followed by XI and then by YAR. The pull of the local factor could thus be reflected in some linguistic patterns for ZBR and XI.

2.5. The linguistic analysis

Three phonological or syntactic variables are examined here from among the many that could have been analyzed: negative contraction, consonant cluster reduction, and intervocalic /t/ voicing. In general, detail on linguistic constraints (see Bell 1977) is kept to the minimum necessary to reveal the nature of the accommodative processes.

Negative contraction: Audience status

Negative contraction (Negcon) reduces *not* to *n't* and attaches it to a preceding auxiliary or modal. Negcon has been largely ignored in the study of linguistic variation, partly because it is so subject to conscious control. In addition, contraction or noncontraction must be specified in any written text, making it unsuitable for a Labovian comparison between scripted and ad lib styles.[7] Negcon also occurs rather infrequently – only about once every two minutes of broadcast speech. Nearly the entire seventeen-hour sample of news language had to be scanned to produce sufficient tokens ($N = 551$).

By the Negcon rule, the item *not* may be variably contracted and joined to an immediately preceding finite modal, *do* (auxiliary), *be* or *have*. The *n't* may attach to the auxiliary (which I use here as a cover term for all the items permitting contraction) either without further phonological change (e.g., *aren't, haven't*) or with a vowel change (*don't, can't*). Regular phonological rules can account for deletion of the final liquid in *will* and *shall* and for reduction of the consonant cluster in *must*. Of the closed set of twenty-three items to which *not* may attach, only *am not* has no negative contraction in standard English, although it is one of the forms covered by nonstandard *ain't* (which, naturally enough, does not appear in news language). *May not* produces the disfavored disyllabic *mayn't*, which did not occur in the sample (see Zwicky and Pullum 1982).

The relative frequencies with which stations applied the variable Negcon rule is displayed in Fig. 1, which graphs the number of times the negative was contracted divided by the number of times it could have been contracted. The most notable feature of the array is that the BBC never contracts negatives – a surprising nonapplication of a very frequent rule of spoken English. This reflects the susceptibility of Negcon to conscious control and probably arose from an explicit style ruling for news reading on the BBC World Service. YA falls closest to the BBC, with a total mean contraction of 27.8 percent. ZB, ZBR, and XI are beyond YA, and XA contracts the most negatives of all at 71.4 percent.

The external station BBC appears to function as a formal standard of noncontraction, a reflection of the prestige of BBC English both worldwide and in the New Zealand speech community (Bell 1982b). There then follow – in three clear groupings – the New Zealand station with the highest-status audience, YA; the mid-status stations ZB, ZBR, and

---

[7] All news copy is scripted. Some contractions are in fact scripted by the journalist or copy editor, others are not. And newscasters apply some of their own contractions and reverse others that had been scripted for them. It is therefore impossible, without access to the written copy, to tell whether the newscaster is responsible for any specific contraction. This (and the low total N) prevents us making comparisons between individual newscasters for their degree of Negcon in the fashion we will undertake later for the two phonological variables.

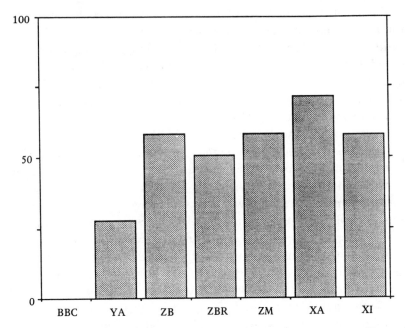

Figure 1. Percentage of negative contraction on seven radio stations, summing all linguistic environments.

XI; and the low-status XA. Only ZM has any suggestion of deviating from the rank its audience indicates it should occupy. At 58.1 percent it is closer to the middle stations than to its expected companion, XA. The stations thus appear to be accommodating their application of the rule to the status of their audience.

These findings closely parallel Brunel's (1970) study of the styles of French-speaking radio stations in Montreal. For affrication of /t/ and /d/ (to t^s and d^z, respectively), the elite CBF station used the lowest frequency (48 percent). The teenage station CJMS used by far the most affrication (90 percent), and the three middle-audience stations used intermediate values (53–54 percent). Yaeger-Dror's (1988) analysis of the use of Hebrew dialects on Israeli radio shows a similar pattern. Apical /r/ in the news language of four stations increases in accordance with their audience's status.

Consonant cluster reduction: Audience solidarity

The most thoroughly studied sociolinguistic variable in English is the rule that simplifies world-final consonant clusters by deleting the stop that is the last member of the cluster (Guy 1980). The reduction (often known as "/*t,d*/ deletion") is an apparently universal marker of less formal speech styles and also registers solidarity within some social groups. Although there have been differences of opinion over what clusters the rule affects and in what manner, the patterns in my data indicated that all clusters with a final stop should be treated as subject to reduction (Bell 1977: 325).

Two linguistic constraints found in all studies to date were also investigated here. The influence of the following phonetic environment was strong, but the presence or absence of a past-tense morpheme boundary (fined vs. *find*) had such an inconsistent effect that it was abandoned as a factor for this study.

Later research on the rule of cluster reduction isolated five classes of following segments: pause, vowel, glide, liquid, and consonant. Vowel disfavors reduction strongly, following consonant favors it, and the other three environments fall less stably in between. In the vowel, pause, and glide environments this rule operates at very low relative frequencies in this sample (generally below 10 percent) – evidence of the general formality of news style. Following pause inhibits the rule almost as much as a vowel (see Guy 1980). I also cross-classify the following segment constraint with a further constraint: whether the cluster occurs in the coordinator *and* or not. The number of tokens is then too few for a full five-factor following-segment constraint, so these are grouped into [+C] (following consonant and liquid) and [−C] (following vowel, glide, and pause).

Figure 2 graphs the percentage of consonant cluster reduction for all stations in the four environments of a following segment by *and* cross-classification. (Phonological variables were not analyzed for the BBC data because of the amount of noise in the shortwave radio channel.) The pattern is very consistent, with a regular rise from the least favored following vowel/non-*and* environment to the most favored consonant/*and* environment. The data confirm the finding that coordinator *and* – excluded from most studies – takes cluster reduction at a consistently higher level (90 percent in Neu 1980) than other lexical items. Equally striking is the regularity of the station ordering. YA reduces the fewest clusters and ZB slightly more. Then come ZM and XA in a central grouping, and ZBR and XI together with the highest cluster reduction, approaching 100 percent in the most favored environment.

This ordering reflects the effect of a local solidarity factor intersecting the status-oriented ordering shown by the Negcon variable. The strongly local station ZBR has shifted well beyond XA and ZM, followed by the

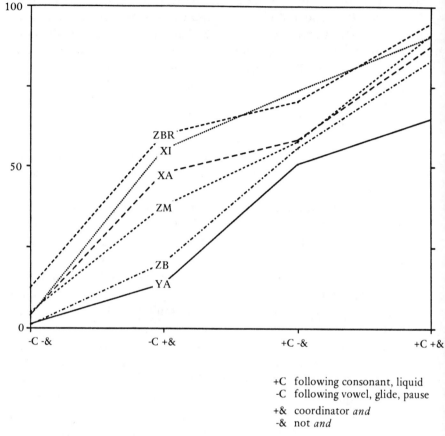

+C   following consonant, liquid
-C   following vowel, glide, pause
+&   coordinator *and*
-&   not *and*

Figure 2. Percentage of consonant cluster reduction on six stations in four linguistic environments.

slightly less locally oriented XI. YA and ZB maintain their positions, with least application of the rule. The orderings are disturbed only by minor crossovers in the [−C, −&] and [+C, +&] environments. Such deviations are not uncommon in environments where rule application is below 10 percent or above 90 percent. The major crossovers are predictable – ZM with XA and ZBR with XI, the two station pairs with similar audiences. The rankings are remarkably consistent, the more so because the spread between stations is in most environments not great. The large N (3,317) has here minimized the effect of fluctuations often caused by insufficient tokens. The presence of the local factor intersecting with status and modifying the rankings we would expect from status alone is confirmed by the distance between ZB and ZBR, the national and local news bulletins broadcast on the single station, 1ZB.

The finding of a local solidarity factor working against status is paralleled by other research on broadcast language. Lipski's (1985) quantitative data from Latin American broadcasting show that use of local phonological variants, especially aspiration and deletion of syllable- and word-final /s/, is stigmatized and minimal in news broadcasts but increases in DJ speech and sports commentary. Lipski notes the strenuous and affected avoidance of local and regional phonology by newscasters in the dozen Spanish-speaking countries he surveyed. Variants that are almost absent from everyday speech are restored in newscasting. Latin American newscasters apply /s/ reduction generally less than 10 percent of the time, although application is 90 percent in everyday speech.

Coupland also shows how status and solidarity linguistic markers mix in the speech of his Cardiff radio presenter, whose show is "no less than a celebration of in-group solidarity" (Coupland 1985: 158), with local dialect serving as a focus and expression of Cardiff identity. Coupland identifies a blend of solidarity and status variants, which are often triggered by different kinds of content. In my data, the national media, YA and ZB, retained a majority of final clusters, but the local community media, ZBR and XI, reduced a majority (Fig. 2). For Negcon, however, these local media followed a national standard (Fig. 1), thus maintaining a necessary link with prestigious media in the formal, high-competence genre of newscasting. Some features were thus used to mark solidarity and others status identities. But where the Cardiff presenter had liberty to range into nonstandard linguistic variants, the New Zealand newscaster used quantitative shifts of standard phonological variants for the same function.

Cluster reduction: Converging on a station style

The extent to which newscasters are accommodating to their audience can be seen in their individual data. Table 2 presents twenty-one newscasters who were grouped by station in Fig. 2 (plus five from the additional sample). They are ranked in implicational order from the least to the greatest overall degree of cluster reduction. The order of speakers coincides strikingly with the station order of Figure 2, to the extent that in most cases it is possible to predict which station a newscaster is on according to his place in the ranking. The speakers fall into three lin-

Table 2. *Percentage of consonant cluster reduction for twenty-six newscasters in four linguistic environments (± following consonant, ± coordinator and)*

News-caster	Station	−C −&	−C +&	+C −&	+C +&	N			
VG	YA	1.8%	6.7%	50.0%	50.0%	55	15	70	16
SD	YA	1.3	17.6	46.7	63.6	79	17	75	22
TE	YA	1.6	11.8	42.3	75.9	61	17	52	29
PB	ZB	0	17.6	43.1	84.8	51	17	65	33
OJ	YA	1.4	18.5	63.8	70.4	71	27	58	27
UF	ZB	1.8	26.3	46.3	84.2	69	19	54	19
OJ	ZB	0	12.5	64.5	85.0	55	16	62	20
YM	ZB		23.5	68.3	77.8	62	17	60	18
AF	ZM	4.2	31.3	46.0	88.5	48	16	63	26
MBR	XA	0	47.8	52.9	81.0	58	23	68	21
BJ	ZM	3.3	31.3	55.7	92.0	61	16	61	25
NV	XA	7.4	43.5	44.8	91.7	81	23	87	24
NH	XI	0	47.1	61.9	78.9	53	17	42	38
KW	XI	2.6	33.3	81.7	90.0	39	18	60	20
MS	ZBR	8.5	44.4	70.9	95.2	59	18	55	21
TA	ZM	6.8	50.0	71.4	92.9	59	16	70	28
GB	XA	4.6	52.4	77.1	89.5	65	21	70	19
JS	XI	1.5	50.0	73.7	100	67	16	57	21
HD	ZBR	8.5	66.7	70.3	93.3	59	21	74	30
TA	ZBR	19.6	68.4	69.4	95.8	51	19	49	24
JP	XI	9.7	90.0	76.1	93.5	62	30	71	31
Additional sample									
PB	YA	0	15.0	32.3	73.9	61	20	62	23
SD	ZB	1.9	29.4	71.4	81.8	54	17	42	22
AF	ZBR	1.4	17.6	54.8	63.3	71	17	73	30
AF	YAR	1.3	14.3	52.7	59.4	79	14	74	32
TA	YAR	0	31.3	57.5	68.2	32	16	40	22

guistic groups: YA and ZB newscasters at the top (with only one ZB speaker breaking the YA sequence), plus one from ZM. The bottom group contains all ZBR newscasters, all but one from XI, plus one each from ZM and XA. In the middle are three ZM and XA newscasters, plus one from XI.

What we see here is individual newscasters converging toward a common style of speech targeted at their audience. This is evidenced in the notably narrow scatter of newscasters from each station. The finding supports the hypothesis proposed earlier that professional consensus is at work among a station's newscasters over what is a suitable style for their particular audience.[8] Individual differences are minimized, and speakers tend to cluster around the station's mean frequency for the variable, giving content to the notion of a "station style" that is accommodated to its audience. The consensus is reflected most obviously in a newsroom's "style book" and the practices of copy editors employed to make news conform to station style (Bell 1984a, 1991). Note, however, that these practices and the linguistic manipulation they involve remain largely below the level of consciousness.

Whether we take the social or the linguistic variables as independent, therefore, the same relationships show up. The natural grouping of newscasters on stations, and of stations according to audience, undeniably stratifies news language styles. On the other hand, linguistically based groups of speakers apparently bear only the roughest resemblance to groupings according to the speakers' individual characteristics. Demographic data were obtained on a sample of Radio New Zealand newscasters to examine the place of the individual communicator. The three top-status speakers were grouped together, as were the three lowest-status speakers. Their pattern for this variable was quite equivocal. In the four cluster reduction environments, the top- and bottom-status groups crossed over twice. In no environment were they separated by more than 8 percent, and the higher-status group in fact used *more* cluster reduction than the lower.

The strongest evidence of all looks not at different newscasters on one station, but at one newscaster on different stations. Several Radio NZ newscasters were recorded on both YA and ZB, and others on YAR and ZBR. These are in effect natural matched guises (Lambert 1967). Listeners record their approval of one of these by their presence in the

---

[8] Compare the notion of "prototypicality" in Gallois and Callan (1988). But note that their concept is of a single speaker who is typical of a group, whereas the finding here focuses on how newscasters speak more like each other than do most groups of speakers.

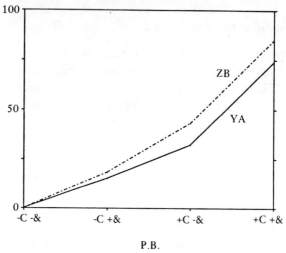

P.B.

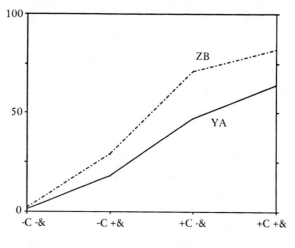

S.D.

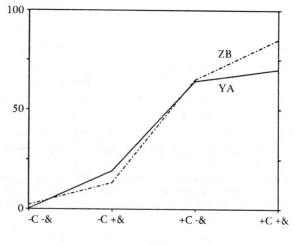

O.J.

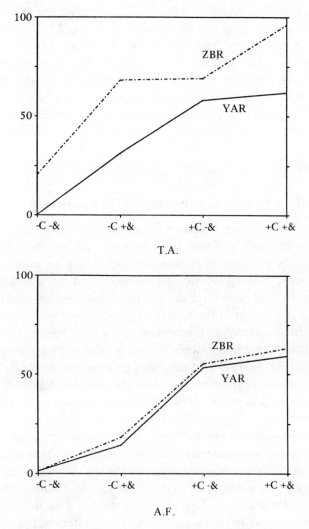

Figure 3. Percentage of consonant cluster reduction for three YA-ZB newscasters (PB, SD, OJ) and two YAR-ZBR newscasters (TA, AF) in four linguistic environments.

audience of the station that broadcasts it rather than of the other station. The prestige of the guise then ranks according to the prestige of the audience who received it.

Figure 3 graphs the performance of three newscasters, P.B., S.D., and O.J., each of whom was recorded on both YA and ZB, and two, T.A.

and A.F., recorded on both YAR and ZBR. Here we see in miniature the same relationships graphed for the stations in Fig. 2.[9] Note that the data for newscaster P.B. on station YA, and those for S.D. on station ZB, came from the additional sample and therefore did not contribute to the station means graphed in Fig. 2. The five newscasters shift in a consistent direction between their two stations, with only one deviant cell in the twenty speaker by environment cells of the comparison. Newscasters S.D. and T.A. in particular shift by 20–30 percent in some environments.

Intervocalic /t/ voicing: One newscaster, two audiences

A third linguistic variable sharpens these style shifts by single newscasters still further and confirms the patterns we have seen so far. Intervocalic /t/ can be realized as an alveolar voiced flap or stop instead of a voiceless stop, making words such as *writer* and *better* sound like *rider* and *bedder*. In American English the rule is now semicategorical (applied more than 90 percent of the time), and the merger with intervocalic /d/ is approaching completion (Fisher and Hirsh 1976; Woods 1979). In New Zealand, however, it is a genuinely variable rule, so that /t/ may be voiced when it follows a vowel and precedes an unstressed vowel. There is a gradient of realization from a voiceless alveolar stop followed by aspiration [t^h], through degrees of fricativization and voicing, to a full voiced alveolar stop [d].

The rankings of stations for their percentage of application of the /t/ voicing rule are less clear-cut than for cluster reduction but generally confirm much of what has already been shown. Most strikingly, all five YA newscasters for whom /t/ voicing was analyzed rank above the four ZB newscasters analyzed. This is despite the fact that, in every case but one, the data come from the same four newscasters heard on both stations. The detail of these style shifts is presented in Fig. 4, together with data for two YAR-ZBR newscasters. Three linguistic constraints on the rule are distinguished: presence of a word boundary after the /t/ (*but##if*), following morpheme boundary (*creat#ing*), or no boundary (*letter*). Although these environments do not order with complete consistency, the shift by individual speakers between stations is very regular. The six newscasters shift, on average, 20 percent in each environment between YA and ZB or YAR and ZBR.

---

[9] YAR was excluded from Fig. 2 because its data were largely from the additional sample.

Accommodation to the audience is the only tenable explanation for the individual speaker shifts shown in Figs. 3 and 4. These graphs display thirty-eight pairwise comparisons of station rankings for newscaster by linguistic environment. Of these, only one environment (newscaster O.J. in $[-C, +\&]$ for consonant cluster) deviates from what we would expect if accommodation is operating. Single newscasters heard on two different stations show a remarkable and consistent ability to make considerable style shifts to suit the audience. These switches between stations are at times very rapid: At off-peak hours, a single newscaster may alternate between YA and ZB news, with as little as 10 minutes between bulletins on the different stations.

2.6. And that is the end of the news

Our analysis of accommodation in the mass media indicates a number of conclusions. Although the one-newscaster/two-audiences comparison is the clearest case, the other evidence also points overwhelmingly to the operation of accommodation in newscasting. For negative contraction, stations rank precisely according to their status, with the external prestige norm, BBC, contracting no negatives at all. For consonant clusters, the pull of local community identity intersects with the status factor, shifting both ZBR and XI to higher levels of cluster reduction. And not only do stations with different audiences differ systematically in their styles, those with similar audiences (ZM-XA and ZBR-XI) share consistently similar styles. News is thus clearly on the responsive dimension posited by audience design.

Sociolinguistic and ethnographic research has, over the years, suggested a variety of factors that can produce such differences within an individual's speech, including topic, setting, and attention to speech. The evidence of newscaster shifts between stations leaves little place for such factors. There is no reason to suppose that newscasters are exercising systematically different amounts of attention on different stations. The physical setting of the communicator in the studio, and the audience anywhere at all, remain constant. The topics of the news are broadly similar across the stations. And in the case of the YA-ZB and YAR-ZBR comparisons, the stations are part of the same broadcasting organization, in the same studios, using the same speakers.

Newscasting also proves to be a case where the speech patterns of individuals are subordinated to corporate style. Mass communicators share a professional consensus about how their audience should be ad-

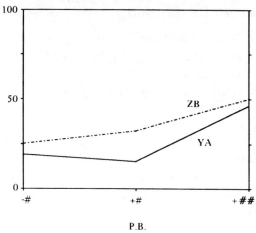

P.B.

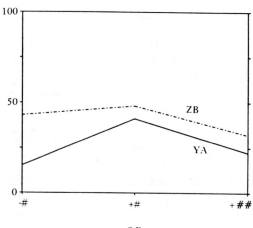

S.D.

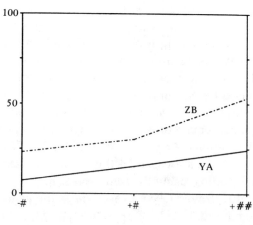

O.J.

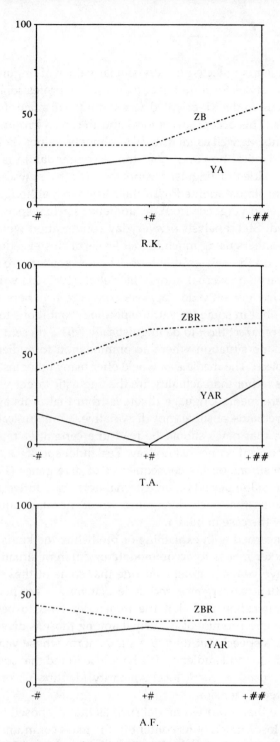

Figure 4. Percentage of intervocalic /t/ voicing for four YA-ZB newscasters (PB, SD, OJ, RK) and two YAR-ZBR newscasters (TA, AF) in three linguistic environments. *Key:* − # no following boundary; + # following morpheme boundary; + ## following word boundary.

dressed, which is reflected in very similar values of linguistic variables and common styles for different audiences. The professional dimension is most evident in the RP-oriented accent unique to a handful of national broadcasters. This accent mixes local and Received Pronunication (RP) vowel variants, as well as intermediate phonetic values (Bell 1986).

We should note, however, that this accommodation is not convergence. The values of linguistic variables used by newscasters are assuredly more status-oriented than their listeners', although the precise degree of their divergence from the audience's actual speech has still to be quantified. Still, analysis of everyday conversation would show the audience members using much higher levels of cluster reduction and /t/ voicing than do the newscasters here. The newscasters are therefore diverging toward an external norm. Giles et al. (1987: 21) write: "It could be argued that not only do speakers converge to where they believe others to be, but in some (as yet, unspecified) conditions to where they believe others *expect them* to be linguistically." The present study specifies at least one situation where accommodation to audience expectations takes place. The media as a whole offer many other instances where expectations rather than actuality are the linguistic target.

Even where media language diverges from that of its audience, the motivation remains positive, not dissociative. Communicators and audience agree that news should be read in a certain way, although the RP-oriented accent is one that no New Zealander speaks naturally. Giles et al.'s propositions on the consequences of divergence (1987: 39) note that the high value placed on an external norm can outweigh the negative evaluations that such divergence would normally attract. This is undoubtedly the case in media.

SAT is concerned with explaining or predicting the kinds of language shifts a speaker makes to accommodate in different situations and the processes involved. We must conclude that some of these strategies – such as mutual convergence and style matching – are inapplicable to mass communication and that the remainder tend to become correspondingly more prominent. Principal among those is divergence from the audience's speech but toward a status norm whose value is shared by communicator and audience. We have also found that some linguistic variables are used to mark local solidarity identity in contrast to the status-oriented dimension.

We can see that a process model such as that proposed by Coupland et al. (1988) loses much of its content in the mass communication situation. The lack of audience presence, feedback, and speaking rights eliminates many of the inputs and processes that are open to the speaker in face-to-face interaction. This by no means invalidates the model as a description of dynamic interaction. In fact, the contrasts illuminate the differences between the two kinds of situations. Nevertheless, this and other models conceived for face-to-face communication would require redesign in order to handle mass communication. The complexity required by face-to-face dynamics is reduced, and their ability to handle different layers of audience and multiple audience roles needs to be enhanced.

As a data context, the media offer a rich source for testing and exemplifying aspects of accommodation theory. The area of accommodation to stereotypes and external targets is of increasing interest to SAT, and it is here that media examples abound. Linguistic stereotyping plays a large role in genres such as advertising (Bell 1986). Here language is used as a shorthand method of calling up associations with desirable target groups. Accommodation to external prestige norms is demonstrable in many different media types, such as record and magazine production, and in genres such as DJ talk. The effects of these strategies on the audience have yet to be researched.

Study of such accommodative strategies will be especially important and fruitful in those many countries that find themselves subject to cultural domination. Here local media products are accommodated – linguistically and in wider communicative ways – to external models (usually Anglo-American) that threaten to swamp the development of truly local genres and styles. The greatest opportunity here is offered by media such as local radio that are comparatively undemanding on resources, flexible in their operation, and responsive to their immediate audience. The many faces of cultural colonialism provide both a variegated field for the study of accommodation in mass communication and a place where findings can be applied for the good of the communities under study.

References

Bauer, R. A. 1964. The communicator and his audience. *In* L. A. Dexter and D. M. White (eds.), *People, Society and Mass Communications*, pp. 125–39. Glencoe, IL: Free Press.

Beebe, L. M. 1981. Social and situational factors affecting communicative strategy of dialect and code-switching. *International Journal of the Sociology of Language*, 32: 139–49.

Bell, A. 1977. The language of radio news in Auckland: A sociolinguistic study of style, audience and subediting variation. Unpublished Ph.D. thesis, University of Auckland. (Ann Arbor, MI: University Microfilms International, 1979).

Bell, A. 1982a. Radio: The style of news language. *Journal of Communication*, 32: 150–64.

Bell, A. 1982b. This isn't the BBC: Colonialism in New Zealand English. *Applied Linguistics*, 3: 246–58.

Bell, A. 1984a. Good copy – bad news: The syntax and semantics of news editing. In P. Trudgill (ed.), *Applied Sociolinguistics*, pp. 73–116. London: Academic Press.

Bell, A. 1984b. Language style as audience design. *Language in Society*, 13: 145–204.

Bell, A. 1986. Responding to your audience: Taking the initiative. Paper presented to the Minnesota Conference on Linguistic Accommodation and Style-Shifting, Minneapolis, Minnesota.

Bell, A. 1988. The British base and the American connection in New Zealand media English. *American Speech*, 63: 326–44.

Bell, A. 1991. *Language of the News Media*. Oxford: Basil Blackwell.

Brown, R., and Gilman, A. 1960. The pronouns of power and solidarity. In T. A. Sebeok (ed.), *Style in Language*, pp. 253–76. Cambridge, MA: MIT Press.

Brunel, G. 1970. Le français radiophonique à Montréal. Unpublished master's dissertation, University of Montreal.

Budd, R. W., Thorp, R. K., and Donohew, L. 1967. *Content Analysis of Communications*. New York: Macmillan.

Burns, T. 1977. *The BBC: Public Institution and Private World*. London: Macmillan.

Coupland, N. 1985. "Hark, hark, the lark": Social motivations for phonological style-shifting. *Language and Communication*, 5: 153–71.

Coupland, N., Coupland, J., Giles, H., and Henwood, K. 1988. Accommodating the elderly: Invoking and extending a theory. *Language in Society*, 17: 1–41.

Coupland, N., and Giles, H. (eds.). 1988. *Communicative Accommodation: Recent Developments (Language and Communication 8/3–4 special issue)*. Oxford: Pergamon Press.

Donsbach, W. 1983. Journalists' conceptions of their audience. *Gazette*, 32: 19–36.

Fill, A. F. 1986. Divided illocution. *International Review of Applied Linguistics*, 24: 27–34.

Fisher, W. M., and Hirsh, I. J. 1976. Intervocalic flapping in English. In S. S. Mufwene, C. A. Walker, and S. B. Steever (eds.), *Papers from the Twelfth Regional Meeting*, pp. 183–98. Chicago: Chicago Linguistic Society.

Gallois, C., and Callan, V. J. 1988. Communication accommodation and the prototypical speaker: Predicting evaluations of status and solidarity. *Language and Communication*, 8: 271–83.

Giles, H. 1973. Accent mobility: A model and some data. *Anthropological Linguistics*, 15: 87–105.

Giles, H., Mulac, A., Bradac, J. J., and Johnson, P. 1987. Speech accommodation theory: The first decade and beyond. In M. L. McLaughlin (ed.), *Communication Yearbook 10*, pp. 13–48. Beverly Hills, CA: Sage.

Giles, H., and Powesland, P. F. 1975. *Speech Style and Social Evaluation*. London: Academic Press.

Glasgow University Media Group, 1980. *More Bad News*. London: Routledge & Kegan Paul.

Guy, G. R. 1980. Variation in the group and the individual: The case of final stop deletion. *In* W. Labov (ed.), *Locating Language in Time and Space*, pp. 1–36. New York: Academic Press.

Howitt, D. 1982. *The Mass Media and Social Problems*. Oxford: Pergamon.

Jones, R. L., and Carter, R. E., Jr. 1959. Some procedures for estimating "news hole" in content analysis. *Public Opinion Quarterly*, 23: 399–403.

Klapper, J. T. 1960. *The Effects of Mass Communication*. New York: Free Press.

Kumar, K. 1975. Holding the middle ground: The BBC, the public and the professional broadcaster. *Sociology*, 9: 67–88.

Labov, W. 1966. *The Social Stratification of English in New York City*. Washington, DC: Center for Applied Linguistics.

Labov, W. 1972. *Sociolinguistic Patterns*. Philadelphia: University of Pennsylvania Press.

Lambert, W. E. 1967. A social psychology of bilingualism. *Journal of Social Issues*, 23: 91–109.

Leech, G. N., and Short, M. H. 1981. *Style in Fiction: A Linguistic Introduction to English Fictional Prose*. London: Longman.

Lipski, J. M. 1985. Spanish in United States broadcasting. *In* L. Elias-Olivares, E. A. Leone, R. Cisneros, and J. R. Gutierrez (eds.), *Spanish Language Use and Public Life in the United States*, pp. 217–33. Berlin: Mouton.

McIntyre, I. 1988. Fall of the smoke blower. *The Times*, June 18, 1988:8.

McQuail, D. 1969. Uncertainty about the audience and the organization of mass communications. *In* P. Halmos (ed.), *The Sociology of Mass-Media Communicators* (*Sociological Review* Monograph No. 13), pp. 75–84. Keele: University of Keele, England.

Milroy, L. 1980. *Language and Social Networks*. Oxford: Basil Blackwell.

Mody, B. 1986. The receiver as sender: Formative evaluation in Jamaican radio. *Gazette*, 38: 147–60.

Montgomery, M. 1988. D-J talk. *In* N. Coupland (ed.), *Styles of Discourse*, pp. 85–104. London: Croom Helm.

Neu, H. 1980. Ranking of constraints on /t,d/ deletion in American English: A statistical analysis. *In* W. Labov (ed.), *Locating Language in Time and Space*, pp. 37–54. New York: Academic Press.

Pool, I. de S., and Shulman, I. 1959. Newsmen's fantasies, audiences, and newswriting, *Public Opinion Quarterly*, 23: 145–58.

Schlesinger, P. 1987. *Putting "Reality" Together: BBC News*. London: Methuen.

Selting, M. 1983. Institutionelle Kommunikation: Stilwechsel als Mittel strategischer Interaktion. *Linguistische Berichte*, 86: 29–48.

Selting, M. 1985. Levels of style-shifting – exemplified in the interaction strategies of a moderator in a listener participation programme. *Journal of Pragmatics*, 9: 179–97.

Solomon, M. 1978. Jimmy Carter and *Playboy*: A sociolinguistic perspective on style. *Quarterly Journal of Speech*, 64: 173–82.

Thakerar, J. N., Giles, H., and Cheshire, J. 1982. Psychological and linguistic parameters of speech accommodation theory. *In* C. Fraser and K. R. Scherer (eds.), *Advances in the Social Psychology of Language*, pp. 205–55. Cambridge: Cambridge University Press.

Trudgill, P. 1972. Sex, covert prestige and linguistic change. *Language in Society*, 1: 179–96.

Trudgill, P. 1974. *The Social Differentiation of English in Norwich*. London: Cambridge University Press.

Trudgill, P. 1983. *On Dialect*. Oxford: Basil Blackwell.

Trudgill, P. 1986. *Dialects in Contact*. Oxford: Basil Blackwell.

Tuchman, G. 1978. *Making News: A Study in the Construction of Reality*. New York: Free Press.

Woods, H. B. 1979. A socio-dialectology survey of the English spoken in Ottawa: A study of sociological and stylistic variation in Canadian English. Unpublished Ph.D. dissertation, University of British Columbia, Vancouver.

Yaeger-Dror, M. 1988. The influence of changing group vitality on convergence toward a dominant linguistic norm: An Israeli example. *Language and Communication*, 8: 285–305.

Zwicky, A. M., and Pullum, G. K. 1982. *Cliticization versus Inflection: English n't.* Bloomington: Indiana University Linguistics Club.

3. Accommodation on trial: Processes of communicative accommodation in courtroom interaction

PER LINELL

3.1. Introduction

This chapter is concerned with discourse in criminal court trials. Hence we will deal with highly asymmetrical social situations, encounters between professionals/experts (judges and lawyers) and laymen/clients (defendants and witnesses), that is, interactants who are widely different in terms of power, status, competence, perspectives, and, presumably, interests and intentions. Specifically, this chapter deals with various accommodative processes (adjustments, attunings) occurring between participants and across trial phases. In my analysis, I use the theoretical framework of speech or communication accommodation theory (SAT or CAT), which has been developed and successively refined over the last fifteen years, chiefly by Howard Giles and his collaborators. As is well known, this theory is designed to elucidate the sociolinguistic mechanisms of, and the social psychological processes underlying, discourse and interaction in various types of social encounters. I assume that the reader is familiar with the basic concepts and major versions of the theory (see recent overviews in Giles et al. 1987; N. Coupland et al. 1988; and the introduction by Giles, Coupland, and Coupland, to this volume). In accordance with recent proposals (e.g., Coupland and Giles 1988), I favor the term "communication accommodation theory (CAT)."

Work in CAT has recognized that accommodative orientations and strategies (and their evaluations by actors and observers) may be quite different under different contextual conditions. Although a major part of this research has used communication in experimental contexts, often but not always (see Thakerar, Giles, and Cheshire 1982) involving subjects of more or less equal status, we are concerned with discourse in an authentic and strongly asymmetrical situation. We would thus contribute to the now rapidly growing number of CAT-based, naturally grounded studies (see Coupland and Giles 1988; Giles, Coupland, and Coupland this volume).

From the point of view of CAT, a court trial may be characterized in terms of speech complementarity (Giles et al. 1987: 14, 33); lawyers and defendants act out very different established interactional roles. It is also a highly ritualized interaction in which actors' conduct is largely predetermined by various situational norms (see Gallois and Callan, this volume). Yet, even such an institutionalized and strongly power-asymmetrical encounter permits, as we shall see, interpersonal accommodations and individual styles. A priori, one might predict several different accommodative orientations and strategies in the trial. Given that professionals and defendants have very different "input values" in terms of language, domain knowledge, status, and power, one might perhaps expect convergence because of, for example, a striving (whether conscious or unconscious) to decrease the gap between parties and to increase intelligibility and efficiency in court procedures. (An explanation in terms of increased chances for social liking, a motive often appealed to in classical SAT-CAT, is not altogether implausible either, at least not in undramatic trials involving petty or nonstigmatizing offenses.) On the other hand, one might also predict that divergent behaviors surface in a court trial. One reason might be the desire to accentuate roles and underscore one's different values and world views. The courtroom is arguably an arena for self-presentation, both for judges and lawyers and for defendants. Discourse and interaction are enacted in front of an audience (the court, members of the general public), so that several types of audience design may occur (see Bell 1984). Accordingly, assumptions of across-the-board accommodations (in either direction) might be quite unrealistic. There is also a wealth of additional contextual factors (e.g., differences in court procedures, case types, defendants' experiences and attitudes, such as cooperation vs. noncooperation) that may affect orientations and behaviors in different directions. Furthermore, in view of the fact that interaction in general is a multilayered phenomenon, one may – solely for that reason – assume several kinds of accommodations to be operative in one and the same trial.

From this microworld of social psychological processes, interactional maneuvering, and linguistic variation, we single out a few dimensions. More specifically, we focus on accommodations in terms of information density and interactional format (the structure of dialogue exchanges). By exploring different layers of the interaction, we investigate further the question raised by N.Coupland et al. (1988) of whether such simultaneous accommodation processes need to be uniform in character and direction.

3.2. Research on courtroom interaction

A substantial amount of research has been carried out in recent years on discourse and interaction in court trials and related judicial settings. The literature has recently been reviewed by Jönsson (1988) (for other reviews and bibliographies, see Danet 1980; Levi 1982, 1985). Some research of special relevance is briefly reviewed here. Except for the research on our Linköping corpus (to be reported later), CAT has – to the best of my knowledge – not been invoked in studies of legal settings (except for Levin and Lin 1988).

Sociolinguistic analyses of variation (mostly at the phonological level) in the speech of defendants in a Viennese traffic court have been conducted by Wodak (1980; Wodak-Engel 1984). Wodak found considerable variation between working-class and middle-class defendants, not the least in their ability to cope with the courtroom situation and have their own stories coherently told and their own opinions voiced. Wodak claimed that there are significant differences in the ways in which the court treat people of varying social-economic status, both in courtroom interaction as such (defendants receive varying types of numbers of questions) and in terms of trial outcomes (verdicts).

In a number of studies collected in O'Barr (1982), William O'Barr and his associates investigated variations in witnesses' testimony styles. They detected two important dimensions of stylistic variation, that is, narrative vs. fragmentary styles and powerful vs. powerless styles. The latter notions were taken from Lakoff (1975), who argued that powerless language was typical of many women's discourse, but O'Barr found that a powerless style characterized many witnesses in court, irrespective of gender. In O'Barr's model, powerless language was characterized by a relatively limited amount of talk, a high incidence of hedges, hesitation forms, polite forms, tag questions and intensifiers, and other features that may be associated with vagueness and a high degree of expressed uncertainty. In a series of experiments, O'Barr showed that differences in testimony styles had clear effects on the attribution of credibility, competence, and intelligence by simulated juries. In other words, differences in witnesses' and defendants' linguistic or interactive styles had social psychological effects. However, neither Wodak nor O'Barr actually investigated such effects in the interaction itself, at least not in regard to possible adjustments of judges' and lawyers' discourse to stylistic differences among witnesses and defendants. This, on the other hand, has been a major objective in our own research.

Other research traditions have studied categories of questions and answers in courtroom hearings. Some examples are Harris (1984), Philips (1984, 1987), Danet and Bogoch (1980), Woodbury (1984), Lane (1985), and McGaughey and Stiles (1983). Most of these use some kind of categorization of speech acts, although not all are quantitatively oriented. Some have looked specifically at differences of question form and their effects on answers (length and linguistic structure of answers). Differences between types of case (serious vs. less serious crimes) and between examination and cross-examination (in the Anglo-Saxon adversarial system) have been specifically attended to. Despite a number of merits, most of this research is fairly atomistic in nature, basically counting tokens of different types of speech acts (particularly with respect to lawyers' questions) without really attempting to capture the *interactional* aspects, that is, the effects of different kinds of questions on witnesses' and defendants' response patterns within longer sequences, and, conversely, the effects of response modes and testimony styles on the professionals' subsequent questioning strategies. Other researchers have analyzed sequential patterns (e.g., Atkinson and Drew 1979) and other conversation analysts of the ethnomethodological school, but as they are interested in structural rather than variable analysis of interaction, they do not attempt a quantitative description of the sociolinguistic variation in interactive styles. Such an analysis is attempted in this chapter, when a model of initiative-response analysis (Linell, Gustavsson, and Juvonen 1988) is used in the analysis of some types of mutual accommodation processes on the part of defendants and legal professionals.

3.3. Accommodative processes in court trials: some earlier findings

In recent years, a number of studies on our Linköping corpus of courtroom discourse have been carried out. In this section, I summarize some findings from this work, particularly some CAT-based studies reported in Aronsson et al. (1987). Later in this chapter, I relate these findings to some data on accommodation processes at the interactional level of courtroom dialogue, reported in Adelswärd, Jönsson, and Linell (1987) but so far not discussed in CAT terms.

The Linköping corpus of courtroom discourse[1] comprises forty criminal trials, which were observed and audio-recorded in a Swedish district court. The charges all concern minor economic offenses, larceny and fraud, representative of the most frequent petty crimes that make up a good deal of the court's everyday reality. After the trials, defendants were individually interviewed about, among other things, their recollections and opinions of the recent trial, opinions about the language used, knowledge of the role structure in the courtroom, and preconceptions of trials and justice in general. Both the court proceedings and the post-trial interviews have been transcribed in extenso.

It should be pointed out that a Swedish criminal trial is different from its Anglo-Saxon counterpart in several respects (see Andenaes 1968). The main actors are the judge, the prosecutor, and (although not in all trials) the defense lawyer. There is no jury, but there are three lay judges, who are seated at the front panel together with the professional judge (chairman of the court) and a clerk. (Henceforth, we will use the term "legal professionals" as a cover term for judges (excluding lay judges), prosecutors, and defense lawyers. Alternatively, we talk about "judges and lawyers," in which case "lawyers" refers to both prosecutors and defense lawyers (unless otherwise stated).) Paraphernalia like wigs or other symbolic garments are not used, and hearings are carried out in a rather informal way. The whole procedure is less adversarial than in the Anglo-Saxon system, and there is seldom any clear difference between examination and cross-examination (such differences have often been documented in American studies of court trials). The judge is often fairly heavily involved during hearings. Trials are open to the general public, although often (at least in petty cases) there are few or no auditors present.

Our corpus includes twenty trials on charges of larceny and twenty of fraud. The majority of the defendants were male (thirty-five of forty). The trials were selected to include twenty defendants who were appearing in court for the first time and twenty defendants who had been tried and convicted at least once in the last ten years. Defendants had either blue-collar jobs or small businesses, or else they were not employed on the open labor market. The latter category (long-term unemployment,

[1] This courtroom corpus is described in more detail in Jönsson (1988). I am deeply indebted to my colleagues Karin Aronsson, Viveka Adelswärd, and Linda Jönsson, whose work and insights I draw on in this chapter. Research on the courtroom corpus has been financed by a grant awarded to Karin Aronsson and Per Linell by the Bank of Sweden Tercentenary Foundation (RJ 84/137).

short-term welfare jobs, early retirement) comprised about half the group (twenty-one of forty).

For the analyses, it seemed natural to assume that the treatment of defendants by judges and lawyers was contingent on the severity of the offense; that is, the professionals' knowledge of this factor, and of the individual defendant's criminal record and social circumstances, might be significant in influencing their behavior. Severity of offense was, for our research purposes, operationalized in terms of the type of penalty (heavy or light); we therefore divided all defendants into two groups of equal size on the basis of their sentences: a serious-offense group (jail, protective supervision, heavy fines) and a minor-offense group (contingent sentences, light fines, not-guilty verdicts). Of course, this operationalization in no way amounts to an assumption that the court's verdict in the individual case is determined in advance. Rather, the logic is, in short, that the court's construction of the individual case (which presumably underlies the verdict) is assumed to be regularly related to the various kinds of background knowledge and the actual interaction in court, and these, in turn, are taken to be strongly interdependent.[2] There was, not surprisingly, considerable overlap between the penalty-based categorization and the division into first-time offenders and those previously tried and convicted. Sixteen of the twenty defendants in the serious-offense group and only four of the twenty in the minor-offense group were previously convicted. Also a defense lawyer is more often present at the serious-offense trial (eighteen, as opposed to seven cases in the minor-offense trials).

Our courtroom discourse corpus, of course, permits numerous analyses on different linguistic and interactional levels and with divergent research objectives. Some discourse patterns, relating primarily to lexical choice and information density, were subjected to a CAT-based analysis in an earlier paper (Aronsson et al. 1987). It was pointed out in the introduction that a court trial is highly ritualized and that, therefore, there are probably strong situational constraints on accommodation processes. In the following review of accommodation processes, we first consider the legal professionals' orientations to the various situational norms of the different phases of the trial and then see what opportunities exist for interpersonal accommodations and individual styles.

A criminal court trial in Sweden involves a number of phases consist-

---

[2]Remember, however, that *all* cases involve *petty offenses*, which in only a few exceptional cases lead to jail sentences. Thus, the terms "serious offense" and "minor offense" are used here only to discriminate between *relatively* more and less serious offenses.

ing of linguistic activities that have separate goals and, partly as a consequence of this, rather different levels of formality. In our studies, it seemed appropriate to distinguish four major phases occurring in the following chronological order: reading the charge (phase I); case for the prosecution (statement of facts) (phase II); examination (and cross-examination) (phase III); and concluding speeches (phase IV). Of these, only the examination (phase III) is dialogical.

These phases are easily identified in the trial and are well suited for comparisons between linguistic styles. On the one hand, they are communicative activities with different goals and purposes. On the other hand, they all treat the same subject matter, that is, the allegedly criminal acts for which the defendant is tried. There is one actor, the prosecutor, who is active in describing and discussing the case in all four phases. In presenting the charge (I), he or she states the formal indictments, most often by reading aloud from a written document. This must be presented in a legally impeccable way, and the language used may therefore be expected to involve rather technical concepts and complex expressions. In his or her statement of facts (II), the prosecutor is supposed to describe the case in detail. Although not directly addressing the defendant specifically, the prosecutor is clearly expected to present the case in such a way that the presentation will allow the defendant to comment on it or to answer questions based on it in the examination phase (III). In this latter phase, the defendant is questioned by the judge and lawyers about the acts with which he or she has been charged and on personal circumstances. In the final speech (IV), the prosecutor then sums up the case and draws conclusions concerning guilt and proposed penalties.

If language is used differently in the various phases of a trial, then this would, first and foremost, be a case of style shifts between activities defined by different situational norms. However, the same phenomena might also be constructed as different (routinized) forms of lawyers' accommodating to a weaker party (the defendant) in a highly asymmetrical encounter. Although topics are kept more or less constant, the prosecutor could be assumed to adapt his or her language to the defendant most often in the examination phase (where the defendant is actually his or her interlocutor) and least often in the charge phase (where the court is the prime addressee and the defendant is more of an overhearer). The statement of facts might be assumed to be intermediate in linguistic style (the defendant is the addressee, although he or she is not allowed to respond immediately). The status of the final speech seems more ambiguous and may hypothetically be placed between the charge and the statement of facts in terms of formality and linguistic complexity. On the one hand, it follows the hearing in time and may be assumed to be responsive to things that have been said there, perhaps by the defendant. Therefore, he or she may seem at least indirectly involved (although now, during the final speech, he or she cannot respond in turn). Yet, the final speech is clearly directed to the court rather than the defendant. A plausible hypothesis would then be that the four major phases focused on here would be related in the following order of decreasing complexity and technicality:

Charge (I) > Final speech (IV) > Statement of facts (II) > Examination (III)

Of course, if there is a systematic stylistic variation following this scale, differences in purposes and recipient categories of the respective speech events need not be the only explanation to be invoked. There is no doubt a parallel decrease in prosecutors' reliance on written texts (in this respect, see the description of simplifications by Philips 1985). Also, one may perhaps understand differences between phases in terms of the varying strength of the social norms governing the respective discourse contexts.

Aronsson et al. (1987) explored this hypothesis on several points. In the following, I only review findings relating to the level of information density in the discourse of the legal professionals.[3] As a measure of information density, we took the number of different content word types (content words: in principle, all nouns, numerals, verbs, and adjectives, plus adverbs derived from these) in a sample of word tokens (running words) in connected discourse. (The size of the samples used in this study was 200 running words). There is reason to believe that this is a good indicator of complexity in actual communication as it tries to measure the amount of new substantive content that is introduced in a given discourse space. Hence, we calculated the information density so defined in the legal professionals' speech in twenty of our trials (those that involved the strong and weak defendants as defined) (Fig. 1). The data clearly confirmed the hypotheses that had been formulated. All differences except those between phases II and IV were significant ($p < .01$). Note especially the range in variation between the highly condensed phase I and the rather diluted speech of the dialogical phase (III).

[3] The distribution of technical language ("legalese") in prosecutors' discourse shows a pattern similar to that of information density (Fig. 1).

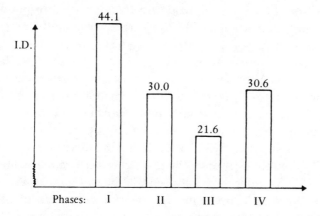

Figure 1. Information density in legal professionals' speech. I.D. = information density in number of content word types per 100 word tokens (see text).

One may take these findings as evidence of forms of speech accommodation through which actors of one category adjust their discourse in situations where they (expect to) address or interact with members of another group (outgroup), whose (stereotypical) communicative characteristics they anticipate. Could the trials also exhibit *interactive* accommodation in which actors adjust to the *actual and varying behaviors or styles* of the individuals with whom they communicate? Does the rather large-scale accommodation described earlier also leave room for more subtle interpersonal adjustments to different categories of defendants? In order to explore these questions, Aronsson et al. (1987) selected two extreme groups of defendants, with *strong* vs. *weak* styles, defined in terms of information density, frequency of hedges, and amount of talk. Accordingly, these styles were, in some respects, reminiscent of O'Barr's (1982) powerful vs. powerless styles. The hypothesis adopted was that these style differences in defendants' linguistic behavior would have social psychological effects in that judges and lawyers would perceive differences among defendants and consciously or unconsciously accommodate their own behavior so as to converge to the speech of their individual interlocutors. A quite strong form of interactive accommodation would then involve the legal professionals mirroring the defendants' language use in terms of information density.

Stated in terms of the number of content word types per 100 running words, the mean values in information density for weak and strong defendants were 19.0 and 23.0, respectively, and the corresponding measures for legal professionals when talking to weak- and strong-style defendants were remarkably similar, 19.4 and 23.7, respectively. Thus, there is a significant relation between professionals' style and defendants' style (Fisher; $p < .01$). Although it cannot be altogether excluded that defendants contribute to convergence in information density too (i.e., that convergence is mutual), it seems highly probable that professionals are responsible for most of the accommodation. As a result of these convergence processes, some dyads come out as relatively strong and others as weak, although, of course, the distinctions are rather subtle in comparison with the differences between trial phases (Fig. 1). When professionals calibrate their speech in terms of information density, it is apparently precisely this property in defendants' speech that counts, not some other aspect of their discourse such as the general activity level (measured in words per turn). There are no differences between the ten most active and ten most passive defendants in terms of information density (means 20.8 vs 21.8, n.s.), and when prosecutors interact with the ten most active and the ten most passive defendants, their mean values for information density were in fact exactly the same (22.8). This is, of course, precisely in accordance with a central CAT prediction.

To summarize, legal professionals have been shown to accommodate interactively (in terms of information density) to defendants. Adjustments to trial phases, on the other hand, are not the effects of immediate, approximative accommodation processes, but seem to be style shifts that occur in response to the situational norms and divergent purposes of the various communicative activities. Yet, these adjustments are also designed for different recipient categories (and recipients in different roles); in fact, they can be regarded as routinized accommodations to situations in which the same recipients (the court, the defendant, the audience, etc.) occupy slightly different roles.

As regards defendants, we could not, of course, compare the different phases of the trials, since defendants are allowed to speak only in the examination (and a few other short dialogical episodes). However, when Aronsson et al. (1987) compared their verbal behavior there with the way they talked about similar matters in the posttrial interviews, they found several kinds of adjustments. For example, defendants use significantly less criminal jargon and swear words in the trials than in the interviews. In general, Aronsson et al. (1987) conceive of the courtroom hearing (i.e. phase III) – the language of which may be characterized as informal, although not really colloquial, conversational style – as a kind of middle ground, which both parties approach by attenuating features of their communicative styles (used about similar topics in other situations), such as features typical of legalese and criminal jargon.

Accommodative processes can be observed at several other points in courtroom discourse. Although not all of these have so far been carefully researched in our corpus, a few should be mentioned. These are several critical speech acts in the trials in which professionals adjust to particular defendant categories. For example, at a rather early point in the trial (immediately after the prosecutor's reading of the charge), the judge asks the defendant about his or her stance with regard to the charge ("the question of admission or denial"). There is systematic variation in the judges' ways of formulating this particular communicative act; it is characterized by formality and conciseness with experienced offenders or when defense lawyers are present (the question would then seem to be only indirectly put to the defendant) and is more conversational and transparent with first-time offenders. Sociolinguistic variation in the realization of other obligatory acts (e.g., pronouncing the sentence, explaining its significance, etc.) can be analyzed along similar lines.

Other variables in professionals' discourse concern forms of address and feedback to defendants' answers. Here too, judges and lawyers tend to approach minor-offense defendants in slightly more conversational ways; the pronoun *du* "you" (second person singular) is used more often than the much more formal *ni* (second person plural), and some sort of restricted feedback or acknowledgment is provided. Serious-offense defendants are more strictly treated (more *ni*, fewer acknowledgments) (Adelswärd, Aronsson, and Linell 1988). As might be expected, when mitigating circumstances are brought up by judges and lawyers, this happens more often with minor-offense defendants. Interestingly, such incidents, which could be intended and interpreted as encouragements, are often misinterpreted (e.g., as ironical or condescending remarks) by these first-time defendants (Adelswärd 1989). In general, instances of miscommunication (overaccommodation, misinterpretation) are more common in trials involving minor-offense defendants (Aronsson 1991).

3.4. Interactive accommodation and the exchange of initiatives and responses

In the analysis of the Linköping courtroom corpus, we now move on to cover some new ground. Whereas CAT has most often been applied to formal linguistic (and paralinguistic) variables in discourse (e.g., phonology, morphology, lexical selection, turn length, pausing behavior, even language choice), we now approach – thereby in a way reflecting the gradual development from SAT to CAT mentioned at the outset – a more functional level, where we look on interactants' conversational contributions as acts and moves in dialogical activities, as turns in the jointly managed interaction. N.Coupland et al. (1988: 27) declare that they "see the discourse management component not only as the broadest but as the most central sociolinguistic category through which interpersonal accommodation is realized." Yet, this functional "level" has only recently begun to be explored in CAT terms (N.Coupland et al. 1988; J.Coupland et al. 1988). Using initiative-response analysis and drawing on some earlier work on our courtroom data (Adelswärd et al., 1987), we attempt to make a contribution to this particular area.

Initiative-response (IR) analysis (Linell et al., 1988) is a system for coding conversational contributions to a dialogue (turns) in terms of *initiatives* and *responses*. By taking a conversational initiative, the speaker tries to govern the ensuing dialogue by requiring or inviting a contribution from his or her interlocutor. Conversely, a speaker gives (tries to give) a response, if he or she complies (partly or completely) with (some of) the conditions that have been set up through the interlocutor's preceding turn (or sometimes, more generally, through the preceding discourse). Thus, initiatives and responses provide links from a turn to its local dialogue context forward and backward respectively. In other words, they are context-determining (predicting) and context-determined (predicted) aspects, respectively (where "context" stands for local dialogue context).[4] In some exchanges (i.e., asymmetrical adjacency pairs like question–answer, promise–acceptance, and order–compliance), the first and second parts may be predominantly initiating and responsive in character, but in many cases, a given conversational contribution comprises both responsive (retroactive) aspects – that is, the speaker ties up with what his or her interlocutor has just done or said – and initiating aspects – that is, the speaker introduces something of his or her own, something that has not been asked for. A question or a promise may therefore also have response properties, that is, if it links up with the current topic or is a relevant reaction to what has just been said. Con-

[4]See Coulthard and Montgomery (1981), Stubbs (1983), and others. Note that, in spite of some terminological affinities ("initiations," "responses"), there are important differences between our theoretical conception and that of the Birmingham school of discourse analysis. For example, we take initiatives and responses to be abstract features of conversational contributions, not utterances or constituents in an exchange structure.

versely, an answer may contain initiating properties if it goes beyond what could be taken as a minimal and adequate response to the preceding question.

The IR coding scheme allows the analyst to code turns in terms of eighteen different types, that is, different sorts of combinations of initiatives and responses. In order to show the coding system in operation, I give a few extracts from the courtroom data (see also the Appendix). The general idea is that each turn is composed of a response part and an initiative part (one of which, however, may be nil). The unmarked response link is symbolized by <, that is, an adequate response to the other's preceding turn. If a contribution also comprises initiating aspects (properties that exceed what could be considered a minimal response), it may be either strong or weak, that is, > and ʌ, respectively. In other words, somebody may either solicit a response (>), and then the other is put under the obligation to provide a topically relevant answer, or he or she may just invite or enable a contribution from the other on the current topic (ʌ). In the latter case, there is a greater degree of optionality; it is easier for the responder to choose to say nothing substantial on the topic.

Court trials are, of course, special in that situational constraints may force the defendant to take all professionals' turns as questions (except, of course, pure acknowledgments and metacommunicative utterances such as "No further questions"). Nonetheless, the empirical reality exhibits a great deal of variation. In the first extract, taken from a trial where the defendant was accused of having overdrawn his bank account, the defendant did nothing but provide minimal answers to the prosecutor's questions.

(Extract 1)

<>   P: And you knew that there was nothing on your account? How else did you make a living during this time?

<   D: Well, I got it through the social welfare.

<>   P: Was it food and accommodation?

<   D: Yes.

<>   P: Yes. And this was evidently . . . this went toward the purchase of liquor, this money, from the Systembolaget [name of the Swedish state company selling liquor].

<   D: Yes.

<>   P: Were you in a period when you did a good deal of drinking?

```
<      D:  Yes.
<>     P:  Yes. Did you treat your mates on this as well?
<      D:  Yes, I did that as well.
```
(Trial no. 28)

Conversely, a defendant may answer the professionals' questions and yet use his or her turns to volunteer some extra information that has not been requested.

(Extract 2)
(The defendant, who ran a small enterprise, was accused of not having delivered the appropriate information to taxation authorities. D argues that this was the duty of the accountant he had hired.)

```
>      P:  I want to ask you now, these VAT [value-added tax] ac-
            counts, you didn't do them yourself either?
<^     D:  No, these are done by Bertil Persson. I cannot do them, not
            those.
<>     P:  You cannot do them, no, but you get them at home. When
            he has done them, you get them to take home?
<^     D:  Yes. Bring home . . . well, I am never there when he does
            this VAT account.
<>     P:  Okay, okay. But you did account for them rather late, many
            times.
<^     D:  Yes, but it was because I didn't have money for them when
            they were due.
<>     P:  You haven't thought of delivering the account and then send-
            ing in the money?
<^     D:  Yes, I have thought about it, but it was a little embarassing
            now and then, so then I held on and sent it once I got the
            money.
```
(Trial no. 6)

In fact, giving expanded responses (coded <^) is the principal method for defendants, at least in our corpus, to occupy at least some of the discourse space in the hearings. In exceptional cases, a defendant may try to oppose the prosecutor's position. To illustrate such a discrepant case, the following extract (3) is given. Here the defendant, who is a young woman accused of petty theft, opposed the prosecutor's suggestions that she had changed addresses too many times lately and that she had earlier been convicted for possession of drugs. This caused her to ask the prosecutor questions and to make metacomments (coded:ʌ) (e.g., turns 2, 12, 22), which are rather strong initiatives, quite unique in our corpus.

(Extract 3)

(. . .)

<ʌ   1.P: Okay. One can see, of course, that you have moved around quite a bit here. You have stayed at different addresses now and then. . . , starts to think it over why you –

:ʌ   2.D: Why so? Yes, why? I think there is no reason to answer that.

–>   3.P: There isn't, no?

<   4.D: I don't think so.

<ʌ   5.P: Um, you have stayed at Trondheimsgatan, for example, and you have stayed at Sjövägen, and we had an address for you in Söderberga here too.

<>   6.D: That's not so many addresses, is it? Do you think so?

<ʌ   7.P: Well, I think that one wonders why you have moved that much.

<>   8.D: Is that a lot? Twice? Or that I stayed at two places. Is that a lot?

<ʌ   9.P: Well, there are three places, where I think you stayed here and, you know that, don't you, we have probably, I guess, tried to reach you on some occasion and we didn't find you either here. You see, I am asking for that reason, you are going to get some kind of punishment for this thing, and one wants to know if you are leading a stable life here in society or if you are floating around, you see –

–>   10.D: Floating around?

<   11.P: Yes.

:ʌ   12.D: If I had to give you an answer why I am doing that, then I think it's odd. That's my business, isn't it? I tell you that I am staying at Västergården and then that will be enough, won't it?

<ʌ   13.P: Well, maybe it will, yes. Because I saw that you had got a penalty for drugs here too.

<>   14.D: Oh, really? That's odd. When was that, then?

=>   15.P: You didn't get that?

–   16.D: Oh, no.

$$
\begin{array}{ccccccc}
\cdot\!\!\cdot> & & \cdot\!\!\cdot\wedge & \cdot\!\!\cdot< & & & \\
:> & & :\wedge & (> & & & \\
<\,=\,> & & <\!=\!\wedge & <) & & & \\
=> & & =\wedge & & -> & & \\
> & \wedge & <\,> & <\!\wedge & < & & - \\
\hline
6 & 5 & 4 & 3 & 2 & & 1 \\
\end{array}
$$

Turns independent   Turns totally dependent
and strongly proactive   and not at all proactive

Figure 2. Turn categories and interactional strength (From Linell et al. 1988: 419).

=>	17.P:	You never got any penalty for that?
<	18.D:	No, I didn't. That's not me.
<∧	19.P:	Maybe it was your pal who got the penalty for this, then, or perhaps it was that way.
<∧	20.D:	But good lord, I am not in the national crime register.
<	21.P:	No, I see.
:∧	22.D:	That, I think, was a bad joke.

(Trial no. 19)

If dialogues, or particular sequences, are coded exhaustively in terms of the IR system, we end up with category profiles that summarize some key aspects of the interaction formats [or "social participation structures," to use a term from Erickson and Shultz (1982: 22)] of the dialogues in question: By what interactive means do actors participate in the social encounter? How are initiatives and responses distributed between the parties? Who dominates? By what means, solicitation of responses (questions) or mutual invitations (many expanded responses on the part of both interlocutors), is the joint discourse brought forward? Is the discourse coherent (many linked, adequate responses) or fragmented (new topics are frequently introduced)? By assigning scores to the various turn types (these scores reflecting the degree of initiation strength or context-(in)dependence; see Fig. 2), we might adduce evidence for determining (a kind of) interactional dominance; the one who takes many initiatives may be said to be interactionally dominant, whereas the one who just provides responses is simply dragged along. If, then, we calculate the respective actors' median scores, it is possible to get overall measures of their participation in the dialogue in terms of initiatives and responses. Taking just Extracts (1–3), these median scores would be as follows for prosecutors (P) and defendants (D)[5]:

Extract no.	P	D	Difference
1	4.00	2.00	2.00
2	4.17	3.00	1.17
3	2.81	3.58	−0.77

We could then take the IR differences (the rightmost column of this table) as one measure of the interactional dominance in the respective dyads.[6] In a courtroom trial, where basically the legal professionals ask the questions and the defendants answer them, there will, of course, normally be a relatively great IR difference. (Extract 3, with its dominance for the defendant [sic!], if, of course, unique in this regard. It is also an exceptional episode in trial 19, whose overall IR difference is 1.51.) If we calculate IR differences for a corpus of dialogues such as the hearings in our trials, it is possible to compare them in terms of interaction format. The absolute measures are hardly important here, but what is interesting is that professionals interact in different ways with different categories of defendants. Adelswärd et al. (1987) showed that levels of interactional dominance (as measured in terms of mean IR differences), types of questions asked (declarative vs. coercive, interrogative questions), and a number of other features of the interaction are different with different types of defendants (Table 1).

As far as question types are concerned, it seems that declarative questions (i.e., questions with declarative syntax) are used as a more conversational way of eliciting information, whereas sequences of interrogative questions (sometimes on mutually unrelated topics) give the interaction an unmistakable ring of interrogation. When it comes to these kinds of accommodations at the level of discourse and interaction, the most clearly predictive factor is a social categorization of defendants into those who have committed more serious vs. less serious offenses (see earlier). In

[5] Of course, sequences as short as these cannot be used to compute reliable IR measures. In our analyses of the court trials, we used samples of 100 turns, starting from the beginning of the examination. The IR difference mean value for the whole corpus was 1.58 (see also Table 2). Intercoder reliability (measured on 10 percent of the data, randomly selected) was 0.81.

[6] Note that "interactional dominance" in terms of the initiatives and responses provided by the parties is just one of several dimensions having to do with dominance and asymmetries in dialogue; see Linell et al. (1988).

Table 1. *Accommodation at the interactional level*

	IR differences (mean values)	Percentage declarative questions
Defendant categories		
Serious-offense group	1.68	43.9
Minor-offense group	1.48	56.4
Mann-Whitney U Test: (See Adelswärd et al. 1988)	$p<.02$	$p<.001$

short, it appears that professionals use somewhat more interrogation-like modes of interaction with the first-mentioned group and more conversation-like modes with the latter group. In other words, if professionals know that defendants are more serious offenders, presumably they stereotypically categorize them as an outgroup that is quite distant from their own group. Therefore they tend to accentuate their own role, and their interrogative style then constitutes a rather clear case of underaccommodation in CAT terms (see N.Coupland et al. 1988). If, on the other hand, defendants are more like "ordinary people" (the minor-offense group), we find a more convergent (conversation-like) pattern.

It is extremely important to realize that, as in any other interaction, interactants—here, professionals and defendants—manage their dyads *jointly*. That is, if judges and lawyers stage the performances in slightly different ways, providing more or less of strict interrogation-like vs. conversation-like contributions, this process must in actuality be attuned to defendants' behaviors, that is, the effects of their ability or willingness to provide answers varying in quantity and quality (e.g., minimal vs. expanded responses). One may perhaps look on defendants' attitudes and strategies as based on the two, at least partly, orthogonal dimensions of activity and cooperativeness (or compliance) (Table 2). As a result, dyads should be treated as units (see Giles et al. 1987: 36), in which the dialogues, collectively accomplished, exhibit different formats. Basically, we can discern three or four types of social participation structures in trials and similar institutional encounters. (In reality, these types, of course, shade into each other with no sharp borderlines.):

Type A: Professionals use sequences of highly controlling questions (e.g., IR categories >, <>), and defendants provide mostly minimal responses (IR: >). (Extract 1 is an illustration of this interaction format.)

Table 2. *Courtroom interaction and defendants' strategies*

Strategy of compliance	Strategies of activity	
	Be active	Be passive
Be compliant (with norms and purposes of court trials)	Type B: volunteer information when opportunity is given (expanded responses: $<\wedge$)	Type A1: answer questions but do not get entangled in lengthy arguments (minimal but adequate responses: $<$)
Be confrontational (noncompliant)	Type C: challenge professionals' right to ask certain questions, raise issues, and state opinions not asked for (IR categories: $:>,:\wedge,<>,<\wedge$, etc.)	Type A2: answer questions in an absolutely minimal manner (sometimes leading to responses considered inadequate by professionals) or sometimes refuse to answer (IR: $-$)

Type B: Defendants expand (some of) their responses, volunteering extra information and providing viewpoints of their own, which is associated with, and probably brings about, more conversation-like comments and follow-up questions from judges and lawyers too (IR: $<\wedge$). (Extract 2 is a short example.) Sometimes this active participation on the part of the defendant may induce professionals to abandon their questioning approach (temporarily) and indulge in a more symmetrical discussion with the defendant.

If trials are assumed to provide opportunities for competition and opposition, one would also expect an interaction format (or social participation structure) involving more combative conduct:

Type C: Defendants oppose or challenge professionals' questions (or their presuppositions) (IR: $:>$), asking counterquestions ($<>$), which sooner or later will bring about stronger countermoves from professionals. (Extract 3 illustrates this type.)

As indicated earlier, type A occurs significantly more often in serious-offense trials, and type B is more typical of minor-offense trials. It may be argued that in both of these examination formats, conduct is more or less compliant with the rules and roles of the criminal trial. Yet, in terms of initiatives and responses, type A leads to polarization (asymmetry, large IR differences) and type B to (somewhat) more symmetry and mutual attuning (more matched, convergent moves of the $<\wedge$ type (expanded responses), especially on the part of defendants but also, although to a much lesser extent, professionals, and hence less pronounced IR differences between parties). Defendants' attitudes, as expressed in the posttrial interviews and possibly also actually entertained during trials, tend to be either cooperative or noncooperative in type A and cooperative in type B. In other words, defendants who are inclined to be noncooperative may (consciously or nonconsciously) exploit their right to answer questions in a minimal way or even to remain silent. Hence, there is a strategy of passive resistance (to be subsumed under type A; see Table 2), which may force professionals to repeat questions (IR: $=>$) (answers are treated as less than adequate, IR: $-$) or to use more closed question types. In our relatively cooperatively oriented corpus, this type (A2) is, however, unusual, occurring only in some passages or episodes (on isolated topics) in few trials.

The combative type (C) certainly exists as a possibility, but it is rarely found in our corpus of petty-offenses trials. [Trial 19 (see Extract 3) is the only fairly clear case; however, as indicated there, this particular defendant used both passive resistance (type A2) and active, combative moves.] Psychologically, this type (C) of speech competition (in the terms of Thakerar et al. 1982) indicates divergence, dissociation, and confrontation, although on the overt level of interaction, both parties tend to use similar strong moves when they pursue their own lines of argumentation, challenge each other, ignore each other's contributions, and so on. In the terms of N. Coupland et al. (1988), it would be a case of under accommodation or even contraaccommodation.

3.5. On the relation between levels of accommodation

I have pointed to patterns of accommodation at two levels: the lexical-grammatical level (particularly as regards information density) and the interactional level (patterns of initiatives and responses). Participants engage in both types of accommodation at the same time, and the question arises of whether we are faced with two mutually more or less independent dimensions of accommodation. Recall that professionals' adjustments of information density were correlated with strong and weak styles of defendants' speech (and not, one should add, with serious- vs. minor-offense categories), whereas the reverse is true of IR patterns. It does not seem possible to predict information density accommodation from interaction format. A more detailed and definitive analysis of the individual dyads cannot be performed (that would necessitate a larger corpus of preferably longer trials), but the data may be used to generate some suggestions (to be further explored using a richer data base).

Our data reveal that judges and lawyers approximate their level of information density in their examination talk to that of their interlocutors, whether *their* level is strong or weak style (as defined earlier). However, this does not mean that professionals accommodate to the same degree in all trials. We do not know the baseline – what would constitute an unmarked level of information density for legal professionals in a courtroom dialogue. But assuming that the defendant's level can be taken as a target value, we may talk about over- and underaccommodation as, in general terms, the relative inaccuracy of accommodations, when prosecutors overshoot or undershoot, respectively, the target by a certain degree. If we define this as three units (in information density, i.e., a difference of three content word types per 100 running words), we get five cases of underaccommodation and three cases of overaccommodation out of seventeen dyads for which data exist.[7] Note that my definitions of over- and underaccommodation are based on objective measures, thus being different from the related concepts of N.Coupland et al. (1988), who base their definitions on the subjective evaluations made by recipients; for them, over accommodation would mean that a recipient perceives a speaker to transcend the sociolinguistic behavior judged necessary for situationally adequate, attuned talk (1988: 32). We do not have access to defendants' evaluations on this point, but it seems plausible to assume that a sizable amount of over- or underaccommodation may be attributed to psychological divergence. The value chosen (three units) is, of course, arbitrary but seems reasonable, given that the difference between strong and weak styles among defendants was about four units, which was evidently sufficient to bring about a consistent difference also in prosecutors' speech (on the aggregated level, not necessarily in every case).

There seems to be no general correlation between IR difference and

---

[7]Three trials out of the twenty under analysis (see earlier) drop out, because the amount of talk by defendants was too small to allow for calculation of information density. (By definition, all these belong to the "weak" group. See Jönsson, 1988).

Table 3. *IR difference and inaccuracy of information density accommodation*

Trial no.	Information density		Over/under- accommodation	IR difference
	Professionals	Defendants		
4 S	26.0	21.5	−4.5	0.85
9 S	26.0	21.0	−5.0	1.54
11 S	21.5	26.0	4.5	2.08
30 S	25.0	20.5	−4.5	1.71
32 S	21.5	25.0	3.5	1.81
7 W	15.5	20.0	4.5	1.25
8 W	21.5	16.0	−5.5	1.35
12 W	20.5	15.5	5.0	1.59

Inaccuracy of accommodation defined as professionals' over- or undershoot of defendants' information density level by three or more units.
S = strong style; W = weak style.

inaccuracy of information density accommodation.[8] As regards the distinction between under- and overaccommodation, one might conjecture that underaccommodation may be assoicated with a large IR difference (i.e., with professionals sticking to a more strict interrogation-like strategy). This does not seem to be the case. Rather, there is a slight but nonsignificant (Mann Whitney $U = 4$, n.s.) tendency toward the reverse (Table 3); information density underaccommodation tends to go with a low IR difference and information density overaccommodation with a high IR difference.

In other words, if defendants take many initiatives (expansions of responses), professionals sometimes fail to accommodate in information density, whereas in the opposite case, when defendants take few initiatives and respond minimally, professionals sometimes overaccommodate informationally. It seems that, in the former case, they may (unconsciously?) perceive defendants as competent enough to cope with more complex language, whereas in the latter case, they react to defendants' passivity by diluting their speech beyond the interlocutors' level. However, once again, the basis for this conjecture is modest indeed. Only more extensive empirical investigations can potentially establish it as a robust finding.

[8] Nor is there any correlaation between inaccuracy of accommodation and strong vs. weak style. Five cases concerned strong-style defendants ($N = 10$) and three cases weak-style defendants ($N = 7$).

3.6. Discussion

Before I proceed to some conclusions, it may be appropriate to voice a possible objection to applying CAT at the interactional level of the initiative–response interplay. On the one hand, this interplay can be regarded as the basis and origin of all accommodative processes; if actors enter a conversation, this amounts to their agreement to play a game together, that is, to coordinate their behaviors (at least at a minimal level) and hence to accommodate mutually to each other's moves. As Heritage (1987: 245) points out with reference to Garfinkel (1963), "accommodative work" is always done at the interactional level. It is inconceivable for one party to remain uninfluenced by the other party's moves (unless he or she completely refuses to communicate). The individual actors' communicative acts (their initiatives and responses in conversation) cannot be understood without the local (and global) contexts in which they are embedded. For example, the notion of answer (or response, reply, etc.) conceptually presupposes accommodation to a local context; an utterance is understood (or intended or taken up) as an answer, or a particular type of answer, only with respect to a preceding initiative (e.g., a question). An initiatory utterance, such as a question or a warning, is more independent in the sense that it projects successive turn(s) more strongly than pure responses, but work on dialogue and discourse, such as activity types (Levinson 1979) or sequential dependence (as in conversation analysis, e.g., Atkinson and Heritage 1984), shows how the speech act status of such initiatives as questions and warnings is negotiated and settled through interaction. The "double contextuality" of conversational contributions (i.e., that utterances are both dependent on and contribute to creating the local context) is built into the basic units of IR analysis. In a sense, dialogue is by definition accommodative in character, and interpersonal accommodation is incorporated into the relevant coding categories themselves. It would then—so the objection goes—simply beg the question to ask whether it is a contingent fact that accommodation is going on there.

Yet, such an argument seems to involve a mixing of levels. It is true that every interaction involves accommodations and adjustments by participants. In a sense, it is impossible not to accommodate. Even the absence of behavioral adjustments, for example, so-called speech maintenance (Bourhis, 1984), is open to interpretation as a special type of orientation or attitude (on the part of the speaker to his or her addressee and/or the purpose of the communicative activity); hence, it too is a kind of "approximation strategy" (in the terminology of N. Coupland et al. 1988). It is also true that accommodation conceptually implies adjustment *to someone and something*, that is, to some perceived communicative attribute of a particular interlocutor (or category of interlocutors) and a specific situation; the conduct of the individual actor can only be understood as part of the dialogical interplay with others (or, if you will, in terms of social psychology rather than individual psychology). However, these insights will, of course, not make CAT empty; there are still many types and degrees of accommodation to discover and explain in empirical research. This also holds for how the management of topics and turns is shared among participants in interaction (how initiative and responses are distributed between the parties). This level of analysis will perhaps more easily make observers see the dialogical essence of discourse and the ubiquity of accommodative processes, but different types of interaction formats are open to empirical investigation just as much as communicative accommodations at "lower" linguistic levels.

Accommodation is present whenever and wherever people interact. Yet, accommodative processes are bound to take very different shapes and directions in different contexts. In a relatively unconstrained and informal conversation between friends, we might expect rather different types than in a highly asymmetrical and strongly routinized and ritualized encounter such as the criminal court trial, where interactants act out of very divergent roles (speech complementarity) and where there are strong situational norms regulating the interaction. Yet, we have seen that there is still room for several types of interpersonal accommodation.

Our courtroom data have confirmed that accommodation in verbal interaction is a multilayered and multimodal phenomenon (see N. Coupland et al. 1988; Giles et al. 1987). Furthermore, simultaneous accommodation processes need not be part of a uniform global process but may encode different, perhaps even contradictory, accommodative orientations. In our data, there are indications that accommodation in information density is largely unconscious and that defendants' differences in style (strong vs. weak) have to do with individual abilities. Accommodation on the initiative–response level might be more dependent on the choice of strategy (whether deliberate or automatic); to the extent that parties select strategies, professionals seem to choose their interactive mode on the basis of their (stereotypical?) perception of the defendant (serious and minor offenders must be treated differently), and defendants entertain different attitudes to the trial as such (cooperative vs. uncooperative) (which does not exclude the possibility that there be differences in their *abilities* to be compliant or cooperative in this situation which is alien to many of them; see Adelswärd et al. 1988).

The criminal court trial involves several monological phases in which professionals speak under rather strong situational norms and using a language that, from the point of view of defendants and witnesses, may seem detached and underaccommodative. Yet, this speech divergence is probably a "means to put order and meaning into the interaction" (Giles et al. 1986: 32) rather than a deliberate attempt to express a dissociative attitude. Even so, a sizable proportion of the defendants sometimes perceive it as off-putting (Adelswärd et al. 1988). Moreover, the court trial is a context where at least newcomers tend to expect negative comments, such as reproaches and blamings. This implies that attempts on the part of judges and lawyers to be strictly impartial or even sometimes encouraging may instead be interpreted as condescending (Adelswärd 1989); if so, we seem to be faced with a case of convergent behavior perceived as inappropriately attuned to the situation (see Giles et al. 1986: 17, 20). Court trials for routine, petty offenses are, at least in our Swedish data and to a limited extent, invaded by more informal, conversation-like features. This process is truly accommodative in character and is probably, for the most part, efficient and beneficial. Yet, when interpreted against background assumptions and expectations of formality and social distance, some symptoms of intended friendliness and empathy may be taken to overaccommodate. Similar effects have been documented in other encounters involving actors who—mutually or unilaterally—perceive the other as socially distant, for example, in communication across generations, as discussed by N.Coupland et al. (1988). Accommodations and attributions are thus embedded in quite complex social psychological realities.

Appendix: The IR category system (simplified)

Each turn type represents a particular combination of initiative and response features. For each category, its interactional weight in terms of a 6-point scoring system is given in parentheses after the category symbol. Here, only eleven out of a total of eighteen categories are described. (For more complete definitions, see Linell et al. 1988.)

a. <> (4): turn with clear properties of both response and initiative, the retroactive part (response aspect) being linked to the main content of the interlocutor's preceding (adjacent) turn and the proactive part (initiating aspect) involving a strong initiative.

b. <∧ (3): same as (a) except that the proactive part is a weak initiative. By "strong initiative" we mean that the speaker explicitly solicits or demands a response from the interlocutor. By "weak initiative" we mean that the speaker asserts something or submits a proposal for comment without explicitly soliciting or demanding (but often inviting) a response from the interlocutor. Where appropriate, we will present categories in pairs of strong and weak initiatives (symbols ending in > and ∧, respectively).

c. > (6) and d. ∧ (5): turn involving an initiative (strong and weak, respectively) on a new and independent topic ("free initiative" with no retroactive part).

e. < (2): turn linked to the interlocutor's adjacent turn and involving no initiating properties *(minimal response)*. The turn is *treated by the interlocutor as satisfying* the demands of (being conditionally relevant to) his or her own preceding initiative *(adequate response)*.

The symbol < appears in other category labels as well. It stands for the unmarked type of response link (local, focal, adequate other-linking).

f. => (4) and g. =∧ (3): turn *linked to the speaker's own preceding turn* (rather than to the interlocutor's turn). The turn is either merely a repetition or simple reformulation of the speaker's preceding initiative or (in case the interlocutor has only given or tried to give a minimal response) a continuation of this preceding turn. (f) or (g) typically occurs when the interlocutor's interjacent utterance is not accepted as an adequate response.

h. :> (5) and i :∧ (4): turn with clear properties of both response and initiative, the retroactive part being nonfocally linked to the interlocutor's preceding turn. A *nonfocal* link usually involves remarking on or challenging the form and/or function of the interlocutor's preceding turn (compare metacommunicative conversational contributions).

j. − (1): turn linked to, or at least possibly linked to, the interlocutor's adjacent turn and involving no initiating properties. The turn is treated by the interlocutor as *not* satisfying the demands of, or as not even conditionally relevant to, his or her own preceding initiative. (j) is a (minimal and) *inadequate response.*

k. −> (2): turn involving a *deferring question* asking for repetition, confirmation, or simple clarification of something contained in the interlocutor's preceding turn.

References

Adelswärd, V. 1989. Defendants' interpretations of encouragements in court. *Journal of Pragmatics*, 13: 741–9.

Adelswärd, V., Aronsson, K., Jönsson, L., and Linell, P. 1987. The unequal distribution of interactional space: Dominance and control in courtroom interaction. *Text*, 7: 313–46.

Adelswärd, V., Aronsson, K., and Linell, P. 1988. Discourse of blame: Courtroom construction of social identity from the perspective of the defendant. *Semiotica*, 71: 261–84.

Andenaes, J. 1968. The legal framework. In N.Christie (ed.), *Scandinavian Studies in Criminology*, Vol. II, pp. 9–17. Oslo and London: Universitetsförlaget and Tavistock.

Aronsson, K. 1991. Social interaction and the recycling of legal evidence. In N. Coupland, H. Giles and J. Wiemann (eds), *"Miscommunication" and Problematic Talk*, pp. 215–43. Newbury Park, CA: Sage.

Aronsson, K., Jönsson, L., and Linell, P. 1987. The courtroom hearing as a middle ground: Speech accommodation by lawyers and defendants. *Journal of Language and Social Psychology*, 6: 99–115.

Atkinson, M., and Drew, P. 1979. *Order in Court: The Organisation of Verbal Interaction in Judicial Settings*. London: Macmillan.

Atkinson, M., and Heritage, J. (eds). 1984. *Structures of Social Action: Studies in Conversation Analysis*. Cambridge: Cambridge University Press.

Bell, A. 1984. Language style as audience design. *Language in Society*, 13: 145–204.

Bourhis, R. 1984. Cross-cultural communication in Montreal: Two field studies since Bill 101. *International Journal of Social Psychology*, 46: 33–47.

Coulthard, M., and Montgomery, M. (eds.). 1981. *Studies in Discourse Analysis*. London: Routledge & Kegan Paul.

Coupland, N. 1984. Accommodation at work: Some phonological data and their implications. *International Journal of the Sociology of Language*, 46: 49–70.

Coupland, N., Coupland, J., Giles, H., and Henwood, K. 1988. Accommodating the elderly: Invoking and extending a theory. *Language in Society*, 17: 1–41.

Coupland, J., Coupland, N., Giles, H., and Wiemann, J. 1988. My life in your hands: Processes of self-disclosure in intergenerational talk. *In* N. Coupland (ed.), *Styles of Discourse*, pp. 201–53. London: Croom Helm.

Coupland, N., and Giles, H. (eds). 1988. Communication accommodation: Recent developments. Special issue of *Language and Communication*, 8, no. 3/4.

Danet, B. 1980. Language in the legal process. *Law and Society Review*, 14: 445–564.

Danet, B., and Bogoch, B. 1980. Context for coercion: Analyzing properties of courtroom "questions." *British Journal of Law and Society*, 7: 61–77.

Erickson, F., and Shultz, J. 1982. *The Counselor as Gatekeeper: Social Interaction in Interviews*. New York: Academic Press.

Garfinkel, H. 1963. A conception of, and experiments with, "trust" as a condition of stable concerted actions. *In* O. J. Harvey (ed.), *Motivation and Social Interaction*, pp. 187–238. New York: Ronald Press.

Giles, H., Mulac, A., Bradac, J. J., and Johnson, P. 1987. Speech accommodation theory: The last decade and beyond. *In* M. L. McLaughlin (ed.), *Communication Yearbook*, vol. 10, pp. 13–48. Beverly Hills, CA: Sage.

Giles, H., and Powesland, P. F. 1975. *Speech Style and Social Evaluation*. London: Academic Press.

Harris, S. 1984. Questions as a mode of control in magistrates' courts. *International Journal of the Sociology of Language*, 49: 5–27.

Heritage, J. 1987. Ethnomethodology. *In* A. Giddens and J. Turner (eds), *Social Theory Today*, pp. 222–70. Cambridge: Polity Press.

Jönsson, L. 1988. *On Being Heard in Court Trials and Police Interrogations*. (Linköping Studies in Arts and Science, 25). University of Linköping, Linköping.

Lakoff, R. 1975. *Language and Woman's Place*. New York: Harper & Row.

Lane, C. 1985. Mis-communication in cross-examinations. *In* J. B. Pride (ed.), *Cross-Cultural Encounters: Communication and Mis-communication*, pp. 196–211. Melbourne: River Seine Productions.

Levi, J. 1982. *Linguistics, Language, and Law: A Topical Bibliography*. Bloomington: Indiana University Linguistics Club.

Levi, J. 1985. Language and the law in the U.S.A. Paper delivered at the Conference on Language in the Judicial Process, Georgetown University, Washington, DC, July 1985.

Levin, H., and Lin, T. 1988. An accommodating witness. *In* N.Coupland and H. Giles (1988), pp. 195–7.
Levinson, S. 1979. Activity types and language. *Linguistics*, 17: 365–99.
Linell, P., Gustavsson, L., and Juvonen, P. 1988. Interactional dominance in dyadic communication: A presentation of initiative-response analysis. *Linguistics*, 26: 415–42.
McGaughey, K., and Stiles, W. 1983. Courtroom interrogation of rape victims: Verbal response mode use by attorneys and witnesses during direct examination vs. cross-examination. *Journal of Applied Social Psychology*, 13: 78–87.
O'Barr, W. 1982. *Linguistic Evidence: Language, Power and Strategy in the Courtroom*. New York: Academic Press.
Philips, S. U. 1984. The social organization of questions and answers in courtroom discourse: A study of changes of plea in an Arizona court. *Text*, 4: 225–248.
Philips, S. U. 1985. Strategies of clarification in judges' use of language: From the written to the spoken. *Discourse Processes*, 8: 421–36.
Philips, S. U. 1987. On the use of Wh questions in American courtroom discourse: A study of the relation between language form and language function. *In* L. Kedar (ed.), *Power through Discourse*, pp. 83–111. Norwood, NJ: Ablex.
Stubbs, M. 1983. *Discourse Analysis*. Oxford, Basil Blackwell.
Thakerar, J., Giles, H., and Cheshire, J. 1982. Psychological and linguistic parameters of speech accommodation. *In* C. Fraser and K. Scherer (eds), *Advances in the Social Psychology of Language*, pp. 205–255. Cambridge: Cambridge University Press.
Wodak, R. 1980. Discourse analysis and courtroom interaction. *Discourse Processes*, 3: 369–80.
Wodak-Engel, R. 1984. Determination of guilt: Discourse in the courtroom. *In* C. Kramarae, M. Schultz, and W. O'Barr (eds), *Language and Power*, pp. 89–100. Beverly Hills, CA: Sage.
Woodbury, H. 1984. The strategic use of questions in court. *Semiotica*, 48: 197–228.

4. Accommodation in medical consultations

RICHARD L. STREET, JR.

4.1. Introduction

During the past several decades, the role of interpersonal communication in health care contexts has been of great interest to medical practitioners and scholars. The communicative exchange between doctor and patient is fundamental to health care delivery for two reasons. First, although sophisticated technologies exist for diagnosis and treatment, talk between provider and patient still represents the primary means by which information is exchanged and understanding is achieved (Shuy 1976; Wasserman and Inui 1983). Second, the affective component of the doctor–patient relationship (e.g., the doctor's display of concern and interest in the patient, and the patient's involvement in the interaction) emerges communicatively through the manner in which doctors and patients coordinate their verbal and nonverbal responses (DiMatteo 1979). Research has demonstrated that informational and affective dimensions of doctor–patient interaction influence an array of health care outcomes including patients' satisfaction, understanding, compliance with prescribed regimens, and utilization of health care services (Ben-Sira 1980; Pendleton 1983).

In spite of its importance, the *process* of communicating in medical consultations remains largely unexplicated. The purpose of this chapter is to (1) critique extant theory and research on doctor–patient communication, (2) present a perspective, communication accommodation theory, for examining doctor–patient interaction, (3) discuss communicative processes and outcomes associated with doctor–patient encounters, and (4) suggest avenues for future research.

4.2. A critique of theory and research on doctor–patient communication

Although making significant contributions to understanding the communicative dynamics of medical interactions, previous research on doctor–patient interaction suffers from several limitations. The following critique is not intended to attenuate the value of previous work; rather, it is hoped that this analysis will provide insight and serve as a useful heuristic for future scholarship in this area.

Dyadic communication is, of course, a cooperative enterprise as participants coordinate their verbal and nonverbal acts in order to accomplish mutual and personal goals. It is a dynamic process as interactants continuously select and modify communicative behaviors in relation to the behavioral choices of interlocutors and to their own communicative objectives (Street and Cappella 1985). One limitation of previous research is the tendency to focus on the *doctor's* communicative acts without considering how the *patient* is communicating (Pendelton 1983). Research in other contexts, such as interviews and social conversation, frequently has demonstrated that an interactant's satisfaction with partners and with the interaction is less the result of what interlocutors do or say per se and more a function of these responses *relative to the interactant's own communicative responses* (for reviews, see Giles et al. 1987; Street, Mulac, and Wiemann 1988). For example, a doctor who holds the floor for periods averaging thirty seconds and who maintains a high level of gaze toward the patient may appear responsive and affiliative to a patient exhibiting similar behaviors but may be perceived as domineering and intimidating by a patient who talks for brief periods and who avoids eye contact.

As Anderson, DeVellis, and DeVellis (1987) have argued, the patient's postconsultation response (e.g., satisfaction or compliance) may depend in large part on how he or she chooses or is able to communicate. For example, were patients able to ask questions? Were they able to give opinions on treatment procedures? Did they feel comfortable looking at the doctor and interrupting if necessary? The fact that previous research had tended to ignore the patient's communicative behavior may account for its failure to discover robust relationships between patients' satisfaction or compliance and specific communicative responses by doctors (Comstock et al. 1982; Roter, Hall, and Katz 1987; Street and Buller 1987).

A second limitation of extant research is that, although some investigators have examined patients' *perceptions* of doctors' communicative behaviors and others have focused on doctors' *actual* behaviors (e.g., body orientation, vocalics, question-asking behavior, informativeness), few have studied patients' perceptual judgments of specific communicative acts by doctors (DiMatteo 1979). For example, patients' satisfaction (and, to some extent, compliance) with medical care is strongly correlated with the extent to which patients *perceive* the doctor's style as caring, concerned, affiliative, responsive, and supportive (Ben-Sira 1980; Buller and Buller 1987; Street and Wiemann 1987). Conversely, doctors perceived to be domineering generally receive negative evaluations from patients (Buller and Buller 1987; Hall, Roter and Rand 1981; Street and Wiemann 1987).

However, there is less conclusive evidence regarding relationships between doctors' actual communicative responses and patients' satisfaction, understanding, and compliance. For example, some investigators have reported that patients' satisfaction is enhanced by the doctor's use of forward leans and direct body orientation when interacting with the patient (Harrigan, Oxman, and Rosenthal 1985; Larsen and Smith 1981); others have not supported these relationships (Comstock et al. 1982; Street and Buller 1987). The extent to which the doctor is authoritative (e.g., giving orders, opinions, and directives) has at times been positively related (Davis 1971; Lane 1983) and has at times been negatively related (Carter et al. 1982; Heszen-Klemens and Lapinska 1984) to patients' compliance with prescribed regimens. In sum, although there is strong support for the claim that patients respond favorably to affiliative and nondominating doctors, there is little empirical consistency regarding what behaviors are *indicative of* doctors' affiliation and communicative dominance.

Finally, until very recently, much of the research on doctor–patient communication was conducted atheoretically (Pendleton 1983). The absence of a comprehensive conceptual framework guiding these investigations has hindered researchers' efforts to remedy the problems stated earlier. On the one hand, there are a host of doctor–patient interaction studies that have examined doctors' verbal behaviors (e.g., Davis 1971; Korsch and Negrete 1972) and, in some cases, the responses of doctors and patients (e.g., Heszen-Klemens and Lapinska 1984; Stiles et al. 1984). The specific coding systems used in these studies—such as Bales's (1950) interaction process analysis, Stiles's (1978) verbal response modes, and the medical communication behavior system (Wolraich et al. 1986)—are frameworks for classifying communicative acts but are not theoretical perspectives for *explicating* doctor–patient interaction. On the other hand, theories that are pertinent to doctor–patient interaction often downplay the role of the communication *process*. That is, they fail to examine contingencies between doctors' and patients' communicative responses (e.g., Becker and Maiman 1975; Ben-Sira 1980; Pendelton 1983).

Admittedly, some recent research has been grounded in theory and has contributed significantly to our understanding of the communicative dynamics of medical consultations. For example, discourse analysts have applied critical theory to verbal exchanges between doctors and patients. These scholars describe how the interface between the participants' utterances functions to maintain the doctor's authority and control over the patient (Fisher 1984; West 1984), regulate information exchange and understanding (Waitzkin 1985), and negotiate the social and communicative roles of the interactants (Byrne and Long 1976; Stiles et al. 1984). While providing insight into doctor–patient interaction, these works are insufficient for *generalizing* relationships between communicative processes (e.g., factors mediating the structure of doctor–patient verbal-nonverbal behavior exchanges) *and* medical care outcomes (e.g., patients' satisfaction, compliance, understanding, and utilization of health care services). For explicating these issues, a communication theory framework should be useful.

4.3. Communication accommodation theory

Communication accommodation theory (CAT) (Giles, Coupland, and Coupland this volume; Giles et at. 1987) has two primary postulates: (1) interactants have motivations for adapting their communication relative to their perceptions of the communicative styles of interlocutors and (2) interactants form impressions and evaluations of partners with respect to their expectations for a partner's communicative style relative to their own style. For example, interactants seeking to win approval, affiliate, establish rapport, communicate effectively, identify socially with partners typically adjust their communicative style toward (i.e., *converge* to) the communicative style of their partners. In these circumstances, convergence usually promotes smooth communicative exchanges and is positively received by partners, presuming that there are no relational or situational norms precluding convergence (Giles et al. 1987; Natale 1975; Street and Giles 1982).

However, some interactions are characterized by role, power, or other social differences between interactants (e.g., doctors and patients, parents and children, interviewers and interviewees). In these situations, conversants may opt to maintain an exchange of communicative dissimilarity (or *complementarity*) that both reflects and reinforces their social differences (Giles 1977). For example, an interactant having greater status may speak for longer periods, initiate most of the conversational topics, speak more slowly, and maintain a more relaxed posture than does the less powerful interlocutor (Street 1986). If both interactants expect and prefer the pattern of communicative differences, complementarity will be postively received, will promote favorable impressions of partners, and will foster a smooth interactive exchange. On the other hand, a communicator may evaluate complementarity unfavorably if he or she wishes that the interaction was characterized by some other pattern of accommodation, such as convergence (Coupland et al. 1988). However, these interactants nonetheless may *maintain* expected communicative differences related to their role or status relationship with a partner because they perceive themselves as powerless to effect a change in the nature of the interaction (e.g., interviewee, sales clerk, patient).

At this point, I should distinguish between accommodation patterns of complementarity and those of *divergence*. Complementarity occurs when interactants *mutually* attempt to maintain their social differences communicatively. For example, an interviewee concerned about impression management may speak quickly, with gestural animation and with high levels of gaze at the interviewer, and will rarely interrupt his or her partner. The more powerful interviewer may speak more slowly, with less gestural animation, and occasionally may interrupt the interviewee or redirect the interview topic. When both partners adhere to these differences, the interaction is typically *stable*, and this exchange may be maintained throughout the interaction (Patterson 1983). Divergence, on the other hand, occurs when an interactant adapts behavior *opposite* to that of a partner. Interactants may diverge in order to (1) distance themselves socially from a partner, (2) render a partner less powerful, or (3) entice an interlocutor to adopt a different communicative style (Giles et al. 1987). For example, on encountering an interlocutor who is smiling, animated, talking quickly and loudly, and maintaining high levels of eye contact, a communicator may exhibit a divergent response (e.g., speak slowly and softly, with neutral facial affect, and be nonexpressive nonverbally) if he or she wants to dissociate from or show disapproval of the partner, to control the interaction by changing the nature of the communicative code (i.e., style-shifting; Scotton 1985), or to encourage the partner to adopt a more serious, reserved style. As such, communicative divergence creates an unstable exchange that may lead to termination of the interaction, unfavorable impressions, and/or changes in the partner's behavior (Giles et al. 1987; Patterson 1983).

In sum, accommodative adjustments are a product of interactants' motivations, perceptions of their own and partners' communicative styles, and situational-relational exigencies. These adaptations, in turn, influence interactants' impressions of partners and the interaction. Given that they may have *multiple* goals during an interaction (e.g., be friendly yet maintain status or authority), conversants may *variously* accommodate different behaviors. For example, interactants may display convergence among body positions, speech rate, and facial expressions yet maintain complementarity among talk durations, frequency of interruptions, topic initiation, and touch (Giles and Smith 1979; Street 1986). That interactants may simultaneously produce various accommodative responses is an important conception when examining doctor–patient interaction.

4.4. Accommodation in doctor–patient interactions

In their conceptions of the ideal doctor–patient encounter, doctors and patients agree that both parties should have mutual goals for the medical visit (i.e., information sharing and helping the patient) and should communicate with one another in an egalitarian fashion, and the patient should be active in the decision-making process (Weiss 1986). Doctors and patients also agree that their relationship is largely a complementary one in that each differs from the other in terms of their knowledge of medicine and their communicative roles in the interaction (expert provider-educator vs. client-learner) (Boreham and Gibson 1978; Stiles et al. 1984). Because of these expectations, two very different forms of accommodation should emerge in medical consultations, with each accomplishing a different communicative function. On the one hand, *complementarity* should be evident among behaviors regulating communicative control and role responsibilities. On the other hand, *convergence* should be exhibited among responses constituting affiliation and communicative involvement. Both communicative patterns may emerge simultaneously because they are largely accomplished through different verbal and nonverbal behaviors (Street 1986).

Complementarity. In most outpatient visits, the doctor is the medical expert and the patient has voluntarily solicited the doctor's help. Thus, the doctor will presume to exercise (and the patient will allow) considerable influence regarding the content and structure of the interaction (Freeling 1983). Hence, although doctors may be more or less dominant with certain kinds of patients (to be discussed later), in most medical consultations doctors and patients will create complementary patterns of communicative exchange reflecting relatively greater dominance and control by the doctor and relatively less by the patient (Boreham and Gibson 1978). In support of this contention, previous research has consistenly demonstrated that doctors verbally control interactions with patients by producing more questions, directives, interruptions, and topic initiations and by talking for a greater proportion of the time (Arntson and Philipsborn 1982; Coulthard and Ashby 1975; Fisher 1984; Shapiro, Najman, and Chang 1983; West 1984). Also, among nonverbal markers of status and dominance, doctors generally hold the floor for longer durations, are allowed more silence within floor holdings, and display more relaxed postures and more nonreciprocated touch than do patients (Smith and Larsen 1984; Street and Buller 1987; 1988; West 1984).

Because of differences in their communicative roles, doctors and patients also tend to complement one another in terms of the functions of their respective utterances. For example, when directing the consultation, the doctor's questions, explanations, and instructions are generally coupled with the patient's answers, acknowledgments, and agreements, respectively; when encouraging the patient to talk, doctors usually provide confirmations and acknowledgments in response to patients' explanations and descriptions of the medical condition (Stiles et al. 1984).

Convergence. If both parties recognize the importance of communicating effectively, exchanging information accurately, and fostering rapport, then many doctor–patient interactions may reveal convergence among behaviors representing affiliation and involvement in the interaction. The *degree* of expressed involvement (e.g., constancy of gaze, frequency of gestures, directness of body orientation toward a partner, and facial expressiveness; Cappella 1983) may vary from interaction to interaction and is contingent on such factors as personal predilections, nature of the task, and relational history between the participants (Giles and Street 1985; Patterson 1983). However, *mutually acceptable expressions of communicative involvement* typically are characterized by *convergent* response patterns as interactants coordinate and match their behaviors around personal, partner, and situational constraints (Cappella 1983; Patterson 1983).

For example, in medical consultations in which the patient is highly anxious about the medical condition, both doctor and patient may display high levels of involvement through directness of body orientation, forward body leans, gaze toward partners, reciprocal topic development, and facial expressiveness. In a routine medical exam with no complications and little need for personal involvement between the interactants, there may be lower levels of affiliative intensity such as less social touching, more gazes away from partners, more indirect body orientations, less facial expressiveness, less intimate talk, more task activity (e.g., physically examining the patient), and more abrupt topic changes (Street and Buller 1988; Street and Wiemann 1987). Nevertheless, in both situations the participants may achieve a mutually acceptable degree of communicative involvement that is indexed by relative similarity among expressive behaviors. Two studies of family practitioner–patient interactions indeed reported that doctors and patients tended to converge nonverbal behaviors related to affiliation and involvement, including forward leans, body orientation, gaze, gestures, and response latencies (Smith and Larsen 1984; Street and Buller 1987).

Another objective highly valued by the doctor and the patient is the efficient, accurate exchange of information. For the doctor, information gathering is crucial for diagnosis and remediation; for the patient, informing and receiving information from the doctor foster understanding, reduce the experience of uncertainty, and help alleviate concerns (Roter et al. 1987; Waitzkin 1985). Thus, reciprocal development of the topic of interaction should characterize most medical consultations. In other words, although the doctor initiates most of the topics in the interaction (Fisher 1984), a particular topic raised by the doctor *or* the patient is typically addressed in the other's subsequent utterance and is mutually developed thereafter. In direct support of this contention, Arntson and Philipsborn (1982) observed a strong reciprocal relationship among socio-emotional comments exchanged between pediatricians and parents. In these interactions, when one participant produced more utterances related to expressing concern, encouraging the other to talk, and signaling understanding, the other participant tended to produce more of the same types of utterances. Also, several studies have indicated that, although doctors may not automically volunteer information, they readily do so in response to the patient's questions and concerns (Boreham and Gibson 1978; Greenfield, Kaplan, and Ware 1985).

In sum, two patterns of accommodation simultaneously emerge during doctor–patient interactions: convergence among behaviors indicative of communicative involvement (i.e., verbal responsiveness, agreements, gaze, body position, gestures, response latencies) and complementarity among behaviors related to control, dominance, and communicative role (i.e., topic initiation, criticism, directives, unilateral touch, extended floor holding durations, interruptions, and pauses within speaking turns). Within specific interactions, however, accommodative response may vary given that doctors appear to exercise greater control and show less involvement with some patients relative to others. These variations have been related to specific characteristics of patients, including sex, age, education and social class, anxiety, and relational history with the doctor.

4.5. Patients' characteristics and accommodation

Patients' age

As previously noted, communicative accommodation is in part contingent on the interactant's attitude toward his or her partners. If positive, the interactant will seek to converge or maintain role-appropriate communicative differences; if negative, the interactant may seek to dissociate via divergence. Harris, Rich, and Crowson (1985) observed that doctors in their study reported positive attitudes toward "middle-aged" and "elderly" patients but negative attitudes toward "adolescent" patients. If these attitudes are characteristic of most doctors, then they may converge to the communicative behavior of middle-aged and older patients more than to that of younger patients (e.g., under twenty-five years of age). In an investigation of forty-one doctor–patient interactions at a family practice clinic, Street and Buller (1988) partially supported this claim. In their study, doctors reciprocated to a greater degree the response latency and floor-holding modifications of patients over thirty relative to those by patients under thirty. Also, doctors generally displayed less communicative involvement (by maintaining greater distance and using fewer vocal acknowledgers such as "uh huh," "I see," "yeah?") and exercised more communicative control (by holding the floor for longer periods) when interacting with younger as opposed to older patients.

On the other hand, Haug and Ory's (1987) review of the literature revealed that many doctors have ageist stereotypes and are not as positively oriented toward elderly patients as they are toward younger patients. Consistent with this observation, Greene et al. (1986, 1987) reported that doctors' utterances to patients over sixty-five were rated as less egalitarian, patient, responsive, and respectful than were utterances to patients under forty-five. Because ageist attitudes are grounded in stereotypic views of older persons, doctors may "overaccommodate" (to be discussed later) to elderly patients because they underestimate the patients' cognitive and linguistic skills (see Coupland et al. 1988). Over accommodation occurs when doctors use simplistic speech registers and exaggerated intonation (as to a child or foreigner), thinking that such a code matches the communicative capabilities of the elderly patient.

In sum, there is some evidence indicating that doctors converge to the communicative behaviors of middle-aged adults more than they do to those of adolescent and young adult patients. Also, from the research reviewed earlier, one could speculate that doctors exhibit little convergence toward the communicative styles of elderly patients if they have ageist attitudes or if they fail to become communicatively involved in consultatons with these patients.

Patients' anxiety

The experience of anxiety about the consultation or the medical condition varies greatly across patients. It can influence the patient's preferences for the doctor's communicative behavior (Ben-Sira 1980; Street and Wiemann 1987), the patient's nonverbal behavior (Harrigan 1985), and the doctor's communicative responses to patients (Waitzkin 1985). Street and Buller (1988) investigated the possibility that doctors vary their accommodation of nonverbal behaviors as a function of the patient's anxiety. Their results, however, revealed few differences in doctors' accommodation to anxious and nonanxious patients. What differences emerged indicated that doctors reciprocated the *less* worried patients' turn durations, body orientations, and vocal backchannels more than those of anxious patients. However, when conversing with more anxious patients, doctors were more consistent in their body orientations and tended to perform fewer activities related to the physical examination of the patient.

In brief, the doctors in Street and Buller's study certainly appeared *responsive* to the patients' anxiety. If these trends characterize most doctor–patient interactions, these phenomena may represent differences in the *roles* interactants assume in response to the patient's anxiety. Patients seeking doctors' care for uncomplicated medical conditions (e.g., common flu, routine physical examination) may approach the medical consultation rather casually and more "socially." Thus, doctors' interactions with these patients may be characterized by smiles, some degree of nonverbal animation (facially and gesturally), small talk, reciprocal response patterns, and periods in which the doctor simultaneously talks to and examines the patient. However, the roles of "sick person" and "health care provider" may be accentuated during doctors' interactions with worried patients. Therefore, these encounters reveal more consistent and complementary forms of interaction as the patient exhibits behaviors indicative of anxiety and uncertainty (e.g., self-touching, gaze avoidance, talkativeness or silence, expressions of concern) and the doctor displays greater communicative involvement and control, perhaps due to their own uncertainty about the disease and its prognosis (Applegate 1986). This explanation is speculative and warrants further empirical attention, especially given evidence that patients' anxiety about medical care significantly influences their response to medical care.

Doctor–patient relational history

Some patients are follow-up, repeat, and regular clients; others are seeing a particular doctor for the first time. The question arises: Are there differences in the manner in which doctors accommodate to repeat patients and first-time patients? Theories of communication in relationships suggest an affirmative answer. When interacting for the first time, interactants often achieve convergence among various behaviors such as speech rate, response latency, accent, intimacy of self-disclosures, and facial and gestural behaviors (Street and Giles 1982). In these encounters, reciprocal response patterns promote communicative efficiency (Giles and Smith 1979; Natale 1975) and facilitate the reduction of uncertainty toward interlocutors (Berger and Calabrese 1975). As relationships develop, response patterns become more idiomatic (Knapp 1984). Although reciprocity may be evident in the interactions of partners who have an established relationship, communication patterns are allowed to vary substantially. In other words, the norm of reciprocity is often attenuated as interactants familiar with one another allow greater response flexibility (Street and Cappella 1985).

Three studies have examined the impact of relational history on doctor–patient communicative behavior. Waitzkin (1985) reported that doctors spend more time with and provide more explanations to patients they have known for longer as opposed to shorter periods of time. Davis (1971) observed that doctors were relatively dominant and first-time patients were relatively submissive regarding who initiated conversational topics, provided directions, made recommendations, and offered evaluative responses. Conversely, doctors' encounters with follow-up patients were characterized by more equality, as patients were more verbally assertive and doctors less controlling. In other words, doctors and repeat patients tended to converge toward the verbal behaviors of their partners such that a more egalitarian interaction was established. On the other hand, Street and Buller (1988) found few differences in doctor–patient communicative accommodation in repeat and first-time consultations. However, of the differences noted, doctors reciprocated the changes in response latency and silence in speaking turns of first-time patients more than of repeat patients.

Although a speculation, there may be two forms of communicative accommodation that emerge as a function of the doctor–patient relational history. First, during the initial visit, doctor and patient may adhere to the traditional roles of a rather submissive patient and a dominant doctor. This adherence is represented among verbal exchanges and may stem from the participants' uncertainty about one another and about the medical condition. However, as in most encounters between strangers, the doctor and patient, to some extent, may converge certain vocal and nonverbal behaviors (e.g., pauses, facial affect) in order to establish a preferred tempo for the interaction and an appropriate level of expressivity. On the other hand, because of their familiarity with one another, both doctors and repeat patients may perceive fewer constraints on their communicative styles. Thus, their interaction may reveal more equality in terms of control of the interaction (in particular, the patient becomes more assertive); however, their individual nonverbal behaviors may show greater variation with respect to that of the other. Overall, however, these studies revealed only a *few* differences in doctor–patient communication as a function of the participants' relational history. Institutional constraints on doctors' and patients' behaviors, as well as the time lag between consultations with a particular patient, may prevent the interactants from communicating in a manner characteristic of other social contexts in which partners have a previously established relational history.

Patients' education and social class

There is substantial evidence indicating that doctors communicate differently with patients of varying social classes and education levels. Doctors typically spend more time with, provide more information to (Pendleton and Bochner 1980; Waitzkin 1985), and are more reassuring and empathic (Wasserman et al. 1984) when interacting with college-educated and high socioeconomic status (SES) patients than when talking to less educated and working-class patients. These response differences may reflect the doctors' attitudes toward patients with varying educations (Cartwright 1967) or to the difficulties doctors encounter when interacting with less educated and lower SES patients (Bennett, Knox, and Morrison 1978; Pendleton, Brouever, and Jaspars 1983). Bochner (1983) has surmised that doctors and upper-class patients experience fewer communicative difficulties because of their relative cultural similarity and, subsequently, their use of similar communicative codes. Thus, one would expect greater verbal and nonverbal behavior convergence during doctors' interactions with more as opposed to less educated patients and with higher as opposed to lower SES patients. Bochner indeed reported less discrepancy between doctors' and patients' mean lengths of utterances during interactions with higher SES patients than during encounters with lower SES patients. However, Street and Buller (1988) reported few differences in doctors' accommodation to the nonverbal behaviors of more and less educated patients.

As previously noted, communicative convergence has been linked to smooth conversational exchanges and favorable impressions of interactants (Giles et al. 1987). Bochner's (1983) review indicates that doctors may converge more to the verbal behavior of more educated and upper-class patients than to that of less educated and working-class patients. These findings, coupled with evidence suggesting that doctors spend less time with and provide less information to working-class and less educated patients (Pendleton and Bochner 1980; Waitzkin 1985), suggest that these patients may be "communicatively disadvantaged" in their consultations with doctors.

Patients' sex

West (1984) reported that male doctors display more communicative dominance when interacting with female as opposed to male patients. Others, however, have found that women tend to receive more time, information, and explanations from doctors (Waitzkin 1985). Also, doctors have been perceived (by independent observers) to display more empathic skill, to leave the examination room less often, and to be more informative when conversing with female as opposed to male patients (Hooper et al. 1982). Street and Buller (1988) specifically examined the question of whether doctors variously accommodated to the nonverbal behavior of male and female patients and found little evidence of such differences. Future research is certainly warranted given that doctors do appear to vary their verbal styles in response to the patient's sex.

4.6. Dysfunctional accommodation in doctor–patient interactions

There are several features of the doctor–patient relationship that can interfere with the interactants' efforts to optimally converge affiliative responses and complement dominance behaviors. These problems may be reflected in one of two forms of dysfunctional accommodative patterns: divergence and misperceived convergence.

Divergence

In some consultations, doctors may intend to exercise power and control contrary to the interests or wishes of patients. For example, doctors and patients have incompatible goals when the doctor wants to finish the consultation quickly and get the patient to accept a recommended course of action, but the patient wants more time to express concerns and discuss treatment alternatives (Dryden and Giles 1987). Relatedly, some critics of medical authority argue that doctors attempt to enhance their power relative to that of the patient, especially when they perceive a threat from the patient's challenge of their diagnosis and recommendations (Fisher 1984; Stimson and Webb 1975; West 1984). When an interactant is threatened by a partner or has goals incompatible with those of a partner, he or she may seek to control the interaction by creating social distance from the interlocutor via communicative divergence (Giles et al. 1987). Some research indeed indicates that doctors sometimes attempt to maximize their power over patients through divergent moves such as topic switches and style shifting.

   When an interactant changes the conversational topic by not linking his or her comment to the partner's previous contribution, he or she is in a sense *diverging* from the content of the partner's utterance. Perceivers generally believe this to be inappropriate conversational behavior

(Tracy 1985), although such liberties are sometimes granted to interactants having status or power (Street 1986). Some doctors exercise this form of divergence when interacting with patients. For example, doctors may produce dramatic topic changes relative to the content of the patient's comment in order to avoid discussion of sensitive issues (Mathews 1983; Segrist 1977 cited in Cicourel 1981) or to counter a patient's challenge or opinion (Danziger 1978; Fisher 1984). Patients rarely pursue their challenge beyond the initial assertion. Thus, by shifting topics, the doctor has effectively controlled the interaction in the way desired.

Related to the notion of topic changes is the more general phenomenon of style shifting. According to Scotton (1985), style shifting occurs when an interactant changes features of the communicative code previously used by the interactants. For example, "What the heck, sir?" juxtaposes the informally connoted by "heck" with the relatively formal "sir." These moves tend to create uncertainty within the interlocutor regarding what communicative style is appropriate for the interaction. Higher-power interactants (such as interviewers and doctors) are able to use style shifting effectively because the lower-power interactants (such as interviewees and patients) tend to follow (converge to) the moves of higher-status individuals and do not perceive themselves as in a position to change the code choices of the other. In medical consultations, style shifting can occur when doctors initially use everyday, lay language when talking to patients and then suddenly switch to medical jargon. Such a move renders the patient less certain and less verbally active because the doctor is now using a code unfamiliar to the patient (Korsch and Negrete 1972; Shuy 1976). Whether intentional or not, such communicative acts reinforce doctors' control over patients in the interaction.

Misperceived convergence

Doctor–patient interactions are quite susceptible to communicative misperceptions and misunderstandings. Not only do they vary in their communicative roles and medical knowledge, but doctors and patients also differ in how each understands disease in terms of its etiology and social effects (Helman 1985). Under such circumstances, empathic understanding is difficult to achieve. Thus, it is not surprising that doctors and patients often misperceive one another's characteristics, intentions, and behaviors. For example, doctors consistently underestimate the patient's desire for information and often misattribute the patient's diffidence in consultations to a lack of interest (Cartwright 1967; Shapiro et al. 1983). Also, doctors generally perceive patients to be more ignorant, dissatisfied, and fearful than they actually are (McKinlay 1975; Pfefferbaum, Levenson, and van Eys 1982). In turn, the patient's reverence for doctors may lead to a perception of the doctor's communicative style that is overly positive and incongruous with what doctors perceive characteristic of themselves (Street and Wiemann 1988).

Given these discrepancies, it is not surprising that there is sometimes little correspondence between how patients and doctors think they are communicating with one another. One form of misperceived convergence occurs when doctors believe they are speaking in a manner understandable to the patient and in fact they are not. For example, Bourhis, Roth, and MacQueen (1988) reported that doctors in their study *thought* they were converging to the patient's linguistic level by using everyday language. However, both nurses and patients perceived little convergence on the part of the doctors. A second form of misperceived convergence may be called "overconvergence" (see Coupland et al. 1988) and occurs when doctors believe that patients have little understanding of medical terminology. Thus the doctor may use very simplistic terms such as "tummy," "bellyache," and "wet your pants" when talking with patients. Some doctor think such lexical choices are convergent to the patient's knowledge base when in actuality they are much below the patient's level of comprehension (Shuy 1976). The recipient of overconvergence typically perceives it to be condescending or patronizing (see Dryden and Giles 1987).

4.7. Accommodation and medical outcomes

As discussed in the previous section, patients and doctors generally prefer interactions that are characterized by convergence among behaviors signaling communicative involvement and by some degree of complementarity among dominance and control behaviors. Thus, one would expect more positive medical outcomes – greater satisfaction, cooperativeness, and understanding – when doctors and patients achieve these communicative formats. Conversely, one would expect patients to be less satisfied, cooperative, and accurate in their understanding when these patterns of interaction are not achieved.

Convergence

In general, patients wish to be active participants in their medical interactions. With respect to the accommodation of verbal behavior, patients' satisfaction, compliance, and understanding should be fostered when both patients and doctors freely discuss issues perceived important to each and reciprocate the exchange of information. This contention receives support if one couples the assumption that doctors are typically active communicators with the research demonstrating that patients' satisfaction and ability to get information from doctors are positively related to the patients' verbal activity (Anderson, De Vellis, and De Vellis 1987; Greenfield et al. 1985). Regarding information exchange, Davis (1968, 1971) reported that one of the situations in which compliance with prescribed treatments was relatively high was in interactions in which doctors and patients mutually exhibited verbal acts of providing information. For example, in that study, patients responded negatively when doctors queried them for information but provided little feedback in return. In essence, during encounters where information exchange was not reciprocated (i.e., patient to doctor only) or infrequent, compliance diminished.

However, research on patients' reactions to doctors' accommodation of nonverbal behaviors remains inconclusive. In counseling sessions, the extent to which counselors "mirrored" clients' postural positions and body orientations has been related to clients' perceptions of rapport and of the counselor's effectiveness (LaFrance 1982; Maurer and Tindall 1983; Trout and Rosenfeld 1980). In experimental studies in which doctors' levels of expressive behaviors were manipulated, Harrigan and her colleagues (Harrigan and Rosenthal 1983; Harrigan et al. 1985) demonstrated that doctors who display more open postures, establish mutual gaze with the patient, lean toward the patient, and use occasional head nods (behaviors often exhibited by patients) were rated more favorably by patients than were doctors who exhibited opposite responses. However, in a naturalistic investigation, Street and Buller (1987) failed to find statistically significant relationships between patients' satisfaction with health care and the degree of similarity between doctors' and patients' nonverbal behaviors.

As reviewed earlier, doctors and patients tend to reciprocate one another's adjustments among expressive behaviors such as gaze, gesture, body orientation, and head nods (Smith and Larson 1984; Street and Buller 1987, 1988). Given patients' self-reports of generally high levels of satisfaction with medical care (Speeding and Rose 1985), these studies perhaps implicitly support the claim that positive medical outcomes can be fostered by some degree of doctor–patient convergence among nonverbal behaviors signaling communicative involvement. However, as a whole, existing research only partially supports this claim.

Complementarity

One of the more difficult communicative tasks for doctors and patients is to negotiate an appropriate pattern of communicative control. As mentioned earlier, both patients and doctors agree that each has different communicative roles and that doctors generally exhibit relatively greater dominance in the interaction than do patients. However, both parties typically agree that there should also be an egalitarian communicative exchange in which the patient may freely express concerns, provide relevant information, and offer opinions on treatment alternatives (Weiss 1986). Compliance and satisfaction appear to be enhanced when doctors and patients are able to meet these expectations for the interaction. For example, several studies have revealed that patients respond favorably in consultations in which patients have opportunities to express their concerns and when their questions and emotional comments are complemented by doctors' responses that offer suggestions, support, inform, and reassure the patient (Carter et al. 1982; Davis 1968; Francis, Korsch, and Morris 1969; Roter et al. 1987).

However, the delicate balance between the interactants' roles and control of the interaction is not always achieved in medical consultations. In particular, there are at least two patterns of communicative exchange related to dominance to which patients respond negatively. On the one hand, patients' compliance and satisfaction diminish when doctors are overly domineering and exhibit numerous directives, disagreements with the patient's comments, rejection of the patient's ideas, and close-ended questioning (Carter et al. 1982; Davis 1968; Heszen-Klemens and Lapinska 1984; Roter et al. 1987). On the other hand, patients also react negatively to patterns of communicative exchange in which the doctor is *insufficiently* dominant and the patient exercises more control over the consultation. Davis (1968) reported lower compliance in interactions in which the patient provided suggestions and directions and the doctor simply agreed with and accepted them.

In sum, patients expect doctors to be receptive, reassuring, directive, attentive, assertive, and involved during consultations. These expectations are generally met when doctors and patients reciprocally develop topics brought up by each, converge (to some extent) affiliative behaviors, and exhibit complementarity among certain role-specific and dominance behaviors. However, among the latter, if doctors are either too passive or too domineering, the patient's positive reaction to the medical consultation is reduced. Given the moderately negative correlations between patients' satisfaction-compliance and perceptions of doctors' dominance (Buller and Buller 1987; Pendleton 1983; Street and Wiemann 1987), it appears that doctors are more apt to be overly rather than insufficiently controlling.

4.8. Directions for future research

In this chapter, I have attempted to demonstrate the viability of a particular communication perspective, communication accommodation theory, for understanding communicative processes and outcomes in doctor–patient interactions. Given the paucity of research on contingencies *between* doctors' and patients' communicative responses and the consequences resulting from these patterns of interaction, the propositions put forth in this chapter are admittedly more suggestive than conclusive. As an epilogue, I discuss several issues that remain problematic. These should be the focus of future research because of their implications for communication theory and health care delivery.

Consistency vs. adaptation in doctor–patient interaction

Much of the evidence reviewed indicates that doctors to some degree accommodate their communication to that of the patient, but that these patterns of accommodation vary for different types of patients. Other evidence demonstrates that doctors tend be rather *consistent* in their manner of interacting with patients, although their individual communicative styles may differ. For example, some doctors have "patient-oriented" verbal response styles (e.g., counseling, providing information, allowing patients opportunities to talk), whereas others have "doctor-oriented" styles (e.g., asking closed-ended questions, giving directions, prescribing courses of action); however, doctors in each group tend to produce their respective styles consistently across interactions with patients (Byrne and Long 1976; Hall, Roter, and Katz 1987; Long 1985). Our own research (Street and Buller 1988), as well as that of Smith and Larsen (1984), suggests that, although somewhat accommodative, doctors nonetheless exhibit considerable consistency in their nonverbal responses to different patients. In other words, doctors may not significantly vary from a baseline style, but some adjustments are made that converge to, diverge from, or complement the patient's response.

A question for future research concerns how doctors manage the maintenance and adaptation of a particular style of interacting with patients. For example, doctors may feel the need to adapt their style given the needs and characteristics of individual patients. However, they also may wish to behave in a rather consistent manner from patient to patient because it is convenient to employ the same generic communicative routine or because institutional and professional constraints limit their flexibility to modify their communication significantly to different patients.

Patients' accommodation to doctors

Much of this chapter has focused on doctors' accommodation to patients' communication. Given that social interaction is mutually constructed by the participants, future research should examine the extent to which *patients* accommodate to the doctor's communicative style. In fact, given that doctors tend to have greater power in the encounter, patients may attempt to accommodate to the doctor more than the reverse (see Giles et al. 1987). Not only is it probable that patients vary in their ability to accommodate to doctors (e.g., using medical language; Bourhis et al. 1988), but their accommodation may preclude opportunities to become sufficiently involved or informed during the encounter. For example, patients may only discuss issues raised by doctors rather than bring up their own topics and concerns (Mathews 1983).

Patients' responses to doctors' accommodation

Individual differences. Different types of patients probably prefer different patterns of doctor–patient communicative exchange. For example, first-time patients tend to be hyperattentive to the manner in which health care providers communicate with them because of uncertainty about the doctor and the medical condition (Friedman 1979). Thus, relative to repeat patients, first-time patients may to a greater degree assess the quality of health care received in relation to ostensible features of a provider's communicative behavior. In support of this contention, three studies have reported that first-time patients expressed lower satisfaction with less affiliative and more domineering doctors than did repeat patients (Buller and Buller 1987; DiMatteo and Hays 1980; Street and Wiemann 1987). Applying CAT, one could hypothesize that new patients may be less tolerant of variations from expected patterns of convergent and complementary doctor–patient communicative exchange than would repeat patients.

Relatedly, the extent to which patients tolerate a range of variability in the doctors' communicative response also has significant theoretical and practical implications. For example, an interactant may expect affiliative behavior from an interlocutor yet may also perceive (or tolerate) an array of responses as sufficiently affiliative. For example, Burgoon (1983) has demonstrated that perceivers often widen their range of tolerance for a partner's behavior when the partner is considered to have high social value (e.g., status or attractiveness). Our own research has indicated that patients indeed accept substantial variability in doctors' nonverbal behaviors without negative sanction (Street and Buller 1987), and that some patients (e.g., less educated) may be less critical of the doctor's style than are others (e.g., more educated) (Street and Wiemann 1988).

Relative importance of verbal and nonverbal behavior. Medical outcomes appear to be more consistently related to doctor–patient *verbal* behavior (e.g., informativeness, directives, reassurance) than to *nonverbal* behavior (e.g., speech rate, body orientation, gaze) (Comstock et al. 1982; Hall et al. 1988). Patients may be more verbally oriented because of the importance of information exchange in medical consultations. Not only is information exchange *primarily* accomplished verbally, but verbal behaviors also play a role in conveying communicative involvement (e.g., elaborating and developing a partner's utterance, counseling, noninterruptive listening, reassuring, and supporting) and dominance (e.g., disagreements, directives, criticism, topic change). This is *not* to say that nonverbal behavior is unimportant in doctor–patient interactions. Rather, because information exchange and problem resolution are the primary functions of these interactions, doctors and patients may be more attentive to verbal rather than nonverbal behavior. Given the previously discussed notion of acceptance ranges for an interlocutor's behavior, one could propose that patients are more tolerant of variability in the doctor's accommodation of nonverbal behavior than of verbal behavior.

4.9. A final comment

As academicians, we know much about the medical outcomes associated with doctors' and patients' beliefs about health and with the attitudes each holds toward the other. However, we still know little about the *process*, which is essentially communicative, linking beliefs, understanding, and medical outcomes. The application of communication theories, such as CAT, to the context of the medical consultation is a promising approach toward filling this void, and should promote the reflexive relationship between good theory and good practice.

References

Anderson, L. A., DeVellis, B. M., and DeVellis, R. F. 1987. Effects of modeling on patients' communication, satisfaction, and knowledge. *Medical Care*, 25: 1044–56.

Applegate, W. H. 1986. Physician management of patients with adverse outcomes. *Archives of Internal Medicine*, 146: 2249–52.

Arntson, P. H., and Philipsborn, H. F. 1982. Pediatrician–parent communication in a continuity of a setting. *Clinical Pediatrics* 21: 302–30.

Bales, R. F. 1950. *Interaction Process Analysis*. Cambridge, MA.: Addison-Wesley.

Becker, M. H., and Maiman, L. A. 1975. Sociobehavioral determinants of compliance with medical care recommendations. *Medical Care*, 13: 10–24.

Bennet, A., Knox, J. D., and Morrison, A. T. 1978. Difficulties in consultations reported by doctors in general practice. *Journal of the Royal College of General Practitioners*, 28: 646–51.

Ben-Sira, Z. 1980. Affective and instrumental components of the physician–patient relationship: An additional dimension of interaction theory. *Journal of Health and Social Behavior*, 21: 170–80.

Berger, C. R., and Calabrese, R. J. 1975. Some explorations in initial interaction and beyond: Toward a developmental theory of interpersonal communication. *Human Communication Research*, 1: 99–112.

Bochner, S. 1983. Doctors, patients, and their cultures. *In* D. Pendleton and J. Hasler (eds.), *Doctor–Patient Communication*, pp. 127–38. New York: Academic Press.

Boreham, P., and Gibson, D. 1978. The informative process in private medical consultations: A preliminary investigation. *Social Science and Medicine*, 12: 409–16.

Bourhis, R. Y., Roth, S., and MacQueen, G. 1988. Communication in the hospital setting: A survey of medical and everday language use amongst patients, nurses, and doctors. *Social Science and Medicine*, 24: 1–8.

Buller, M. K., and Buller, D. 1987. Physicians' communication style and health care satisfaction. *Journal of Health and Social Behavior*, 28: 375–88.

Burgoon, J. K. 1983. Nonverbal violations of expectations. *In* J. M. Wiemann and R. Harrison (eds.), *Nonverbal Interaction*, pp. 77–111. Beverly Hills, CA: Sage.

Byrne, P. S, and Long, B. 1976. *Doctors Talking to Patients: A Study of the Verbal Behavior of General Practitioners Consulting in Their Surgeries*. London: Her Majesty's Stationery Office.

Cappella, J. N. 1983. Conversational involvement: Approaching and avoiding others. *In* J. M. Wiemann and R. P. Harrison (eds.), *Nonverbal Interaction*, pp. 113–48. Beverly Hills, CA: Sage.

Carter, W. B., Inui, T. S., Kukull, W. A., and Haigh, V. H. 1982. Outcome-based doctor–patient interaction analysis: Identifying effective provider and patient behavior. *Medical Care*, 20: 550–68.

Cartwright, A. 1967. *Patients and Their Doctors*. London: Routledge & Kegan Paul.

Cicourel, A. V. 1981. Language and medicine. *In* C. A. Ferguson and S. B. Heath (eds.), *Language in the USA*, pp. 407–29. Cambridge: Cambridge University Press.

Comstock, L. M., Hooper, E. M. Goodwin, J. M., and Goodwin, J. S. 1982. Physician behaviors that correlate with patient satisfaction. *Journal of Medicine Education*, 57: 105–12.

Coulthard, M., and Ashby, M. 1975. Talking with the doctor. *Journal of Communication*, 25: 140–47.

Coupland, N., Coupland, J., Giles, H., and Henwood, K. 1988. Accommodating the elderly: Invoking and extending a theory. *Language in Society*, 17: 1–41.

Danziger, S. K. 1978. The uses of expertise in doctor–patient encounters during pregnancy. *Social Science and Medicine*, 12: 359–67.

Davis, M. 1968. Variations in patients' compliance with doctors' advice: An empirical analysis of patterns of communication. *American Journal of Public Health*, 58: 274–88.

Davis, M. 1971. Variations in patients' compliance with doctors' orders: Medical practice and doctor–patient interaction. *Psychiatry in Medicine*, 2:31–54.

DiMatteo, M. R. 1979. A social-psychological analysis of physician–patient rapport: Towards a science of the art of medicine. *Journal of Social Issues*, 35: 12–33.

DiMatteo, M. R., and Hays, R. 1980. The significance of patients' perceptions of physicians' conduct. *Journal of Community Health*, 6: 18–34.

Dryden, C., and Giles, H. 1987. Language, social identity, and health. *In* H. Beloff and A. Coleman (eds.), *Psychology Survey 6*, pp. 115–39. Levister: British Psychological Society.

Fisher, S. 1984. Institutional authority and the structure of discourse. *Discourse Processes*, 7: 201–24.

Francis, V., Korsch, B. M., and Morris, M. H. 1969. Gaps in doctor–patient communication: Patients' response to medical advise. *New England Journal of Medicine*, 280: 535–40.

Freeling, P. 1983. The doctor–patient relationship in diagnosis and treatment. *In* D. Pendleton and J. Hasler (eds.), *Doctor–Patient Communication*, pp. 161–76. London: Academic Press.

Friedman, H. S. 1979. Nonverbal communication between patients and medical practitioners. *Journal of Social Issues*, 35: 82–99.

Giles, H. 1977. Social psychology and applied linguistics: Toward an integrative approach. *ITL: Review of Applied Lingusitics*, 33: 27–42.

Giles, H., Mulac, A., Bradac, J., and Johnson, P. 1987. Speech accommodation theory: The next decade and beyond. *Communication Yearbook*, 10: 13–48.

Giles, H., and Smith, P. 1979. Accommodation theory: Optimal levels of convergence. *In* H. Giles and R. St. Clair (eds.), *Language and Social Psychology*, pp. 45–65. Oxford: Basil Blackwell.

Giles, H., and Street, R. L., Jr. 1985. Communicator characteristics and behavior. *In* M. Knapp and G. Miller (eds.), *Handbook of Interpersonal Communication*, pp. 205–62. Beverly Hills, CA: Sage.

Greene, M. G., Adelman, R., Charon, R., and Hoffman, S. 1986. Ageism in the medical encounter: An exploratory study of the doctor–elderly patient relationship. *Language and Communication*, 6: 113–24.

Greene, M. G., Hoffman, S., Charon, R., and Adelman, R. 1987. Psychosocial concerns in the medical encounter: A comparison of the interactions of doctors with their old and young patients. *The Gerontologist*, 27: 164–68.

Greenfield, S., Kaplan, S., and Ware, J. 1985. Expanding patient involvement in care. *Annals of Internal Medicine*, 102: 520–8.

154   R. L. Street, Jr.

Hall, J. A., Roter, D. L., and Katz, N. R. 1987. Task versus socioemotional behaviors in physicians. *Medical Care*, 25: 399–412.
Hall, J. A., Roter, D. L., and Katz, N. R. 1988. Meta-analysis of correlates of provider behavior in medical encounters. *Medical Care*, 26: 657–75.
Hall, J. A., Roter, D. L., and Rand, C. S. 1981. Communication of affect between patient and physician. *Journal of Health and Social Behavior*, 22: 18–30.
Harrigan, J. A. 1985. Self-touching as an indicator of underlying affect and language processes. *Social Science and Medicine*, 20: 1161–8.
Harrigan, J. A., Oxman, T. E., and Rosenthal, R. 1985. Rapport expressed through nonverbal behavior. *Journal of Nonverbal Behavior*, 9: 95–110.
Harrigan, J. A., and Rosenthal, R. 1983. Physicians' head and body positions as determinants of perceived rapport. *Journal of Applied Social Psychology*, 13: 496 509.
Harris, I. B., Rich, E. C., and Crowson, T. W. 1985. Attitudes of internal medicine residents and staff physicians toward various patient characteristics. *Journal of Medical Education*, 60: 192–5.
Haug, M. R., and Ory, M. G. 1987. Issues in elderly patient–provider interactions. *Research on Aging*, 9: 3–44.
Helman, C. G. 1985. Communication in primary care: The role of patient and practitioner explanatory models. *Social Science and Medicine*, 20: 923–31.
Heszen-Klemens, I., and Lapinska, E. 1984. Doctor–patient interaction, patients' health behavior, and effects of treatment. *Social Science and Medicine*, 19: 9–18.
Hooper, E. M., Comstock, L. M., Goodwin, J. M., and Goodwin, J. S. 1982. Patient characteristics that influence physician behavior. *Medical Care*, 20: 630–38.
Knapp, M. 1984. *Interpersonal Communication and Human Relationships*. Boston: Allyn and Bacon.
Korsch, B., and Negrete, V. 1972. Doctor–patient communication. *Scientific American*, 227: 66–74.
LaFrance, M. 1982. Posturing mirroring and rapport. In M. Davis (ed.), *Interaction Rhythms: Periodicity in Communicative Behavior*, pp. 279–97. New York: Human Sciences Press.
Lane, S. D. 1983. Compliance, satisfaction, and physician–patient communication. *Communication Yearbook*, 7: 772–98.
Larsen, K. M., and Smith, C. K. 1981. Assessment of nonverbal communication in the patient–physician interview. *Journal of Family Practice*, 12: 481–8.
Long, B. L. 1985. A study of the verbal behavior of family doctors. *International Journal of the Sociology of Language*, 51: 5–25.
Mathews, J. J. 1983. The communication process in clinical settings. *Social Science and Medicine*, 17: 1371–8.
Maurer, R. E., and Tindall, J. H. 1983. Effects of postural congruence on clients' perceptions of counselor empathy. *Journal of Counseling Psychology*, 30: 158–63.
McKinlay, J. B. 1975. Who is really ignorant – physician or patient? *Journal of Health and Social Behavior*, 16: 3–11.
Natale, M. 1975. Convergence of mean vocal intensity in dyadic communication as a function of social desirability. *Journal of Personality and Social Psychology*, 32: 790–804.
Patterson, M. L. 1983. *Nonverbal Behavior: A Functional Perspective*. New York: Springer-Verlag.
Pendleton, D. 1983. Doctor–patient communication: A review. In D. Pendleton

and J. Hasler (eds.), *Doctor–Patient Communication*, pp. 5–56. London: Academic Press.

Pendleton, D., and Bochner, S. 1980. The communication of medical information in general practice consultations as a function of the patients' social class. *Social Science and Medicine*, 14A: 669–73.

Pendlteon, D., Brouwer, H., and Jaspars, J. 1983. Communication difficulties: The doctor's perspective. *Journal of Language and Social Psychology*, 2: 17–36.

Pfefferbaum, B., Levenson, P. M., and van Eys, J. 1982. Comparison of physician and patient perceptions of communication issues. *Southern Medical Journal*, 75: 1080–3.

Roter, D. L., Hall, J. A., and Katz, N. R. 1987. Relations between physicians' behaviors and analogue patients' satisfaction, recall, and impressions. *Medical Care*, 25: 437–51.

Scotton, C. 1985. What the heck, sir? Style shifting and lexical colouring as features of powerful language. In R. L. Street, Jr., and J. N. Capella (eds.), *Sequences and Pattern in Communicative Behavior*, pp. 103–19. London: Edward Arnold.

Shapiro, M. C., Najman, J. M., and Chang, A. 1983. Information control and the exercise of power in the obstetrical encounter. *Social Science and Medicine*, 17: 139–46.

Shuy, R. W. 1976. The medical interview: Problems in communication. *Primary Care*, 3: 365–86.

Smith, C. K., and Larsen, K. M. 1984. Sequential nonverbal behavior in the physician–patient interview. *The Journal of Family Practice*, 18: 257–61.

Speedling, E. J., and Rose, D. N. 1985. Building an effective doctor–patient relationship: From patient satisfaction to patient participation. *Social Science and Medicine*, 21: 115–20.

Stiles, W. B. 1978. Verbal response modes and dimensions of interpersonal roles: A method of discourse analysis. *Journal of Personality and Social Psychology*, 36: 693–703.

Stiles, W. B., Orth, J. E., Scherwitz, L., Hennrikus, D., and Vallbona, C. 1984. Role behaviors in routine medical interviews: A repertoire of verbal exchanges. *Social Psychology Quarterly*, 47: 244–54.

Stimson, G. V., and Webb, B. 1975. *Going to See the Doctor: The Consultation Process in General Practice*. London: Routledge & Kegan Paul.

Street, R. L., Jr. 1986. Interaction processes and outcomes in interviews. *Communication Yearbook*, 9: 215–50.

Street, R. L., Jr., and Buller, D. 1987. Nonverbal response patterns in physician–patient interactions: A functional analysis. *Journal of Nonverbal Behavior*, 11: 234–53.

Street, R. L., Jr., and Buller, D. 1988. Patients' characteristics affecting physician–patient nonverbal communication. *Human Communication Research*, 15: 60–90.

Street, R. L., Jr., and Cappella, J. N. 1985. Sequence and pattern in communicative behavior: A model and commentary. *In* R. L. Street, Jr., and J. N. Cappella (eds.), *Sequence and Pattern in Communicative Behaviour*, pp. 243–76. London: Edward Arnold.

Street, R. L., Jr., and Giles, H. 1982. Speech accommodation theory: A social-cognitive approach to language and speech behavior. *In* M. Roloff and C. Berger (eds.), *Social Cognition and Communication*, pp. 193–226. Beverly Hills, CA: Sage.

Street, R. L., Jr., Mulac, A., and Wiemann, J. M. 1988. Speech evaluation differences as a function of perspective (participant versus observer) and presentational medium. *Human Communication Research*, 14: 333–64.

Street, R. L., Jr., and Wiemann, J. M. 1987. Patients' satisfaction with physicians' interpersonal involvement, expressiveness, and dominance. *Communication Yearbook*, 10: 591–612.

Street, R. L., Jr., and Wiemann, J. M. 1988. Differences in how physicians and patients perceive physicians' relational communication. *Southern Speech Communication Journal*, 53: 420–40.

Tracy, K. 1985. Conversational coherence: A cognitively grounded rules approach. *In* R. L. Street, Jr., and J. N. Cappella (eds.), *Sequence and Pattern in Communicative Behaviour*, pp. 30–49. London: Edward Arnold.

Trout, D. L., and Rosenfeld, H. M. 1980. The effect of postural lean and body congruence on the judgment of psychotherapeutic rapport. *Journal of Nonverbal Behavior*, 4: 176–90.

Waitzkin, H. 1985. Information giving in medical care. *Journal of Health and Social Behavior*, 26: 81–101.

Wasserman, R. C., and Inui, T. S. 1983. Systematic analysis of clinician–patient interactions: A critique of recent approaches with suggestions for future research. *Medical Care*, 21: 279–93.

Wasserman, R. C., Inui, T. S., Barriatua, R. D., Carter, W. B., and Lippincott, P. 1984. Pediatric clinicians' support for parents makes a difference. An outcome-based analysis of clinician–parent interaction. *Pediatrics*, 74: 1047–53.

Weiss, S. J. 1986. Consensual norms regarding patient involvement. *Social Science and Medicine*, 22: 489–96.

West, C. 1984. *Routine Complications: Troubles with the Talk Between Doctors and Patients*. Bloomington: University of Indiana Press.

Wolraich, M. L., Albanese, M., Stone, G., Nesbitt, D., Thomson, E., Shymansky, J., Barkley, J., and Hanson, J. 1986. Medical communication behavior system: An interactional analysis system for medical interactions. *Medical Care*, 24: 891–904.

5. Accommodation and mental disability

HEIDI E. HAMILTON

5.1. Introduction

Coupland et al. (1988) introduce a "sociolinguistically elaborated model" of speech accommodation theory (SAT) in which the speaker attends to the interlocutor's productive performance (the focus of more traditional SAT) and projected ability to comprehend, as well as conversational needs, and to the role relations between the conversational partners. Of its four components, the discourse management component that responds to the addressee's conversational needs is understood to play the central role in what has been recast as "communicative accommodation theory (CAT)" (see, e.g., Coupland et al. 1990). The purpose of this expanded accommodation framework is "to model and explain degrees and types of communicative 'attuning' in discourse, and contextualise these with considerations of social norms, beliefs and expectations, self- and other-categorizations, and interactional goals, as they influence both encoding and decoding choices." (Coupland et al. 1990: 3).

In this chapter, I apply this interactionally grounded sociolinguistic framework of accommodation theory to a situation of potential and actual miscommunication – conversations between normal and mentally disabled interlocutors, including Alzheimer's disease patients, schizophrenics and the mentally retarded.[1] First, I discuss the disability-linked

I wish to thank Justine Coupland, Nikolas Coupland, Howard Giles, and Deborah Tannen for their many helpful and insightful comments on earlier drafts of this chapter.
[1] My decision to use the term mental "disability" rather than "impairment" or "handicap," is based on St. Claire's (1989) discussion of Wood and Badley's model of disablement (1978a, 1978b, 1980), which distinguishes between *impairment* as a medical disorder (pathological condition), *disability* as the expression of impairments in terms of deviations from performance norms (physical, psychological, and social tasks, skills and behaviors), and *handicap* as the disadvantage for a given individual resulting from an impairment or disability. Within this tripartite distinction, this chapter deals primarily with performance deviations (i.e., disabilities) and not with their cause or whether they result in disadvantage.

decreased ability to accommodate the conversational partner along dimensions of interpretive ability and discourse management, viewing this as a contributing factor to communicative breakdown. Second, in the face of this type of breakdown, I examine the normal other's use of accommodation both to the mentally disabled partner's perceived interpretive competence and to his or her conversational needs, seen as a way to maintain a balance between accomplishing what one wants to propositionally while maintaining both the speaker's and the hearer's face (see Brown and Levinson 1987; Goffman 1967; Lakoff 1973, 1979) in the interaction. Thus, the notion of accommodation is shown to be related both to the cause and to the consequence of interactional breakdown.

The kinds of studies in which one is most likely to locate such interactional nonsuccesses and resultant accommodative strategies are those based on spontaneously occurring interactions between normal and mentally disabled interlocutors in natural settings. Studies of language use in mentally disabled groups tend, however, to examine isolated language problems of the mentally disabled individual, ignoring his or her ability to communicate in context, as well as the influence that the normal conversational partner has on the interaction (see Coupland et al. 1988; Crystal 1984; Price-Williams and Sabsay 1979; Rochester and Martin 1979). Because of the unfortunate lack of published studies including analyses of *interaction* between members of these three mentally disabled populations and normal interlocutors, the section on accommodative strategies by the normal interlocutor in response to communicative breakdowns is informed primarily by my own research.

5.2. Disability syndromes

Alzheimer's disease, which was first described by Dr. Alois Alzheimer (1907), is a condition that results in a gradual deterioration of intellectual and physical abilities, including memory loss, change in personality, loss of reasoning capacity, and language loss. Because Alzheimer's disease has been identified as the major cause of senility (Katzman 1985: 1), it is usually associated with the elderly, although the condition is thought to be the same regardless of the age of the victim (Reisberg 1981: 15). Definitive diagnosis of Alzheimer's disease can be made only by biopsy or autopsy of the patient's brain and the subsequent location of the characteristic abnormal structures called "neuritic" (or "senile") plaques, consisting of degenerating nerve endings, and neurofibrillary tangles, consisting of thousands of pairs of abnormal, twisted filaments in specific areas of the brain tissue. However, because there is at present no cure or treatment for Alzheimer's disease, a diagnosis of exclusion by ruling out a wide variety of other possible causes for the condition, including vitamin deficiencies, infections, and brain tumors, is usually preferred to the much riskier diagnosis by biopsy. Likely candidates for the cause of Alzheimer's disease are genetic factors, chromosomal abnormalities, slow-acting or dormant viruses, accumulation of environmental toxins such as aluminium, or a combination of these factors (Katzman 1985; Reisberg 1981).

Mental retardation, according to the American Association on Mental Deficiency, "refers to significantly subaverage general intellectual functioning resulting in or associated with concurrent impairments in adaptive behavior and manifested during the developmental period" (cited in Szymanski and Crocker 1985: 1636). For all levels of mental retardation "linguistic deficits are almost a defining feature" (Sabsay and Platt 1985: 2). The importance of language problems to the picture of mental retardation is supported by St. Claire (1986), who administered a semantic differential test to lay people and psychologists who were both acquainted and unacquainted with retarded individuals. Of eighty-one items offered to describe a mentally retarded individual, "speech unclear" was one of only six items identified to a significant degree by all groups. According to Sabsay and Platt (1985: 2), 85 percent of the people in the United States classified as retarded have no evident organic disorder or brain pathology. St. Clarie's (1989) multidimensional model of mental retardation discusses the various senses in which individuals may be considered retarded, including organic abnormalities or pathologies, subnormal performance (including IQ scores), and socially constructed retardation.

Schizophrenia, according to Lehmann and Cancro (1985: 680), is consistently characterized by a group of symptoms, despite the fact that no consistent course, outcome, or single cause has been ascertained and no characteristic morphological changes in the brains of schizophrenics have been demonstrated. Characteristic symptoms include hallucinations, thought disorder, and disorders of verbal behavior, such as use of neologisms, echolalia, excessive concreteness, and general incoherence (Lehmann and Cancro 1985: 681ff). Although space constraints do not allow a discussion, it should be noted that much controversy surrounds research into the relative degrees of genetic and environmental influence on schizophrenia. [For example, see Helmchen and Henn (1987) for biological perspectives of schizophrenia and Blakar (1985) and Käsermann and Altorfer (in press) for a discussion of the possible influence of parents' language use on children diagnosed as schizophrenic.]

The common element in the three populations in this study is cognitive disability. Although accompanying language disabilities are generally observed in all three populations, these groups as a whole must be treated differently than individuals with the classic forms of aphasia who are intellectually sound despite having varying degrees and types of language disorders (see Andresen 1985, Obler and Albert 1980, and Wertz 1978 for discussion). What differs among the three cognitively disabled groups is the age of onset of the disability; whether or not the disability has an organic cause; and whether or not the disability is reversible, stable, or progressive. Given the diversity of specific pathologies represented in the following analyses, it is hoped that any similarities found with regard to accommodation processes may point to generalizations regarding communicative problems involving the cognitively disabled as a whole.

In addition to a review of interactional problems and processes associated with these syndromes, many of the observations and analyses reported in this chapter are based on fourteen naturally occurring conversations involving one Alzheimer's disease patient that were tape-recorded in a 121-bed Washington, D.C.-area private health care center between November 1981 and March 1986.[2] The total duration of the transcribed conversation is four hours and twenty-four minutes. At the time of the interactions, the patient, who will be called Elsie, was eighty-one to eighty-six years old. She had earned an advanced degree and had been professionally active until ten years before the beginning of this study. According to the Global Deterioration Scale (GDS) for Age-Associated Cognitive Decline and Alzheimer's Disease (Reisberg, Ferris, and de Leon 1982), Elsie was at the stage of moderately severe cognitive decline (state 5) at the onset of our conversations in 1981 and had reached the stage of very severe cognitive decline (stage 7) by 1986. GDS stage 5

[2]During 1981–3 I worked as a volunteer once a week at the Hermitage in northern Virginia, a private health care center for the elderly. My weekly activities included coleading an armchair exercise class and a baking class; engaging in one-to-one conversations with residents; reading to a blind resident; and escorting residents to and from in-house activities. I wish to thank Ms. Jill Bergen, Coordinator of Volunteer Services, for arranging permission for me to tape-record interactions in which I was involved at the health care center, and Elsie, a wonderful woman whom I never saw only as an informant but came to love as a friend.

corresponds to the clinical phase "early dementia"; stage 7 corresponds to the clinical phase "late dementia." At the beginning of the study, Elsie could walk and eat independently; by 1985 she needed assistance. By March 1986, Elsie was bedridden and her verbal production consisted solely of the responses *mmm, mhm, hmm?* and *uhhuh*, although her systematic use of these indicates a degree of comprehension on her part, especially of personally important utterances.

5.3. Unintentional underaccommodation

There is overwhelming evidence that breakdown or nonsuccess in interactions between normal interlocutors and the mentally retarded, schizophrenics, and Alzheimer's patients occurs primarily at the discourse level. With the possible exception of the severely mentally retarded (see Price-Williams and Sabsay 1979), morphosyntactic structures in speakers belonging to the mentally disabled groups seem to be virtually intact (Chaika 1974; Kempler 1984; Rochester, Martin, and Thurston 1977; Rutter 1985; and Sabsay and Kernan 1983). Although mentally disabled speakers' utterances may be identified as grammatically correct, their use is still perceived as problematic. It appears that speakers in these populations are not fully able to take the role of the other in the interaction, that is, they have difficulty in designing their utterances in such a way that their conversational partners can understand what they are saying (Herbert and Waltensperger 1982; Rochester et al. 1977; Rutter 1985; and Sabsay and Kernan 1983).

Coupland et al. (1988) discuss underaccommodation to conversational needs as a phenomenon sometimes found in discourse directed to young interlocutors by the healthy elderly. Characteristics of this underaccommodation include greater focus on the self than on the addressee and lowly attuned discourse management. Recipients' evaluation of underaccommodation is said to be generally negative, for example, that the speakers are "inconsiderate" or "unhelpful" (Coupland et al. 1988: 32), passive or egocentric.

This notion of underaccommodation appears to be a common thread running through the literature on communicative difficulties in contexts involving mentally disabled individuals, although other terms are used to describe the phenomenon. An important distinction must be made, however, between *intentional* or *strategic* underaccommodation, in which the speaker to some degree designs his or her talk to be unhelpful to his or her conversational partner, and *unintentional* or *nonstrategic* underaccommodation, which appears to characterize the discourse of the mentally disabled. It is generally not the case that these individuals do not *wish* to take the role of the other; it is that they *cannot* take the role of the other to the extent that normal interlocutors can. Unfortunately, this critical difference between strategy and disability on the part of the mentally disabled speaker is not always perceived by the normal recipients of this underaccommodation, leading to misattributed and undeservedly negative evaluations of the mentally disabled speaker's behavior.

Role taking is, of course, critical to an individual's success as a conversational partner. It is only by figuratively stepping into the mind of the addressee that we are able to accomplish conversational coherence and maintain mutual face in interaction. The full range of linguistic and social decisions in interaction – such as whether to use a pronoun or a full noun phrase; when to take a turn at talk; and which speech acts, register, and conversational style to choose – is contingent on role taking. Mead (1934: 253) considers role taking to be "basic to human social organization"; Sacks, Schegloff, and Jefferson (1978: 42–3) suggest that "recipient design" is "perhaps the most general principle particularizing conversation." In taking the role of the other, interlocutors operate with various types of assumptions – including what constitutes shared background knowledge, social expectations, common sense, and cultural, ethnic, sex, and other stereotypes. When these assumptions prove to be wrong, and knowledge assumed to be shared is *not* shared, expectations are *not* met, or stereotypes are *not* confirmed in the interaction, interlocutors may experience interactive difficulties. Social and sociopsychological characteristics of the conversationalists, as well as their relationship to each other, will in turn influence the discourse strategies used in reaction to communicative breakdown. The frustration resulting from such difficulties can lead normal individuals to construct or confirm a stereotype of the mentally disabled group as a whole, similar to the reinforcement of racial and ethnic stereotypes discussed in Gumperz (1982). For disabled individuals, to the extent to which they are aware of their disability, the communicative difficulty may heighten their own feeling of incompetence, leading to a potentially serious breakdown of mutual face in the interaction.

Difficulties in taking the role of the other are manifested in a variety of ways. The following examples taken from the literature on language use by schizophrenics, the mentally retarded, and Alzheimer's patients, as well from my own study on Alzheimer's disease, illustrate some of the interactional problems that result from difficulties in taking the role of the others.[3] Space constraints prevent a more complete examination of the problem.

Information problems

Probably the most obvious manifestation of the difficulty in taking the role of the other in conversation is the misuse of the information system. That is, information that is *not* known to the listener is presented as given by the speaker or information that *is* known to the listener is presented as new by the speaker. Referencing problems (Rochester et al. 1977; Rutter 1985; and Sabsay and Kernan 1983) fall within this category, as do ill-constructed orientation or complicating action sections of narratives (Labov and Waletzky 1967).

In the following extract from Sabsay and Kernan (1983: 28), a mentally retarded woman, Pat, has been talking about two boyfriends, Luke and John. When Pat uses the pronoun *he* in line 2, it is obvious to her who the referent is. The fact that she has not taken the role of the researcher in designing her utterance is evidenced in line 5 by the researcher's incorrect guess as to the referent (*John* instead of *Luke*).

Extract 1

1.	Pat:	So we went out there. Outside.
2.		Y'know, <u>he</u> says, "Wanna go outside?"
3.		<u>He</u> says, "Come on, go outside, it's
4.		too stuffy in here."
5.	Researcher:	Who's this? You and <u>John?</u>
6.	Pat:	<u>Luke.</u>
7.	Researcher:	Luke. Okay.

Rochester et al. (1977) further observe that a person listening to a schizophrenic speaker often has to search for information that in fact is

---

[3]Transcription conventions by Tannen (1984):

Brackets between lines indicate overlapping speech
Two people talking at the same time
Brackets on two lines
      indicate second utterance latched onto first without a perceptible pause
: elongation of the preceding sound (e.g., choo:se)
. . noticeable pause or break in rhythm
<u>underlinings</u> direct the reader's attention to portions of the extract discussed in the text

In addition, where deemed relevant to the analysis or interpretation, the length of a pause is given to the nearest tenth of a second; for example, (0.6) = pause of six-tenths of one second.

never given or is given in ambiguous form. Extract 2 from Sabsay and Kernan (1983: 289) supports a view of mentally impaired speakers forcing their normal interlocutors to do whatever work is necessary to make sense of what was just said. In this extract, Elva omits parts of the complicating action of her narrative that would provide information critical to the listener's understanding.

Extract 2
1. Researcher: Hi, Elva, how are you doing?
2. Elva: I just asked this guy where he worked. I threw the
3.   paper on the ground. Do you think I should go back
4.   for it?

As the conversation progressed, the researcher was able to reconstruct approximately what had happened. At a bus stop, Elva had seen a man whom she thought she knew. When she asked him where he worked, he started to write his name on a piece of paper. She took the paper and threw it on the ground because she was afraid of strange men making advances to her. Elva's paranoid belief that people were following her at the time caused her to think about going back and getting the paper before they could use the fingerprints on it to find her. The fact that Elva thought she had provided the researcher with enough information to formulate an answer to her question *Do you think I should go back for it?* indicates a severe problem on her part in taking the role of the other.

Lexical problems

Manifestations of production problems at the lexical level are neologisms, which include coinage of new words as well as reassignment of the meaning of common words and overuse of empty words. In her examination of the discourse of thought-disordered schizophrenics, Carpenter (1982: 568ff.) relates schizophrenics' use of neologisms, such as *corpuller, eyecudescence,* and *torron,* to their inability or unwillingness to take the role of the other in conversation. She observes that, when using a neologism, schizophrenics do not pause to allow themselves a moment in which to gauge whether the listener is "with them" or to "set off" their neologisms with special intonation to alert the listener to pay special attention. Their intonation could be described as an "excited monotone" not amenable to interruption or interaction. Often schizophrenic speakers do not respond at all to queries, interruptions, or other obvious signs of lack of comprehension.

Besides the coinage of new words, a common word may be assigned a different meaning. In an example cited in Carpenter (1982: 567), the lexical item *apartment* is used by a schizophrenic speaker to mean not a place to live but a "thing apart."

Extract 3
1.   As a child, I was already an apartment.

This unconventional meaning is a source of confusion to the listener and provides evidence that the speaker is unable (or unwilling) to recognize that the conversational other is incapable of immediately decoding the idiosyncratic meaning. This reassignment of meaning is not always a one-time occurrence. The Alzheimer's patient in my study, Elsie, used the word *dress* in conversations six months apart to refer to paintings in two different locations in the health care center.

Another lexical phenomenon that causes difficulty for the conversational partner is the use of what are called "empty words" in the literature. These words include (*some*)*thing* or *kind* for inanimate objects, *somebody* or *one* for people, *place* for locations, and so on. In extract 4, Elsie and I are looking at a group photograph containing her husband. It was not possible for me to determine what "things" Elsie was referring to.

Extract 4
1. Elsie: There's mine. My husband⌐
2. Heidi: ⌊That's your husband
3. Elsie: this, uh. uhhuh. And that was when he was younger
4.   and now he's of course older⌐and they
5. Heidi: ⌊uhhuh
6. Elsie: have.. you see they have a whole lot of *things*
7.   around⌐
8. Heidi: ⌊yes⌐
9. Elsie: ⌊getting into these different *things*
10.   and having (em in) and getting a lot of *things*
11.   done.
                                        (March 5, 1982)

When Elsie had problems finding a word in our conversations through fall 1982, she occasionally used circumlocutions or semantically related words that indicate a greater orientation to the other than do newly coined words, inexplicit words, or completely unrelated words reassigned to take the place of the "lost" words. After that point, she stopped using circumlocutions and semantically related words. The fact that Elsie provided a decreasing number of clues to her intended meaning suggests that she was becoming less able to provide the informational help she needed to offer her partner in order to maintain a successful conversation.

Topical problems

Topic shifts perceived as inappropriate by the conversational partner are another manifestation of an underlying difficulty in taking the other's perspective in the interaction. In their pragmatic evaluation of the senile elderly, Hutchinson and Jensen (1980) found that senile elderly frequently introduced new topics before previous topics were brought to a close. In her case study of a thought-disordered schizophrenic referred to as X, Chaika (1974: 269) provides an example of change of topic within the patient's own monologue. While talking about her pets, X says:

Extract 5
1. (pause, drop to low pitch, as in an aside) I had a little goldfish too like a clown.
2. (pause, higher pitch) Happy Halloween down.

Chaika observes that utterance 2 does not fall within the general topic of pets or goldfish, but appears to have been triggered by the phonetic features (*down* and *clown* rhyme) or possibly a semantic association between *clown* and *Halloween*. It is not so much the topic switch within the monologue that is problematic, Chaika argues; it is that the switch is not marked as such for the listener's benefit by a phrase such as *oh, that reminds me* or *not to change the subject*.

Problems with indirectness

The preceding discussion of problems in underaccommodating the conversational partner has been limited to utterances produced by mentally disabled interlocutors. It is important, however, to understand that this distinction between disabled and normal is not hard and fast and that others besides the mentally disabled have trouble taking the perspective of a conversational partner. In extract 6, I underaccommodate to Elsie's ability to comprehend by overestimating at that point the amount of interpretive work Elsie is able to contribute to the discourse. Comprehension problems are the result.

Extract 6
1. Heidi: Okay, now I'll take the people to third and fifth first and
2. then *I'll come back for people who go to second,* so *I'll be back*
3. *for you* ⟨to Elsie⟩. . . .
4. *I'll come back for the people on second,* cuz I can't I
5. can't take everybody, okay?
6. So *I'll be I'll be right back.* . . .
7. Elsie: (Are we going) Are we going now?
8. Heidi: *I'll be right back*
9. Elsie: We're leaving?
10. Heidi: *I'll be right back* . . *for people who live on second.*
11. so
12. Elsie: (does that mean) am I to go?
13. Heidi: No you just stay right here. *I'll be right back*
14. *for you.* Okay?

(November 27, 1981)

In this extract, Elsie appears to be unable to infer what *she* is supposed to do from *my* statements about *my* actions. Elsie has to ask three times whether she is leaving (*Are we going now?*, *We're leaving?*, *Am I to go?*), the third time explicitly asking whether what I said meant that she should go too (pinpointing her problem in making the inference). Only after that do I specifically say *no* and tell her what *she* should do (*you just stay right here*) before repeating what *I* was going to do.

Elsie's difficulty in interpreting indirectness (to which I underaccommodate) may be related to her difficulty in taking my perspective. If she cannot take my perspective, she is unlikely to be able to attribute my possible motivation for using indirectness (I was in fact attempting to downplay the residents' relative dependence on me by not telling them directly what to do). Brown and Levinson (1987: 268) suggest that this is a general problem of indirect uses of language: "Decoding the communicative intent relies on the mutual availability of a reasonable and particular motive for being indirect."

The decreased ability of the mentally disabled to take the role of the other in conversation does not appear to be uniformly distributed across all facets of language use. Whereas numerous examples of underaccommodation to the conversational partner in terms of his or her ability to comprehend or to overall coherence requirements (such as those discussed earlier) can be found in conversations involving the mentally disabled, it appears that these individuals can accommodate quite normally to their interlocutor's more procedural conversational needs. The conversations between Elsie and me contain numerous instances of intricate structural manipulations. These include Elsie's repeating a portion of her utterance that was overlapped by my question and then continuing on to respond to the overlapped question, and asking follow-up questions to a question I posed before giving an appropriate response to my question. Price-Williams and Sabsay (1979) observe that even the severely mentally retarded are able to take question-answer turns, although they are often unable to fill those turns with an appropriate answer.

Examination of my longitudinal data with reference to the discourse management processes discussed in Coupland et al. (1988) indicates that Elsie's ability to attend to face concerns remained intact longer than her ability to accommodate to overall coherence and the addressee's ability to comprehend but deteriorated earlier than her ability to accommodate to the more mechanical needs in conversation. As Elsie expended increasingly less effort on communicative tasks over time, the situation was manifested differently in her own language use and in interactions with others. Ramifications of less effort by Elsie for her *own language use* included greater use of automatic language as opposed to creative language. Ramifications of less effort expended in *interactions* included taking the role of another person less completely and less frequently, carrying out only those mechanical tasks that were most critical for conversational maintenance. This resulted in the conversational partner's having to do more of the total discourse work if the interaction was to be maintained at a relatively successful level.

5.4. Discourse attuning processes in reaction to communicative nonsuccess

We have just seen how underaccommodation (unintended though it may be) can be the cause of interactional nonsuccess. In this section, we examine accommodative strategies that the normal conversational partner may employ in the face of this nonsuccess by attending to the disabled individual's ability to comprehend as well as to her conversational needs. These conversational needs are attended to by discourse management strategies that are understood by Coupland et al. (1988) to be directed toward "discourse field" (ideational content construction), "discourse tenor" (management of interpersonal positions, roles, and faces), and "discourse mode" (formal procedural-textual dimensions of interaction) [see Gregory and Carroll (1978) and Halliday (1978) for discussion of this tripartite distinction].

Before we look at the specific manifestations of this accommodation, however, it is important to note that the decreased ability of the mentally disabled speaker to take the role of the other results in more than problems of understanding for the normal other. Such nonsuccesses are a source of interpersonal feelings of embarrassment or inadequacy and contribute heavily to the stigma that is associated with mental disability. In their discussions of stigma, Goffman (1963) and Katz (1981) suggest that stigmas related to speech or communication (which we have seen to be a part of mental disability) are worse than physical stigmas, which can more easily be concealed, because the communicative stigmas are made obvious each time the individual speaks. These communicative difficulties increase the tension found in virtually all conversations between getting information across and maintaining face, as the interlocutors try *not* to draw attention to the problems caused by mental disability in the interaction.

Because this section examines *my own* use of language in interactions with Elsie, it is important to establish the methodological legitimacy of the analysis. Although my discourse analytic approach here is introspective and informed by ethnographic detail available through my own participation, my own communicative behavior could not have been affected by my research interests, since I had not considered the role accommodation was playing in the conversations until after the final recording had been made. Because determinations of the extent to which one partner is taking the role of the other *in a natural setting* rely on an insider's knowledge of what has been shared over time [see Blakar (1985) for discussion], I argue that it is legitimate (if not imperative) for the analyst to be in the role of participant-observer. Of course, this methodology has limitations, as do all methodologies, and should be understood as a personal research approach, such as the one for which Kitwood (1988: 176) argues to *supplement* the technical approach generally used. (Kitwood's argument addresses senile dementia specifically, but I suggest that it can be expanded to include the populations discussed in this chapter.)

The key to a personal approach is that it does not "stand outside," taking the position of a detached and unaffected observer. At its core, it works interpretively and empathically, going far beyond the measurement of indices or the codification of behaviour. In all of this the researcher takes a personal risk. . . . *It is on the ground of our own experience in relationship that we can gain some inkling of what is happening to another.* (My emphasis)

Question strategies

The analyses of question and response strategies in this chapter were carried out on five conversations that took place between Elsie and me in March 1982, September 1982, March 1984, July 1985, and March 1986. These conversations, selected from among the fourteen conversations in the corpus, are lengthy exchanges that represent different phases of Alzheimer's disease. In the course of the five conversations, 598 questions were asked – 217 by Elsie and 381 by me. The fact that these conversations comprise 60.2 percent of the total speaking time (two hours and thirty-nine minutes out of a total four hours and twenty-four minutes) and contain 59.7 percent of the total questions asked (598 of 1,002) indicates that the distribution of questions in these conversations is representative of the entire corpus. In preparation for an examination of the appropriateness of the responses to these questions (Hamilton 1989), this set of 598 questions was reduced to 521 according to the following criteria: A question was discarded from further analysis if (1) because of overlap, the question was apparently not heard; (2) the speaker gave the conversational partner no time to respond and immediately followed with a reformulation of or an answer to her own question; (3) the question was addressed to a third party; or (4) the response was not discernible to the degree necessary to evaluate its appropriateness.

Besides examining syntactically marked questions, I included in the analyses declarative questions (see Quirk et al. 1972: 392) whose syntactic form is that of a statement (e.g., *You don't know how to do that?*) but that are spoken with a final rising question intonation, as well as sentence fragments containing no finite verb (e.g., *The most things to order? The most books here?*), which are spoken with a final rising question intonation. Contextually defined questions that may be interrogative in force but not in form were excluded from the present examination. Considering the comprehension and production difficulties in the conversations under study, it seems to be more straightforward to work with grammatically defined questions (which may have functions other than interrogation) rather than to attempt to determine what may or may not function as a question in a given context.

Within a framework of division of labor in discourse, this section examines my accommodation in question strategies to Elsie's interpretive comprehension and to discourse mode over the four-year period. Elsie's continually decreasing ability to carry out her share of the discourse work necessitated constant reassessment on my part as I attempted to make adequate and appropriate compensation in order to buoy up what I perceived to be her competence level in the interactions. Overestimation regarding the extent of Elsie's problems occasionally led to overaccommodation on my part.

A division of labor perspective on discourse holds that a speaker's encoding work is counterbalanced by a listener's decoding and interpretation work. "Division of labor" refers to the relative amounts of work that the conversational partners contribute to the superordinate goals of making sense of what is going on, attempting to achieve conversational coherence, saving mutual face, and sustaining the interaction. This discourse work can be in the form of structural-sequential work ("mode"), such as taking or relinquishing a turn at talk, which keeps the conversational mechanism going; face work ("tenor"), such as saving the partner from embarrassment; and ideational content work ("field"), such as selecting a topic (speaker's work) or drawing an inference (listener's work) from an indirectly stated utterance.

The listener may be asked to call on knowledge from shared experiences with the speaker or from generally known cultural and world knowledge in order to make sense of what the speaker is saying. Regarding work on the speaker's side, he or she needs to realize when pieces of information critical to the understanding of his or her linguistic contribution are, for example, not yet part of the listener's knowledge bank.

The division of labor in discourse can be charted in each of the two fundamental discursive domains – production and comprehension. The speaker has an easier time in the production of discourse if the listener takes some of the "load" off the speaker, for example by being able to infer or generalize from what the speaker has said. And the listener has an easier time comprehending the discourse if the speaker takes over a larger share of discourse work by keeping the listener's perspective in mind.

Within the terms of this general framework, it has been possible to chart a progressive shift in the division of labor in my own interactions with Elsie. An examination of the distribution of the 521 questions across the five conversations under study reveals that Elsie's part in asking questions became smaller and smaller over time, beginning with 57 percent of the questions asked in March 1982 and ending with 4 percent

Table 1. *Relative percentages of questions asked by Elsie and Heidi in five selected conversations (N = 521; actual number of questions in parentheses)*

	Heidi		Elsie	
March 1982	43%	(44)	57%	(59)
September 1982	44%	(52)	56%	(66)
March 1984	63%	(66)	37%	(39)
July 1985	93%	(110)	7%	(8)
March 1986	96%	(74)	4%	(3)
Average	66%	(346)	34%	(175)

four years later in March 1986. Of course, as Elsie asked an increasingly smaller proportion of the questions, my proportion became larger and larger, beginning with 43 percent of the questions asked in March 1982 and ending with 96 percent in March 1986. As Elsie became increasingly unable over time (due to progression of the disease) to use questions to initiate new topics and to follow up on current ones, I attuned to the procedural consequences of this conversational disability by producing an increasing proportion of the total number of questions in our interactions.

Not only did Elsie's production of questions decrease over time, her ability to respond appropriately to wh-questions simultaneously decreased. That I was subconsciously attuning to this disability became clear to me in the process of investigating the appropriateness of responses made by Elsie and me to each other's questions.[4] Contrary to my expectation that, along with the progression of Alzheimer's disease, an increasingly lower percentage of Elsie's responses would be appropriate, no clear trend could be determined. The highest percentage of

[4]Space limitations preclude a full discussion of the considerations that led up to the response appropriateness criteria used in this investigation. Briefly, each response was assigned a number from 1 to 5 to represent its type of appropriateness as a response. The numbers (2–5) representing types of inappropriate responses are *not* meant to designate increasing degrees of inappropriateness; rather, they indicate different *orders* and are meant to help track the types of inappropriateness over time that correspond to the progression of Alzheimer's disease.

1 = fully appropriate response: not necessarily correct, but at least not inexact (2), grammatically or lexically mismatched (3), mismatched type (4), or change in topic/silence (5);
2 = inexact response: information given is too vague to be of use to the questioner;
3 = incorrect response: "incorrect" does not refer to mismatch with real-life facts, but rather to grammatical or lexical disagreement with respect to the question;
4 = disagreement of question type: yes–no answer to a wh-question;
5 = no response (e.g., change of topic or silence).

appropriate responses made by Elsie occurred in September 1982 (62 percent of total responses). The lowest percentage occurred in March 1984 (38 percent), with 51 percent of Elsie's responses in March 1986 being interpreted as appropriate.

It is likely that the answer to this puzzling situation lies with me as Elsie's conversational partner. On closer examination of the data, it appears that in selecting the *type* of question to ask her, I was attuning in view of my preconceptions of Elsie's ability to answer various types of questions. This strategy enabled Elsie, *despite decreasing abilities*, to continue to give a high proportion of appropriate responses. In March 1984, when Elsie had the lowest percentage of appropriate responses in the five conversations (38 percent), I asked the greatest number of wh-questions (38 percent) and the smallest number of yes–no questions (51 percent) of all five conversations. Keeping this in mind, it comes as no surprise that Elsie's proportion of appropriate responses actually *increased* in the July 1985 (45 percent) and March 1986 (51 percent) conversations when I used a decreasing number of wh-questions (11 percent in July 1985 and 8 percent in March 1986) and an increasing number of yes–no questions (63 percent in July 1985 and 72 percent in March 1986). In adjusting my questioning strategies to match what I perceived to be Elsie's decreasing ability to provide appropriate responses to wh-questions, I not only attuned to Elsie's interpretive comprehension but also facilitated her next move.

Extract 7 illustrates how this accommodative shift of question type can take place in real-time interaction as the listener's inability to deal with the more difficult question types becomes apparent to the speaker. The extract begins with Elsie asking me a question (line 1) that I am unable to understand. As the conversation progresses, Elsie's actions indicate that she wants me to push away the protective railing that runs along the side of her bed.

Extract 7

1. Elsie: Will you keep will you keep (till it) please? (0.7)
2. Heidi: *What would you like me to do?* (2.2)
3. Heidi: *Will I what?* (3.5)
4. Elsie: And they (get uh get themselves) to push this
5.   (here. I didn't, here. right) (0.4)
6. Heidi: *What would you like to be pushed?* (0.3) *This?*

(July 1985)

The accommodation begins with my reformulation of an unmarked, open-ended wh-question (*What would you like me to do?*) into a marked, open-ended wh-question (*Will I what?*) when the unmarked version receives no response (2.2-second pause). This marked form, which echoes the syntactic structure of Elsie's question on line 1, can be seen as an attempt to facilitate Elsie's next turn, the reproduction of her original question. Following a somewhat confusing utterance 3.5 seconds after the marked open-ended question (lines 4 and 5), which, contrary to my expectations, was not posed within the *will X . . . ?* framework, I incorporate the verb that Elsie's response contained (*push*) into an unmarked, but focused, wh-question (*What would you like to be pushed?*). I then immediately continue with a focused yes–no question (*This?*), pointing to the railing on the side of her bed. This question asks only for confirmation of its contents by Elsie, allowing her to do an even smaller share of the discourse work. Thus, this sequence clearly shows the continual adjustments made in question formation to accommodate to Elsie's apparent inability to comprehend my question, with the intent to facilitate her next conversational move. This question sequence is typical of Elsie's and my exchanges in the later conversations of 1985 and 1986, as Elsie becomes less able to do discourse work.

Another characteristic of these later conversations is a relatively higher proportion of questions to request actions (e.g., *Can you sit up a little more?*, *Can you drink some?*, and *Can you suck on the straw?*). Fourteen percent of the questions posed in July 1985 and 18 percent of those posed in March 1986 were primarily requests for action compared with no such occurrences in March 1982, 8 percent in September 1982, and 1 percent in March 1984.[5] It appears that my questions were being used less in *verbal* interchanges (such as would be precipitated by the use of a question to request information) and more in situations where an appropriate response to a question could be an *action* rather than a verbal response. This procedural attuning strategy served as a successful means of continuing to carry on a "dialogue" – albeit one composed of verbal questions and nonverbal (action) responses.[6]

Sometimes attempts by the healthy conversational partner to accommodate to the decreasing abilities of the impaired interlocutor are off target. That is, instead of attuning perfectly to the impaired individual's changes in interpretive comprehension or discourse management abili-

---

[5] The primary function of each question asked in the conversation between Elsie and me was determined and the percentage of each type tracked over time. The questions were seen to fulfill the following functions: requesting information, requesting action, checking one's own understanding (or indicating one's own problems in understanding), checking the other's understanding or agreement, exclaiming, and testing-tutoring.
[6] See Snow (1977) for a discussion of this phenomenon in mother–infant discourse.

ties, the healthy interlocutor overaccommodates to these abilities. In their examination of accommodation and the elderly, Coupland et al. (1988) suggest that younger speakers may regularly overaccommodate their speech to the elderly. This overaccommodation occurs because the younger speakers "are accommodating *not* to individuals' communicative characteristics per se, but rather, to those they stereotype the elderly as possessing" (Coupland et al. 1988: 9).

Investigations of question production uncovered two examples of this kind of overaccommodation on my part to Elsie's abilities. Both seem to be related to the characterization of Alzheimer's patients as being context- (or stimulus-) bound (see Appell, Kertesz, and Fisman 1982: Obler 1981), which implies the patient's ability to function at a higher level when talking about the here and now than about distant times and places. Whereas 78 percent (236 of 301) of my questions that make temporal references refer to the present time, only 64 percent (104 of 162) of Elsie's questions with temporal reference do. In addition, a detailed examination of the wh-questions produced by Elsie and me in all fourteen of our conversations reveals that whereas 34 percent (40 of 119) of my wh-questions are *what*-questions that refer to concrete objects in the environment (e.g., *What is this figurine?*), only 7 percent (8 of 112) of Elsie's wh-questions are. This imbalance is especially pronounced in the conversations between May 1982 and July 1985. Although space constraints do not allow a detailed discussion of these examples of overaccommodation, it appears that my perception of the degree of Elsie's context boundedness did not always match reality. This mismatch turned my attempts at accommodation into overaccommodation, the result being a greater amount of talk about the concrete environment and the present time than would have been necessary.

Sabsay and Platt (1985: 114) discuss the detrimental effects of the tight control exerted by nonretarded interlocutors in order to decrease the possibility of nonsuccess in their conversations with retarded individuals. Through their overaccommodation, well-meaning nonretarded individuals may reduce the opportunities for retarded speakers to show their level of competence, making them look more incompetent than they actually are.

Response strategies

As a starting point, utterance design in response to a communicative breakdown can be seen as being designed to negotiate between coherence and face maintenance, as in Lakoff's discussions (1973, 1979) of clarity and politeness. Lakoff (1973) maintains that in most informal conversations, face issues take precedence over clarity, because "actual communication of important ideas is secondary to merely reaffirming and strengthening relationships" (Lakoff 1973: 298). For greater precision, however, it is necessary to incorporate Brown and Levinson's (1987) extension of Lakoff's thinking on politeness, which differentiates between positive and negative politeness. Negative politeness takes into account the interlocutor's need for independence; positive politeness takes into account the interlocutor's need to be liked and to have his or her wishes understood and appreciated. I suggest that the interactional goals of coherence, positive face maintenance, and negative face maintenance should be seen as three axes defining a tridimensional space in which response strategies can be placed[7] (Fig. 1). My claim here is not that particular strategies can be distinguished quantitatively from one another by exact placement in that space, but rather that they can be compared to one another regarding relative focus on the three goals.

Response strategies aimed at reversing the *linguistic* consequence of communicative breakdown, incoherence, would have coherence as their goal; strategies aimed at reversing one of the *social* consequences of communicative breakdown, a feeling of helplessness and dependence, would have negative face maintenance as their goal; and finally, strategies aimed at reversing another *social* consequence of communicative breakdown, a feeling of being an undesirable person, would have positive face maintenance as their goal. In Coupland et al.'s (1988) terminology, the first set of strategies seems to be accommodative in terms of management of the discourse field, the second and third sets in terms of management of the discourse tenor.

In what follows, I discuss strategies used to respond to communicative breakdowns in interactions involving Elsie and me with reference both to Fig. 1 and to the accommodative taxonomy outlined in Coupland et al. (1988). The dichotomy of strategies for dealing with face problems discussed by Goffman (1967), corrective and avoidance strategies, serves as the basic framework for this discussion. However, this framework is expanded to specify a range of other strategies that attempt partial accomplishment of the goals of coherence, positive face maintenance, and negative face maintenance.

First, if I perceive understanding to be more important than face is-

---

[7] I wish to thank the editors of this volume for suggesting that I think beyond a one-dimensional continuum for placement of response strategies.

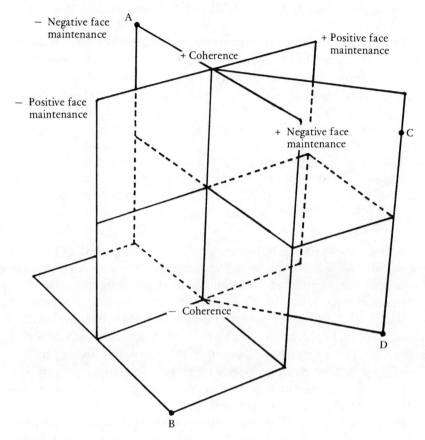

Figure 1. Tridimensional response strategy space.

sues in the interaction, I can take actions to *correct* the misunderstanding inherent in Elsie's question. Other-initiated repairs, however, conflict with the preference for self-correction in conversation (see Schegloff et al. 1977). Brown and Levinson (1987: 38) maintain that correction by the conversational partner threatens the mistaken person's positive face by implying that he or she is incompetent or misguided. I suggest, however, that in the context of disabled speakers, such other-initiated repair seems to represent an equal (or even greater) threat to the negative face, to the extent that pointing out a mistake may highlight the degree of helplessness and dependence of the disabled individual. Furthermore, the threat to the disabled interlocutor's positive face is somewhat offset by the consideration to the positive face shown by the fact that individual's question was answered at all (see the next section on avoidance strategies).

In extract 8, Elsie thinks incorrectly that the current time of day is 2 o'clock (it is actually 11:30 A.M.) because she sees a big wooden "2" on the wall above the nurses' station indicating the second floor. Because this misunderstanding occurs in the context of talking about a party to take place that afternoon, it is important to me that Elsie realize that the party will begin at 2 o'clock, not that it is 2 o'clock now.

Extract 8

1. Elsie: Well this is nu two now, isn't it?⌐
2. Heidi: ⌐yes. no. no.
3.   no. It's only about 11:30 now.

(November 20, 1981)

Following my initial *yes* to her question, either influenced by her use of a negative tag question or by my thinking that she was referring to her floor number, I corrected her explicitly by using three *no*'s followed by the correct time. This example of discourse accommodation seems to be primarily at the levels of field and mode, to the detriment of tenor, in that ideational content and sequential ordering take priority over face concerns. The approximate location of this corrective strategy in Fig. 1 is represented by point A, which takes into account the emphasis on coherence, the threat to negative face, and the somewhat offsetting consequences with regard to positive face.

Second, if I perceive face issues to be more important than the understanding of a proposition in the situation, I can *avoid* talking about Elsie's misunderstanding. Specifically, I can choose for *interactional* reasons not to fulfill her structural discourse expectations, for example, to blatantly not answer Elsie's question. Brown and Levinson (1987: 34) suggest that the choice not to answer can be perceived as a threat to the mistaken person's positive face, in that nonanswers may imply lack of consideration because they show that the interlocutors are not "cooperatively involved in the relevant activity" (ibid.: 125). This strategy carries with it face-threatening consequences for the person carrying out the act as well, which are, of course, not modeled in Fig. 1, in that he or she has been shown to be uncooperative or inept in terms of the sequential necessities of conversations. Because the avoidance strategy by definition avoids direct reference to the source of the misunderstanding, it also avoids threatening the mistaken person's negative face (as discussed earlier). Sacrificing the disabled partner's positive face to save her negative face points to an underlying assumption that the feeling of independence is more important than the feeling of being liked. In extract 9, the staff member and I appear to be accommodating to a stereotype regarding a strong desire on the part of the elderly to be independent [see Pincus (1981), chapter 4, for discussion of the need for dependence-independence in old age].

The precontext to extract 9, which occurs after extract 8, involved continued confusion on Elsie's part regarding when and where the party would be that afternoon. My reminding Elsie that she lives on the second floor prompts her to conclude incorrectly that the party will be on the second floor. When Elsie will not relent in asking if her understanding of the situation is correct (it is not), a staff member and I avoid answering her question, choosing instead to change the topic of conversation from the upcoming party to the lunch Elsie is about to eat. (Elsie's use of the word *side* most probably refers to the wing of the building.)

Extract 9

1. Elsie: Is that right? (on) which side will it? on
2.   which on which side will will it be?
3. Staff: You have a good lunch.⌐
4. Heidi: ⌐Have a good lunch.
                                        (November 20, 1981)

It appears that this discourse accommodation is primarily at the level of tenor, to the detriment of mode and field, in that negative face concerns take priority over the creation of coherence, which would have been facilitated by a more predictable response to Elsie's question. This avoidance strategy is represented schematically at point B, which shows prioritization of negative face concerns and the negative effects on positive face and coherence.

Price-Williams and Sabsay (1979) point out that this type of avoidance of direct reference to the source of the communicative breakdowns may not be as helpful to the mentally disabled as it at first appears. They argue that the distress in conversations between retarded and nonretarded interlocutors is at least partially attributable to the failure of the nonretarded individual to report his or her comprehension difficulties to the retarded speaker.

Third, if I do not wish to point directly to Elsie's misunderstanding by using *no* or some similar linguistic feature, but I do want to get across the correct information, I can change the relevant lexical item or grammatical category that is incorrect in my partner's utterance in the design of my own next utterance. In extract 10, after I tell Elsie that I cannot stay to look at her magazines because I am planning to go downtown with some friends who have arrived from New York, she responds with a tag question (lines 10, 12) including the pronoun *he*, which triggers the disagreement in number (plural vs. singular) in my response (lines 13, 16) to her question. Note the elongation of the *m* in *my* in line 13, which may be due to hesitation caused by my having to design a grammatical disagreement. Elsie's incorporation of my change in number into her next turn (lines 17, 19) indicates the success of this strategy.

Extract 10

```
 1.  Heidi:   I think I'll have to come back another time to
 2.           look at those┌because I'm I'm waiting. I have
 3.  Elsie:               └yes
 4.  Heidi:   some friends from out of town who are here
 5.           now.┌in from New York. So┌I'm going┌downtown
 6.  Elsie:       └mhm                 └Goo:d.  └Goo:d.
 7.  Heidi:   with them.┌but I wanted to stop by and see you
 8.  Elsie:            └oh that's fine
 9.  Heidi:   first.
10.  Elsie:   └Uhhuh. Good.┌Good. He's gonna be here for a
11.  Heidi:               └uhhuh.
12.  Elsie:   while then, isn't he?
13.  Heidi:   M: My friends will just be here until tomorrow
14.           morning.┐
15.  Elsie:          └uhhuh┐
16.  Heidi:               └so they won't be here too long.
17.  Elsie:   Oh I see. So they'll get together and go,┌won't
18.  Heidi:                                           └mhm
19.  Elsie:   they?
20.  Heidi:   mhm mhm.
```

(September 5, 1982)

This response strategy, unlike the corrective and avoidance strategies just discussed, seems to carry out all three discursive tuning processes (field, tenor, and mode). Coherence is established to a greater extent than in avoidance strategies, although arguably not to the degree of corrective strategies. Both Elsie's positive and negative faces are protected, as I cooperate by giving her an answer (which is not the case with avoidance strategies) but simultaneously protect her negative face more than in corrective strategies by giving no direct signal of the problem. The approximate location of this strategy in the tridimensional space is accordingly represented by point C in Fig. 1.

Finally, if I do not wish to draw attention to the fact that I do not understand, but would like to make some linguistic contribution to the conversation, I can incorporate one or more of the lexical items in Elsie's utterance into my response. In this case, accommodation assists in faking understanding, which in turn helps to move the conversation along. In extract 11, Elsie switches the topic with the question *Have they said anything what they're gonna do?* Although I have no idea who the referents for *they* are, I am able to transform Elsie's question into a negative response (*They haven't said anything*) followed immediately by what I wanted to say in the first place (*I'll just be here a few minutes*). The negative form of the response allows me to make an almost effortless link to Elsie's question, despite lack of understanding, and to get on with my own conversational goals.

Extract 11

1.	Elsie:	*Have they said anything* what they're gonna
2.		do?
3.	Heidi:	*They haven't said anything* but I'll just be here a few
4.		minutes.
5.	Elsie:	Oh.
6.	Heidi:	So we'll take you back.
7.	Elsie:	Alright. Sure. You'll just sit down for however long you
8.		want to.

(September 5, 1982)

This response strategy seems to accommodate both the Elsie's positive and negative faces (tenor) while carrying out the procedural-textual needs of the conversation (mode), to the detriment of overall coherence (field). My incorporation of Elsie's words into my next utterance provides a cohesive (i.e., textually attuned) response to her question, as well as a nonthreatening one to her negative face by virtue of no explicit reference to the communicative misunderstanding. The approximate location of this strategy in the tridimensional space is represented by point D in Fig. 1.

It is interesting to compare this strategy of accommodation used by a normal interlocutor of giving lip service to what the disabled individual said (without understanding it) and getting on with his or her own interactional goals with a strategy used by schizophrenics as described by Herbert and Waltensperger (1982: 237): "the situation in which a patient will respond to an interviewer's questions using many of the same words that the questioner has employed." Lehmann (1980), as cited in Herbert and Waltensperger (1982: 238), suggests that "the patient, aware of his ideational shortcomings, uses this strategy as a compensatory mechanism in order to maintain a rapport with the interviewer." Obler (1981) also notes the similarity between normal and disabled behavior. In her discussion of a chapter in Irigaray (1973) that outlines the language behavior of the examiner who is testing Alzheimer's patients, Obler (1981: 379) states, "curiously enough, we note that several of the experimenter behaviors Irigaray lists parallel the dementing behaviors she describes elsewhere."

5.5. Conclusions

The importance of a conversational process often comes into much clearer focus when that process is absent or unsuccessfully carried out than when it is effectively used (Gumperz and Tannen 1979). Analyses of interactions between mentally disabled individuals, such as Alzheimer's patients, schizophrenics, and the mentally retarded, and normal individuals underscore the role accommodation plays in buoying up social interaction. When an interlocutor, because of a psychological, physiological, or developmental dysfunction, cannot take the role of his or her conversational partner, this unintentional underaccommodation can result in communicative breakdown, manifested in incoherence and problems of mutual face.

Maintaining coherent interaction of mutual social acceptability against this backdrop is not easy. Choices need to be made regarding how to deal with the nonsuccess. In an attempt to ward off or lessen the threat of a breakdown, the normal interlocutor can accommodate before the fact to the disabled partner's abilities and disabilities, allowing the disabled interlocutor to function at a higher level than would otherwise be possible. This preventive strategy is effective, of course, only if the normal individual's perceptions of the disabled individual's abilities match actual abilities, that is, that they do not result in overaccommodation. On the other hand, if a specific breakdown has already occurred and must be dealt with immediately, an after-the-fact strategy is selected according to the relative importance of the interactional goals. The intricate intertwining of the goals of coherence, positive face maintenance, and negative face maintenance motivates the fine-tuned linguistic and social accommodation that occurs in response to the breakdown.

The central role that discourse management plays in the sociolinguistically elaborated communicative accommodation theory introduced by Coupland et al. (1988) and Coupland et al. (1990) makes accommodation theory potentially much more attractive and useful to discourse analysts than earlier versions. Its "more integrated recipiency-interested approach" (Coupland et al. 1990) allows us to determine the degree of accommodation at a variety of levels within a single utterance, and to relate it to interactional strategies and goals. For example, the CAT model paved the way for a more intricate discussion of those response strategies to communicative breakdown that fall between the traditional avoidance and correction dichotomy.

In his discussion of Mead, Cottrell (1980) points to the difficulty of designing empirical research involving Meadian concepts for use in applications to problems of social life. The CAT model enabled a systematic discussion of Mead's concept of "taking the role of the other," encouraging us to tease apart the notion into the variety of levels on which the role of the other can be taken. This approach can be helpful both to longitudinal studies in the future, such as in the examination of the "slow and progressive loss of self" in senile dementia suggested by Kitwood (1988: 176), and in studies contrasting the various types of mental disability. In the former case, it is likely that the identification of the gradual deterioration in degree and type of role taking could have consequences for assessment of the level of the disability. In the latter case, it is imaginable that various groups of mentally disabled would have different degrees and types of abilities in taking the role of the other in conversation, which could have consequences for diagnosis. It is hoped that such longitudinal and contrastive studies will be able to elaborate on the discussions in this chapter.

The observations of accommodation discussed in this chapter lead to a methodological recommendation against one-sided analyses of interactions involving a mentally disabled individual in which only the disabled individual's language use is examined. As we have seen, the normal conversational partner's subconscious attuning to the disabled individual's language ability (or as it is perceived by the partner) can steer the interaction in a direction that suggests greater or lesser abilities on the part of the disabled person than exist in actuality. It is imperative that the normal partner's language use be examined as well, so as to be able to assess its influence on the disabled individual's performance.

In closing, it is hoped that insights gained into the causes and consequences of communicative difficulties of the mentally disabled will help us not only to appreciate the vital functions that communicative accommodation fulfills in keeping inconspicuous interaction from becoming noticeably abnormal, but also to determine how our knowledge can best be used to benefit those groups studied here.

References

Alzheimer, A. 1907. Über eine eigenartige Erkrankung der Hirnrinde. *Allgemeine Zeitschrift für Psychiatrie,* 64: 146–8.
Andresen, H. 1985. Selektiv erhaltene sprachliche Fähigkeiten bei schwerer Aphasie. *In* H. Andresen and A. Redder (eds.), *Aphasie: Kommunikation von Aphatikern in Therapiesituationen,* pp. 43–69. Osnabrück: *OBST* 32.
Appell, J., Kertesz, A., and Fisman, M. 1982. A study of language functioning in Alzheimer patients. *Brain and Language,* 17: 73–91.
Blakar, R. M. 1985. Towards a theory of communication in terms of preconditions. *In* H. Giles and R. N. St. Clair (eds.), *Recent Advances in Language, Communication, and Social Psychology,* pp. 10–40. London: Erlbaum.
Brown, P., and Levinson, S. 1987. *Politeness: Some Universals in Language Usage.* Cambridge: Cambridge University Press. [Reprint of Brown, P., and Levinson, S. 1978. Universals in language usage: Politeness phenomena. *In* E. Goody (ed.), *Questions and Politeness: Strategies in Social Interaction,* pp. 56–310. Cambridge: Cambridge University Press.]
Carpenter, K. 1982. Neologisms in "word salad": How schizophrenic speakers make themselves misunderstood. *Berkeley Linguistics Society,* 8: 562–71.
Chaika, E. 1974. A linguist looks at "schizophrenic" language. *Brain and Language,* 1: 257–76.
Cottrell, L. S. 1980. George Herbert Mead: The legacy of social behaviorism. *In* R. K. Merton and M. W. Riley (eds.), *Sociological Traditions from Generation to Generation,* pp. 45–65. Norwood, NJ: Ablex.
Coupland, N., Coupland, J., Giles, H., and Henwood, K. 1988. Accommodating the elderly: Invoking and extending a theory. *Language and Society,* 17: 1–41.
Coupland, N., Henwood, K., Coupland, J., and Giles, H. 1990. Accommodating troubles talk: The management of elderly self-disclosure. *In* J. McGregor and R. White (eds.), *Reception and Response: Hearer Creativity and the Analysis of Spoken and Written Texts,* pp. 112–44. London: Croom Helm.
Crystal, D. 1984. *Linguistic Encounters with Language Handicap.* Oxford: Basil Blackwell.
Goffman, E. 1963. *Stigma: Notes on the Management of Spoiled Identity.* Englewood Cliffs, NJ: Prentice-Hall.
Goffman, E. 1967. *Interaction Ritual.* Garden City, NY: Doubleday.
Gregory, M., and Carroll, S. 1978. *Language and Situation: Language Varieties and their Social Contexts.* London: Routledge & Kegan Paul.
Gumperz, J. (ed.). 1982. *Language and Social Identity.* Cambridge: Cambridge University Press.
Gumperz, J., and Tannen, D. 1979. Individual and social differences in language use. *In* C. Fillmore, D. Kempler, and W. S.-Y. Wang (eds.), *Individual Differences in Language Ability and Language Behavior,* pp. 305–25. New York: Academic Press.
Halliday, M. A. K. 1978. *Language as Social Semiotic.* London: Edward Arnold.

Hamilton, H. 1989. Inappropriateness of response: Longitudinal case study of one Alzheimer's patient. Paper presented at the 64th Annual Meeting of the Linguistic Society of America, Washington, DC.

Helmchen, H., and Henn, F. A. 1987. *Biological Perspectives of Schizophrenia.* Chichester: Wiley.

Herbert, R. K., and Waltensperger, K. Z. 1982. Linguistics, psychiatry, and psychopathology: The case of schizophrenic language. In L. K. Obler and L. Menn (eds.), *Exceptional Language and Linguistics,* 217–46. New York: Academic Press.

Hutchinson, J. M., and Jensen, M. 1980. A pragmatic evaluation of discourse communication in normal and senile elderly in a nursing home. *In* L. Obler and M. Albert (eds.), *Language and Communication in the Elderly,* pp. 59–73. Lexington, MA: Lexington Books.

Irigaray, L. 1973. *Le langage des déments.* The Hague: Mouton.

Käsermann, M.-L. and Altorfer, A. In press. The obstruction of conversation: A polylogue case study. *Journal of Language and Social Psychology.*

Katz, I. 1981. *Stigma: A Social Psychological Analysis.* Hillsdale, NJ: Erlbaum.

Katzman, R. 1985. Current frontiers in research on Alzheimer's disease. *In* V. L. Melnick and N. N. Dubler (eds.), *Alzheimer's Dementia: Dilemmas in Clinical Research,* pp. 1–11. Clifton, NJ: Humana Press.

Kempler, D. 1984. *Syntactic and Symbolic Abilities in Alzheimer's Diesese.* Ph.D. dissertation, UCLA.

Kitwood, T. 1988. The technical, the personal, and the framing of dementia. *Social Behaviour,* 3: 161–79.

Labov, W., and Waletzky, J. 1967. Narrative analysis: Oral versions of personal experience. *In* J. Helm (ed.), *Essays on the Verbal and Visual Arts,* pp. 12–44. Seattle: University of Washington Press.

Lakoff, R. 1973. The logic of politeness. *Chicago Linguistics Society,* 9: 292–305.

Lakoff, R. 1979. Stylistic strategies within a grammar of style. *In* J. Orasanu, M. Slater, and L. L. Adler (eds.), *Language, Sex, and Gender,* pp. 53–78. *Annals of the New York Academy of Science,* 327.

Lehmann, H., and Cancro, R. 1985. Schizophrenia: Clinical features. *In* H. Kaplan and B. Saddock (eds.), *Comprehensive Textbook of Psychiatry IV,* pp. 680–712. Baltimore: Williams & Wilkins.

Mead, G. H. 1934. *Mind, Self, and Society.* Chicago: University of Chicago Press.

Obler, L. 1981. Review of *Le langage des déments* by Luce Irigaray. *Brain and Language,* 12: 375–86.

Obler, L., and Albert, M. 1980. Language and aging: A neurobehavioral analysis. In D. S. Beasley and G. A. Davis (eds.), *Aging, Communication Processes and Disorders,* pp. 107–21. New York: Grune & Stratton.

Pincus, L. 1981. *The Challenge of a Long Life.* London: Faber and Faber.

Price-Williams, D., and Sabsay, S. 1979. Communicative competence among severely retarded persons. *Semiotica,* 26: 35–63.

Quirk, R., Greenbaum, S., Leech, G., and Svartvik, J. 1972. *A Grammar of Contemporary English.* Essex: Longman.

Reisberg, B. 1981. *A Guide to Alzheimer's Disease.* New York: Free Press.

Reisberg, B., Ferris, S. H., and de Leon, M. J. 1982. The global deterioration scale (GDS): An instrument for the assessment of primary degenerative dementia (PDD). *American Journal of Psychiatry,* 139: 1136–9.

Rochester, S. R., and Martin, J. R. 1979. *Crazy Talk.* New York: Plenum Press.

Rochester, S. R., Martin, J. R., and Thurston, S. 1977. Thought process disorder in schizophrenia: The listener's task. *Brain and Language,* 4: 95–114.

Rutter, D. R. 1985. Language in schizophrenia: The structure of monologues and conversations. *British Journal of Psychiatry*, 146: 399–404.

Sabsay, S., and Kernan, K. 1983. Communicative design in the speech of mildly retarded adults. In K. Kernan, M. Begab, and R. Edgerton (eds.), *Environments and Behavior*, pp. 283–94. Baltimore: University Park Press.

Sabsay, S., and Platt, M. 1985. Weaving the cloak of competence: A paradox in the management of trouble in conversations between retarded and nonretarded interlocutors. In S. Sabsay, M. Platt, et al. (eds.), *Social Setting, Stigma, and Communicative Competence*, pp. 95–116. Amsterdam: John Benjamins.

Sacks, H., Schegloff, E., and Jefferson, G. 1978. A simplest systematics for the organization of turn-taking for conversation. In J. Schenkein (ed.), *Studies in the Organization of Conversational Interaction*, pp. 7–55. New York: Academic Press. [Paper first published in *Language* 50 (1974).]

Schegloff, E., Jefferson, G., and Sacks, H. 1977. The preference for self-correction in the organization of repair in conversation. *Language*, 53:361–82.

St. Claire, L. 1986. Mental retardation: Impairment or handicap? *Disability, Handicap and Society*, 1: 233–43.

St. Claire, L. 1989. A multi-dimensional model of mental retardation: Impairment, subnormal behavior, role failures and socially constructed retardation. *American Journal of Mental Retardation*, 94: 88–96.

Snow, C. 1977. The development of conversation between mothers and babies. *Journal of Child Language*, 4: 1–22.

Szymanski, L., and Crocker, A. C. 1985. Mental retardation. In H. Kaplan and B. Sadock (eds.), *Comprehensive Textbook of Psychiatry IV*, pp. 1635–71. Baltimore: Williams & Wilkins.

Tannen, D. 1984. *Conversational Style*. Norwood, NJ: Ablex.

Wertz, R. T. 1978. Neuropathologies of speech and language: An introduction to patient management. In D. F. Johns (ed.), *Clinical Management of Neurogenetic Communicative Disorders*, pp. 1–101. Boston: Little, Brown.

Wood, P. H. N., and Badley, E. M. 1978a. Setting disablement in perspective. *International Rehabilitation Medicine*, 1: 32–7.

Wood, P. H. N., and Badley, E. M. 1978b. An epidemiological appraisal of disablement. In A. E. Bennett (ed.), *Recent Advances in Community Medicine*. Edinburgh: Churchill Livingstone.

Wood, P. H. N., and Badley, E. M. 1980. *People with Disabilities*. New York: World Rehabilitation Fund.

6. Accommodation in therapy

KATHLEEN FERRARA

6.1. Introduction

Support for the original statement of speech accommodation theory (SAT) (Giles 1973) has been amply provided by experimental studies on intercultural convergence of general speech phenomena, such as language choice, accent, and speech rate (Bourhis and Giles 1977; Bourhis et al. 1979). However, recent challenges to the theory to (1) achieve more precision in detailing specific linguistic features involved in convergence or divergence (Coupland 1984; Thakerar, Giles, and Cheshire 1982; Trudgill, 1981, 1986), (2) apply to style shifting evidenced in intracultural as well as intercultural accommodation of speech between speakers of unequal status (Putnam and Street 1984), and (3) account for cooperative encounters in *natural* settings (Coupland 1984) have resulted in further refinement of the theory about language adaptation in response to interlocutors. Increasingly, accommodation theory is becoming concerned with the socially constituted nature of language behavior.

In light of these advances, the central aims of this chapter are to expand the range of naturally occurring settings for which information is available and to offer a close linguistic analysis of accommodated speech in the natural setting of psychotherapy. At the same time, the chapter offers methodological criticism and suggestions for innovations that may result in a clearer understanding of accommodative processes.

The setting to be examined, psychotherapy, is a highly focused dyadic experience between a client and a trained psychotherapist. Paradoxically, in psychotherapy, language serves both as the method of diagnosis and as the medium of treatment. Relatively little is known about the processes involved in the interaction because the speech event has emerged only in the twentieth century. Since World War II, psychother-

187

apy has gained wide recognition and increasing acceptance. Unlike psychoanalysis, an often lengthy and expensive undertaking of up to five years, short-term psychotherapy in the United States has become widely available to working-class people through a broad range of company-paid insurance programs at their place of employment. These employer-sponsored programs typically pay up to 80 percent of the cost of weekly sessions; as a result, psychotherapy is affordable to a growing number of blue-collar workers. This trend, and the increasing familiarity of the public with mental health opportunities, place many speakers of lower-class social dialects in contact with highly educated, typically middle-class professionals who speak different dialects. The fluidity or geographical mobility of Americans, who frequently move from region to region for employment, also increases the incidence of contact between speakers with different regional dialects. Such dialect contact, and the resulting opportunity for accommodative behavior in a cooperative situation, serve as a basis for this chapter's focus on dialect differences. Quite often, clients may speak a different regional or social dialect from that of their therapist [see Giles (1973) for an examination of regional differences in dialects].

A specific reason for assuming that accommodative behavior is evident in therapy lies in the general belief of therapists that all successful therapy clients become more like their therapists in beliefs and values and that, in part, good therapists model what they consider appropriate behavior for their clients. The chief means of this modeling is through language behavior. Although it is difficult to measure convergence in such intangibles directly, considerable progress has been made by communication accommodation theory (CAT) in measuring convergence (and divergence) of language behavior. Language behavior, which is more readily measurable, may thus be an excellent tool to gauge more fundamental convergence between therapist and client and to measure how well therapy is progressing.

An understanding of speech accommodation processes may provide a powerful predictive tool for therapists interested in assessing or researchers interested in measuring the progress and possible outcome of therapy. Lennard's (1962: 225) suggestion that growing similarity in the verbal formulation of experience may also correlate with a growing similarity on deeper, more lasting aspects of patient attitudes and behavior can be utilized to make predictions about therapeutic outcomes. That is, convergence on the linguistic level may precede a change on other levels of behavior. Conversely, the documentable absence of accommodation might prove fruitful in confirming a therapist's suspicion of resistance, a frequent clinical problem.

An additional advantage of looking at psychotherapy from a CAT perspective is that if concerted language behavior or speech accommodation is indicative of increased rapport between client and therapist, and if objective measurements can specify which variables change, then such findings can be incorporated into training manuals for beginning therapists. Making explicit to therapist-trainees what are conscious or unconscious processes of experienced therapists could facilitate more rapid utilization of rapport-building techniques. Given current economic pressures that influence the trend to briefer therapies, such explicit training could be valuable.

Whereas early advances in SAT development relied heavily on experimental manipulation, work by Bell (1984) and Coupland (1984, 1985) has increasingly sought to refine the theory to account for language as it is actually used in a wide variety of everyday settings. The present chapter follows this trend but acknowledges that a full range of techniques of analysis is needed. Just as both subjective and objective measurements are informative, it is necessary to continue to test the applicability of current formulations with both experimental *and* observational studies in order to advance our understanding of how people accommodate and why some situations and some individuals produce different types and rates of accommodation. The present work is based on tape-recorded observational data supplemented by interviews with clients and therapists.

It is interesting that most previous studies look at short-term contact between speakers with *socially* different dialects. However, as Giles (1973) and Trudgill (1981, 1986) point out, accommodation is also possible between speakers with *regionally* different dialects, as well as in long-term contacts over a period of years.

Coupland's (1984) travel assistant study, for example, a thorough and linguistically precise study of phonological accommodation, examines within-speech community variability between a Cardiff travel assistant and fifty-one clients, only one of whom had previously conversed with the assistant. The conversations recorded lasted for five to ten minutes. Likewise, most interview situations are between strangers. What results from such studies is an accounting of *instant accommodation*. This involves nearly immediate shifts based on early recognition by the interlocutor of salient interpersonal accent differences. It is no mistake that the linguistic level of accommodation most readily measured in a short span of time is the phonological level. This is the case because a single utterance can contain many tokens of an individual variable. These large numbers result in a valid and reliable picture. But this is not the whole picture. As research on CAT continues, we should remember that any adequate theory of communication accommodation will account for shifts in short-term, long-term, and mid-range lengths of contact. Likewise, an adequate theory should account for speech accommodation on levels other than the phonological. It should not surprise researchers if the findings from each type differ somewhat.

For speech accommodation, it is conceivable that different linguistic levels – phonological, morphological, syntactic, semantic, and discourse – would favor differential lengths of time for accommodation to develop. For example, in order to study syntactic shifts, we might need long stretches of discourse or small samples over time. The current study is concerned with accommodation on more than one linguistic level. Bell's (1984) statement that "different linguistic variables are differentially affected by accommodation" is worthy of exploration. It would be useful to know if individual speakers are more willing, or more able, to accommodate on one linguistic level than another and to achieve an understanding of the factors involved. Trudgill's (1986) question. "What are the limits of accommodation?," and his observation that it could be claimed that morphology and phonology are likely to behave differently in accommodation further invite linguistic analysis of the extent of the phenomenon at varying linguistic levels.

Trudgill (1986) cites Nordenstam's (1979) research on Swedish–Norwegian accommodation, on the lexical and morphological levels, and Rogers (1981) study of English English–Australian English intonation acquisition, on the suprasegmental level, as two examples of work that probes the linguistic levels of accommodation. Notably, as described, both works involve accommodation "beyond the speech community," over time, on levels other than that of segmental phonology.

Unfortunately, little inquiry has been made into accommodation at the grammatical level; the current study attempts to address this issue. Longitudinal studies such as Trudgill (1981), Shockey (1984), and Nicholson (n.d.), examining long-term accommodation between English and American interlocutors, demonstrate the value of adding a time dimension. In a 1978 study. Douglas-Cowie provided a semilongitudinal analysis by dividing speech recorded in a two-hour interview in half. We would anticipate that with longer exposure to an interlocutor, the participants would be afforded additional time to build their *expectations* of the speech pattern frequency of their conversational partner and, after processing them, be able to track or converge on even complex syntactic patterns.

Expectation is an important variable that has been little studied but that undoubtedly affects the amount and extent of accommodation. I argue that objective measurement of short-term accommodation between interlocutors who have little or no expectation of further interaction may underrepresent the extent of linguistic convergence between speakers of unequal status. It may be that speakers who intend or expect to have further discourse in future cooperative encounters are more highly motivated to attend to the relative frequencies of salient interpersonal differences in language.

For these reasons, one portion of the current study investigates rates of accommodation at three different times in weekly, hour-long sessions between interlocutors who expect to have further cooperative interchanges on a weekly basis: a therapist and client in psychotherapy. A separate segment investigates whether accommodation is visible on the discourse level.

The chapter is organized as follows. Section 6.2 contains a brief review of previous research on language in psychotherapy and an overview of prior research dealing specifically with speech accommodation in psychotherapy. Section 6.3 describes the methods of the study, and Section 6.4 reports on the findings. Section 6.5 examines the possibility of communication accommodation on the level of discourse. The chapter closes with a brief discussion of the potential applicability of such studies for enhancing understanding and control of psychotherapy outcomes.

6.2. Language, accommodation, and psychotherapy

Despite Sapir's (1927) proposal some sixty years ago that linguistics could provide valuable insights for psychological research, only a handful of studies have attempted such interdisciplinary or applied work, and none until mid-century. Nonetheless, the intricacy and subtlety of therapists' language behavior with their clients has commanded the interest of sociolinguists (e.g., Ferrara 1988a; Labov and Fanshel 1977; Wodak 1981) and ethnomethodologists (Sacks 1970–1; Turner 1972). As a result of advances in linguistic science, a growing number of psychologists and psychiatrists have recently begun to pay close attention to language in psychotherapy (e.g., Elliott et al. 1987; Havens 1978, 1979, 1980, 1984; Hill 1978; Russell 1987; Russell and Stiles 1979). This increased attention to language is appropriate since, perhaps more than any other professional service encounter, psychotherapy is dependent on language.

In this section, I review some of the important studies of therapeutic language by linguists, anthropologists, psychologists, and psychiatrists and discuss those few studies that have examined accommodative language behavior in therapeutic interchanges. Prior research tended to focus on only one side of the therapeutic dyad – examining either client or therapist speech but typically not both. Such studies fail to take into account a concern with communication behavior and psychotherapy as an *interpersonal* creation of a situation. In fact, interlocutors show continual adjustment to the immediate context of ongoing talk, and CAT affords a vantage point from which to survey such interaction. Likewise, previous studies of language use in psychotherapy failed to take into account the possible effects of dialect differences between client and therapist despite the fact that more and more working-class clients are availing themselves of therapy from largely middle-class therapists. The present study assumes that discrepancies at the dialect level are a primary ground on which client and therapist seek to establish rapport.

In the early 1950s, an interdisciplinary group of linguists, anthropologists, and psychologists began working together at the Center for Advanced Study in the Behavioral Sciences on a project to apply the then recently developed tools of phonetic description and kinesics to video recordings of psychotherapy. Because therapists make interpretations and assess effectiveness largely on the basis of impressions gained through evanescent data (language interaction in real time), the prospect of an objective record with which to verify or modify clinical assessments was (and is) appealing. In 1957 a rationale for such work was proposed by Pittenger and Smith. McQuown (1957: 86) optimistically saw the potential applicability and relevance to other fields:

> It is to be hoped that workers in the field of psychiatry may eventually be able to call upon linguists and other social scientists doing research in these areas to provide them with useful tools for the purposes of critical diagnosis, for checking on the progress of therapy, for prescriptions as to therapeutically desirable personal and social contacts, and for the communication of their intuitions in demonstrable and testable form to their fellow psychiatrists and to their trainees in the practice of psychiatry.

Pittenger, Hockett, and Danehy (1960) present an encompassing treatment of the beginning minutes of an initial therapy session with a thirty-year-old female outpatient who claims she would be happier if her husband died. The microanalysis is divided physically into two parts: (1) a transcription that includes intonation, duration of pauses, features such as hesitation, sighs, gasps, coughs, throat clearings, and variation in speech rate, volume, and tone quality, and (2) an exploration of what actually happens during the interview in an interpretive analysis that closely parallels the transcription. The authors proceed on the assumption that overall impressions of a person can be subdivided into specifiable observations of language use. The analysis benefits from the additional insights of two psychiatrists but is beset by the same problem faced by McQuown's analysis: The reader has no principled way to follow the leap from description to interpretation.

From an ethnomethodological perspective, Turner (1972) describes the social-organizational features of *group* therapy, using segments of actual language to illustrate various properties of "therapy talk." Turner is concerned with how group therapy is officially begun, how newcomers are ratified, what constitutes pretherapy talk, how the therapist exercises control, and the role of silence. Turner raises ethnographically sensitive questions about how therapy talk differs from other kinds of talk and the different entitlements of the participants. Sacks (1970–1) also bases a number of observations about sequentiality in ordinary conversation on extracts from group therapy.

Similarly, the work of Duncan (1972), influenced by Goffman's insights on face-to-face interaction, bases observations of signals and rules for turn taking on videotapes of therapy. Although Duncan's research utilizes therapeutic discourse not so much to illuminate aspects of the speech event as to illustrate strategies of turn taking, and includes no segments of language in use, his work is important in that it highlights the problematic nature of categorizing verbal behavior.

A parallel but independent avenue of research on language in psychotherapy involves the attempts of numerous psychologists to achieve an adequate categorization schema for encoding the types of verbal behavior that occur there. Such coding devices are useful in quantitatively measuring verbal responses, increasing objectivity, and increasing reliability. Bales (1950), Gottschalk and Gleser (1969), Gottschalk, Lola, and Viney (1986), Russell and Stiles (1979), and Stiles (1978, 1979) offer proposals for categorizing response modes or discourse. However, different labels and definitions have hindered comparability across studies.

In recognition of this, Elliot et al. (1987) is an attempt by six psychologists to promote comparability across coding studies by synthesizing seven of the more than twenty category systems that have been developed to distill six primary response modes (or types of talk) from the various coding schemes in the literature. These are question, advisement, information, reflection, interpretation, and self-disclosure. The authors base their findings on a common set of seven tape-recorded therapy sessions by seven diverse practicioners. Russell (1987) presents an overview of established coding systems.

In addition to being a major interdisciplinary effort, Labov and Fanshel (1977) has firmly established discourse analysis as an important approach in linguistics. Even a decade later, it represents the most faithful textual study of discourse to date. The book builds upon two works: Pittenger, Hockett and Danehy's (1960) *The First Five Minutes* and *Playback: A Marriage in Jeopardy Examined*, Fanshel and Moss's (1971) analysis of six sessions of a family interview.

The success of Labov and Fanshel (1977) lies in their making the basis of their insights more explicit than previous works had done and in their proposal of twenty general rules of discourse. The research assumes that therapeutic interaction is sufficiently comparable to all types of conversation that general principles about ordinary talk emerge from a study of therapeutic discourse.

Subsequent to Labov and Fanshel, Wodak and Flader (1979) contains an article by Trömel-Ploetz and Franck investigating startling deviations from the normal expectations of therapeutic conversations in the form of paradoxical retorts to inpatients. The study is valuable in that these violations help elucidate the unspoken norms and principles that hold in the therapeutic situation. Elsewhere, Wodak (1981) explores problem presentations in group therapy. She concludes, contrary to Hallum (1978), that lower-class speakers can effectively participate in the "talking cure." Wodak also empirically establishes the difference between the two speech events, interview and psychotherapy.

Realizing that "the therapist had to express himself in particular words and these words have received comparatively little attention," Havens (1978: 336), a psychiatrist, applies structural linguistics and argues that different schools or styles of therapy characteristically employ preferred grammatical modes. He claims that psychoanalysis characteristically uses imperatives, whereas existential therapy uses exclamations and rhetorical questions, and counterprojective techniques are characterized by declarative sentences. Havens (1978) explores what he terms "simple emphathic speech" by therapists (e.g., "It hurt." "How much you must feel about him.") in which the therapist puts "the other's state of mind into words." Havens's work is especially attractive to students of language because he provides actual extracts to illustrate his points. Havens (1980: 60) also acknowledges that "the selection of the language in which therapists work has been so largely neglected." Havens (1984) is an attempt to apply Austin's concept of performatives to identify four types of therapeutic behavior: (1) appraising or reckoning, (2) commending or admiring, (3) hoping for, and (4) wishing for.

Phoenix and Lindeman (1982) in DiPietro (1982), like Havens (1978), see different schools of therapy as preferring to employ different syntactic forms. They concentrate on categorizing the use of past, present, and future tenses. However, this categorization is probably premature given the frequent borrowing and eclecticism of the majority of psychotherapists. Leaffer (1982) uses both experimental and descriptive data in a psycholinguistic framework to develop a list of cues to indicate Freud's concept of clinical denial.

Work on metaphor in psychotherapy (e.g., Ferrara 1988a; Lentine 1988; Pollio et al. 1977) shows the ubiquity and importance of figurative language to therapeutic insight. Ferrara (1988a) is a discourse analysis of naturally occurring psychotherapy from an ethnographic perspective that focuses on various discourse strategies utilizing the cohesive devices of repetition and contiguity. Specific chapters deal with narrative structure, the phenomenon of retellings, dream telling through narrative syntax, jointly constructed extended metaphor, repetition as rejoinder, and joint sentence productions in psychotherapeutic dyads.

An early attempt to increase understanding of the interactive process in psychotherapy and counseling is Pepinsky and Karst's (1964) discussion paper titled "Convergence: A Phenomenon in Counseling and Psychotherapy." The study was informed by Lennard's (1962: 225) earlier suggestion that "during therapy there is a growing similarity in verbal behavior between therapist and patient," such that over time they become more alike in the categories of verbal expressions they employ to describe thoughts, feelings, and actions. A quarter of a century later, this statement invites investigation in terms of a more mature CAT. Lennard's content-based study of eight clients and four therapists found that talk about therapy and client–therapist roles decreased over time, whereas affective communication (talk about feelings) increased during the same period. Although the tendency in the small body of research on accommodation in therapy has been to focus on *clients'* shifts in verbal behavior, a few studies have examined therapists' speech with equal care. Pepinsky and Karst acknowledge that therapists' speech may also be characterized by accommodation.

Two related studies utilizing a shared data base, Bieber, Patton, and Fuhriman (1977) and Patton, Fuhriman, and Bieber (1977), found more specific linguistic evidence for a phenomenon akin to convergence (which they term "concerted action") in the verb types they tape-recorded for the first, eleventh, and twenty-fifth psychological counseling sessions of three counselor–client dyads. We can assume that these interchanges bear a great deal of similarity to psychotherapy sessions. Using case-grammar theory, Patton et al. (1977) classified verbs according to case role in three client–counselor dyads and found evidence of "concerted action." They found that across time, counselor and client increased their use of stative verbs but decreased their use of agentive verbs.

Expanding the study to include case roles of noun phrases referring to the client as well as those of verb phrases, Bieber et al. (1977) used a computer-assisted language analysis system (CALAS) to identify diminishing differences in verb-type usage between a single counselor and client. They measured the total frequency of each verb type on stative, experiencer, benefactive, and agentive verbs. They suggest that "tracking" (Jaffee 1964) and convergence between participants in counseling may indicate that clients learn to talk about themselves using the counselor's ways of speaking. An interesting finding is that although they observed "concertizing" of speaking throughout the series of three sessions, in the final (twenty-fifth) session they report client divergence in that "interesting dissimilarities begin to occur." This finding has bearing on the data to be investigated here.

Two subsequent studies, Meara, Shannon, and Pepinsky (1979) and Meara et al. (1981), also bear on linguistic convergence, but in psychotherapy rather than counseling. In an ingenious research design, excerpts from a demonstration film in which three famous psychotherapists, representing three different major theoretical approaches to therapy, meet individually with the same client, Gloria, are analyzed using CALAS. The three orientations are (1) client-centered with Carl Rogers, (2) gestalt with Fritz Perls, and (3) rational-emotive with Albert Ellis. The middle and final three minutes of each session were compared for stylistic complexity as measured by (1) number of sentences, (2) average sentence length, (3) average block length, and (4) average clause depth. As expected, Meara et al. (1979) found that the therapists were significantly different from one another on all four measures. More important, the same client, Gloria, exhibited stylistic complexity that varied in the direction of the particular therapist with whom she communicated. Her speech was simple with Perls and most complex with Ellis. Meara et al.

(1979) cautiously suggest that the data indicate the social influence that therapists exert in therapy and illustrate the modeling of linguistic style that may be preliminary to other possibly substantive concerted actions, such as changes in attitudes, beliefs, and/or behavior.

The second study of the pair, Meara et al. (1981), examines semantic dimensions of verb types from a revised case grammar perspective. Although the data show that the same three therapists (see Bieber et al. (1977) differ in preferred semantic categories, the client, Gloria, did not appear to be influenced in her initial interviews with any of the three therapists. No further sessions were undertaken or analyzed, leaving open the question this study addresses of whether accommodation will ensue in subsequent sessions of serial therapeutic interchanges.

6.3. Description of the study

Selected for analysis in the first segment were audiotape recordings made of the first six sessions of individual psychotherapy between a male therapist and a female client, both in their mid-thirties. Both the therapist and the client gave advance written permission to be recorded. For detailed analysis here, the first meeting, the second meeting, and the sixth meeting were chosen, allowing a look at three important periods in therapy: the initial meeting, the subsequent meeting, and a meeting one month later. These tape recordings and those in the second segment on discourse are part of a corpus of thirty-six hours of therapeutic discourse collected from four therapists and eight clients in Austin, Texas. All of the clients were in therapy with therapists with higher-status dialects who were originally from the northeastern United States. As described by Labov and Fanshel (1977) in *Therapeutic Discourse: Psychotherapy as Conversation*, psychotherapy is composed of a wide array of speech acts, from questions and answers to personal experience narrative to extended metaphor and conversation about the weather. [See Ferrara (1988a) for further discussion.] Because participants are discussing intimate concerns, often of a highly charged nature, fully natural, largely unselfconscious speech is easily obtainable. The findings for therapeutic discourse are similar to yet different from those for other types of focused, cooperative, face-to-face exchanges between interlocutors of unequal status, such as professor and student, supervisor and nurse, lawyer and client, or doctor and patient.

For this case study, the clients and therapists volunteered to have their sessions tape-recorded. No one but the client and the therapist was present at the time of recording, which occurred in the therapists' offices. The female client in the early part of the study, Wilma, is a low-status speaker of highly stigmatized Ozark English (south Midland dialect), similar to Appalachian English. She has complained to the male therapist, Gerry, of low self-image and relationship problems. It is notable that she has recently moved to Texas from her home in the Ozarks, "back in the hills, in a town of 400" in Missouri. She is twice divorced, living with a boyfriend, and has left her two children, aged nine and twelve, with their paternal grandparents in the Ozarks. She is employed as a secretary and hopes to own her own beauty salon. The experienced therapist, Gerry, works in a large mental health office connected with a prominent medical insurance company. He sees clients whose employer pays health care benefits covering 80 percent of their session costs. His dialect was developed in Richmond, Virginia, and Baltimore, Maryland. It is characterized by pronunciation of *rather* as [raðə] instead of the more common American pronunciation, [ræðə]. The therapist's dialect is relatively high in status in the United States because it originates in a focal area; the client's dialect, Ozark English, is comparatively low in status, as it emanates from a relic area that is not a cultural hub. The Ozarks comprise a hilly or mountainous, geographically isolated area roughly at the intersection of three American states: Missouri, Arkansas, and Oklahoma. [See Christian, Wolfram, and Dube (1987) for details of the similarity of Ozark and Appalachian English.]

For the study, four specific linguistic variables from among those detailed for Ozark and Appalachian English by Christian et al. (1987), Wolfram and Christian (1976), and Wolfram (1980) are measured by frequency. Two of the variables to be quantified are phonological and two are morphosyntactic. The variables are detailed here and shown in outline form with examples in (1):

(1)   Linguistic Variables

Morphosyntactic	*Examples*
1. Irregular preterite in place of past participle	I had went to the store.
2. Subject–verb nonconcord	Me and Billy was scared.

Phonological	
3. initial /w/ deletion	When I 'uz (was) a freshman
4. intrusive /t/, especially after /s/	Oncet I had to throw him out

Coupland (1984) has highlighted the problem: How do we determine when a speaker's speech style has shifted? (We can use objective measurement, lay judges' evaluation, or self-report data.) The baseline for the therapist here is usage with another client from the upper middle class, speech to colleagues, and speech to the researcher, but in this study we join the client on her first meeting with the therapist and thus have no information. I assume, along with Meara et al. (1979), that the initial meeting is fairly representative of the client's speech. The presence of over twenty-five nonstandard features reflecting Ozark English in the client's first session provides further support for this assumption.

Both client and therapist in the study provide self-report evidence of psychological convergence, manifested by increasing rapport over time. They engage in what the therapist considers successful therapy. It is important to note that the mutually agreed upon goal for those who enter psychotherapy is to effect change in behavior and attitudes over a series of meetings, and that quite often the therapist becomes a model for the client (Frank 1961).

As formulated by Thakerar et al. (1982), the broad notions of (1) desire for social approval and (2) increased communicative efficiency as psychological motivations for accommodation behavior are sufficiently general to account for the linguistic behavior observed. However, it is essential to note that in this type of professional service encounter, as with Coupland's (1984) travel assistant, there are competing claims on a trained professional. The psychotherapist must walk a thin line between displaying high competence and high benevolence. He or she must foster an atmosphere of acceptance and mutual confidence in order to effect change while also appearing professionally competent. These can often be conflicting demands.

Before considering the longitudinal findings, we will discuss an interpretive model of convergence across time that I propose for psychotherapy. The model is useful in evaluating the data here, and possibly other data as well. An interpretive model along the line of Fig. 1 would show linguistic convergence for psychotherapy at a midpoint in the series of encounters. We might expect *downward* accommodation by the high-status therapist along with *upward* accommodation by the low-status client as they seek a trusting, working relationship. As this relationship continues past the trust-building stage in subsequent psychotherapy sessions, we might expect the therapist to resume normal speech habits while modeling alternative behavior and attitudes for the client.

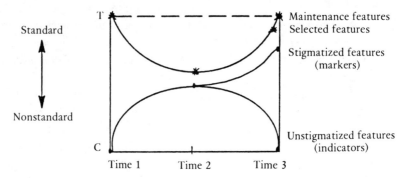

Figure 1. A model of client–therapist convergence across time.

As Fig. 1 illustrates the client over time could be expected to pattern speech so as to continue accommodating on those variables that are heavily evaluated socially (called "markers") and to resume former language patterns on those features that are not stigmatized (called "indicators"). Labov (1972) has observed that linguistic variables can be divided into two types: *markers*, which are subject to both social class and stylistic variation, and *indicators*, which are subject only to social class variation. Labov argues that markers are relatively high in a speaker's consciousness (i.e., are more salient) compared to indicators. Trudgill (1986) has carefully evaluated those factors that contribute to salience and finds that "stigmatization" is one of the leading factors.

To summarize the model, over the *midrange* time period in psychotherapy, and possibly in other serial encounters, we might find fairly rapid convergence after a period of assessment, followed by resumption of individual patterns of linguistic behavior, except on those variables that are perceived as stigmatized. There we would expect longer-term upward accommodation.

This model is confirmed by two clinical psychologists, who state that linguistic accommodation is just one technique, along with nonverbal accommodation, that trained therapists can regularly employ to establish rapport as they begin psychotherapy. The model is also consistent with the finding of Bieber et al. (1977), who found "linguistic convergence in counseling [to be] a policy making process."

In general, the results of the current study show clear support for the hypothesis (Thakerar et al. 1982) that lower-status speakers converge more in the direction of higher-status speakers than vice versa. The findings also illustrate an incidence of hyperconvergence to a point beyond the addressee. In the following section, we consider the four variables and briefly examine the findings to see how they fit the proposed model for midrange accommodation.

6.4. Findings of the study

The first variable: Irregular preterite equal to past participle

In Ozark-Appalachian English (OE and AE), the preterite form of many irregular verbs is extended to the past participle, as in *he has wrote,* whereas Standard English uses *he has written.* This results in identical surface forms for the preterite and past participle for many common verbs, including those in (2).

(2)   went, bit, broke, tore, took, wore, saw, wrote

It is possible that OE and AE speakers use a generalized past form. Some examples from the corpus, including uses of *had did, had saw, have took,* and *have wrote,* are shown in (3).

(3)   But I <u>had went</u> with this engineer from work.
      We were discussin' what he <u>had did</u>.
      I <u>had went</u> to church down South a few times.
      I had talked to him in September I think that year on the phone and <u>I'd saw</u> him once or twice out places but he didn't want to have anything to do with me.
      I <u>would have took</u> time with her.
      Some doctor <u>had wrote</u> that on there.

A summary of the results for all four variables over three sessions is shown in Table 1.

The results for the first variable (irregular past tense equivalent to past participle) are illustrated in Fig. 2. All graphs show the percentage of <u>nonstandard</u> use. The downward projection visible in Fig. 2 indicates that the client shows dramatic accommodation to the standard over time. As illustrated, in the fist session, she uses verbs like <u>had went</u>, <u>has did</u>, and <u>have wrote</u> 83 percent of the time. Fifteen tokens of nonstandard verbs occur. By the second session, the graph shows that she has decreased to 50 percent nonstandard usage. By the sixth session, over a month later, she has accommodated to the standard, which the therapist has maintained. In this session, she uses no irregular past tense as the past participle.

We can be relatively certain that this pattern is not caused by in-

Table 1. *Summary of client and therapist usage of variables over three therapy sessions*

| | Irregular preterite = past participle | | Subject–verb nonconcord | | Deletion of initial unstressed /ʊ/ | | Intrusive /t/ | |
	C	T	C	T	C	T	C	T
First session	83%	0%	17%	10%	23%	0%	50%	0%
Second session	50%	0%	14%	17%	29%	0%	0%	0%
Sixth session	0%	0%	8%	0%	21%	0%	66%	0%

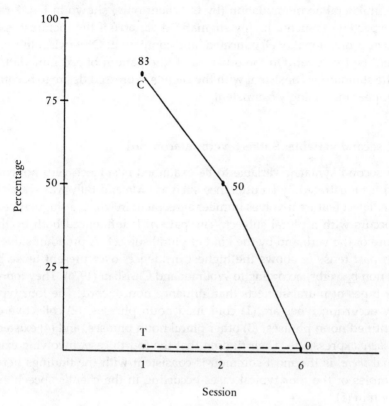

Figure 2. IRREG past tense equivalent to past participle. *Key:* C = —.
T = --.

creased attention to speech because in (4) (taken from the first minutes
of the first session), we see (see the Appendix at the end of this chapter)
that the client maintains an OE nonstandard construction and repeats it
a second time despite a Labovian opportunity for careful speech when
the therapist asks, 'What?'

(4) GW(1):2
    T: So you're not engaged or anything.
    C: No. I took the ring off that night (.) that I found out he <u>had</u>
    <u>went</u> AWOL.
    T: That he had WHAT?
    C: That he <u>had went</u> to San Antonio (.) to get his stuff.
    T: Oh. So you just <u>re</u>cently broke off the engagement?
    C: Uh-huh.

The unilateral accommodation (by the client only) shown in Fig. 2 can be expected on such a highly stigmatized variable if the therapist is to appear professional, well educated, and competent. Otherwise, the cost would be too great. On the other hand, the pattern of accommodation to the standard is consistent with the client's expressed desire to become or appear increasingly competent.

The second variable: Subject–verb nonconcord

The second syntactic variable to be examined is subject–verb nonconcord, as illustrated by an utterance such as "Me and Billy was scared." This dialect feature involves number agreement in which a singular verb co-occurs with a plural subject. The pattern is influenced both by the nature of the verb and by the kind of plural subject. A pronoun subject with past tense *be* shows the highest incidence, over present tense be and non-be verbs, according to Wolfram and Christian (1976). They found four types of plural subjects that influence nonconcord. The four typically occurring types are (1) conjoined noun phrases, (2) collective or quantified noun phrases, (3) other plural noun phrases, and (4) existential *there* expressions. Their finding that the fourth case, involving existential *there*, is the most common is consistent with the findings here. Examples of the four typical cases occurring in the client's speech are shown in (5).

(5)   Subject–Verb Nonconcord
    Conjoined Noun Phrases
      And I didn't know what it WAS until this one night Martín and I was talkin'.
      Her and my daughter gets along real well.
    Collective/Quantified Noun Phrases
      But it seems like a lot of my nightmares has to do with him.
    Other Plural Noun Phrases
      Was those meetings that good?
    Existential There
      There's days that I told myself, "Just block Martín out."
      There's three girls and three boys.
      I'd like to think that there's both sides of me now.

The graph in Fig. 3 for subject–verb nonconcord shows that in Session 1, the client uses singular verbs with plural subjects, as in "This one night Martín and I was talkin' " 17 percent of the time, decreasing to 14

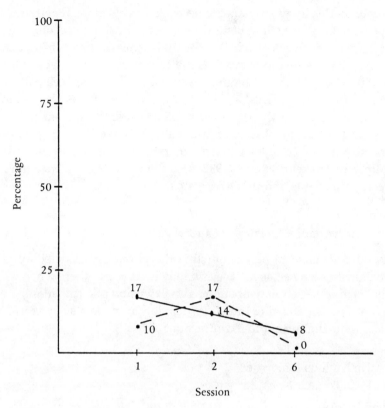

Figure 3. Subject–verb nonconcord. *Key:* C = —. T = --.

percent and then to 8 percent of nonconcord, a reduction of half by Session 6.

The graph indicates a degree of hyperconvergence by the therapist in session 2. Examples of this usage by the therapist are shown in (6).

(6) Therapist Subject–Verb Nonconcord

> T: There's times when you'd want to be able to be very cool and there's times when you'd want to (.) show what's inside.

> T: Uh, does the country girl and the city girl handle that any differently?

As Wolfram and Christian (1976) observe, subject–verb nonconcord is fairly common in informal standard American English, so that utterances like "There was a lot of people there" are not heavily stigmatized in spoken American English. Thus we have a partial explanation for the high rate of convergence shown by the therapist. He is <u>able</u> to accommodate on this linguistic variable because it exists in his repertoire. This appears to be a case of linguistic divergence signaling psychological convergence (Thakerar et al. 1982). A possible explanation of the pattern in Fig. 3 is that the therapist matches the 17 percent he had tracked for the client in Session 1 and accommodates to her previous speech pattern. In the meantime, the client has lessened her frequency, as she continues to do. By Session 6, the therapist no longer utilizes this technique. To do so in light of the client's differentially decreased rate might appear patronizing. The complex pattern illustrated here is consistent with the findings of Thakerar et al.'s (1982) study of a cooperative encounter between participants of differential status.

The third variable: Deletion of initial /w/

The third variable to be examined is the phonological deletion of the initial unstressed /w/, as in "Me and Billy used to fish there when we 'uz kids." This deletion may operate as an extension of a rule in most varieties of English allowing initial /w/ deletion in modals such as *will* and *would*, reducing further to a contraction, as in (7).

(7)
　　He'll tell us tomorrow.
　　He'd come if he could.

For OE-AE, the environments that allow deletion are an unstressed syllable or a position that is not syntactically exposed, (e.g., not clause final or prepausal), as predicted by Wolfram and Christian (1976). Most commonly the pattern involves the past form of the copula or auxiliary be, that is, <u>was</u> or <u>were</u>, as shown in the examples in (8). Quite often it involves the deletion of a following vowel, as in the client's statements in (9).

(8)　*Initial /w/ Deletion*
　　We 'uz lookin' down there at his old car.
　　The girls were both gone when I 'uz a freshman in high school.

(9)　I flew off the handle 'cause I knew he'z at a bar.
　　And it's about fifteen miles from where I'z born and raised.

In cases involving the third-person singular subject pronoun, *he* or *she*, there is resulting homophony with contracted present, past, and present perfect forms, as in (10). We note that in OE-AE, 'He'z gone' can have three readings:

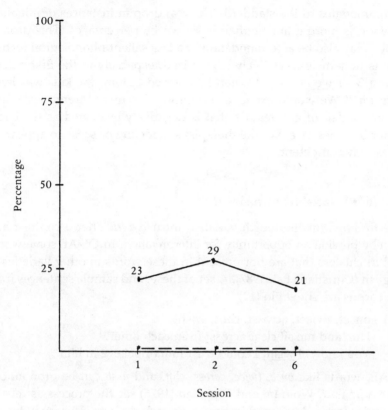

Figure 4. Deletion of initial /w/ in unstressed syllable. *Key:* C = —.
T = --.

	Standard English		OE-AE
(10)	He is gone	–>	He'z gone
	He was gone	–>	He'z gone
	He has gone	–>	He'z gone

This phonological process also affects the pronoun *one* and the discourse marker *well*, shown in (11).

(11) I brought this'n for you to read.
'Ell he makes good money right now but oh I don't know.

The results for deletion of initial /w/ are shown in Fig. 4. What the percentages in Fig. 4 do not reflect is the actual decrease in the client's usage, from eleven and twelve nonstandard tokens in the first two sessions to only five tokens in the sixth session. The low-status speaker accommodates to the standard. The real drop in instances of initial /w/ deletion is more dramatic than is shown by percentages. This drop in usage may also be accommodation of a less salient phonological feature that is nonetheless relatively stigmatized, especially in the first person form (I'z or we'z), as in "When I'z married to him, the kids was livin' with me." We would expect a continuing downward trend, according to the model, of any feature that is negatively evaluated as the client either becomes aware of the therapist's modeling or seeks to appear increasingly competent.

The fourth variable: Intrusive /t/

The findings for the fourth variable, intrusive /t/, offer a contrast and thereby provide an opportunity for interpretation. In OE-AE some words end in clusters that are not present in these words in other varieties of English (Christian et al. 1987). A set of these, and sample sentences from the corpus are shown in (12).

(12)   oncet, twicet, acrosst, clifft, wisht
       Him and me sit clear acrosst from each other.
       You know, I wisht I could trust him or believe in him.

In AE, words like *once, twice, across, cliff,* and *wish* can be pronounced with a final /t/. Wolfram and Christian (1976) see the process as related to earlier forms developed in British English dialects. They may be the survival of archaic forms, along with a set like *amidst, amongst.* If this is the case, this variable may be more accurately described as lexical, not phonological. At any rate, the intrusion of /t/ is more frequent following a spirant, especially /s/, and when the following word begins with a vowel. Wolfram and Christian (1976) point out that in Appalachia this pronunciation is common among different social and age groups and is not particularly stigmatized. Because it is an indicator, not a marker, we would expect, given the model in Fig. 1, that there would be a short period of accommodation, followed by resumption of usage levels. The graph in Fig. 5 shows an unusual pattern of dip and rise at Sessions 2 and 6. This is interpretable in light of the model if we see this as a case of *temporary accommodation* followed by resumption of an unstigmatized usage.

To summarize the findings so far, before turning to the section on accommodation at the discourse level, we have examined four specific variables on which speakers exhibit variable rates of accommodation.

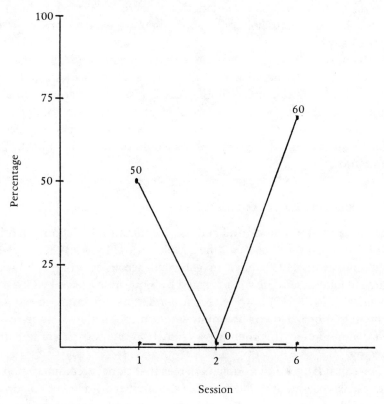

Figure 5. Intrusive /t/.

The findings in this study lend additional support to CAT. The results broadly support the prediction that low-status speakers will conform more to the speech of a high-status interlocutor than vice versa. The study attempted to add linguistic precision to the measurement of accommodation, and to advance beyond description by providing an interpretive model that was shown to account for another type of accommodation in a professional work setting. It revealed a pattern of psychological convergence and explored dynamic rather than static accommodation over a midrange length of time. Additional sampling will show whether the model in Fig. 1 has applicability for other naturally occurring data of midrange time. The case study approach, of course, is not without limitations. The methodological choice that allows depth does not favor breadth. The argument was made that as one more technique of observation, a case study approach over time does allow us to investigate syntactic accommodation, a level of inquiry where we have scarcely begun to gather evidence but where we expect many more discoveries await.

In the next section, I advance the notion that accommodation may also be visible at the discourse level, and that this source, as well as the syntactic, morphological, and phonological levels, can be tapped with longitudinal studies. By analyzing stretches of conversation going beyond the sentence, researchers may discover new dimensions of speech accommodation that will help reveal the extent of the sociolinguistic phenomenon.

6.5. Accommodation at the discourse level

If accommodation is a central process in human interaction, then it is natural to presume that it will be visible on multiple levels of speech. Coupland et al. (1988) have investigated accommodation at the discourse level. Such inquiry is presaged by a question posed by Giles and Powesland (1975: 169) in their recommendations for future research on accommodation: "How is accommodation through speech style related to accommodation in other ways – such as by speech content (e.g. agreeing)?"

Two candidates for discourse variables that signal accommodation are discussed subsequently. Most people are familiar with the often surprising synchrony or well-coordinated speech evidenced by some spouses, couples, boss–employee dyads, and others with frequent contact in longstanding relationships. Hearing a couple tell a story in tandem, simultaneously or with one partner speaking in echolike fashion, is a not unusual social occurrence. Two types of well-coordinated speech evidenced in psychotherapy and in other close relationships are (1) joint sentence productions (collaborative utterances) and (2) repetition used as rejoinder. Two kinds of repetition as rejoinder will be differentiated, *echoing* and *mirroring*. These differences reflect differences in client and therapist modes of communication accommodation.

"Collaboratives" is the term introduced by Sacks (lec. 1, fall 1965) to designate the extention or completion by one person of a sentence begun by another. The syntactic and prosodic clues to juncture points where extension or completion are possible are examined more fully in Ferrara (1988a), but it is sufficient here to note that pauses, word stretches, particles such as *uh*, rising intonation, and conjunctions are the principal juncture points for such spliced utterances. The phenomenon appears to indicate that "one knows what the other person has in mind by saying it for him, as in completing his sentence," according to Schegloff (1984: 42). The linguistic evidence offered by such jointly constructed utterances points to a finely tuned accommodation of thoughts and words. An example from the same client and therapist described earlier follows:

(13)

    GW(1)19

    C: And uh (2) I told him that night I said, "You need to find you somebody that doesn't know anything about you," 'cause I know an awful lot about his past and it's not good. He was a male whore and he was or is and –

    T: **Boy, you sure talk about him in =**

    C: **= a negative way**

    T: Yeah.

    C: Most definitely. Think I hate him? I think a part of me does. The love–hate syndrome? ((laugh))

In the preceding example, Gerry, the therapist (T), initiates a proposition that Wilma, the client (C), completes. A second example from Wilma and Gerry's second session further illustrates joint sentence productions. Data from four therapists and five clients show that a proposition can be completed by either participant. The privilege of completing or extending another's thought in a syntactically and semantically consistent manner is symmetrical between interlocutors regardless of gender or role in therapy.

(14)

    GW(2)21

    C: I I don't understand that part of me. Why why do I do that?

    T: [You kinda play chicken.]

    C: [Like I try to be bad] and then I turn around and try to scare –

    T: You kinda play chicken with yourself, [don't you?]

    C: [Mmhmm] (8)

    T: Well, I don't know. People play chicken to prove something (1) in my estimation. I mean there's a thrilling part to it. **But (.) there's also a uh =**

    C: **= destructive part too.** ((sniffling))

    T: Uh-huh. That's right. Certainly can be. It certainly can be.

Consider a third example of attuned talk taken from the transcript of a session between a different client and therapist, both female. Here the therapist is the completer of the sentence begun by the client (They are discussing the client's use of dreams as a smoke screen to prevent discussion of deeper issues.)

(15)

> MS (2) 16
> T: Oh, you're throwing me little . little [scraps]
> C: [tidbits] Yeah =
> T: = to   distract
>   me. I see. All right.
> C: If I just throw enough tidbits, yeah. **If I throw enough tidbits**
>   **then finally maybe =**
> T: **= I'll get off the path.**

As measured by the SoundCap application to a Macintosh computer, the latched time (=) in the next example of a therapist producing a collaborative sentence with her client is 2/10ths of a second.

(16)

> MS 5(12)
> C: . . . but I think it's gonna be okay when I get back to Belle-
>   meade and I'm working with new people. The woman I worked
>   with this afternoon will be my boss. She's –
> T: You like her?
> C: Yeah. I think we'll be okay. I don't like her calling me honey,
>   though. **I'm gonna have to find some way =**
> T: **= to tell her.**
> C: to tell her. And this is not a person that (2) Somebody that's
>   forty years old I mean maybe can call me honey, but this is a
>   woman that's not even my age. She's mid twenties and she's
>   calling me honey.

Such close tracking of another's thoughts and words, resulting in tightly interlocked utterances and jointly arrived at sentences, far from constituting interruption, appears to be a concertizing of speech indicative of accommodation. Close examination of thirty collaboratives in twelve hours of discourse between therapists and clients indicates that interlocked utterances occur more frequently, up to one every seven minutes, between client–therapist dyads who have worked together over a period of a year or more.

The second type of discourse accommodation to be examined involves the repetition of another's utterance in an adjacent utterance, using the same declarative intonation. Such contiguous repetition is of two varieties. The first, called "echoing," is typically clausal and client generated and ranges from four to nine words. The other, termed "mirroring," is typically phrasal and therapist generated and ranges from three to five words. Discounted here are formulaic echoes characteristic of greetings: A: *Hi*, B: *Hi;* or leave takings: A: *Bye*, B: *Bye*. The focus is on novel, contentful utterances of three or more words. Also excluded is clarification echo, distinguished by <u>rising</u> intonation; this is a separate phenomenon.

The accommodative character of these occurrences is all the more clear when it is noted that languages allow for alternative constructions such as paraphrase and substitution of pro-forms to aid speakers in avoiding exact matching of another's speech (repetition). In English a sentence sequel in agreement can simply be *Yes* or its colloquial variants (e.g., *Yeah*).

To illustrate, for example, in response to a statement such as

A: Their boss rarely goes to meetings.

it is common to hear a paraphrase, such as

B_1:   Yeah, he hardly ever attends them.

or a pro-form, such as

B_2:   Yeah. He seldom does.

A repetition with the identical downward intonation, word choice, and syntax (echoing), as in the following dyadic interchange, is indicative of accommodation:

A: Their boss rarely goes to meetings.
B_3:   Their boss rarely goes to meetings.

When such repetition does occur, the highly accommodative behavior may have social significance.

In the following example, consider the highly accommodative way in which the client Sharon chooses to agree with the therapist Marian's interpretive summary of Sharon's attitude towards her paternalistic boss.

(17)
MS(1)28
C: ((angry tone)) He thinks he's doing me a favor, I'm afraid, by letting me get on my feet financially, and as long as I'm doing $10 a month better than I was doing before, they don't have to consider anything else.
T: (4) So this father is not a real good father.
C: (1) Well, he's helpin' his kids out.

T: (2) **You don't want to be one of his kids.**

C: (2) **I don't want to be one of his kids.** I would never have told him some of those things if he hadn't asked me something about "what did he use" (3) had to do with the word "mistake" or whatever. I don't know what it is.

The client's echo of the therapist's entire nine-word statement stands out from a more usual reply, such as "No, I don't," and appears more emphatic. Echoing in therapy typically occurs after a therapist makes a declarative statement about a client's condition or feeling, based on previous discourse by the client, and when the client wishes to signal emphatic agreement. These echoings represent very important moments in therapy when the therapist has made an insightful interpretation of the client's experience that is so accurate that the client adopts the statement wholesale, accommodating speech to an exact match of the interlocutor's semantic, syntactic, and prosodic features.

(18)   MS(3)

T: You were closed out.

C: I was closed out.

Compare the echoed responses in (17) and (18) to the unaccommodated potential replies, "No, I don't" for (17) and "Yeah, I was" for (18). Both the actually recorded rejoinders display the minimal deictic shift from *you* to *I* that is common in such echoes.

In another example, Marian the therapist and Sharon the client are discussing how Sharon's previous male employer, like her present one, offered her a sympathetic ear and then seemingly turned on Sharon later, in her opinion.

(19)

MS(1)35

C: But (2) you know, I've been in his office too when I was real upset and he stood up and put his arms around me, and I know he felt supportive at the time ((upset tone)) and for the support I got my feet tied to the floor.

T: **You were run over.**

C: (1) **I was run over.** I refused to tell him as much as he wanted to know. I – he said that I agreed to check in with him every week. That's why I got fired. I didn't check in with him. I missed two class meetings at the end of the semester.

By choosing to repeat the statement of another (often about one's own feeling or condition), using the same word choice, syntax, and downward intonation pattern, rather than avoiding repetition with pro-forms or paraphrase, a speaker exhibits an extreme form of accommodation. This matching behavior exhibits a kind of convergence on the discourse level.

Mirroring, on the other hand, is a discourse strategy utilized by therapists. It involves partial repetition by a therapist of a client's statement. In echoing, the client repeats the therapist's speech, whereas in mirroring, the therapist repeats a key portion of the client's utterance with downward intonation. An example from Wilma's session with Gerry will illustrate.

(20)
GW(1)34

> C:) I never knew for a long time what it WAS. **I always felt like there was kind of a turmoil.**
>
> T: **Turmoil**↘
>
> C: Within myself. And I didn't know what it WAS (.) until this one night Martín and I was talkin' (2) and (.) and uh (3) I forgot what that was. I had (.) I wrote it down (.) in a book. And I've got the book out in the car. I should have brought it up. (1) How I'z feelin' that night.

By picking out a phrase from the client's preceding discourse and repeating it (often with a thoughtful, even tone), therapists attempt to draw out an elaboration or further comment on a topic of particular value. Mirroring indicates a willingness to hear more. It is the discourse equivalent of "Go on, tell me more." It indicates that the therapist is actively attending to the talk by the client.

The difference between echoing and mirroring is especially clear in the following discourse segment, where both occur. The extract is again from a session between Marian and Sharon. (They are discussing Sharon's persistent pent-up anger.) Note that both client and therapist converge in speech behavior, using different discourse strategies: one to signal emphatic agreement, one to request elaboration indirectly. Echoing is shown in boldface, and mirroring is underlined.

MS(5)23

> T: . . . You have much to be angry about. It'd probably be better you know, if we can keep it here . for the time being, but you know, **it doesn't always (.) work that way.**
>
> C: **No, it doesn't always work that way.** (11) But I don't feel in <u>danger of exploding</u> at Larson Management. I'm hardly in the office anymore.
>
> T: (1.7) <u>In danger of exploding</u>. ((thoughtful, even tone))

Neither echoing nor mirroring is fully comprehensible from a sentence-level analysis alone. Both are distinct from the type of speech (with rising intonation) characterized by Quirk et al. (1980) as echo utterances. Both echoing and mirroring signal attentiveness to the speech of another and evidence a willingness to take up the word choices of another. They manifest content covergence. To support the claim that these discourse strategies involve convergence, it may be useful to consider a nonaccommodated example from a segment of a talk show. The following example from Scotton (1989), illustrating divergence, may serve as relief against which the other type may be evaluated. The interviewee (a sociologist) chooses not to repeat the exact words of the talk show host, apparently distancing himself somewhat.

(22)
Phil Donahue show (discussion of police brutality)
Interviewee: They see brutality, they work with it, real and imagined,
               and it becomes an everyday occurrence for them (pause).
               And this is the way they perceive the world.
Donahue: Us and them.
Interviewee: We and they. That's right.

Both echoing and mirroring underscore the nature of the social interaction in psychotherapy. Clients and therapists alike are engaged in a collaborative effort wherein both are intently focused on examining a single subject: the beliefs and actions of the client. Their goals for a session may differ, but their intent is to enhance the client's well-being. To facilitate this, each seeks, through communication behavior, to establish rapport. One means of accomplishing this is through speech accommodation.

Analysis of therapy session transcripts from clients and therapists who have worked together for two years shows a high incidence of such occurrences – as many as four in a five-minute period. These findings suggest that the use of longitudinal case studies (as in Shockey 1984; Trudgill 1981) is a methodological approach that may shed additional light on the question of the extent of speech accommodation to another and lead to a fuller understanding of the linguistic levels on which accommodation occurs.

6.6. Conclusion

Studies of speech accommodation in psychotherapy are interesting, but are they also useful? As demonstrated by several studies, objective measurements of specific linguistic variables ranging from sentence complexity (Meara et al. 1979) and characteristics of verbs (Bieber et al. 1977) to the current investigation of phonological, morphosyntactic, and discourse-level phenomena indicate that the verbal behavior of client and therapist evidences accommodation over time.

Because individual psychotherapy is an intensely focused dyadic experience conducted largely through the medium of speech, the likelihood is strong that speech accommodation will be dramatically in evidence. Therapists who learn to understand the process can also harness its potential for quickly establishing rapport, for gauging the progress or predicting the success of therapy, and for interpreting the behavior of an increasingly wide social range of clients. Work on speech accommodation in therapy has barely begun. Future studies in this important context should investigate the extent to which such accommodative behavior is unconsious or conscious, whether in fact it is a learnable technique. Another area for future research is examination of those styles of therapy that depend on low or contra-accommodative styles (challenges and adversarial exchanges). These exceptions to the premises of CAT may underscore their validity in the majority of cases.

In conclusion, this sociolinguistic study has attempted to add precision to the social psychological theory of speech accommodation and to broaden the base of contexts in which accommodation occurs by measuring specific linguistic variables in naturally occurring, face-to-face encounters between a psychotherapist and a client.

In order to move beyond description, use was made of an interpretive model that helped explain why speakers accommodate at differential rates. The argument was additionally made that previous work advancing our understanding of short-term phonological accommodation can be paired with studies of long-term or midrange accommodation, and that a fruitful avenue of research is to consider accommodation on other linguistic levels such as the syntactic or discourse level. It was further suggested that the true extent of speech accommodation may only emerge with studies of extended contact such as is possible in longitudinal studies. We can conclude that the fundamental concepts of CAT regarding the social psychological motivation for accent convergence and divergence provide a framework for interpreting the complex process by which changes in language behavior in psychotherapy can both signal and enhance rapport, an often essential element in successful conduct of therapy. Ongoing research on speech accommodation should be guided by the question of whether accommodation is differentially realized on varying levels of language.

Appendix

TRANSCRIPTION CONVENTIONS

Symbol	Example	Explanation
[ ]	C: Well [maybe I need] to T: [you should]	Brackets indicate simultaneous utterances by differing speakers. The left-hand bracket marks the onset of simultaneity; the right-hand bracket marks the end of simultaneous speech.
:	We:ll no::	Colons indicate that the preceding syllable has been elongated. two colons indicate twice as long a syllable as one.
——	I <u>hate</u> that woman.	Underlining is used to indicate heavier emphasis (in the speaker's pitch or loudness.)
°	T: °Secrets. secrets°	A raised degree sign indicates a soft or low voice.
=	C: I don't like = T: = any hassles.	Equal signs indicate that no perceptible time has elapsed between the words latched by the marks. They are used when a speaker starts to speak, with little or no break between his and the previous speaker's utterance.
(1) or (.5)	C: I uh (1) wish I could. T Why (.5) can't you?	Numbers in parentheses indicate the seconds and tenths of seconds of pauses between words or speaker turns.
(·)	C: I never (·) hurt so much.	A nonsentence final period surrounded by parentheses indicates a pause of less than half a second.
( )	C: She was wearing a ( )	Empty parentheses indicate that something was uttered but that the transcriber was unable to determine the actual words spoken.
(monster)	T: He was a (monster).	Parentheses around a phrase or word indicates an estimation of what the actual words were when the transcriber is uncertain.
(( ))	T: ((laugh)) That's more like it.	Double parentheses enclose descriptions of additional relevant sounds that are not words (e.g., ((cough)), ((throat clear)).
↗	T: Do you think it's the tape? ↗	An upward arrow indicates rising intonation.

Symbol	Example	Explanation
↘	T: You felt betrayed. ↘ C: I felt betrayed. ↘	A downward arrow indicates falling intonation.
	C: I tho-	A hyphen on an incomplete word indicates speaker break off, with a glottal stop.

References

Bales, R. F. 1950. A set of categories for the analysis of small group interaction. *American Sociological Review*, 15: 257–63.

Bell, A. 1984. Language style as audience design. *Language in Society*, 13: 145–204.

Bieber, M. R., Patton, M. J., and Fuhriman, A. J. 1977. A metalanguage analysis of counselor and client verb usage in counseling. *Journal of Counseling Psychology*, 24: 264–71.

Bourhis, R. Y., and Giles, H. 1977. The language of intergroup distinctiveness. In H. Giles (ed.) *Language, Ethnicity and Intergroup Relations*, pp. 119–36. London: Academic Press.

Bourhis, R. Y., Giles, H., Leyens, J.-P., and Tajfel, H. 1979. Psycholinguistic distinctiveness: Language divergence in Belgium. In H. Giles and R. St. Clair (eds.) *Language and Social Psychology*, pp. 158–85. Oxford: Basil Blackwell.

Christian D., Wolfram, W., and Dube, N. 1987. Variation and change in geographically isolated communities: Appalachian English and Ozark English. Publication No. 74 of the American Dialect Society. Tuscaloosa: University of Alabama Press.

Coupland, N. 1980. Style-shifting in a Cardiff work-setting. *Language in Society*, 9: 1–12.

Coupland, N. 1984. Accommodation at work: Some phonological data and their implications. *International Journal of the Sociology of Language*, 46: 49–70.

Coupland, N. 1985. Hark, hark, the lark: Social motivations for phonological style-shifting. *Language and Communication*, 5: 153–71.

Coupland, N., Coupland, J., Giles, H., and Henwood, K. 1988. Accommodating the elderly: Invoking and extending a theory. *Language in Society*, 17: 1–41.

DiPietro, R. J. (ed.) 1982. *Linguistics and the Professions*. Norwood, NJ: Ablex.

Douglas-Cowie, E. 1978. Linguistic code-switching in a Northern Irish vallage: Social interaction and social ambition. In P. Trudgill (ed.), *Sociolinguistic Patterns in British English*, pp. 37–51. London: Edward Arnold.

Duncan, S., Jr. 1972. Some signals and rules for taking speaking turns in conversations. *Journal of Personality and Social Psychology*, 23: 283–92.

Elliott, R., Stiles, W. B., Mahrer, A. R., Hill, E. E., Friedlander, M. L., and Margison, F. R. 1987. Primary therapist response modes: Comparison of six rating systems. *Journal of Consulting and Clinical Psychology*, 55: 218–23.

Fanshel, D., and Moss, F. (1971). *Playback: A Marriage in Jeopardy Examined*. New York: Columbia University Press.

Ferrara, K. 1987. Repetition as rejoinder in therapeutic discourse. Paper presented at the annual meeting of the Linguistic Society of America, San Francisco.

Ferrara, K. 1988a. The structure and construction of therapeutic discourse. Ph.D. Dissertation, University of Texas at Austin.

Ferrara, K. 1988b. Variation in Narration: Retellings in therapeutic discourse. *In* K. Ferrara, B. Brown, K. Walters, and J. Baugh (eds.) *Linguistic Change and Contact* (Proceedings of the 16th Annual New Ways of Analyzing Variation in Language Conference), Texas Linguistics Forum 30, pp. 100–12. Austin: University of Texas, Department of Linguistics.

Frank, J. D. 1961. *Persuasion and Healing: A Comparative Study of Psychotherapy* (revised edition 1973). Baltimore: Johns Hopkins University Press.

Giles, H. 1973. Accent mobility: A model and some data *Anthroplogical Linguistics*, 15: 87–105.

Giles, H. (ed.) 1984. Dynamics of speech accommodation: Special Issue of *International Journal of the Sociology of Language*, 46.

Giles, H., Mulac, A., Braodac, J. J., and Johnson, P. 1987. Speech accommodation theory: The first decade and beyond. *In* M. L. McLaughlin (ed.), *Communication Yearbook 10*, pp. 13–48. Beverly Hills, CA: Sage.

Giles, H., and Powesland, P. F. 1975. *Speech Style and Social Evaluation*. New York: Academic Press.

Giles, H., and Smith, P. 1979. Accommodation theory: Optimal levels of convergence. *In* H. Giles and R. St. Clair (eds.), *Language and Social Psychology*, pp. 45–65. Oxford: Basil Blackwell.

Giles, H., and St. Clair, R. (eds.) 1978. *Language and Social Psychology*. Baltimore: University Park Press.

Gottschalk, L. A., and Gleser, G. C. 1969. *The Measurement of Psychological States Through the Content Analysis of Verbal Behavior*. Berkeley: University of California Press.

Gottschalk, L. A., Lola, F., and Viney, L. L. 1986. *Content Analysis of Verbal Behavior: Significance in Clinical Medicine and Psychiatry*. Berlin: Springer-Verlag.

Hallum, K. C. 1978. Social class and psychotherapy: A sociolinguistic approach. *Clinical Social Work Journal*, 6: 188–201.

Havens, L. 1978. Explorations in the uses of language in psychotherapy: Simple empathic statements. *Psychiatry*, 41: 336–45.

Havens, L. 1979. Explorations in the uses of language in psychotherapy: Complex emphathic statements. *Psychiatry*, 42: 40–8.

Havens, L. 1980. Explorations in the uses of language in psychotherapy: Counterprojective statements. *Contemporary Psychoanalysis*, 16: 53–67.

Havens, L. 1984. Explorations in the uses of language in psychotherapy: Counterintrojective statements (preformatives). *Contemporary Psychoanalysis*, 20: 385–99.

Hill, C. E. 1978. Development of a counselor verbal response category system. *Journal of Counseling Psychology*, 25: 461–8.

Jaffee, J. 1964. Verbal behavior analysis in psychiatric interviews with the aid of digital computers. *In* D. M. K. Roch and E. A. Weinstein (eds.) *Disorders of Communication*, vol. 42, pp. 289–399. Baltimore: Williams & Wilkins.

Labov, W. 1966. *The Social Stratification of English in New York City*. Washington, DC: Center for Applied Linguistics.

Labov, W. 1972. *Sociolinguistic Patterns*. Philadelphia: University of Pennsylvania Press.

Labov, W., and Fanshel, D. 1977. *Therapeutic Discourse: Psychotherapy as Conversation*. New York: Academic Press.

Leaffer, T. 1982. Applications to psychoanalysis and psychotherapy. *In* R. J. DiPietro (ed.), *Linguistics in the Professions*, pp. 13–26. Norwood, NJ: Ablex.

Lennard, H. L. 1962. Some aspects of the psychotherapeutic system. *In* H. H.

Strupp and L. Luborsky (eds.), *Research in Psychotherapy*, vol. 2, Washington, DC: American Psychological Association.

Lentine, G. 1988. Metaphor as cooperation in therapeutic discourse. *In* K. Ferrara, B. Brown, K. Walters, and J. Baugh (eds.), *Linguistic Change and Contact* (Proceedings of the 16th Annual New Ways of Analyzing Variation in Language Conference), Texas Linguistics Forum 30, pp. 192–9. Austin: University of Texas, Department of Linguistics.

McQuown, N. A. 1957. Linguistic transcription and specification of psychiatric interview materials. *Psychiatry*, 20: 79–86.

Meara, N. M., Pepinsky, H. B., Shannon, J. W., and Murray, W. A. 1981. Semantic communication and expectation for counseling across three theoretical orientations. *Journal of Counseling Psychology*, 28: 110–18.

Meara, N. M., Shannon, J. W., and Pepinsky, H. B., 1979. Comparison of the stylistic complexity of the language of counselor and client across three theoretical orientations. *Journal of Counseling Psychology*, 26: 181–9.

Nicholson, J. (n.d.). The theory of speech accommodation: Speakers of British English in the USA. Manuscript, Department of Linguistics, University of Texas at Austin.

Nordenstram, K. 1979. *Svenskam i Norge*. Gothenburg: University Press.

Patton, M. J., Fuhriman, A. J., and Bieber, M. R. (1977). A model and a metalanguage for research on psychological counseling. *Journal of Counseling Psychology*, 24: 25–34.

Patton, M. J., and Meara, N. M. 1987. The analysis of natural language in psychological treatment. *In* R. L. Russell (ed.), *Language in Psychotherapy: Strategies of Discovery*. New York: Plenum Press.

Payne, A. 1980. Factors controlling the acquisition of the Philadelphia dialect by out-of-state children. *In* W. Labov (ed.), *Locating Language in Time and Space.*, pp. 143–78. New York: Academic Press.

Pepinsky, H. B., and Karst, T. O. 1964. Convergence: A phenomenon in counseling and psychotherapy. *American Psychologist*, 19: 333–8.

Phoenix, V. G., and Lindeman, M. I. 1982. Language patterns and therapeutic change. *In* R. J. DiPietro (ed.), *Linguistics and the Professions*, pp. 3–12. Norwood, NJ: Ablex.

Pittenger, R. E., Hockett, C. F., and Danehy, J. J. 1960. *The First Five Minutes*. Ithaca, NY: Paul Martineau.

Pittenger, R. E., and Smith, H. L., Jr. 1957. A basis for some contributions of linguistics to psychiatry. *Psychiatry*, 20: 61–78.

Pollio, H. R., and Barlow, J. M. 1975. A behavioral analysis of figurative language in psychotherapy: One session in a single case study. *Language and Speech*, 18: 236–54.

Pollio, H. R., Barlow, J. M., Fine, H. J., and Pollio, M. R. (eds.). 1977. *Psychology and the Poetics of Growth: Figurative Language in Psychology, Psychotherapy and Education*. New York: Halsted Press.

Putnam, W. B., and Street, R. L., Jr. 1984. The conception and perception of noncontent speech performance: Implications for speech accommodation theory. *International Journal of the Sociology of Language*, 46: 97–114.

Quirk, R., Greenbaum, S., Leech, G, and Svartvik, J. 1980. *A Grammar of Contemporary English*. Harlow, Essex: Longman Group.

Rogers, I. 1981. The influence of Australian English intonation on the speech of two British children. *Working Papers of the Speech and Language Research Centre, Macquarrie University*, 3: 25–42.

222   K. Ferrara

Russell, R. L. (ed.), 1987. *Language in Psychotherapy: Strategies of Discovery*. New York: Plenum Press.
Russell, R. L., and Stiles, W. B. 1979. Categories for classifying language in psychotherapy. *Psychological Bulletin*, 86: 404–19.
Sacks, H. 1970–1. Unpublished mimeograph lecture notes.
Sapir, E. 1927. Speech as a personality trait. *American Journal of Sociology*, 32: 892–905.
Schegloff, E. 1984. On some questions and ambiguities in conversation. In J. M. Atkinson and J. Heritage (eds.), *Structures of Social Action: Studies in Conversation Analysis*, pp. 28–52. Cambridge: Cambridge University Press.
Scotton, C. M. 1989. Marked code-switching to negotiate discourse power. Or, when speech is not audience designed. Talk presented at Texas A&M University.
Shockey, L. 1984. All in a flap: Long-term accommodation in phonology. *International Journal of the Sociology of Language*, 46: 87–95.
Stiles, W. B. 1978. Verbal response modes and dimensions of interpersonal roles: A method of discourse analysis. *Journal of Personality and Social Psychology*, 36: 693–703.
Stiles, W. B. 1979. Verbal response modes and psychotherapeutic technique. *Psychiatry*, 42: 49–62.
Thakerar, J., Giles, H., and Cheshire, J. 1982. Psychological and linguistic parameters of speech accommodation theory. In C. Fraser and K. R. Scherer, (eds.), *Advances in the Social Psychology of Language*, pp. 205–55. Cambridge: Cambridge University Press.
Trömel-Ploetz, S., and Franck, D. 1979. "I'm dead": A linguistic analysis of paradoxical techniques in psychotherapy. *Journal of Pragmatics*, 1: 121–42.
Trudgill, P. 1981. Linguistic accommodation: Sociolinguistic observations on a sociopsychological theory. In C. Masek, R. A. Hendrich, and M. F. Miller (eds.), *Chicago Linguistic Society 1981 Papers from the Parasession on Language and Behavior*, pp. 218–37. Chicago: University of Chicago Press.
Trudgill, P. 1983. *On Dialect: Social and Geographical Perspectives*. New York: New York University Press.
Trudgill, P. 1986. *Dialects in Contact*. Oxford: Basil Blackwell.
Turner, R. 1972. Some formal properties of therapy talk. In D. Sudnow (ed.), *Studies in Social Interaction*. New York: Free Press.
Wodak, R. 1981. How do I put my problem? Problem presentation in therapy and interview. *Text*, 1: 191–213.
Wodak, R., and Flader, D. (eds.) 1979. *Therapeutische kommunikation*. Königstein-Taunus: Scriptor.
Wolfram, W. 1980. Beyond Black English: Implications of the Ann Arbor decision for other non-mainstream varieties. In M. F. Whiteman (ed.), *Reactions to Ann Arbor: Vernacular Black English and Education*. Arlington, VA: Center for Applied Linguistics.
Wolfram, W., and Christian., D. 1976. *Appalachian Speech*. Arlington, VA: Center for Applied Linguistics.
Woods, H. G. 1979. A socio-dialectology survey of the English spoken in Ottawa: A study of sociological and stylistic variation in Canadian English. Ph.D. dissertation, University of British Columbia, Vancouver, as cited by Bell (1984: 155).

7. Accommodation in native–nonnative interactions: Going beyond the "what" to the "why" in second-language research

JANE ZUENGLER

7.1. Introduction

In recent years, an increasing amount of research on second-language acquisition (SLA) has shifted away from studying aspects of the learner's second language (L2) behavior in isolation. The emphasis in the 1970s was on analyses of errors in the learner's language, in support of linguistic theory stating that there are certain universals that govern all SLA. By implication, it was assumed that all learners make the same, or similar, errors (see e.g., Burt and Dulay 1975; Oller and Richards 1973; Richards 1974; Schumann and Stenson 1975). Although there is still some theoretical support for such a research orientation, a growing number of SLA researchers have begun to study L2 learners as they interact with others, whether it be native speakers (NSs) of the language they are learning or other nonnative speakers (NNSs). The shift toward interactionally situated research can be credited, in large part, to theoretical assertions by Krashen (1981, 1982) that comprehensible input from the L2 learner's interlocutor is crucial for language acquisition to take place. Also influential are claims by Long (1981, 1983, 1985), Hatch (1983), and others that in interactions, it is the negotiations toward meaning that are necessary for L2 development.

The growth in research on NS–NNS interactions clearly represents an important step toward the study of language as communication. However, much of the research is atheoretical, confined to linguistic descriptions of the NNS's or NS's speech. Since NNSs and NSs communicate within a social context that they both influence and are influenced by, it is essential to tie the research to sociolinguistic theory. In so doing, we can go beyond linguistic description to an explanation of how NSs and NNSs communicate.

223

Given the need for a theoretical perspective, this chapter assesses the potential of one sociolinguistic theory, communication accommodation theory (CAT), to explain dynamics in NS–NNS interactions (i.e., to account for variation at a given time). The chapter first discusses the current extent of acceptance of CAT in general in the literature. Then it critically discusses the research studies on L2 performance variation that directly test, or are indirectly relevant to, CAT. Following that, the chapter describes the phenomenon of "foreigner talk (FT)" by native speakers when interacting with L2 learners and argues that CAT should be invoked to explain its occurrence in context.

7.2. CAT as a theory of L2 variation

Beebe and Giles's (1984) paper represents one of the first theoretical discussions of the relevance of CAT to L2 data (see also Beebe and Zuengler 1981). Since then, CAT has been increasingly cited in the SLA literature. However, as indicated later, CAT is either assigned a limited scope or discussed with little or no L2 empirical data as support.

In some of the recent literature (e.g., Ellis 1985; Pennington and Richards 1986), CAT is considered only with respect to explaining variation in long-term and ultimate L2 acquisition (and not variation in performance at a given time). Indeed, these have been the loci of most empirical research in the accommodation tradition (see, e.g., Ball, Giles, and Hewstone 1984; Garrett, Giles, and Coupland 1989; Giles and Byrne 1982).

The literature that refers to CAT as a major theory of L2 performance (e.g., Tarone 1989) typically presents the argument with little or no L2 data, relying instead on non-L2 data. For example, Beebe's (1988) volume on SLA contains an account of CAT-related variation that is almost entirely devoid of L2 data support. Faerch and Kasper (1987), in a discussion of language transfer, devote a section to CAT as an explanation of how social psychological factors such as the desire to mark ethnic group membership can cause an L2 speaker to diverge linguistically from an NS interlocutor by transferring features of the native language into the L2. However, Faerch and Kasper, like Beebe, have little L2 empirical evidence to cite as support, and instead rely heavily on anecdotes.

What the foregoing discussion suggests is that the field of SLA appears to consider CAT a sound and potentially useful theory of L2 variation (see, e.g., Tarone 1989), particularly, perhaps, in explaining differences in ultimate L2 acquisition. However, there is not yet a body of clear supporting evidence. The following section contains a discussion of the existing research.

7.3. CAT-related research on L2 interactional variation

Two related research reports suggest that L2 speakers can accommodate to the ethnic identity of their interlocutors, thus causing variation in their L2 across interlocutors. Beebe (1981) reports a study of sixty-one Chinese-Thai children and seventeen adults who were interviewed in Thai by one interviewer who was ethnically Thai and a second who was ethnically Chinese (although she spoke Thai without a Chinese accent). Analyzing the pronunciation of six vowels in the subjects' L2 Thai, Beebe found that subjects pronounced five of the six vowels significantly more Thai-like when interacting with the ethnic Thai interviewer than with the Chinese interviewer. In other words, when talking to the ethnic Chinese interviewer, they increased their Chinese accent in Thai. In interpreting the results, Beebe drew on CAT in suggesting that ethnic solidarity caused the subjects to make their speech less Thai-like with the Chinese interviewer. Although the subjects were not converging *linguistically* directly toward the interlocutor (since the interviewer's actual speech did not have a Chinese accent), they were converging *psychologically* toward sterotypical Chinese-Thai speech (see also Thakerar, Giles, and Cheshire 1982).

Combining the Chinese-Thai data with other data from Puerto Rican children, Beebe and Zuengler (1983) argue that CAT should be applied to L2 interactional variation. Although the Chinese–Thai data showed phonological convergence in the L2, the data from the Puerto Rican children exhibited convergence toward the interviewer in terms of amount of talk. That is, in interviews in English, the children talked a lot if the interviewer talked a lot. When the interviewer spoke less, the children spoke less as well.

A caveat should be attached to the assertions in Beebe (1981) and Beebe and Zuengler (1983), however. Both articles cite data from research that was not originally conducted to test CAT. The articles represent post hoc applications of CAT to the research results. Although there is nothing wrong with that in itself, what is needed as well is research that is conceptualized and conducted to test CAT directly. The research study that is reported next comes somewhat closer to meeting that need.

Young (1988) claims that it is not interlocutor ethnicity per se that induces L2 variation, but the overall degree of social convergence existing between interlocutors (of which ethnicity is but one component). Young hypothesized that for L2 speakers in informal settings, there would be a positive relationship between degree of social convergence and degree of L2 linguistic convergence toward the interlocutor. [Giles and Johnson (1987) made a similar claim and provided evidence that when an NNS and an NS share important social identities, ethnic or not, the NNS will be likely to converge toward the NS's language use.] Young measured social convergence by determining how many of six attributes – ethnicity, sex, occupation, educational level, place of origin, and age – the interlocutors shared. Twelve L2 subjects who were native Chinese speakers participated in the study. The subjects were adults residing in the United States. They were divided into high and low L2 English proficiency based on performance on the Test of English as a Foreign Language (TOEFL). Each subject was interviewed twice in English, once by a native English speaker (NS) and once by another NNS (who was a native Chinese speaker). In order to encourage an informal setting, the interviews were conducted in the subjects' home. The dependent measure of linguistic convergence was regular plural marking in English. Young predicted that degree of social convergence with the NS would correspond positively to degree of native-English-like plural production in the subjects' L2 English and that degree of social convergence with the NNS would correspond positively to degree of nonnative-like plural production. The results were significant for high-proficiency subjects who were interacting with NSs. (Results were nonsignificant for low-proficiency subjects overall and for high-proficiency subjects interacting with NNSs.) Young interprets the findings as indicating that the high-proficiency subjects had acquired sociolinguistic competence, whereas the low-proficiency subjects had not. According to Young, the findings also prove that it is not interlocutor ethnicity alone that causes linguistic variation, but a *collection* of attributes (of which *one* is ethnicity) by which interlocutors assess their relative similarity to each other. As such, these findings differ somewhat from Beebe's (1981) and Beebe and Zuengler's (1983) accounts, while at the same time providing clear support for the similarity-attraction aspect of CAT.

A weakness of the study is that Young used rather gross categorical measures of each of the six components of social convergence in order to come up with a "convergence index." For example, although marking sex as either "same" or "different" may involve a simple decision, it is more problematic to determine whether education and occupation are the same or different. The subjects' own perceptions of these components should be elicited (provided that they find them perceptually salient). Nevertheless, since Young attempted to measure a more complex set of attributes than the foregoing investigators, his findings are noteworthy and provide compelling support for CAT.

The remaining set of studies to be discussed share the same focus: They have investigated whether CAT explains phonological variation in the L2 English of native Spanish and Greek speakers. Two of the studies investigated the influence of ethnicity on L2 performance. Instead of considering differences between interlocutors in ethnic group membership, however, the studies investigated whether L2 pronunciation would vary as a result of a native-English-speaking (i.e., Anglo) interlocutor conveying positive or negative attitudes toward the L2 speaker's ethnic group.

Zuengler (1982) asked whether ethnically threatening remarks by an American English-speaking Anglo interlocutor would affect L2 pronunciation. The study was influenced by results of Bourhis and Giles (1977) and Bourhis et al. (1979). In the former study, subjects responded to ethnic threat by making their native language more ethnic-sounding, whereas in the latter, subjects switched from the Anglo's language (their L2) to their native language. Zuengler predicted that compared to speech in response to an ethnically neutral question, subjects' L2 English would, under ethnic threat, diverge phonologically from a standard English-speaking Anglo interlocutor by becoming more nonnative-sounding. The subjects were thirteen adult native Spanish and Greek speakers. They responded twice; the first response was to a neutral topic, namely, suggestions about language learning. The second response was to an ethnically threatening remark. The speaker said that bilingual education was stupid, that New York (the setting of the study) should be English only, and that Greek and Spanish were unimportant languages. Anyone wanting to speak Spanish or Greek should go back to his own country. The speaker then said, "You agree with me, don't you?" The analysis compared subjects' production, across the conditions, of three phonological variables. They were prevocalic /r/, /I/ (the vowel in *bit*) and word-final /z/; a preliminary analysis had shown that all three varied in the Greek and Spanish speakers' English. Results showed variation according to the type of response to the ethnically threatening question. That is, the subjects who gave a very personal response, and/or who made clear ethnic references in their answer, decreased in native English-like pronunciation of the sounds (i.e., displayed psychological divergence through their pronunciation). Other subjects responded to the Anglo's threats by objectifying their answer (i.e., speaking in the third person) and making no clear references to their particular ethnic group. These subjects made their pronunciation more standard, native English-like, and converged psychologically toward the Anglo. Zuengler concluded that some of the subjects may have identified strongly as ethnic group members and defended their ethnic solidarity by making their L2 phonologically distinct from that of the Anglo interlocutor. The other subjects, who made their speech more like that of the Anglo interlocutor, possibly had weaker ethnic identification and chose, in responding, to maintain a distinctiveness from their ethnic group.

Zuengler's (1982) results thus suggest that L2 pronunication can vary, by converging or diverging, under conditions of perceived ethnic threat. As Giles and Johnson (1987) have claimed, speakers who choose to deemphasize their ethnic identity will do so by attenuating their ethnic speech markers, whereas speakers who choose to make their ethnic identity more salient will accentuate their ethnic speech markers. Replication studies are necessary, however, before any conclusions can be drawn, as Zuengler's results should be considered tentative. It is only a conjecture that subjects might have differed in strength of ethnic identification. Dividing subjects according to the nature of their response was a post hoc analysis, and no information had been gathered on subjects' degree of ethnic identification. In addition, since only thirteen subjects were tested, the results were not submitted to statistical analysis. Finally, there are several plausible strategic intents that may have been mediating convergence, for example, concern for the face needs of the interlocutors, dissimulation, and so on.

Whereas Zuengler (1982) looked at subjects' response to a perceived ethnic threat, Berkowitz (1986) investigated subjects' response to perceived empathy toward the subjects' ethnic group. The hypothesis was that there would be linguistic divergence away from an NS interviewer whom subjects perceived as culturally empathic toward them. That is, performance in the L2 would be less nativelike. Berkowitz predicted linguistic divergence as an outcome of psychological convergence; subjects would feel more comfortable with an empathic interviewer and therefore would not be concerned about producing their "best" (i.e., most standard) L2 English. Fifty-two adult Dominican Spanish-speaking women, half of whom were assessed as having high L2 proficiency and half low, were assigned to experimental and control groups. The treatment consisted of showing the subjects a videotape of a class in which the teacher, through how and what she talked about with the students, displayed what was intended to be culturally empathic behavior toward them. The teacher discussed with the class a story they had read about a Dominican woman who had moved to New York City and then returned to the Dominican Republic. People there found that she had changed. The teacher asked the students whether they had had similar experiences, how they felt about the woman, and so on. In other words, the teacher acted as if she was trying to understand the students' experiences as foreigners. The control subjects, on the other hand, viewed a discussion of the same story, with the same teacher acting neutral. That is, the teacher showed no affect, paid no attention to the content of the story, and focused instead on questions regarding grammar and vocabulary. All subjects were then interviewed by the teacher. A posttreatment questionnaire included a scale to elicit the subjects' perception of the teacher's degree of cultural empathy. Dependent phonological measures consisted of standard American English production of the following: prevocalic /r/; the stressed and unstressed central vowels /ʌ/ and /ə/ (in *but* and *alike*, respectively); consonant clusters; and specific consonant clusters that are word-initial and begin with /s/ (e.g., *school*). Native Spanish speakers tend to produce nonnative variants of all the foregoing measures; for example, an initial vowel is often added before the consonant cluster in *school*, and *but* may be pronounced with /a/ instead of /ʌ/.

Results were nonsignificant when experimental and control groups were compared. The lack of differences may have been due to the absence of a clear and valid difference between treatment and control videotapes, because there were no differences between the experimental and control subjects ' ratings of teacher empathy on the posttreatment questionnaire. Berkowitz suggests that subjects may have had a general desire to please the interviewer (a number of subjects in the control group rated the interviewer as culturally empathic).

Berkowitz then grouped subjects according to their rating of interviewer empathy on the posttreatment questionnaire. Here some differences did emerge. For both high- and low-proficiency subjects, there was a significant negative correlation ($r = -.23$) between ratings of cultural empathy and standard pronunciation of consonant clusters (which supported the hypothesis). However, at both proficiency levels, two of the measures showed a significant positive correlation with ratings of cultural empathy. The measures were degree of standard pronunciation of /r/ ($r = .29$) and of initial consonant clusters beginning with /s/ ($r = .31$). These positive correlations represented a direction opposite that predicted. (The other measures were nonsignificant.)

Although Berkowitz's (1986) results suggest the influence of perceived cultural empathy on L2 pronunciation, not all of the phonological variants represented the linguistic divergence that was predicted. It could be argued, however, that CAT could predict linguistic *convergence* in this study as well. Subjects would converge toward an interlocutor they liked and with whom they wanted to promote social attractiveness.

It should be noted that whereas Young (1988) found significant effects only for the high-proficiency subjects, results for both low- and high-proficiency subjects in the Berkowitz (1986) study were significant. The matter of when L2 learners develop sociolinguistic competence remains an unanswered question.

Zuengler (1987) studied CAT processes focusing on task expertise. The research partially replicated Thakerar et al.'s (1982) set of studies on the effects of unequal status on native language speech in pairs of L1 subjects. Thakerar et al. created a status imbalance by forming pairs of subjects in which one interlocutor had more training or expertise than the other (e.g., with respect to dental training or performance on a block design task). Each pair was asked to discuss a topic that made their status imbalance salient. Subjects' degrees of standardness were analyzed as dependent measures. Since both low- and high-status interlocutors were NSs, they were considered linguistically comparable because they presumably possessed the same standard-nonstandard speech repertoire. Findings indicated that relative to interlocutors in equal-status pairs, low-status subjects made their speech more standard, whereas high-status subjects made their speech less standard. Measures included listeners' judgments of standardness, as well as objective measures of speech rate and word-final pronunciation of the nonstandard glottal stop /?/ versus the standard variant /t/. Although the findings indicate that, objectively, linguistic divergence occurred, the speakers were subjectively *converging*, Thakerar et al. argue. They were converging toward what they expected their interlocutor's speech style to be, based on stereotypical notions of how high- and low-status speakers speak. The authors suggest that the subjects may have had different motives for their convergence. It is possible that the low-status subjects subjectively converged as a face-saving act, since they needed to recoup their self-esteem. The speech shift would function to maintain their identity. High-status subjects, on the other hand, did not suffer any loss of self-esteem. They shifted their speech, according to Thakerar et al., as a means of ensuring comprehension by their partner.

Zuengler's (1987) study investigated whether a status imbalance in interactions between NSs and NNSs would cause phonological variation in both speakers' English. Status imbalance was operationalized as perceived unequal expertise in performing a task, a test of artistic judgment (Meier 1963). Forty-five NS–NNS dyads of adult women were formed; the NNSs were native Spanish speakers, whereas the NSs were English-speaking American women who had been raised in the New York City metropolitan area. The predictions, based on Thakerar et al. (1982), were that subjective convergence would occur, with subjects shifting toward what they expected their partner's speech style to be. That is, compared to a control group in which subjects were not aware of their relative expertise, (1) relative task "experts" would decrease their pronunciation standardness and (2) relative task "nonexperts" would increase theirs. Unlike Thakerar et al., it was not possible to make predictions about objective *linguistic* divergence or convergence by interlocutors in each pair. In Zuengler (1987), the NSs and NNSs were not considered linguistically comparable, since most of the NNSs had not yet acquired the same standard-nonstandard speech repertoire as the NSs, and the sounds that underwent shift by the NNSs did not necessarily match those on which the NSs shifted. The choice of different speech measures for the NNSs and NSs reflects this noncomparability.

Subjects completed part of the art judgment test, which involved looking at sets of four slightly different pictures and ranking them from aesthetically "best" to "worst." After finishing one section of the test, they were asked to have a ten-minute conversation about their judgments. Following that, they completed a second section of the test. Prior to the next conversation, the pairs in the experimental groups were told how they had performed on the test (compared to art experts). In fifteen of the pairs, the NNS was led to believe she had done very well (i.e., was the relative expert), whereas the NS partner had not. In fifteen pairs it was the opposite, with the NS being told she was the relative expert. (The performance scores they were given did not reflect their actual performance but were manipulations created by the investigator.) Finally, fifteen pairs comprised the control group, which was not informed of its task performance. All pairs then had a second conversation about the test. A posttest questionnaire measured subjects' perceptions of their relative expertise. Analyses involved comparisons of pronunciation standardness across the two conversations midway through and at the end of the task. For the NNSs, degree of standardness was determined by analyzing subjects' pronunciation of (1) the voiced interdental fricative /ð/ found in *them;* (2) /r/; (3) any word-final consonant clusters; (4) the stressed and unstressed vowels /ʌ/ and /ə/ (found in *but* and *alive,* respectively); and (5) the low front vowel /æ/ found in *man.* For the NSs, standard pronunciation of the following sounds was determined: (1) /ð/; (2) the voiceless interdental fricative /θ/ (found in *think*); (3) /r/; and (4) /ə/, the mid-back rounded vowel in *off.* The particular NS measures chosen were those that Labov (1966) indicates are sociolinguistic variables in New York City speech; how frequently the standard variants are produced varies according to social class and formality of task. In the literature, all of the NNS measures except /ʌ/ and /æ/ have been shown to undergo variation in the English of native Spanish speakers with respect to formality of task, occupational interests, gender, or other factors (see, e.g., Anisman 1975; Hartford 1978). It was felt that they therefore would be good candidates for variation due to expertise differences. The other two measures selected, /ʌ/ and /æ/, were found to vary in preliminary analysis of the data, and they were included to determine whether they were sensitive to expertise. Although the data analysis could have focused on the nature of nonstandard variants as well as the frequency of standard variants, it was decided to limit the analysis to the latter, since the hypotheses solely concerned shifts in standardness.

Only a small set of the results were significant; they were limited to nonexperts and occurred on one measure for both NNSs and NSs. NS nonexperts significantly increased their standardness of /ɔ/, whereas NNS nonexperts significantly *decreased* their standardness of /r/. That is, results of /ɔ/ for the NSs supported the hypothesis, but the significance of /r/ for the NNSs occurred in a direction *opposite* to that predicted. [The bidirectionality of results is not the same as that reported in Berkowitz (1986), however, as her subjects were all NNSs, whereas Zuengler's (1987), bidirectionality contrasts NNSs and NSs.] Zuengler's NS results correspond to Thakerar et al.'s (1982) outcomes: The NS nonexperts were attempting to recoup any lost self-esteem by making their speech more standard again. As an interpretation of the NNS outcomes, possible ethnolinguistic dominance by the NSs is suggested. If NNSs tend to be treated as subordinate in general, being assigned nonexpert status could cause them to simply give up aiming for correctness, thus displaying a kind of passive divergence. There did not seem to be any motivation to recoup self-esteem, as there was for the NSs. Although only a limited pattern of shift occurred in the study, CAT is capable of explaining the phonological variation observed. Further research should consider measures other than the variables chosen in the previous studies to determine whether a status imbalance affects aspects of language production that have not been studied to date.

However, what is lacking in CAT research on L2 (and native language as well) is a theory-based rationale for selecting particular linguistic items to study. The criterion for selecting linguistic measures in the previously cited research has been simply to choose items that are already known to vary. Although variability is, of course, a prerequisite for variation research, much research in SLA indicates that L2 is full of variation, some of which is developmental, rather than "sociolinguistic" in the usual sense. [See Beebe and Giles (1984), as well as the later discussion.] It is important for language acquisition researchers to determine whether particular variables are subject to *social* conditioning, and if so, why. Trudgill (1981), writing about native language, suggests that sounds that are likely to undergo accommodative shifts may be those that speakers are most conscious of. In other words, they might be the category of variables that have traditionally been called "stereotypes" (see Labov 1970, 1972).

Noting that a number of early and recent research studies of Spanish speakers' L2 English indicate that /r/ is sensitive to social conditioning (see several of the studies discussed earlier), Zuengler (1988) tested Trudgill's suggestion on L2 speakers. She sought to determine whether /r/, and any other sounds, were held as stereotypes in Spanish speakers' English. Forty-five adult native Spanish speakers were asked to mimic an American native English speaker trying to speak Spanish. Analyses were conducted of which sounds the subjects chose to alter and which ones they were most conscious of altering. The most frequently reported item was /r/, which they pronounced as the American English retroflex [ɻ]. This result would appear to support Trudgill's (1981) theory and, as such, to offer an explanation (albeit limited and applicable so far only to native Spanish speakers) for which sounds undergo accommodation-influenced variation.

In summary, what can be said about CAT research on L2 interactional variation is that there are, to date, a small number of investigations, and some of them have inconclusive results. That this is the case is not a problem with CAT itself, however. As discussed earlier, the inconclusiveness of results may be due to problems in interpreting unpredicted directions of shift in several of the cases, the possibility of choosing the wrong variables (and revealing only limited effects), small numbers of subjects in some of the studies, and post hoc analyses in others. Despite such problems, CAT appears promising as a theory of L2 sociolinguistic variation. It is essential that further research be conducted within a CAT paradigm to determine the extent to which the theory can help us explain the complexities of nonnative speech.

7.4. Foreigner talk (L1 variation when talking to L2 speakers)

The particular linguistic adjustments that NSs make when interacting with L2 speakers have been observed for a long time. It was in the early 1970s that the adjustments, named "foreigner talk (FT)" by Ferguson (1971, 1975), began to be studied. Since then, researchers have accumulated information about the linguistic characteristics of FT. The questions of *why* and *when* FT is used, however, remain unanswered. Instead, there are points of disagreement, undoubtedly due to the fact that there has been no unifying theory to explain the dynamics of FT.

In this section, the observed characteristics of FT are briefly summarized. Then CAT is invoked as an explanation of the dynamics of FT. Specifically, it is shown that a number of CAT dimensions presented by Coupland et al. (1988) in discussing interactions with the elderly are relevant to explaining the use of FT.

When it was first researched, FT was usually presented in conjunction with baby talk (i.e., how adults speak to infants), because the two were considered similar in form and function. Since then, FT has been studied separately by SLA researchers. Those interested particularly in NS modifications in L2 classroom settings have used the term "teacher talk" (e.g., Chaudron 1988), but the latter is usually considered a type of FT rather than a distinct phenomenon (e.g., Kleifgen 1985; Schinke-Llano 1983).

The formal features of FT are well documented; for summaries, see Ellis (1985), Hatch (1983), and Larsen-Freeman (1985). Some of the features comprising FT are (relative to NSs interacting with other NSs) slower speech rate, shorter and simpler sentences, more questions and question tags, greater pronunciation articulation, less use of contractions, fewer pronouns, and vocabulary that is restricted to high-frequency words. It has been found, however, that not all NSs use FT when interacting with NNSs, nor does FT, when employed, contain all of the features just listed. There is no uniform explanation provided in the literature for such variation in FT use.

Another phenomenon observed in FT use is variation in grammaticality. That is, NSs sometimes make syntactic alterations to their FT that would be considered ungrammatical within the NS speech community. The lack of an overriding theory to explain FT use is evident in the fact that ungrammaticality has become a point of disagreement in the literature. Instead of looking for reasons why variation in FT grammaticality occurs, researcher disagreement focuses on whether FT *in general* should be described as grammatical or ungrammatical. Thus, one finds, for example, that some of the literature points out that FT can be ungrammatical (e.g., Ellis 1985; Snow, van Eeden, and Muysken 1981), and other literature portrays FT as usually *not* ungrammatical (e.g., Clyne 1981; Freed 1981; Long 1983). Arthur et al. (1980) resolve the "problem" of grammaticality by suggesting that we use the term "foreigner talk" to describe NS ungrammatical speech to NNSs and "foreigner register" to describe NS grammatical speech to NNSs. Lacking an overriding theory of FT variation, the literature is thus restricted to the level of disagreements about descriptive adequacy.

By invoking CAT dimensions, we can move the FT literature beyond the descriptive level to an explanation of the dynamics underlying FT use. Viewing FT within a CAT framework will clarify much of the variation observed in FT use and bring a coherence to the literature.

The following discussion of FT is based on the formulation of the CAT model presented in Coupland et al. (1988). Their focus is on elucidating interactions between the young and the elderly. The CAT model is extended to explain the strategies underlying such interactions. Four dimensions of CAT presented in Coupland et al. (1988) will be invoked to explain the dynamics inherent to NS interactions with NNSs: (1) NS interactional goals; (2) NS perceptions of the NNS; (3) NS encoded strategies; and (4) NNS decoding of NS strategies.

Native speaker's interactional goals

To understand the NS's use (or nonuse) of FT, we must first assume that the NS has a certain interactional goal or goals in communicating with an NNS. According to CAT (Coupland et al. 1988), speakers may (consciously or unconsciously) wish to communicate effectively, ensure that their message is comprehensible, gain their partner's social approval, or emphasize distinctiveness from their partner.

There is support in the FT literature for the speaker goals that are conceptualized by CAT. A number of writers have described FT as reflecting the NS's desire for communication efficiency and mutual comprehension (e.g., Clyne 1981; Freed 1981; Hatch 1983; Kleifgen 1985; Snow et al. 1981; Valdman 1981). Ensuring comprehension might be a particularly strong goal in certain types of interactions. For example, observers note greater FT use when the NS and NNS are involved in a two-way exchange of information than in a one-way communication by the NS (Ellis 1985; Hatch 1983; Long 1981). The NS displays a greater degree of FT use (and possibly more concern about comprehensibility) when the interaction is spontaneous rather than planned (Long 1983), and when the topics discussed are abstract and complex (Snow et al. 1981).

Other literature on FT points to NS goals of displaying liking for the NNS and obtaining the NNS's social approval. Clyne (1981) and Evans (1987) provide data illustrating that through the use of FT, the NS can signal that he or she identifies with the NNS and supports the NNS's language efforts.

Another goal that a speaker may have, as indicated by CAT, is to maintain distinctiveness from the interlocutor. This goal could be manifested in NS–NNS interactions by the *nonuse* of FT, and thus provide one explanation for the observation that FT does not always occur in NS–NNS interactions.) There is support for this goal in the FT literature. Perdue (1984) and Clyne (1981) emphasize the NS's goal of maintaining distinctiveness rather than ensuring communication success, and Valdman (1981) concurs, describing the function of FT as enabling NSs to increase the social distance between themselves and their NNS interlocutor. Perdue (1984) suggests that NSs often display ethnocentrism in interacting with NNSs and implies that FT use may reflect this practice.

Native speaker's perceptions of the nonnative speaker

Speakers' interactional goals are influenced by their perceptions of the interlocutor. These perceptions may be based on a sample of the interlocutor's behavior or on stereotypes of the interlocutor (Coupland et al. 1988). In NS–NNS encounters, the NS forms impressions of the NNS that can serve to alter or strengthen the NS's interactional goals (which, of course, can change through the interaction).

There are two dimensions that are salient to many NSs in perceiving their NNS interlocutor. One dimension concerns perceived ethnic and cultural differences. The NS's perception of such differences could, in turn, strengthen his or her goal of maintaining distinctiveness (if he or she felt threatened, for example, by the NNS's ethnicity or wished to display ethnocentrism). In such circumstances, the NS might choose to *not* use FT or to use it in an overaccommodating manner (see later). The same perception may have an opposite effect, too. An NS who perceived great social and cultural distance between the self and the NNS interlocutor could choose to downplay any distinctiveness and work to increase social liking and approval instead. The NS's use of FT would reflect this goal.

Several researchers have argued that NNSs are not necessarily viewed as members of specific ethnic groups but are often perceived more generically as "foreign," and foreignness is itself a role or identity (see Harder 1980; Janicki 1986). Beebe and Giles (1984) state that NNSs, because of their nonnativeness, are generally assigned a low-status role when interacting with NSs.

Another dimension that is salient in perceptions of the NNS interlocutor is the NNS's linguistic or communicative competence. Some NSs assess the NNS's productive and receptive competence by attending to the NNS's behavior (usually throughout the conversation). Other NSs simply base their perceptions of NNS competence on stereotypes they hold of NNSs. If an NS perceives that the NNS is weak in communicative competence, the interactional goal of mutual comprehensibility will become an important one for the NS. This could, in turn, lead to increased use of FT in the interaction. There is evidence that an increased amount of FT does indeed occur with NNS interlocutors who may be perceived as having low levels of communicative competence (see Ellis 1985; Kleifgen 1985; Long 1983; Scarcella and Higa 1982).

Native speaker's encoded strategies

Having one or more of the interactional goals listed earlier, and perceiving characteristics of the interlocutor, the speaker will encode certain language strategies. These strategies, which we will apply to the NS speaker, consist of speech "convergence," "divergence," "maintenance," and "complementarity" (Coupland et al. 1988).

Speech "convergence" refers to a strategy by which a speaker adjusts his or her speech in the direction of what he or she perceives the interlocutor's speech to be. FT adjustments in speech rate, pronunciation, vocabulary, and so on, can be explained as a manifestation of the strategy of speech convergence. Convergence occurs on a continuum from very few adjustments to an almost exact matching of the NNS's speech. The observations in the literature that NSs employ different degrees of FT in their talk, and that most FT adjustments occur with low-proficiency NNSs (Ellis 1985; Kleifgen 1985), are descriptions of varying degrees of speech convergence. So is the evidence that FT can contain features that mirror the NNS's mistakes (e.g., Evans 1987; Snow et al. 1981), since it illustrates the fact that in making their speech more similar to the NNS's, NSs may include ungrammatical features in their FT. Thus, we can explain grammatical variation in FT as a convergence strategy that is influenced by the NNS's degree of grammaticality.

NS speakers can also choose to employ the strategies of speech known as "maintenance" or "divergence." Neither strategy would involve the use of FT. Use of such strategies provides an explanation for the observation in the literature that some NS–NNS interactions do not contain any FT. An NS may have the interactional goal of maintaining distinctiveness from the NNS (as discussed earlier) for reasons of ethnocentrism, as a response to a negative stereotype held of the NNS, and so on (see Perdue 1984; Valdman 1981). The NS can attempt to distinguish himself or herself by not making any adjustments in personal speech style. Otherwise, if the NS perceives that the NNS's language is already very similar to the NS's (and that speech maintenance wouldn't make him or her distinctive enough), the NS might use speech divergence to ensure greater distinctiveness. In such circumstances, the NS could make his or her speech more standard (if that will distinguish it from the NNSs), or could shift away from the NNS into his or her regional dialect, or use certain jargon, a special register, and so on. In other words, the NS would be diverging away from the NNS into a speech variety differing from the one the NNS is using.

A fourth speech strategy that speakers can use is "complementarity" (Coupland et al. 1988). This is a strategy by which speakers emphasize perceived role differences between interlocutors. NS–NNS interactions can typify several sets of role relationships. Beebe and Giles (1984) discuss such interactions as composed of high-status–low-status participants, with the NNS assigned the lower status role. Others indicate that NS–NNS interactions are composed of nonforeigner–foreigner role relationships (e.g., Harder 1980; Janicki 1986). Most NS–NNS interactions that occur in the classroom exemplify a teacher–student role relationship.

If the NS chooses to emphasize the role differences by employing the speech strategy of complementarity, he or she may or may not use FT to do so. The types of adjustments the NS makes will be a function of what he or she perceives the appropriate speech styles to be for the particular role relationship chosen for emphasis. For example, an NS in a teacher–student interchange may slow down his or her speech and display careful articulation in what he or she perceives is an appropriate style for a teacher. An NS to whom the foreigner–nonforeigner role dynamics are salient (see Harder 1980; Janicki 1986; Katz 1981) might choose the standard speech style if he or she considers that to be the expected style of the nonforeigner. Perceiving himself or herself as the higher-status interlocutor (see Beebe and Giles 1984), the NS could slow down his or her speech rate and decrease standardness (see Thakerar et al. 1982; Zuengler 1987).

Nonnative speaker's decoding of the native speaker's strategies

An important part of the dynamics of NS–NNS interactions is the effect of the NS's language strategies on the NNS. Obviously, how the NNS perceives the strategy can, in turn, influence the dimensions just discussed, inform the NNS's perception of the NS, and influence future interactions between the NNS and other NSs. We discuss one effect in particular, since it is an important one that signals the potential for "miscommunication" (Coupland et al. 1988) in many NS–NNS interchanges. Moreover, there is evidence for it in the literature on FT.

"Overaccommodation" is a label given to a speaker whom the addressee considers is overdoing it. That is, the speaker is perceived as making more adjustments than are necessary or appropriate to the interaction. The speaker may in fact have positive intentions, but he or she is instead perceived by the addressee as being condescending or contolling (Coupland et al. 1988: 32). Such miscommunication (i.e., the speaker has one intention but the addressee perceives another) is common to young–elderly interactions, Coupland et al. argue.

It is not just young–elderly interactions that experience miscommunication caused by overaccommodation, for the use of FT in NS–NNS interactions can give rise to the same problem. Specifically, three types of overaccommodation can occur. [These were first formulated by Ryan et al. (1986) and are cited in Coupland et al. (1988)]. According to Ryan et al., the speaker may be practicing "sensory overaccommodation," which means that the speaker overdoes it when he perceives that the addressee is handicapped. Aplying this phenomenon to NS–NNS interactions, the NS may overproduce FT features if he or she judges (rightly or wrongly) the NNS to be linguistically handicapped and the goal is to make the NNS comprehend his or her message. The NNS might experience this as the NS "talking down," placing the NNS in a childlike position. Ellis (1985), Snow et al. (1981), and Valdman (1981) all point out such negative aspects of FT use.

Another type of overaccommodation is "dependency overaccommodation" (Ryan et al. 1986, discussed in Coupland et al. 1988). Such overaccommodation is perceived by the addressee as placing him or her in a lower status role, where the speaker controls the interaction and the addressee is made to feel dependent on the speaker. Some of the FT literature suggests that dependency overaccommodation can occur in NS–NNS interactions. As pointed out earlier, Beebe and Giles (1984) have argued that due to the NNS's nonnativeness, he or she is usually "assigned" a lower status role when interacting with NSs. The NS goal in the interaction may be a positive one (e.g., to show liking for the NNS or to help the NNS comprehend the message). However, the NNS might perceive the FT adjustments as signifying that he or she is in a lesser position. The FT adjustments can also be perceived as helping the NS control the conversation. A number of researchers have indeed observed that NSs often control interactions with NNSs (e.g., Long 1981; Scarcella 1983).

A third type of overaccommodation that can take place in NS–NNS interactions is "intergroup overaccommodation" (Ryan et al. 1986). Here the addressee evaluates the speaker's language strategies as making the addressee feel that he or she is being treated as a group member, not an individual. This perception can occur in NS–NNS interactions in which the NNS perceives that he or she is being labeled a "foreigner" or "language learner." As discussed earlier, some researchers argue that NSs often lump all NNSs together as "foreigners," regardless of personality or ethnic group, and "foreign" becomes a social identity of its own (see Harder 1980; Janicki 1986). If this is a common phenomenon, we would expect that many NNSs would evaluate NS adjustments negatively as intergroup overaccommodation.

It is important to determine how often such NNS evaluations are made of NS overaccommodation. Although FT adjustments may be intended by the NS to promote successful communication, they may instead be evaluated by the NNS recipient as *undermining* communication. Having repeated experience with NSs who appear to be overaccommodating could cause the NNS to lose motivation for further language acquisition, avoid interactions with NSs, and develop negative attitudes toward them, their society, and their language. These circumstances would in turn affect NSs, and social and psychological distance would increase. In studying FT, we must attend to the NNS's affective response to it. As we have seen, the NS cannot assume that FT adjustments will lead to successful communication. Since miscommunication can have such a significant impact on the NNS's language learning and attitudes, we must look to ways of helping NNSs and NSs to effectively communicate.

7.5. Conclusion

We have seen that CAT enables us to explain much of the variation observed in L2 production. CAT can be invoked both as a theory of variation in acquisition over time and of variation in a speaker's L2 performance at a given time. The evidence for NS variation (i.e., FT use) in interactions with language learners can benefit, as well, by invoking CAT. The theory brought a unifying perspective to a body of FT literature that lacked explanation and coherence. We look forward to more research conducted within a CAT paradigm in our effort to understand the complexity of variation in language use.

References

Anisman, P. H.. 1975. Some aspects of code switching in New York Puerto Rican English. *Bilingual Review*, 2: 56–85.

Arthur, B., Weiner, R., Culver, M., Lee, Y. J., and Thomas D. 1980. The register of impersonal discourse to foreigners: Verbal adjustments to foreign accent. *In* D. Larsen-Freeman (ed.), *Discourse Analysis in Second Language Research*, pp. 111–24. Rowley, MA: Newbury House.

Ball, P., Giles, H., and Hewstone, M. 1984. The intergroup theory of second language acquisition with catastrophe dimensions. *In* H. Tajfel (ed.), *The Social Dimensions*, Vol. 2, pp. 668–94. Cambridge: Cambridge University Press.

Beebe, L. M. 1981. Social and situational factors affecting the communicative strategy of dialect code-switching. *International Journal of the Sociology of Language*, 32: 139–49.

Beebe, L. M. (ed.). 1988. *Issues in Second Language Acquisition: Multiple Perspectives*. New York: Newbury House.

Beebe, L. M., and Giles, H. 1984. Speech-accommodation theories: A discussion in terms of second-language acquisition. *International Journal of the Sociology of Language*, 46: 5–32.

Beebe, L. M., and Zuengler, J. 1981. A word before the final vows. Review of H. Giles and R. St. Clair (eds.), *Language and Social Psychology*. *Contemporary Psychology*, 26: 279–80.

Beebe, L. M., and Zuengler, J. 1983. Accommodation theory: An explanation for style shifting in second language dialects. *In* N. Wolfson and E. Judd (eds.), *Sociolinguistics and Language Acquisition*, pp. 195–213. Rowley, MA: Newbury House.

Berkowitz, D. 1986. The effects of perceived cultural empathy on second language performance. Unpublished Ph.D. dissertation, Columbia University.

Bourhis, R. Y., and Giles, H. 1977. The language of intergroup distinctiveness.

242   J. Zuengler

In H. Giles (ed.), *Language, Ethnicity and Intergroup Relations*, pp. 119–35. London: Academic Press.

Bourhis, R. Y., Giles, H., Leyens, J. P., and Tajfel, H. 1979. Psycholinguistic distinctiveness: Language divergence in Belgium. In H. Giles and R. St. Clair (eds.), *Language and Social Psychology*, pp. 158–85. Baltimore: University Park Press.

Burt, M., and Dulay, H. (eds.) 1975. *New Directions in Second Language Learning, Teaching and Bilingual Education*. Washington, DC: Teachers of English to Speakers of Other Languages.

Chaudron, C. 1988. *Second Language Classrooms: Research on Teaching and Learning*. Cambridge: Cambridge University Press.

Clyne, M. G. 1981. "Second generation" foreigner talk in Australia. *International Journal of the Sociology of Language*, 28: 69–80.

Coupland, N., Coupland, J., Giles, H., and Henwood, K. 1988. Accommodating the elderly: Invoking and extending a theory. *Language in Society*, 17: 1–41.

Ellis, R. 1985. *Understanding Second Language Acquisition*. Oxford: Oxford University Press.

Evans, M. 1987. Linguistic accommodation in a bilingual family: One perspective on the language acquisition of a bilingual child being raised in a monolingual community. *Journal of Multilingual and Multicultural Development*, 8: 231–35.

Faerch, C., and Kasper, G. 1987. Perspectives on language transfer. *Applied Linguistics*, 8: 111–36.

Ferguson, C. 1971. Absence of copula and the notion of simplicity: A study of normal speech, baby talk, foreigner talk and pidgins. In D. Hymes (eds.), *Pidginization and Creolization of Languages*, pp. 141–50. New York: Cambridge University Press.

Ferguson, C. 1975. Towards a characterization of English foreigner talk. *Anthropological Lingusitics*, 17: 1–14.

Freed, B. 1981. Foreigner talk, baby talk, native talk. *International Journal of the Sociology of Language*, 28: 19–40.

Garrett, P., Giles, H., and Coupland, N. 1989. The contexts of language learning: Extending the intergroup model of second language acquisition. In S. Ting-Toomey and F. Korzenny (eds.), *Language, Communication and Culture*, pp. 201–21. Newbury Park, CA: Sage.

Giles, H., and Byrne, J. 1982. An intergroup approach to second language acquisition. *Journal of Multilingual and Multicultural Development*, 3: 17–40.

Giles, H., and Johnson, P. 1987. Ethnolinguistic identity theory: A social psychological approach to language maintenance. *International Journal of the Sociology of Language*, 68: 69–99.

Harder, P. 1980. Discourse as self-expression—on the reduced personality of the second-language learner. *Applied Linguistics*, 1: 262–70.

Hartford, B. S. 1978. Phonological differences in the English of adolescent female and male Mexican-Americans. *International Journal of the Sociology of Language*, 17: 55–64.

Hatch, E. M. 1983. *Psycholinguistics: A Second Language Perspective*. Rowley, MA: Newbury House.

Janicki, J. 1986. Accommodation in native speaker–foreigner interaction. In J. House and S. Blum-Kulka (eds.), *Interlingual and Intercultural Communication*, pp. 169–78. Tübingen: Gunter Narr Verlag.

Katz, J. T. 1981. Children's second-language acquisition: The role of foreigner talk in child–child interaction. *International Journal of the Sociology of Language*, 28: 53–68.

Kleifgen, J. 1985. Skilled variation in a kindergarten teacher's use of foreigner talk. *In* S. M. Gass and C. G. Madden (eds.), *Input in Second Language Acquisition*, pp. 59–68. Rowley, MA: Newbury House.

Krashen, S. 1981. *Second Language Acquisition and Second Language Learning*. Oxford: Pergamon.

Krashen, S. 1982. *Principles and Practice in Second Language Acquisition*. Oxford: Pergamon.

Labov, W. 1966. *The Social Stratification of English in New York City*. Washington, DC: The Center for Applied Linguistics.

Labov, W. 1970. The study of language in its social context. *In* P. P. Giglioli (ed.), *Language and Social Context*, 1972, pp. 283–307. Harmondsworth, Middlesex: Penguin.

Labov, W. 1972. *Sociolinguistic Patterns*. Philadelphia: University of Pennsylvania Press.

Larsen-Freeman, D. 1985. State of the art on input in second language acquisition. *In* S. M. Gass and C. G. Madden (eds.), *Input in Second Language Acquisition*, pp. 433–44. Rowley, MA: Newbury House.

Long, M. H. 1981. Questions in foreigner talk discourse. *Language Learning*, 31: 135–57.

Long, M. H. 1983. Linguistic and conversational adjustments to non-native speakers. *Studies in Second Language Acquisition*, 5: 177–93.

Long, M. H. 1985. Input and second language acquisition theory. *In* S. M. Gass and C. G. Madden (eds.), *Input in Second Language Acquisition*, pp. 377–93. Rowley, MA: Newbury House.

Meier Art Tests. 1963. *II. Aesthetic Perception*. Chicago: Stolting.

Oller, J. W., and Richards, J. C. (eds.). 1973. *Focus on the Learner: Pragmatic Perspectives for the Language Teacher*. Rowley, MA: Newbury House.

Pennington, M. C., and Richards, J. C. 1986. Pronunciation revisited. *TESOL Quarterly*, 20: 207–26.

Perdue, C. (ed.). 1984. *Second Language Acquisition by Adult Immigrants: A Field Manual*. Rowley, MA: Newbury House.

Richards, J. C. (ed.). 1974. *Error Analysis*. London: Longman.

Ryan, E. B., Giles, H., Bartolucci, G., and Henwood, K. 1986. Psycholinguistic and social psychological components of communicaation by and with the elderly. *Language and Communication*, 6: 1–24.

Scarcella, R. C. 1983. Discourse accent in second language performance. *In* S. M. Gass and L. Selinker (eds.), *Language Transfer in Language Learning*, pp. 306–26. Rowley, MA: Newbury House.

Scarcella, R. C., and Higa, C. A. 1982. Input and age differences in second language acquisition. *In* S. Krashen, R. Scarcella, and M. Long (eds.), *Child–Adult Differences in Second Language Acquisition*, pp. 175–201. Rowley, MA: Newbury House.

Schinke-Llano, L. A. 1983. Foreigner talk in content classrooms. *In* H. W. Seliger and M. H. Long (eds.), *Classroom Oriented Research in Second Language Acquisition*, pp. 146–64. Rowley, MA: Newbury House.

Schumann, J. H., and Stenson, N. (eds.). 1975. *New Frontiers in Second Language Learning*. Rowley, MA: Newbury House.

Snow, C. E., van Eeden, R., and Muysken, P. 1981. The interactional origins of foreigner talk: Municipal employees and foreign workers. *International Journal of the Sociology of Language*, 28: 81–92.

Tarone, E. 1989. Accounting for style-shifting in interlanguage. *In* S. Gass, C. Madden, D. Preston, and L. Selinker (eds.), *Variation in Second Language Acquisition: Psycholinguistic Issues*, pp. 13–21. Clevedon: Multilingual Matters.

Thakerar, J. M., Giles, H., and Cheshire, J. 1982. Psychological and linguistic parameters of speech accommodation theory. *In* C. Fraser and K. R. Scherer (eds.), *Advances in the Social Psychology of Language*, pp. 204–55. Cambridge: Cambridge University Press.

Trudgill, P. 1981. Linguistic accommodation: Sociolinguistic observations on a sociopsychological theory. *In* C. Masek, R. A. Hendrich, and M. F. Miller (eds.), *Papers from the Parasession on Language and Behavior, Chicago Linguistic Society*, pp. 218–37. Chicago: University of Chicago Press.

Valdman, A. 1981. Sociolinguistic aspects of foreigner talk. *International Journal of the Sociology of Language*, 28: 41–52.

Young, R. 1988. Variation and the interlanguage hypothesis. *Studies in Second Language Acquisition*, 10: 281–302.

Zuengler, J. 1982. Applying accommodation theory to variable performance data in L2. *Studies in Second Language Acquisition*, 4: 181–92.

Zuengler, J. 1987. Effects of "expertise" in interactions between native and nonnative speakers. *Language and Communication*, 7: 123–37.

Zuengler, J. 1988. Identity markers and L2 pronunciation. *Studies in Second Language Acquisition*, 10: 33–50.

8. Interethnic accommodation: The role of norms

CYNTHIA GALLOIS AND VICTOR J. CALLAN

8.1. Introduction

Researchers in the area of cross-cultural communication have long recognized the crucial role that norms and their violations play in contributing to understanding and misunderstanding across groups. Indeed, Hall (1959) argued cogently that socially determined norms (or rules), and misinterpretations of rule violations by members of outgroups, are the most important cause of prejudice. Hall pointed out that people tend to see their own norms as natural and as having moral force. He suggested that cross-cultural misunderstandings could be greatly reduced if people were sensitized to the norms of their own and other cultures; many cross-cultural training programs have been developed from his ideas.

Over the intervening years, other explanations of prejudice and hostility between ethnic and cultural groups have overshadowed to some extent the part played by norms in misunderstanding between ethnic groups [see Kim and Gudykunst (1988) for a recent review of some relevant theories]. Speech accommodation theory (SAT), for one, has been employed extensively to analyze cross-ethnic and cross-cultural communication. Research directed by this theory points to important issues addressed in cross-cultural training packages. Among the more obvious considerations are the status of the interactant from the other culture, the nature of the contact (formal, informal), and the attributions gener-

The research presented in this chapter was partially supported by grants from the Australian Research Grants Scheme and the University of Queensland.

We would like to thank Pat Truesdale, Catherine O'Hara, Clive Williams, and Amanda Fulcher for their help in data collection and coding. We are especially grateful to Angela Bryan for her help in developing the questionnaires and content categories, as well as for data collection. We are also grateful to the editors for their helpful comments.

Correspondence concerning this chapter should be addressed to Cynthia Gallois, Department of Psychology, University of Queensland, Queensland 4072, Australia.

ated about speakers due to their use of particular accommodative strategies.

Even though SAT has included a role for norms, it is only recently that the need for researchers in this area to deal explicitly with them has been fully acknowledged. As Ball et al. (1984) point out, SAT was originally developed as a reaction to the overuse of roles and norms in explaining communicative behavior. SAT instead emphasized the interpersonal relationship between conversational partners, the motivation to converge to or diverge from the partner's speech forms, and the attributions made about the communicative behavior of other speakers. In this view, although norms do play some role, it is the immediate interaction, along with the aspects of personal and social identity involved (Tajfel and Turner 1979; Turner 1986), that are crucial in explaining accommodative shifts by speakers and listeners, especially those across ethnic groups. Thus, in earlier years, little attention was paid to the influence of norms in the accommodation process.

This chapter aims to explore further the manner in which norms work in interethnic encounters and to suggest some ways they may influence communication accommodation. Our review examines the role of SAT (or "communication accommodation theory, or CAT," as it is now more appropriately called; see Giles et al. 1987) in directing research on interethnic communication. In addition, we describe the findings of research guided by CAT and the value of developing a more comprehensive understanding of situational factors in communication accommodation. In order to function effectively and happily in a new culture, people must gain cultural skills and knowledge about the communication-based norms that facilitate daily interactions with people in all aspects of the host culture.

8.2. Norms and immigrants

The bulk of research on CAT has involved convergence to or divergence from an interlocutor within the framework of a single interaction. Sometimes this has involved only a few sentences, as in the field work on accommodation across languages done by Bourhis (1983). In these studies, the measure of accommodation has been the extent to which speakers change (or think they change) their behavior with respect to a specific conversational partner. Some researchers, however, have looked at another related phenomenon—accommodation by a member of one speech community to the behavior of another over an extended period of time.

The motivation by immigrants to converge over time has been addressed directly by CAT and by ethnolinguistic identity theory [ELIT; e.g., Beebe and Giles 1984; Giles and Johnson 1981]. ELIT makes predictions about individual differences in the desire to learn a new language and to speak it with members of the new speech community, which are similar to its predictions about initial orientation to accommodate to a conversational partner who is a member of an ethnic outgroup (Giles and Johnson 1987; see also Gallois et al. 1988). Research using either CAT or ELIT has revealed much about the communicative issues that can be addressed in cross-cultural training packages. For instance, Shockey (1984) found that American immigrants in England converged to British speech forms for interpretability motives; that is, these people adopted characteristic British pronunciations of sounds that were necessary for clear understanding but retained their American accent when comprehension was not an issue. Trudgill (1986), indeed, has suggested that long-term accommodation to the behavior of one speech community by members of another may be the major mechanism in dialect change.

Communication accommodation over time, and the perception of it by members of the host community, are very relevant in countries where there is substantial immigration, such as Australia. In spite of the multicultural policy adopted by the government, Australia is a very monolingual country (Callan and Gallois 1987; Clyne 1982), and both aborigines and immigrants are thus under considerable pressure to learn and speak Australian English, the majority language.

Immigrants are aware of this pressure, and the tendency to shift to English is strong for most groups, although the tie to the original language remains strong for some (Clyne 1982). We have also found that although the children of Greek immigrants still value their parents' language (Callan and Gallois 1982; see also Giles, Rosenthal, and Young, 1985), at the same time they reject immigrant accents (Callan, Gallois, and Forbes, 1983). In a very recent unpublished study (with Gaiero and Lopez), we found that Italian immigrants and their children rated Australian-accented speech more positively than Italian-accented speech, in some cases even when the Australian-accented speech contained norm-violating grammatical errors. On the other hand, Hispanic immigrants and their children, who represent a more recently arrived community in Australia, showed considerably more solidarity for Spanish accents relative to Australian ones. On the basis of other research, we might speculate that their solidarity will diminish over time.

In some cases, convergence by immigrants may be to the most common or typical behavior of the new group. One possibility is for speakers to converge to the behavior that is most distinctive of the new community. Turner (1986) suggests that peopel who hold certain beliefs or attitudes, or who behave in particular ways, are *prototypical* for their groups. Their attitudes or behavior most clearly distinguish their group from other groups. Immigrants may be especially likely to converge to prototypical behavior.

In other cases, immigrant speakers may converge to a norm, or a perceived norm, in the new community rather than to prototypical behavior. Convergence by immigrants may also be evaluated by natives as norm-following behavior, or it may be seen as behavior that is prototypical for the host community. Gallois and Callan (1988), for example, studied the way Anglo-Australian viewers judged Australian, British, and Italian speakers. The viewers also judged the speakers' nonverbal behavior, and we computed indexes of the degree to which the immigrants used behavior that was prototypical for the Anglo-Australian speakers. We found that Australian and immigrant speakers were judged more positively on traits related to solidarity both when they were perceived as prototypical and when they followed norms for the expression of positive emotion.

Members of the majority community also have sterotypes, and may hold norms, about how immigrants do and/or should use the majority language. It is helpful for immigrants and members of a host community to be aware of these norms, which are often not made explicit, in order to minimize misunderstanding (see Furnham and Bochner, 1986).

Findings from studies testing CAT highlight the importance of training immigrants and visitors to countries with other cultures to be sensitive to several key variables. Convergence that is perceived by members of the host community as inappropriate to the speaker's status, the relationship, or the norms of the situation may be labeled as ingratiating, condescending, or gauche, and the speaker may be evaluated negatively as a person. Platt and Weber (1984), for example, described a variety of convergence attempts by Australian businessmen in Singapore to their Sinaporean staff, and by immigrant workers to Australian coworkers in Australian factories, all of which resulted in negative rather than the positive evaluations, which were the motivations behind the convergence. All these examples involved violations of norms in the host culture.

To understand the part played by norms in cross-ethnic interactions and their impact on communication accommodation, it is worthwhile to examine briefly the ways in which norms have been conceptualized and studied by sociolinguists and social psychologists. Such an examination also gives some insight into why norms were not included in SAT for many years, as well as how they could be incorporated into an accommodation model.

8.3. Conceptualizations of norms

From the earliest days of role theory, norms have been defined as expectations about behavior that members of a community feel should (or should not) occur in particular situations [e.g., see Biddle and Thomas (1966) for clear examples of this use of the concept]. The emphasis is on expectations, that is, on socially shared *ideas* about appropriate and inappropriate behavior. Argyle and his colleagues have developed this conception of norms in their research on social situations and social rules (see Argyle, Furnham, and Graham 1981). Their work, however, has in general not touched on the fine detail of communicative shifts that has characterized CAT. Rather, it has been concerned with the more general aspects of relationships.

On the other hand, sociolinguists from Fishman (1971) on have studied the effects of norms on the fine details of communication, particularly code switching in multiethnic communities, whether the code is a language or another type of speech variety. Indeed, one can see even earlier evidence of this concern in linguistics. One thinks especially of the fascinating analysis of style done by Joos (1961), where speaking styles ranging from "intimate" to "frozen" are triggered by situational factors, including norms. Since this early work, sociolinguists have tended to look at norms as involving changes in communicative codes that are triggered by *features of the situation.*

Within this tradition, the role of place in determining code choice has loomed large, and sociolinguists have looked at the influence of churches, courtrooms, and the like in determing the use of a high rather than a low variety. Other factors, of course, have also been well documented. One well-studied variable is situational formality, along with norms for courtesy and politeness. This is opposed to informal or intimate situations, with their norms of solidarity, which may trigger the use of a low variety (see Fishman 1971; Gumperz and Hymes 1972; Rubin 1968). Labov (1972) extended the concept of situational influences to include value systems and ideology. In his view, speakers choose from the linguistic repertoire available to them, in part as a means of signaling their loyalty to a speech community. In more recent years, researchers such as Milroy (e.g., 1980, 1987) and, here in Australia, Horvath (1985) have taken this tradition even further by exploring in depth the code choices made by speakers that can be related to the type, complexity, and variability of their social networks.

For all these researchers, Fishman's (1971) aphorism, "who says what to whom, where, and when," has guided the search for situational and normative influences on linguistic and code choices. There has been a tendency to view these choices as rather automatic functions of situational influences, however. It is as if, because a speaker is in, say, a formal situation, talking to a stranger from another ethnolinguistic group about a topic of mutual interest and value neutrality, the speaker must choose a high form of the language. It is probably this conceptualization of the role of situations and norms that led psychologists such as Giles (1977) and Bourhis (1979) to describe sociolinguistics as treating speakers as linguistic automata.

In fact, to conceive of norms simply as features of a situation that determine a speaker's code choices is a mistake. Rather, the choices are mediated by expectations and ideas that the speaker holds about appropriate and inappropriate behavior. It is only relatively recently that sociolinguists have explicitly acknowledged this aspect of norms. Gibbons (1987), for example, points out that situations themselves cannot trigger language or communication choices. Instead, the roles and relationships within situations, mediated by the expectations of speakers and listeners, are the direct influences on the choices.

As sociolinguists have come in recent times to take a more psychological view of norms, so social psychologists, especially those working within the framework of CAT, have also returned to the use of norms, particularly to explain anomalous or unpredicted results in speech accommodation studies. Bourhis (1979, 1985) was probably the first to do this in a systematic way. He suggested, on the basis of experimental evidence, that initial linguistic choices in interthnic encounters may be made as a function of situational norms and expectations. Once the situation has been established, however, Bourhis suggests that interpersonal motives govern later linguistic choices. Thus, he argues, speakers accommodate to one another within social situations containing norms about code choice.

Genesee and Bourhis (1982, 1988) investigated the idea that both norms and interpersonal motives govern code choices in interethnic encounters between strangers. They found that they could predict evaluations of French and English Canadian salesmen's initial communications with customers in Montreal on the basis of a situational norm that salesmen use the preferred language of their customers. Later interchanges, however, were evaluated mainly on the basis of reactions to convergence and divergence as interpersonal acts. Interestingly, in a replication of this work in 1986, Stieblich found that although the sequence of norm-governed evaluations followed by interpersonal evaluations was maintained, the norms themselves had changed. Now it appears that French Canadians believe that salesmen should always address their customers initially in French [Genesee and Bourhis (1988) also found this in Quebec City].

Bourhis (1985) and Genesee and Bourhis (1988) have argued that this conceptualization of linguistic choices represents a way to integrate sociolinguistic and sociopsychological approaches to speech accommodation and to code switching. Ball et al. (1984), for example, found that Australians who converged in a job interview toward the more working-class accent of the interviewer were evaluated as negatively as divergent speakers. In addition, speakers who converged upward were seen as attempting to ingratiate themselves. In the first case, the evaluations may have resulted from a perception of norm violation in the job interview situation. In the second case, on the other hand, the attributions may have been caused by a perception that the speaker waas only following a situational norm and not being honest [early work in attribution theory, e.g., Jones and Davis (1965) would predict this effect]. Norms, it should be noted, are seen here as expectations influencing speakers' motivation, and not as situational triggers per se. Other researchers have given similar explanations in studies where the predicted effects of convergence and divergence did not appear.

McKirnan and Hamayan (1984a,b) attempt to bring an entirely social psychological analysis of norms and their role in communication into the general ambit of cross-ethnic and cross-cultural communication. They describe norms as shared cognitions that concern our expectations about the behavior of others in social situations, as well as providing rules for our own behavior. Thus, they emphasize the psychological and motivational character of these variables. In this way, they parallel the emphasis in CAT on subjective accommodation and its importance for both speakers and listeners in ingroup and intergroup encounters (Beebe and Giles 1984; Giles, Bourhis, and Taylor 1977; Thakerar, Giles, and Cheshire 1982).

McKirnan and Hamayan (1984a) describe norms as varying in content, clarity (including range and distinctiveness), and evaluation (including strength and tone). First, they argue, as others have (see Argyle et al. 1981), that the content of norms varies from one situation and one role relationship to another. Thus, the same behaviors may be perceived differently in different situations and for different role relationships. For example, whispering and pointing might be norm-violating between guests at a party but norm-following between students in a library. Second, they argue that norms differ in their clarity and range (i.e., in the extent to which appropriate behavior is perceived to have distinct boundaries). They suggest that intergroup attitudes influence the clarity and range of norms in interethnic encounters. In particular, people with more negative attitudes toward an ethnic outgroup may have clearer norms and a narrower range in regard to the behavior to outgroup members. Finally, norms differ in the extent to which following them and deviating from them is evaluated positively or negatively and in the intensity of evaluations. In this way, McKiman and Hamayan's work has close parallels with that of the Burgoons and their colleagues (Burgoon 1983; Burgoon and Hale 1984; Burgoon and Miller 1985) on violations of expectations. These researchers also argue that violations of expectations can result in positive and negative consequences of varying strength, depending on the norm, the situation, and the role relationships.

8.4. Norms and CAT

Obviously, this analysis of norms has implications for communication accommodation, in both verbal and nonverbal behavior. First, intergroup attitudes influence norms, as both McKirnan and Hamayan's (1984a,b) work and ELIT (Giles and Johnson 1981, 1987) propose. McKirnan and Hamayan found that norm violations in American English involving the intrusion of Spanish words were much more severely evaluated by Anglo-American children than were violations involving syntactic intrusions from Spanish or phonological errors associated with Hispanic accents. They also found that the strength of negative evaluations of these violations was related to subjects' ethnocentrism and their attitudes toward Hispanics. One might speculate that severe evaluations of lexical intrusions resulted from an attribution by the subjects that the intrusions were deliberate, and could not simply be explained by lack of knowledge or skill in English. The other side of this coin, of course, involves the influence of norms on intergroup attitudes and, thus, evaluations of accommodation. Situational norms and expectations about behavior influence the extent to which intergroup membership is salient, and therefore the strength of an evaluation in a particular case.

There is another reason for the explicit investigation of communication norms from the perspective of CAT. Norms put constraints of varying degree and strength on the accommodative moves that are perceived as desirable in an interaction. For example, Giles and Johnson (1986), in one study, found that, contrary to predictions, their subjects paid more attention to the higher status of a speaker than to what the speaker said or to the speaker's ethnic group. This may be a case where strong norms with regard to persons of higher status override the impact on listeners of convergence and divergence by an ethnic outgroup member. Giles and Johnson found in another study, however, that strong attitudes toward a topic, in their turn, could override normative considerations and produce evaluations of a speaker based on intergroup factors. Therefore, it is important to identify those situations whose norms are likely to constrain strongly the accommodative moves that are available to speakers and listeners. In the same way, we can identify those situations where, because the strength of norms is low, evaluations of violations are not very negative and those situations that, because normative range is high, leave maximum room for communicative shifts based on interpersonal or intergroup motives. Native speakers have this knowledge intuitively; immigrants may be judged by these rules whether they know them or not.

The theoretical and empirical work by Coupland et al. (1988) is perhaps the clearest example of the trend in CAT to integrate sociolinguistic variables. Their work adds to the initially proposed speaker strategies of convergence and divergence three other types: interpretability strategies, discourse management strategies, and interpersonal control strategies, together called "nonapproximation strategies." Coupland et al.'s version of CAT brings together the two traditions in communication described earlier: the social psychology of language, of which CAT is now one of the major theoretical models, and sociolinguistic studies of code switching and dialect change.

Recent versions of CAT also address the influence of social setting on speaker and listener behavior in cross-ethnic interactions. Gallois et al.

(1988) proposed that situational variables add to a person's initial orientation toward a conversational partner in influencing the addressee focus taken, and thus the strategies used and the evaluations made. They considered two main aspects of situations. The first is situational norms, in particular, formality. The second consideration is the extent to which a situation is threatening. Situations can be threatening by virtue of their norm structure; that is, formal situations, with their stricter norms, may be more threatening than less formal situations, where there is more range and tolerance in norms. Situations are also threatening, though, because of the topic, the social group memberships of interactants, and differences in power and status (Giles and Johnson 1986, 1987).

Gallois, Callan, and Johnstone (1984) looked at the relationship between ethnic group, situational norms, and threat. Following the argument of Lambert (1967), we proposed that judgments of social distance based on ethnic group membership are made early in intergroup encounters. When social distance is very high (as it is between many Anglo-Australians and Australian aborigines), all other considerations, including normative ones, are overridden in favor of strategies (both speech production and evaluation) designed to maintain social distance. At lower levels of social distance, like that between Anglo-Australians and Italians, situational factors related to threat become paramount. Threatening situational factors include formal or status-marked settings, intimate settings, male others, norm-violating behavior, and high-dominance behavior. Giles and Johnson (1986) also included in their analysis topics about which the person has strong beliefs or feelings. Thus, violations of norms or high-dominance behavior by members of ethnic outgroups, especially in formal or status-marked settings, pose a threat and are met with very negative evaluations. Informal public settings, submissive behavior, communication from females, and norm-following behavior, on the other hand, are labeled as nonthreatening and are evaluated more positively.

By contrast, Giles and Johnson (1987) proposed that there is a higher, rather than lower, tolerance for the behavior of ethnic outgroup members when they have high social status and when the situation is formal. This may occur because of general norms prescribing deference to high-status others. This proposal from ELIT leads, first, to the prediction that violations of norms or high-dominance behavior may be less negatively evaluated in formal than in informal situations when the behavior comes from a high-status outgroup member. In addition, there may be a greater normative range in formal situations for high-status than for equal-status others, even when these others are members of ethnic outgroups. This difference in normative range may not apply in informal situations. Although these two formulations lead to different predictions, they are not incompatible. Rather, they emphasize different aspects of status and formality, and thus highlight the importance of situational norms. In addition, they point to the possibility of general norms (such as "be polite"; see Argyle et al. 1981) and role- or situation-specific norm conflict. This possibility makes the detailed investigation of communication norms even more interesting.

8.5. An inquiry into communication norms in Australia

Social psychological research on interethnic communication in Australia has mainly been concerned with the acceptance by Australians of speakers with a foreign accent, the evaluation of standard and nonstandard speakers, and studies of communication accommodation. CAT has often been the framework guiding these studies. Several studies have examined personality evaluations by listeners of speakers with various Australian native accents (e..g., cultivated vs. broad: Seggie, Fulmizi, and Stewart 1982) and comparisons of evaluations of Australian, European, and Asian accents (Ball 1983; Gallois and Callan 1981; Seggie 1983). These studies generally confirm that educated Australian and British speakers are evaluated more positively. Extensions of this research to incorporate situational variables, as well as the sex of the speaker and listener, have permitted more complex normative interpretations of these evaluations (see Gallois and Callan 1985).

Australia is an ideal setting for communication accommodation research because of the existence of a large range of native and immigrant accents, which vary in status and prestige. Once norms are defined and evaluated, inferences about their role can be replaced by more direct evidence of their significance in the shaping of language attitudes and accommodative strategies. There are also questions about the significance of norms to speakers and listeners; the relationship between normative expectancies and causal attributions; and the importance of norms as the social, political, and linguistic status of various immigrant groups changes. All these factors must impinge on the relationship between norms and communication accommodation by putting more or fewer constraints on the accommodative moves allowed in a situation.

We have begun an initial investigation into the content, range, and intensity of the norms Anglo-Australians hold in situations that are emotionally arousing. We have chosen to look at formal situations (in this case, university lectures or job interviews), which are potentially somewhat threatening. We have compared norms as a function of sex and ethnicity (Australian and Italian) among interactants who are of equal or unequal status. Finally, we have compared expectations for oneself with expectations for the behavior of others. This research does not constitute a test of CAT. Instead, it is informed by CAT, and it aims to fill a gap in the situational component in recent models of accommodation.

The situations we are studying involve the expression of positive feelings (compliments) or negative feelings (criticism). Research on assertive communication suggests that both of these behaviors cause difficulty (see Lange and Jakubowski 1976; Leah, Law, and Snyder, 1979). There appear to be conflicts between general rules ("be polite" or "don't be immodest") and interpersonal goals ("stand up for your rights"). In addition, giving compliments and criticism has been shown to have a different impact on receivers as a function of speaker and receiver sex (e.g., Wilson and Gallois 1985) and interpersonal relationship (Lewis and Gallois 1984). In interpersonal terms, CAT predicts different reactions to them: convergence (at least in nonverbal behavior) as a response to compliments, especially if the speaker's motives are explained in positive ways, and divergence as a response to criticism, especially if the speaker's behavior is attributed to personal motives. These reactions, however, may change with variations in normative constraints and the ethnic group memberships of interactants. We tried, thus, to determine the norms for Anglo-Australians, and whether these norms are applied in the same way to Australians and Italians.

Our method involved the use of questionnaires. This method was chosen in order to elicit subjects' expectations about appropriate and inappropriate behavior rather than the behavior itself. We inquired about both appropriate and inappropriate behavior, since many researchers into social rules (e.g., Argyle et al. 1981) have suggested that it may be easier to recognize a rule violation than to express the rule in a positive form. Needless to say, actual behavior in a situation cannot be predicted accurately from knowledge of norms and expectations alone, any more than expectations and norms can be postdicted from behavior alone (the usual method). Nonetheless, research on both actual behavior and norms is necessary for a complete understanding of speakers' reactions to members of their ingroups and outgroups, and thus to the development of CAT.

Our subjects were forty male and forty female Anglo-Australian students. They gave their reactions to a series of written vignettes. Each vignette described a social context where two people, one of them the subject, conversed. Here is an example:

You have recently turned in the first major report for your sociology subject. You are worried about the result, because your lecturer, Dr. Antonia Petri, is known as a perfectionist. She passes out the marked reports in class. When she get to you, she compliments you on your good work, saying yours is one of the best reports in the group. (Compliment from a higher status Italian female other)

After reading the vignette, subjects were asked to write either the verbal response they should make or the appropriate response to the situation by the other person. Using seven-point bi-polar scales, subjects also rated how they should present an appropriate reply in terms of the amount of nine nonverbal behaviors: vocal pitch, loudness, tempo, variability, tension, accent (broad vs. cultivated and Australian vs. foreign), eyebrow raise, and gaze. All nonverbal behaviors were selected from the literature on expression of emotion and on intergroup communication as being associated with social status, power, interest-arousal, or solidarity-affiliation.

Next, subjects rated the importance of five motives for the response they wrote (using five-point scales varying from "not important" to "very important"). The motives were "to be effective in attaining the goal," "to strengthen the relationship," "to be fair," "to be polite and do the appropriate thing," and "pleasing the other person" (for compliments) or "standing up for your rights" (for criticism). These motives were taken from the literature on assertive communication and on social rules, and are strongly associated with power and solidarity. Motives, of course, are crucial to the evaluation process proposed by CAT; Taylor and Royer (1980) were the first researchers in this tradition to elicit motives retrospectively. Finally, subjects wrote a second sentence in which they indicated what should *not* be said or done in the situation.

In order to code subjects' written responses to the vignettes (what they or the other person should or should not say), we constructed nine major content categories. These were polite responses, positives, negatives, information, taking action, strong negatives (rudeness), sexist or racist comments, nonverbal behaviors, and miscellaneous. These main categories were then further divided into subcategories. Each response was coded into one or two subcategories. The questionnaires were coded by a trained assistant who waas not aware of the hypotheses of the study.

Table 1. *Norms for responses to compliments: what to say, how to say it, and why*

═══

Equal-status other
What: You and the other person should say "thank you."
        You should give more information to Australian others, and Italian
        others should give more information to you.
How: No significant effects.
Why: Being fair and pleasing the other person are more important for you
        than for the other person.

Higher-status other
What: You should thank the other person.
        The other person should make positive comment to you.
        You should not speak rudely to Italians; all others should not speak
        rudely to you.
How: You should use a tenser voice than the other person.
        You and the other person should use more cultivated accents when
        the other is an Australian man than when the other is an Italian man
        or a woman.
        You and the other person should use more eyebrow raise when the
        other is Australian and of the opposite sex or Italian and of the same
        sex.
        Males: You should speak with higher pitch, faster, more variably,
                 and with more gaze than the other person.
        Females: The other person should speak with more of these traits than
                 you should.
Why: Being fair to you is the most important motive for the other person.
        Being polite is more important with males than with females.
        Males: Strengthening the relationship and pleasing the other are
                 more important with Italians than with Australians.
        Females: Pleasing the other is more important with Italians than with
                 Australians.
                 Strengthening the relationship is more important with Aus-
                 tralians than with Italians.

═══

A second assistant independently coded a 20 percent sample of the questionnaires; agreement between the coders was 95 percent. Frequency counts of content subcategories were made separately for each vignette. Where 50 percent of the subjects' responses to a vignette were coded into the same subcategory, it was considered to be socially shared normative response. Where no subcategory was used by a majority of subjects, responses were combined into main categories, using the same 50 percent criterion.

Table 1 presents a summary of the results for responses to compli-

Table 2. *Norms for responses to criticism: what to say, how to say it, and why*

Equal-status other
What: You should not say negative things to Italians.
        Others should not be rude to you.
        Australian others should apologize to you.
How: You should use more eyebrow raise and higher pitch than the other person.
        You and the other person should use higher pitch when the other is Australian than when he or she is Italian.
Why: Being effective and standing up for your rights are more important for you than for the other person.
        Being polite is more important for the other person.

Higher-status other
What: You should not say negative things to Italians.
        Others should not say negative things to you.
        Australian others should justify themselves or apologize to you.
How: You should use a tenser voice than the other person.
Why: Being effective, standing up for your rights, and strengthening the relationship are more important for you than for the other person.

---

ments, and Table 2 presents a summary for responses to criticism. To give the most complete view of the norms that emerged, we have combined the results for content (all of them met the 50 percent criterion specified earlier) with the results of multivariate analyses on ratings of nonverbal behavior and motives. The biggest differences appeared between responses to compliments and those to criticism. Nevertheless, some differences also emerged between subjects' own responses and the responses they expected from others, and between ingroup and intergroup contexts.

Norms about content: What should you say?

There was very strong agreement to compliments should involve thanks. The only exception to this was higher-status others, who were expected to give general positive comments (such as "I really enjoyed the project" and "You're joking—that's fantastic!"), rather than specific thanks for the compliment. Interestingly, a second response appeared for two of the equal-status conditions ("you" when responding to an Australian and "they" when the other person was Italian). This was giving clarifying information (such as "I really enjoyed doing it" or "I had a lot of help from other people"). This norm may be a specification of the oft-mentioned Australian tendency to play compliments down and not to praise oneself. Such a suggestion is given further support by the fact that a substantial minority of subjects wrote self-praising responses as what should *not* be said.

Subjects were not as consistent in indicating what should not be said, at least in equal-status interactions. Rather, this norm seems to be positive—thank the other person for the compliment. For higher-status interactions, a constraint did appear consistently—not to respond rudely. This norm may have arisen from the formal context, as it applies to both the lower-status and the higher-status person. It may also indicate that, even in positive contexts, concern about inappropriate behavior is more salient with unequal-status others, where the lower-status person may be more vulnerable and more eager to please.

In responses to criticism, subjects agreed, especially when the other person was Italian, that rude, abusive, or other very negative comments (such as "Get lost" or obscenities) should not be made (see Table 2). They also expected apologies from Australian others (or justifications-excuses if the other person was of higher status). Subjects did not agree about what they themselves should or should not say in *ingroup* interactions as a response to criticism. Inspection of the data indeed revealed that appropriate responses were split among apologies, excuses, clarifications, suggestions for corrective action, and negative remarks (even abuse), as were inappropriate responses. Instead, the norm of avoiding impoliteness seemed to be confined to interactions with Italians. Subjects generally seemed to be more concerned about impoliteness and negativity when the other person was Italian.

Norms about nonverbal behavior: How should you say it?

As Table 1 shows, many of the significant differences in subjects' ratings of appropriate nonverbal behavior occurred in response to compliments, but always for higher-status interactions. In equal-status contexts, there were no significant effects (other than for foreign accent, where Italians were expected to sound more foreign than Australians, as they were in every case). For higher-status interactions, all of the nonverbal behaviors that produced significant effects are associated with high arousal (Gallois, Pittam, and Callan 1989; Mehrabian 1972; Scherer 1986). In addition, fast tempo and vocal tension are associated with status and dominance (Scherer 1986; Street, Brady, and Putman 1983).

Female subjects seemed to feel it was appropriate to adopt a somewhat more reserved nonverbal stance than the other person, perhaps in deference to the formality of the situation and the higher status of the other. Male subjects, however, reacted in almost the opposite way, expecting to behave in a more animated way than the other person. They may have felt that this nonverbal behavior was a good way of compensating for their lower status when they were less powerful but not under any real threat. Subjects of both sexes, however, said they should use more cultivated accents with Australian men than with others; this behavior may indicate deference to what some would argue is the highest-status group in these vignettes. These norms, in addition, are in accord with actual behavior (see Kramarae 1981; Smith 1985).

In this study, eyebrow raise was probably strongly associated with positivity, as it was paired in the response scales with lowered eyebrows, a part of the facial expressions for anger and sadness (Ekman and Friesen 1975). Noller and Gallois (1986) found that men were particularly likely to use eyebrow raise as a sign of positive affect in a structured message-sending task. Thus, it is reasonable to suggest that our subjects believe it is appropriate to adopt a positive facial expression with same-sex Italians of higher status and with opposite-sex Australians of higher status when the other person has given a compliment. Once again, a norm of emphasizing positive affect seems to be operating.

The norms our subjects hold for nonverbal behavior in response to criticism, compared to compliments, seem to vary less with the social group memberships of the interactants. As the results for verbal behavior also indicate, there are constraints on behavior in negative situations, but there may be fewer positive rules. Rather, reactions in these rather threatening situations may involve greater care by lower-status people, who are more vulnerable and wish to be positive, even though they may not expect this response from others.

Motives: Why do you say it?

As Table 1 indicates, most significant differences in subjects' ratings of the importance of the five motives in response to compliments appeared for higher-status vignettes. In equal-status vignettes, subjects thought it was more important for them than for the other person to be fair and to

please the other person. This tendency to attribute more positive motives to oneself than to others is widespread in studies of attribution [see
Watson (1982) for one review]. When the other person was of higher
status, on the other hand, Table 1 indicates several other interesting
effects. Here again, men seemed to place more importance on good relations with Italians than with Australians, whereas women showed more
deference to a higher-status person from an ethnic outgroup. In previous research, we have found, as have others, that women evaluate
outgroup speakers more positively than do men. This tendency may be
reflected in what women see as the appropriate motives in interacting
with people of other ethnic groups at low or moderate levels of social
distance. If so, this goal seems to exist even though they feel, contrary
to men, that the relationship is more important with an ingroup member.

In the case of responses to criticism in equal-status vignettes (see Table 2), subjects felt that it was more important for them than for the
other person to be effective in obtaining their goal and to stand up for
their rights, but more important for the other person than for them to
strengthen the relationship, to be fair, and to be polite. Thus, the same
self-serving attributions that characterized responses to compliments were
evident here. When the other person was of higher status, however,
subjects rated it as more important for them than for the other person
to be effective, to strengthen the relationship, and to stand up for their
rights. This suggests that the self-serving tone of their attributions was
somewhat qualified by the higher status of the other.

8.6. Conclusions

The influence of norms on responses to these vignettes has some interesting implications for CAT, as well as for the development of intercultural training programs. First, the prediction from CAT (and ELIT) that
in friendly contexts, where the interpersonal relationship is salient, situational factors themselves make convergence likely, was supported by
these results. The general rule "be polite" (Argyle et al. 1981) seems to
be translated as "be positive, verbally and nonverbally." We might predict, thus, that convergence in speech or nonverbal behavior, as well as
positively attuned strategies of discourse management and interpersonal control (Coupland et al. 1988), would be positively evaluated in
these contexts for both ingroup and interethnic interactions. These strat-

egies, in many cases, have the effect of emphasizing the *personal* nature of the encounter. Importantly, such strategies can be taught fairly easily to people about to enter another culture, either through experiential training or through culture awareness techniques.

There is still plenty of room, in responses to compliments, for interpersonal accommodation to vary, particularly in view of the lack of agreement about inappropriate behavior. Given the strong normative pressure to thank the other person (or to speak positively in other ways), one would expect counterattuning to take mainly the form of divergence in nonverbal behavior. Interestingly, the variable of accent, which looms so large as a marker of both social class and ethnicity, did not enter very much into our subjects' norms. Accent shifts thus may constitute a way to diverge from a disliked outgroup member who gives a compliment without violating any norms. Future studies using actual shifts in speech, rather than questionnaire vignettes, are an obvious step in examining these findings.

For negative situations, counterattuning may be independent of conversational norms. Our subjects did feel that it is inappropriate to be very negative or rude in response to criticism from Italians and thus (perhaps) to reciprocate the behavior of the other person. They also felt that an important motive for behavior was being effective and standing up for your rights, that is, defending yourself against the criticism. On the other hand, there was no agreement among our subjects that group-based divergence, either verbal (such as racist remarks) or nonverbal (including accent shift), is an appropriate response to criticism. Counterattuning thus is likely to take other forms than the nonverbal expression of negative emotion. Indeed, the lack of agreement about what *should* be said in response to criticism indicates that counterattuning strategies, when they are used, may be more likely to appear in verbal behavior, whereas the nonverbal channels preserve a norm-driven positive tone (that is, say what you think, but say it with a smile).

The analysis of responses to insults, criticism, or other negative remarks may require additions to the strategies proposed in Coupland et al.'s (1988) model of CAT. These situations imply a threat to personal or group-based power and esteem. Speaker strategies in response to criticism, therefore, may have different motives from those in other situations. For example, communication that is highly divergent in words, accent, and nonverbal behavior may be motivated by a strong desire to express personal dislike, dominate the other, and increase social distance when one is feeling very vulnerable. Our subjects saw this type of prejudiced response as inappropriate (norm-violating), especially in cross-ethnic contexts.

We should point once again to the importance of status as a situational factor, as well as to the influence that status has on communication norms. In general, our subjects indicated that norms in formal situations where status is unequal are more constraining than where status is equal; the constraints involve politeness, reserve, and positive emotion. Sex of subject differences qualified this impression somewhat, revealing that men may feel justified in competing for status (or at least compensating for their lower status) to a greater extent than women. If the higher-status person in an interaction does nto share this view, one would expect a greater potential for conflict, and thus for attuning strategies based on intergroup factors, in interactions where a man has lower status.

Norms in this study did change somewhat as a function of the ethnic group membership of the other person. In the main, subjects seemed especially concerned with being positive when the other person was Italian. This suggests that norms may exist in Australia for showing positive prejudice toward Italians, who represent an old and well-established immigrant group. Norms are likely to be different for inter-actions with Australian aborigines or for newer immigrant groups such as the Vietnamese. As van Dijk (1988) found in South Africa, however, racism is more often communicated subtly than overtly; norms for extra-positive behavior toward certain ethnic outgroups may be one means for doing this. An interesting topic for future research would be to com-pare norms for interactions with outgroup members who represent varying degrees of social distance and threat. We predict fewer norma-tive contraints on one's own behavior when social distance or threat is high but more constraints on the behavior of ethnic outgroup members. Again, this prediction could be tested using actual speech, as in tradi-tional investigations of CAT.

The results of research on people's shared beliefs about what they should and should not do in various contexts helps to fill out the "situ-ational influences" component in CAT (e.g., Gallois et al. 1988). Our findings also suggest a useful framework for organizing the basic prin-ciples of an intercultural training program. First, situations can be di-vided at least into positive and negative, as well as into formal and in-formal. Second, questions about norms must be answered: Do the norms involve verbal or nonverbal behavior (or both)? Do they prescribe behav-ior, or restrict it, or both? The results of our research give further support to the proposal that threat is an important situational influence that, along with status and formality, has an impact on norms themselves. It is well established that prejudiced reactions toward ethnic groups are often spurred on by a sense of threat produced by the economic success and social mobility of many ethnic minorities. In addition, we have found, as have others, that norms vary for different intergroup encounters.

All of these results suggest that the "situational influences" and "initial orientation" components of CAT need to be more strongly linked than they have been to date (e.g., by Giles and Johnson 1987 or by Gallois et al. 1988). The connections go in both directions, from situations and norms to initial orientation, and vice versa. Finally, our results indicate direct links between norms and attributions by listeners about speakers' motives, as is already implied by CAT (see Giles et al. 1987). Listeners may make their evaluations after answering this question: Is this person's behavior norm-following, norm-violating, or not affected by norms?

There are clearly many questions still to examine. We do not know, for example, the extent to which the expressed norms we found are modified in actual behavior. Norms, especially those obtained via questionnaires, represent beliefs about socially desirable behavior, and not people's less than ideal responses to real situations. In addition, we have explored only a small subset of the large number of situational variables, group memberships, and conversational types that can interact with norms to influence people in encounters across ethnic and cultural groups. Nonetheless, we belive that this method, in which behavioral norms are explored in some detail for very specific situations, has the potential for greatly increasing our knowledge of normative content, clarity, and range. Such specificity permits the comparison of norms with behavior observed using sociolinguistic methods, as well as comparisons with evaluations of speakers. If we are to negotiate the intricate terrain of interethnic communication and to develop better cross-cultural communication packages, we must come to grips with the connections between social identity, social context, norms, and behavior. Further development of CAT seems to provide a fruitful means to this end.

References

Argyle, M., Furnham, A., and Graham, J. A. 1981. *Social Situations*. Cambridge: Cambridge University Press.

Ball, P. 1983. Stereotypes of Anglo-Saxon and non-Anglo-Saxon accents: Some exploratory Australian studies with the matched guise technique. *Language Sciences*, 5: 163–83.

Ball, P., Giles, H., Byrne, J. L., and Berechree, P. 1984. Situational constraints on the evaluative significance of speech accommodation: Some Australian data. *International Journal of the Sociology of Language*, 46: 115–29.

Beebe, L. M., and Giles, H. 1984. Speech accommodation theories: A discussion in terms of second-language acquisition. *International Journal of the Sociology of Language*, 46: 5–32.

Biddle, B. I., and Thomas, E. J. (eds.). 1966. *Role Theory: Concepts and Research*. New York: Wiley.

Bourhis, R. Y. 1979. Language in ethnic interaction: A social psychological approach. *In* H. Giles and B. St. Jacques (eds.), *Language and Ethnic Relations*, pp. 117–41. Oxford: Pergamon.

Bourhis, R. Y. 1983. Language attitudes and self-reports of French-English language usage in Quebec. *Journal of Multilingual and Multicultural Development*, 4: 163–79.

Bourhis, R. Y. 1985. The sequential nature of language choice in cross-cultural communication. *In* R. L. Street and J. N. Capella (eds.), *Sequence and Pattern in Communicative Behaviour*, pp. 120–41. London: Edward Arnold.

Burgoon, J. 1983. Nonverbal violations of expectations. *In* J. Wiemann and R. P. Harrison (eds.), *Nonverbal Interaction*, pp. 77–112. Beverly Hills, CA: Sage.

Burgoon, J., and Hale, J. L. 1984. The fundamental topic of relational communication. *Communication Monographs*, 54: 19–46.

Burgoon, M., and Miller, G. R. 1985. An expectancy interpretation of language and persuasion. *In* H. Giles and R. N. St. Clair (eds.), *Recent Advances in Language: Communication and Social Psychology*, pp. 199–229. London: Erlbaum.

Callan, V. J., and Gallois, C. 1982. Language attitudes of Italo-Australian and Greek-Australian bilinguals. *International Journal of Psychology*, 17: 345–58.

Callan, V. J., and Gallois, C. 1987. Anglo-Australians' and immigrants' attitudes toward language and accent: a review of experimental and survey research. *International Migration Review*, 11: 48–69.

Callan, V. J., Gallois, C., and Forbes, P. 1983. Evaluative reactions to accented English: Ethnicity, sex role and context. *Journal of Cross-Cultural Psychology*, 14: 407–26.

Clyne, M. 1982. *Multilingual Australia*. Melbourne: River Seine.

Coupland, N., Coupland, J., Giles, H., and Henwood, K. 1988. Accommodating the elderly: Invoking and extending a theory. *Language in Society*, 17: 1–41.

Ekman, P., and Friesen, W. 1975. *Unmasking the Face*. Englewood Cliffs, NJ: Prentice-Hall.

Fishman, J. A. 1971. *Sociolinguistics: An Introduction*. Rowley, MA: Newbury House.

Furnham, A., and Bochner, S. 1986. *Culture Shock: Psychological Reactions to Unfamiliar Environments*. London: Methuen.

Gallois, C., and Callan, V. J. 1981. Personality impressions elicited by accented English speech. *Journal of Cross-Cultural Psychology*, 12: 347–59.

Gallois, C., and Callan, V. J. 1985. Situational influences on perceptions of accented speech. *In* J. P. Forgas (ed.), *Language and Social Situations*, pp. 159–73. New York: Springer-Verlag.

Gallois, C., and Callan, V. J. 1988. Communication accommodation and the prototypical speaker: Predicting evaluations of solidarity and status. *Language and Communication*, 8: 271–83.

Gallois, C., Callan, V. J., and Johnstone, M. 1984. Personality judgments of Australian aborigine and white speakers: Ethnicity, sex, and context. *Journal of Language and Social Psychology*, 3: 39–57.

Gallois, C., Franklyn-Stokes, A., Giles, H., and Coupland, N. 1988. Communication accommodation theory and intercultural encounters: Intergroup and interpersonal considerations. *In* Y. Y. Kim and W. B. Gudykunst (eds.), *Theories in Intercultural Communication (Intercultural Communication Annual,* Vol. 12), pp. 157–85. Newbury Park, CA: Sage.

Gallos, C., Pittam, J., and Callan, V. J. 1989. Encoders and decoders: Non-verbal behaviour, bias, and decoding emotional messages. Manuscript submitted for publication.

Genesee, F., and Bourhis, R. Y. 1982. The social psychological significance of code switching in cross-cultural communication. *Journal of Language and Social Psychology*, 1: 1–27.

Genesee, F., and Bourhis, R. Y. 1988. Evaluative reactions to language choice strategies: The role of sociostructural factors. *Language and Communication*, 8: 229–50.

Gibbons, J. 1987. *Code Mixing and Code Choice: A Hong Kong Case Study*. Clevedon: Multilingual Matters.

Giles, H. 1977. Social psychology and applied linguistics: Towards an integrative approach. *ITL Review of Applied Linguistics*, 35: 27–42.

Giles, H., Bourhis, R. Y., and Taylor, D. M. 1977. Towards a theory of language in ethnic relations. *In* H. Giles (ed.), *Language, Ethnicity and Intergroup Relations*, pp. 307–48. London: Academic Press.

Giles, H., and Johnson, P. 1981. The role of language in ethnic group relations. *In* J. C. Turner and H. Giles (eds.), *Intergroup Behaviour*, pp. 199–243. Oxford: Basil Blackwell.

Giles, H., and Johnson, P. 1986. Perceived threat, ethnic commitment, and interethnic language behaviour. *In* Y. Y. Kim (ed.), *Interethnic Communication: Current Research*, pp. 91–116. Newbury Park, CA: Sage.

Giles, H., and Johnson, P. 1987. Ethnolinguistic identity theory: A social psychological approach to language maintenance. *International Journal of the Sociology of Language*, 68: 69–99.

Giles, H., Mulac, A., Bradac, J. J., and Johnson, P. 1987. Speech accommodation theory: The first decade and beyond. *In* M. McLaughlin (ed.), *Communication Yearbook 10*, pp. 13–48. Beverly Hills, CA: Sage.

Giles, H., Rosenthal, D., and Young, I. 1985. Perceived ethnolinguistic vitality: The Anglo- and Greek-Australian setting. *Journal of Multilingual and Multicultural Development*, 6: 256–69.

Gumperz, J., and Hymes, D. (eds.). 1972. *Directions in Sociolinguistics: The Ethnography of Communication*. New York: Holt, Rinehart and Winston.

Hall, E. T. 1959. *The Silent Language*. New York: Doubleday.

Horvath, B. 1985. *Variation in Australian English: The Sociolects of Sydney*. Cambridge: Cambridge University Press.

Jones, E. E., and Davis, K. E. 1965. From acts to dispositions: The attribution process in person perception. *In* L. Berkowitz (ed.), *Advances in Experimental Social Psychology*, Vol. 2, pp. 219–66. New York: Academic Press.

Joos, M. 1961. *The Five Clocks*. New York: Harcourt Brace Jovanovich.

Kim, Y. Y., and Gudykunst, W. B. (eds.). 1988. *Theories in Intercultural Communication (Intercultural Communication Annual,* Vol. 12). Newbury Park, CA: Sage.

Kramarae, C. 1981. *Women and Men Speaking*. London: Newbury House.

268   C. Gallois and V. J. Callan

Labov, W. 1972. *Sociolinguistic Patterns*. Philadelphia: University of Pennsylvania Press.

Lambert, W. E. 1967. A social psychology of bilingualism. *Journal of Social Issues*, 23: 91–109.

Lange, A., and Jakubowski, P. 1976. *Responsible Assertive Behavior: Cognitive/Behavioural Procedures for Trainers*. Champaign, IL: Research Press.

Leah, J., Law, H. G., and Snyder, C. W. 1979. The structure of self reported difficulty in assertiveness: An application of three mode common-factor analysis. *Multivariate Behavioral Research*, 4: 443–62.

Lewis, P. N., and Gallois, C. 1984. Disagreements, refusals, or negative feelings: Perception of negatively assertive messages from friends and strangers. *Behavior Therapy*, 15: 353–68.

McKirnan, D. J., and Hamayan, E. V. 1984a. Speech norms and perceptions of ethno-linguistic group differences: Toward a conceptual and research framework. *European Journal of Social Psychology*, 14: 151–68.

McKirnan, D. J., and Hamayan, E. V. 1984b. Speech norms and attitudes toward outgroup members: A test of a model in a bicultural context. *Journal of Language and Social Psychology*, 3: 21–38.

Mehrabian, A. 1972. *Nonverbal Communication*. Chicago: Aldine-Atherton.

Milroy, L. 1980. *Language and Social Networks*. Oxford: Basil Blackwell.

Milroy, L. 1987. *Observing and Analysing Natural Language: A Critical Account of Sociolinguistic Method*. Oxford: Basil Blackwell.

Noller, P., and Gallois, C. 1986. Sending emotional messages in marriage: Nonverbal behaviour, sex and communication clarity. *British Journal of Social Psychology*, 25: 287–97.

Platt, J., and Weber, H. 1984. Speech convergence miscarried: An investigation into inappropriate accommodation strategies. *International Journal of the Sociology of Language*, 46: 131–46.

Rubin, J. 1968. *National Bilingualism in Paraguay*. The Hague: Mouton.

Scherer, K. R. 1986. Affect expression: A review and model for future research. *Psychological Bulletin*, 99: 143–65.

Seggie, I. 1983. Attribution of guilt as a function of ethnic accent and type of crime. *Journal of Multilingual and Multicultural Development*, 4: 197–206.

Seggie, J. L., Fulmizi, C., and Stewart, J. 1982. Evaluatioins of personality traits and employment suitability based on various Australian accents. *Australian Journal of Psychology*, 34: 345–57.

Shockey, L. 1984. All in a flap: Long-term accommodation in phonology. *International Journal of the Sociology of* Language, 46: 87–95.

Smith, P. 1985. *Language, the Sexes, and Society*. Oxford: Basil Blackwell.

Stieblich, C. 1986. Interpersonal accommodatoin in a bilingual setting. *Language Problems and Language Planning*, 10: 158–76.

Street, R. L., Brady, R. M., and Putman, W. B. 1983. The influence of speech rate stereotypes and rate similarity on listeners' evaluations of speakers. *Journal of Language and Social Psychology*, 2: 37–56.

Tajfel, H., and Turner, J. C. 1979. An integrative theory of intergroup conflict. *In* W. G. Austin and S. Worchel (eds.), *The Social Psychology of Intergroup Relations*, pp. 33–47. Monterey, CA: Brooks/Cole.

Taylor, D. M., and Royer, L. 1980. Group processes affecting anticipated language choice in intergroup relations. *In* H. Giles, W. P. Robinson, and P. M. Smith (eds.), *Language: Social Psychological Perspectives*, pp. 185–92. Oxford: Pergamon.

Thakerar, J., Giles, H., and Cheshire, J. 1982. Psychological and linguistic parameters of speech accommodation theory. *In* C. Fraser and K. R. Scherer (eds.), *Advances in the Social Psychology of Language*, pp. 205–56. Cambridge: Cambridge University Press.

Trudgill, P. 1986. *Dialects in Contact*. Oxford: Basil Blackwell.

Turner, J. 1986. *Rediscovering the Social Group: A Self-Categorization Theory*. Oxford: Basil Blackwell.

van Dijk, T. 1988. *Communicating Racism*. Newbury Park, CA: Sage.

Watson, D. 1982. The actor and observer: How are their perceptions of causality different?. *Psychological Bulletin*, 92: 682–700.

Wilson, L. K., and Gallois, C. 1985. Perceptions of assertive behavior: Sex combination, role appropriateness, and message type. *Sex Roles*, 12: 125–41.

9. Organizational communication and accommodation: Toward some conceptual and empirical links

RICHARD Y. BOURHIS

9.1. Introduction

Since its articulation in the early 1970s, speech accommodation theory (SAT) has evolved into a complex and rich conceptual framework that helps account for a broad range of communicative behaviors in both laboratory and field settings (Giles et al. 1987). During the 1980s, the accommodation framework was successfully adapted as a conceptual tool to better understand communicative processes in an ever-increasing range of applied settings, as indeed this volume attests. One aim of this chapter is to extend the accommodation framework to yet another applied setting: the rapidly developing field of organizational communication (Goldhaber and Barnett 1988; Jablin et al. 1987). Given the expanding scope of both the accommodation and organizational communication literatures, this *first* attempt to link these two fields of research is neces-

The author would like to thank the following individuals for their very helpful comments on earlier drafts of this chapter: Richard Clément, Nik Coupland, Justine Coupland, Howard Giles, Uus Knops, Gary Kreps, Miguel Strubell, Stella Ting-Toomey, Richard Tucker, Janina Walker, and Margaret Weiser.

The author wishes to thank the Canadian Commissioner of Official Languages, D'Iberville Fortier, for providing the grant support and human resources needed to conduct the New Brunswick Linguistic Work Environment (LWE) Survey. The author wishes to thank Maurice Heroux and Pierre Nadon of the Office of the Commissioner of Official Languages, who provided support for the LWE projects since 1985. Special thanks are due to Jan Carbon and Jean Guy Pattenaude, whose experience with bilingual work environments in the Canadian Federal Administration greatly contributed to the development of the LWE Survey. Jan Carbon and Jean Guy Pattenaude are also thanked for their enthusiasm and patience in administering the LWE Survey Project. The author is also grateful to the deputy ministers and New Brunswick department heads who approved and supported the project within the Federal Administration. A thank-you is also due to all the New Brunswick civil servants who completed the LWE Survey and without whom this research would not have been possible.

Comments concerning this chapter are much appreciated and should be addressed to Richard Y. Bourhis, Département de Psychologie, Université du Québec à Montréal, P.O. Box 8888, Station A, Montréal, Québec, Canada, H3C 3P8.

sarily quite focused and selective. It is hoped that linking the accom-modaton with the organizational communication field will provide the needed impetus for researchers in both these fields to join forces in ad-dressing ever more pressing communication problems within organiza-tions throughout the world.

The first section of this chapter provides a brief overview of the ac-commodation framework especially in relation to language switching in bilingual environments such as those found in Canada. The reason for this focus on accommodation research conducted in the Canadian set-ting is twofold. First, the earliest empirical studies supporting key fea-tures of the accommodation framework were conducted in the bilingual setting of Montreal, where instances of linguistic convergence and main-tenance could be unequivocally monitored through clear-cut French–English language switches (e.g., Giles, Taylor, and Bourhis 1973). Sec-ond, the field settings chosen in this chapter to explore the linkage be-tween the accommodation framework and organizational communica-tion are also Canadian and bilingual, namely, the language of work in the Federal Civil Administration of Canada. Thus, historical and meth-odological reasons account for our choice of bilingual work environ-ments as the first testing ground for exploring possible SAT contribu-tions to the organizational communication literature.

In the second section of the chapter, we briefly identity some of the areas of the organizational communication field that could be enriched with features of the accommodation framework. Although this is not the aim of the chapter, a thorough conceptual integration of the accommo-dation framework in the organizational communication field would most likely warrant a review article of its own. A more modest aim of this chapter is to apply features of the accommodation framework to selected issues characteristic of the organizational communication literature.

The third section of the chapter presents selected features of a recent empirical study dealing with the language of work in the Canadian Fed-eral Administration (Bourhis 1989, in press). Key aspects of the accom-modation framework and of the organizational communication litera-ture were used to conceptualize and design this study. This survey study of French-English language use in the Canadian Federal Administration was conducted among more than 2,400 bilingual Francophone and An-glophone civil servants posted in the Province of New Brunswick. As in the earliest empirical tests of the accommodation framework, it is per-haps in the ethnically and politically volatile area of bilingual language use in Canada that one can best explore the validity of combining the accommodation and organizational communication fields for studying communication problems in work environments.

It is noteworthy that in the predominantly U.S.-based organizational communication literature, little mention is made of bilingual issues in the workplace, perhaps reflecting the hegemonic position of the English language and of white unilingual males in North American business and civil administrations. Thus, in its own right, the discussion of bilingual issues in the workplace presented in this chapter may contribute to the development of an organizational communication field that is more sensitive to issues related to multilingualism and multiculturalism in the work world (see Banks 1987; Coleman 1985; Triandis and Albert 1987).

9.2. Aspects of speech accommodation theory

First developed in the United Kingdom as a model of interpersonnal communication (Giles 1973), key features of SAT were soon found relevant for cross-cultural communication in multilingual countries such as Canada. Indeed, Giles, Taylor, and Bourhis (1973) obtained some of the earliest empirical support for the SAT framework in a cross-cultural study conducted in the bilingual city of Montreal. In this study, it was found that bilingual Anglophone students perceived Francophone bilinguals more favorably when the latter converged to English than when they maintained French. Furthermore, the Anglophone students were more likely to switch to French with their Francophone interlocutor if the latter had previously converged to English than if he had maintained French in his communication. Since both the Anglophone and Francophone interlocutors communicated in each other's weaker language, this study showed that mutual language convergence could be used as a strategy to promote interpersonal liking and ethnic harmony even at the possible cost of communicative effectiveness. This study was important since it supported the basic SAT notion that speakers often adapt or "accommodate" their speech toward that of their interlocutors through the strategy of speech convergence. The encoding of this strategy was shown to reflect speakers' conscious or unconscious need for social integration with their interlocutor and was explained in terms of social psychological notions such as similarity-attraction and social exchange theory (Giles and Powesland 1975).

The SAT framework also proposed that speakers may wish to maintain or diverge linguistically from their interlocutors either because they dislike their interlocutors as individuals or because speakers as group members wish to differentiate themselves from outgroup interlocutors (Bourhis and Giles 1977). Using key notions from Tajfel's (1978) social identity theory, speech maintenance and speech divergence were conceptualized as group distinctiveness strategies reflecting speakers' need to maintain or assert their positive group identity vis-à-vis outgroup speakers (Giles, Bourhis, and Taylor 1977). The clearest empirical evidence for the strategies of divergence and maintenance emerged in cases of language switches occurring within cross-cultural encounters in multilingual settings. Empirical evidence for language divergence was obtained in Belgium with trilingual Flemish students communicating with a Francophone interlocutor (Bourhis et al. 1979), and evidence for language maintenance was obtained in cross-cultural encounters between Francophones and Anglophones in Montreal (Bourhis 1983, 1984a). The Montreal field studies showed that overall, 30 percent of the Anglophone pedestrians sampled in the studies maintained English in their responses to a plea for directions voiced in French by a Francophone interlocutor (Bourhis 1984a). These language maintenance responses were obtained even though the Anglophone respondents had sufficient linguistic skills to utter a few words of French in their replies to the Francophone interlocutor. Given the anonymity of these casual encounters, indications were that English language maintenance was indeed being used by Anglophones as a dissociative response aimed against the Francophone speaker simply because the Francophone was categorized as an outgroup speaker. The traditionally high status and power position of the Anglophone minority within the Francophone majority setting of Montreal was also invoked to help explain English maintenance among Anglophone pedestrians, who may also have felt threatened by recent Quebec Government efforts to increase the status of French relative to English through language legislation (Bourhis 1984b). In contrast, the studies showed that only 3 percent of Francophone pedestrians maintained French when providing directions to the English-speaking interlocutor and that 97 percent accommodated to the interlocutor by converging to English. These results were in line with studies showing that speakers who perceive themselves as subordinate group members often tend to converge linguistically to the speech style of speakers they categorize as dominant group members (Bourhis 1979; 1984a; Giles et al. 1977).

In the 1980s, communicative strategies such as convergence, maintenance, and divergence were documented within the SAT framework in numerous cultural and applied settings across a broad range of channels, including speech style, verbal, vocal, and nonverbal communication (this volume; Coupland and Giles 1988; Giles et al. 1987). The accommodation framework has also been reformulated and expanded to incorporate sociolinguistic notions such as discourse management strategies pertinent to the content and relational aspects of conversations (Coupland et al. 1988). As such, these developments should be pertinent to many applied settings, including the field of organizational communication, which is the topic of concern in the next section.

9.3. Organizational communication and accommodation

"Organizations cannot function without one vital component: communication. With the rapid expansion of corporations and technology, the quickly evolving field of organizational communication has undergone enormous, unprecedented growth . . . and change" (Jablin et al. 1987: 7).

Interest in the area of organizational communication has grown greatly in the last decade, as is evident from the numbers and breadth of research articles recently published in this field (Goldhaber and Barnett 1988; Jablin et al. 1987). It is not possible in these few pages to do justice to this expanding field. Thus, only key themes in this research area will be discussed as they relate to the accommodation framework and to the empirical concerns developed in this chapter.

A useful definition of organizations is provided by Kreps (1986: 5), who states that organizations are groupings of people who "develop ritualized patterns of interaction in an attempt to coordinate their activities and efforts in the ongoing accomplishment of personal and group goals." Usually, people in organizations join their efforts to achieve individual or collective goals, which may be financial, affiliative, educational, productive, or cultural. Thus organizations to which individuals can belong range from business firms to government departments, academic institutions, unions, fraternities, political parties, and social and cultural organizations. The preceding definitions also implies that organizing is a repetitive activity, since groups of persons never totally fulfill all their goals and constantly set new ones.

An important premise of the organizational communication literature is that *communication* is the social force that enables individuals to work cooperatively to achieve mutually recognized goals (Kreps 1986). Thanks to the process of communication, people can establish functional interpersonal relationships that allow them to work together toward the attainment of organizational goals. Indeed, Weick (1987: 97–8) succinctly states the key role of communication in organizations and in the process defines much of what organizational communication is about:

> Interpersonal communication is the essence of organization because it creates structures that then affect what else gets said and done and by whom. Structures form when communication uncovers shared occupational specialties, shared social characteristics, or shared values that people want to preserve and expand. The structures themselves create additional resources for communication such as hierarchical levels, common tasks, exchangeable commodities, and negotiable dependencies. These additional resources constrain subsequent contacts and define more precisely the legitimate topics of further communication.

As in the case of accommodation theory, it is noteworthy that organizational communication also assigns a central role to interpersonal communications in its field. Thus it seems pertinent to review briefly some key components of organizational communication and to note how the accommodation framework can be related to these basic features of the field.

Basic elements and themes of organizational communication

As in the other fields of communication, the basic components of organizational communication include the message, the channel, the sender-receiver, encoding-decoding, meaning, feedback, and communication effects. Whereas the "message" usually refers to the verbal, rhetorical, vocal, and nonverbal cues that are conveyed by communicators in organizational settings, the "channel" is the medium in which the message travels, such as the visual, auditory, or written channel. The "sender" is the source or individual who emits the message, and the "receiver" is the target or person who receives it. "Encoding" and "decoding" refer to the processes of creating and interpreting messages, thus allowing individuals to formulate meaning from messages. "Feedback" is a message sent in response to the initial message and facilitates the interpretation of messages between senders and receivers. The outcome or result of the message exchange process is commonly known as the "communication effects." It is because communication effects can have such dramatic positive or negative impacts on key aspects of organizational life such as job satisfaction, job productivity, and the very survival of organizations that the field of organizational communication has become so important in the last two decades.

In the organizational communication literature, much research has been conducted on "internal communications," which refer to the interpersonal and small group communications that occur between members of the organization within the work units, administrative sections, and departments of their organization (Kreps 1986). Internal communication also includes communications between superiors and subordinates, as well as those between colleagues and associates of the same organization. "External communication," which is less well researched, refers to the communications that an organization and its members have across its boundaries with the environment, such as with their competitors, suppliers, clients, government agencies, the public, and so on.

Internal organizational communications have both formal and informal channels. Formally prescribed channels of communication determine who speaks to whom, when, and through what channels in an organization. Formal channels are dictated by the officially planned structure of the organization, which includes power and status hierarchies, as well as the specific responsibilities, job positions, and job definitions of individual members of the organization. Formal channels of communication include downward, upward, and horizontal communication message flow, each serving different functions (Kreps 1986).

Downward communication flows from upper management to lower levels in the organization and is meant to be used as a tool for directing the performance of subordinates in accomplishing their task. However, downward communication is often contradictory and unclear, and may lead to role conflict and low morale among employees. Downward communication is sometimes used by superiors to assert their status and power differentials over their subordinates (e.g., use of jargon, divergence), resulting in employee resentment of management and the organization. Upward communication flows from lower-level employees to upper-level management personnel in the organization. Although channels for upward communication are often underdeveloped, they serve a crucial function, since individuals at the lowest level of the hierarchy are often the most knowledgeable contributors to managerial decision making. However, the risks of retribution involved in upward communication of unfavorable information can result in employees communicating only positive messages to their superior (the "mum" effect), thus contributing to the isolation of executives (Dansereau and Markham 1987). Horizontal communication flows among organizational members at the same hierarchical level. It can facilitate task organization and promote information sharing and social support among peers. It may also contribute to conflict management in organizations (Kreps 1986).

Although much research effort has been devoted to problems of upward and downward communication, this area could gain from the addition of the accommodation framework as a conceptual tool for analyzing communication breakdown in organizations (see Coupland, Giles, and Wiemann in press). Indeed, the pertinence of the accommodation framework to formal communications in organizations seems implicit in Kreps's (1986: 202) observation that the key to effective formal message flow in organizations, whether it be downward, upward, or horizontal, "is the development of meaningful interpersonal relationships among organizational members. . . . Only through the development of effective relationships can organization members develop trust in one another, communicate meaningfully with one another, and elicit cooperation." The accommodation framework is a theory that focuses on the interpersonal needs of communicators as they relate to each other. As such, this approach would seem ideally suited to contribute to this field of organizational communicatioin.

In contrast to formal channels, informal channels of communication are not planned and do not usually follow the formal structures of organizations. Informal networks emerge out of natural social interactions among organization members that are usually task related but may also be based on interpersonal attraction and shared interests reflecting common cultural, linguistic, age, or sex-based group memberships. Given the limitations of the information provided through formal channels of communication in complex organizations, informal channels allow members to know more about who is doing what in their organization, as well as to gain insights about projected changes in the organizations. The "grapevine" allows members to learn more about how their organization really works and can help members plan how to adapt better to their organization. Restricted information flow can increase ambiguity and uncertainty about the organization such that reliance on information transmitted through the grapevine increases. Even though attention is often paid to the deviant aspects of the grapevine (e.g., gossip, false rumors), this informal channel of communication usually transmits quite accurate information that travels quickly through the organization. Kreps (1986) concludes that formal and informal communication channels serve complementary roles and that managers have an interest in coordinating these channels rather than favoring the formal over the informal channel. The application of the accommodation framework to research on informal communication in organizations could be fruitful given that both fields consider interpersonal communication processes as central to their concerns.

Basic theories of organizational communication

A number of important communication theories have been articulated to guide the research and analytic efforts of organizational communication researchers. Recently, Krone, Jablin, and Putnam (1987) adapted Fisher's (1978) four human communication perspectives to theorizing in organizational communication. They proposed that most middle-range theories and models of organizational communication can be situated within one or more of these perspectives. These four theoretical perspectives are (1) the mechanistic perspective, (2) the systems-interaction perspective, (3) the psychological perspective, and (4) the interpretive-symbolic perspective. Krone et al. state that these theoretical perspectives are complementary, as each serves to elucidate different features of communicative processes in organizations. As regards research strategy, Krone et al. propose that the field of organizational communication will advance conceptually and empirically to the degree that researchers make the effort to situate their own research approaches properly within one or more of the four perspectives that characterize much of the current organizational communication literature.

A brief account of these four theoretical perspectives is now given to situate the possible contribution of SAT within aspects of each of them. It seems worthwhile to attempt to situate the accommodation framework within these theoretical perspectives, since SAT is not represented as a communication theory in the Krone et al. review or in any of the chapters of the two most recently published *Handbooks of Organizational Communication* available today (Goldhaber and Barnett 1988; Jablin et al. 1987). It is hoped that this brief overview is sufficient to suggest at least some of the potential contributions of the accommodation framework (Giles et al. 1987) to aspects of the organizational communication field.

The *mechanistic perspective* considers communication as a transmission process in which messages travel across a channel from one point to another in a linear and transitive way within well-established communication structures. This approach ensures that the source convey accurate messages to the receiver. Means are sought to minimize noise and barriers to information transmissioin, which can lower message fidelity and lead to communication breakdowns. Gatekeepers serve as information filters, controlling information flow to receivers.

The mechanistic approach is often used in "network analysis" research, a field that uses communication flow to analyze the social and formal authority networks that develop between individuals in organizations (Monge and Eisenberg 1987). Classic research on the downward transmission of oral and written messages from superiors to subordinates also tends to use the mechanistic approach, since it focuses on message transmission patterns down the organizational hierarchy and seeks to identify the points in the hierarchy where communication breakdowns occur. The mechanistic approach tends to oversimplify communication processes and is somewhat dehumanizing, as it pays little attention to the needs of the sender and receiver and the role of meaning in communication. The accommodation framework could add a complementary dimension to traditional network analysis and downward message transmission research, since much of the focus of the accommodation perspective is on how senders accommodate the form and content of their messages to the actual and perceived needs of their receivers.

The systems-interaction perspective also deals with communicative messages but does so by focusing on how such acts recur in meaningful ways and change gradually through time. Such changes reveal systematic sequential patterns of communicative behaviors whose probability of recurrence can be predicted. In this approach, it is the patterns of sequential messages transmitted through time rather than single messages that are more important and that ultimately reveal, through their redundancy, the structure and function of the communication system under scrutiny.

Studies of superior–subordinate communications have used the systems-interaction approach to study the dominance patterns of manager–subordinate interactions and have linked such findings to shifts in how the job performance of subordinates is attributed through time. Studies of labor–management bargaining have analyzed sequences of communicative behaviors during negotiations to distinguish sequences of tactics that lead to settlement from those that lead to conflict and impasse. Krone et al. (1987) note that a drawback of the research using the systems-interaction approach is that such studies often ignore the meaning and salience of the messages for participants and may thus limit the external validity of some findings.

Although the system-interaction perspective is not at the root of the accommodation framework, it is interesting to note that some SAT studies have used sequential analyses to understand better the dynamic nature of conversations in organizational settings (Bourhis 1985). For instance, in the linguistically tense setting of Montreal, Genesee and Bourhis (1982) demonstrated that language choices made in the first speaker turns of a French–English client–clerk encounter had a dramatic impact on the evaluation of language choices made in subsequent speaker turns of the conversation. Results of this study showed that when both French and English interlocutors showed their mutual "good will" and "respect" through mutual language convergence at the onset of their cross-cultural encounter, subsequent language choices seemed emptied of their divisive ideological content and had little impact on listeners' evaluations. In contrast, when the French and English interlocutors maintained their respective ingroup languages at the onset of their cross-cultural encounter, their subsequent language choices became evaluatively quite costly and were rated in discriminatory intergroup terms. Based on such findings, Bourhis (1985) presented a number of conceptual and empirical proposals that pointed the way to a partial integration of notions from both the system-interaction perspective and the accommodation framework.

The psychological perspective is characterized by a focus on how the information processing capacities of human senders and receivers of messages affect their communications in organizational settings (Kroner et al. 1987). Attention is also paid to the conceptual filters of individuals (e.g., cognitions, motives, and values), who must attend to, process, and structure a chaotic stimulus environment into managable and meaningful messages. For instance, in a job interview setting, this approach would focus on how the interviewer processes and integrates the job applicant's vocal activity, rhetorical communication strategies, and nonverbal communication to assess the applicant's employment suitability. The purposive and instrumental nature of communicative behavior of both receivers and senders of information is also of concern in research using this approach. Unlike the mechanistic approach, issues of encoding-decoding, communication barriers, gatekeeping, and noise are viewed as psychological processes characteristic of human senders and receivers rather than as message transmission processes characteristic of communication channels.

The psychological perspective is a popular conceptual framework in the organizational communication discipline. As Krone et al. (1987) note, studies using this approach have dealt with important organizational communication topics such as superior–subordinate communication, perceptions of leader communication style, distortion in upward communication, communication climate, superior–subordinate semantic-information distance, and the relationship between openness in communication and job satisfaction.

Analysis of how the psychological approach is used to address these organizational topics makes it evident that the accommodation framework is most pertinent to this aspect of the organizational communication literature. This is not surprising given that SAT originated as a social psychologial theory having as a focus the motivational, affective, and cognitive processes guiding individuals' communicative strategies with their interlocutors. Recent SAT developments (Coupland et al. 1988) focusing on how receivers perceive and interpret communicative acts as accommodative, underaccommodative, overaccommodative, or contra-accommodative attest to the concerns of the SAT framework for considering dynamically the production and reception processes of individual communicators. As such, the accommodation framework could serve as an ideal theoretical and empirical complement to many aspects of the organizational communication literature that have been inspired by the psychological perspective. To illustrate, a few tentative suggestions regarding how the SAT framework could contribute to some of the research topics listed earlier are presented here.

The topic of superior–subordinate communication (Dansereau and Markham 1987) is one area of the organizational communication literature that could benefit from the accommodation framework. Jablin (1979: 1202) defined superior–subordinate communication as "those exchanges of information and influence between organizational members, at least one of whom has formal authority to direct and evaluate the activities of other organizational members." In his review of this literature, Jablin notes that one-third to two-thirds of a supervisor's time is spent communicating with subordinates and that face-to-face discussion is the dominant mode of interaction. The majority of superior–subordinate interactions concern job task issues, with conversational topics focused more on impersonal than personal issues. Although superiors are more likely to initiate interactions with subordinates than the converse, superiors tend to be less positive and less satisfied in their interactions with their subordinates than with their bosses. However, evidence suggests that subordinates' job satisfaction is positively related to estimates of amount of communication contact with superiors.

As reviewed in Jablin (1979), research by Webber (1970) attests to the perceptual differences that exist between superiors and subordinates. This research shows that superiors perceive that they communicate more with subordinates than subordinates perceive they do, whereas subordinates feel that they send more messages to their superiors than the latter perceive they receive. The potential for communicaton breakdown is evident, since superiors and subordinates often perceive that the other fails to keep them adequately informed.

These patterns of superior–subordinate communications deal mostly with the quantity rather than the quality of communicative acts. Research using the SAT framework could complement the preceding findings through its focus on the quality of sender–receiver communications. This is implied in the accommodation notion that despite their positions as superiors or subordinates, speakers may, for motivational reasons of their own, choose to accommodate or not accommodate to the communicative needs of their interlocutors (Bourhis 1979; Genesee and Bourhis 1982, 1988).

Attention to the quality of superior–subordinate communication is evident in the research dealing with "open communications" in organizational settings. Openness in communication focuses on the content of messages communicated between superiors and subordinates. Redding (1972: 330) defined openness in message sending as the "candid disclosure of feelings, or 'bad news', and important company facts," and openness in message receiving as "encouraging, or at least permitting, the frank expression of views divergent from one's own; the willingness to listen to 'bad news' or discomforting information" (ibid). Studies reviewed by Jablin (1979) suggest that open communication relationships are characterized by superiors and subordinates who perceive the other interactant as a willing and receptive listener and who refrain from giving responses that might be perceived as providing negative relational or disconfirming feedback. Jablin (1982) has shown that subordinates at the lowest levels of their organizational hierarchies perceive less openness in superior–subordinate communication than do subordinates at the highest level. Studies suggest that employees are more satisfied with their jobs when openness of communication exists between superiors and subordinates than when relationships are closed. Furthermore, openness of communication between superiors and subordinates is seen as an essential element for an effective organizational climate and has been linked to employee job performance.

In SAT terms, one would expect openness of communication between superiors and subordinates to be characterized by accommodative communication strategies, whereas closed communicative relationships would be characterized by underaccommodative and/or contra-accommodative strategies. The openness vs. closedness of communication notions could be complemented and expanded using the newer aspects of the accommodation framework (Coupland et al. 1988). Thus messages characteristic of open vs. closed communications could not only be scrutinized for their discursive contents, but could also be analyzed in terms of their approximation (e.g., speech style convergence and divergence), interpretability (e.g., syntax and complexity modifications), and interpersonal control (e.g., politeness, interruptions, and form of address usage) strategies. Such analyses could also serve to test hypotheses related to both the SAT framework and the notion of openness of communication. The motivational and cognitive bases of open vs. closed communication orientations could also be explored using key psychological features of the accommodation framework such as social exchange, similarity-attraction and uncertainty reduction (Giles et al. 1987).

The perceptual gaps in understanding and information that exist between superiors and subordinates concerning their work environment are known as "semantic information distance." Jablin (1979) considers this notion one of the most robust concept in the organizational communication literature. Large semantic distance between superiors and subordinates has been linked to many organizational problems, such as low morale among subordinates, difficulties in agreeing on basic job duties and demands facing subordinates, communication breakdowns, and reduction of organizational effectiveness. In his review of this expanding literature, Jablin states that future research should pursue the development of valid and reliable techniques to reduce the extensive semantic gap that exists between superiors and subordinates in numerous organizational settings. One way of achieving this goal could be to introduce features of the accommodation framework. Helping superiors and subordinates to be more aware of their respective communicative needs, as demonstrated within the accommodation framework, could be a first step in increasing understanding and information flow between superiors and subordinates in organizational settings.

Many other suggestions regarding how the accommodation framework could contribute to some of the other research topics listed earlier could also be developed. Note that in a future chapter, efforts could also be made to articulate how the SAT framework could be used to develop research issues that have not yet emerged in this area of the organizational communication literature. The main point here is that much theoretical, conceptual, and empirical potential lies in linking key features of accommodation theory within selected areas of the organizational communication literature.

The interpretive-symbolic perspective views organizational communication as behavior that has the capacity to create, maintain, or dissolve the structure of organizations (Daft and Weick 1984). Like the symbolic interactionism tradition, the interpretive-symbolic perspective proposes that given their ability to communicate, individuals are capable of creating and shaping the social and symbolic reality of their organizational settings. This approach stands in sharp contrast to the mechanistic and psychological approaches, which share the premise that the structure and characteristics of organizations can be taken as givens and have properties that determine communication processes within them (i.e., communication as a dependent variable). In the interpretative-symbolic perspective, communication occurring during work-related role taking contributes to the negotiation and creation of shared meaning for words and actions pertinent to organizational life. "Congruence" refers to a consensus of meaning for interpreting organizational events, which in turn contribute to the articulation of an organizational culture that itself shapes consensual meaning in organizations (Smircich and Calas 1987).

Using research methodologies such as case studies, participant observation, and ethnomethodology, organizational communication researchers using this perspective have focused on topics such as communication rules, organizational culture, organizational myths, the management of meaning, and the legitimization of power and politics in organizations. Researchers guided by the interpretative-symbolic tradition usually seek to account for the full richness and complexity of the organizational communication phenomena under study, and propose correspondingly dense and complex theories to account for their findings. Krone et al. (1987) note that the intersubjective nature of the methods used by researchers in this traditioin can make it difficult to draw generalizations from researchers' analyses of case studies.

Although the conceptual origins of the accommodaton framework had little to do with the interpretative-symbolic tradition, recent theoretical extensions of the SAT framework do include concerns about taking better account of the negotiated and intersubjective nature of communicative behavior. Indeed, in their recent article, Coupland et al. (1988) seek to integrate conceptually within the accommodation framework key notions from discourse analysis, role taking, and constructivist research traditions. This integration is most evident in Coupland et al.'s discussions of "discourse management strategies" and "interpersonal control strategies." Thus, as with many other middle-range theories presented in the review by Krone et al. (1987), we find that even though the accommodation framework could paint a basically psychological picture of organizational communication, it is an evolving communication theory that borrows from complementary perspectives and, as such, could blend well with interpretive-symbolic and systems-interaction traditions.

Each of the four communication perspectives just presented contributes in its own way to a better understanding of communication issues in organizations. As Krone et al. (1987) point out, it is the responsibility of researchers to decide which combination of perspectives is most apt to address effectively the organizational communication issues they wish to explore. These authors state that it is also the researcher's task to operationalize and execute studies in ways that befit the underlying premises of the communication perspective they have adopted. One can add that this goal can be reached only if researchers also correctly identify which communication perspectives lies at the root of the middle-range theories they are using to guide their research efforts in the field. Our analysis of accommodation theory as a potentially new conceptual framework for addressing organizational communication issues was such an exercise in matching middle-range theory to existing fundamental communication perspectives. With this task tentatively accomplished, the path is clear to test *empirically* the applicability of the SAT framework to concrete sets of organizational communication problems and issues. Selected findings from the first such study are presented in the fourth section of this chapter.

9.4. Organizational communication in bilingual settings: An empirical study

Despite increasing interest in problems of cross-cultural communication within and between organizations (Banks 1987; Gudykunst, Stewart, and Ting-Toomey 1985; Triandis and Albert 1987), much of the organizational communication research has been conducted in monolingual environments where the question of bilingual language use was not an issue. However, given the global nature of much of today's business activity, bilingual work environments are becoming a fact of life for a growing number of individuals working in organizations throughout the world. Economic trade alliances between nation-states such as those making up the European Community (EC) have brought to the fore the issue of bilingual use at work both in business organizations and in important sectors of government administrations dealing with trade, defense, and diplomacy. The recent EC push to liberalize trade relations further by 1992 through the free flow of goods and services across the national boundaries of the EC will quite likely increase the pressure on individuals and institutions to work bilingually. Although not without its problems (Hamers and Blanc 1989), bilingualism can be seen as linguistic capital (Bourdieu 1982) imbued with considerable value for both individuals and institutions in multilingual settings. It seems clear that the issue of bilingualism in the workplace is destined to emerge as an important topic of concern in the field of organizational communication in the 1990s.

Canada is an example of a nation that has gained much experience with official bilingualism as a language policy within its organizational structure. In 1969 the Canadian Federal Government passed the Official Languages Act, which declared both French and English as equal-status official languages of Canada. The act was adopted by the Federal Government as a partial response to the rise of the Québécois Francophone independence movement (Coleman 1984). This bilingualism policy was promulgated to demonstrate that being Francophone was possible not only within the Francophone majority Province of Quebec but also throughout Anglo-Canada, thanks to federally sponsored bilingual services introduced since passage of the act (Bourhis 1984b).

One organizational goal of the policy was to create work environments within the Federal Administration that would allow Francophone civil servants to envisage the possibility of a successful career conducted not solely in English, as in the past, but also through the use of French (Canada 1988). This official policy sought to enshrine the notion that bilingual rather than unilingual usage was favored as the form of communication for civil servants working in relevant sectors of the Canadian Federal Administration. However, after years of implementation a lack of French language use has prevailed despite the government's relative success in increasing the proportion of Francophones employed at different levels of the Federal Administration (Canada 1988; Mackay 1983). Furthermore, the implementation of extensive French language training programs for Anglophone public servants did not result in greater use of French in the administration, as originally anticipated by policy makers (Bibeau et al. 1976). Thus, despite the implementation of costly organizational measures, the use and status of French as a language of work has remained far below targeted goals among both Anglophone and Francophone civil servants working in the Canadian Federal Administration.

To explore some of these organizational communication problems, a recent study using the accommodation framework was conducted within the Canadian Federal Administration (Bourhis 1989, in press). The study sought to identify key factors likely to account for French and English language use among bilingual civil servants working in the Federal Administration. From an organizational communication perspective this issue remains important, since language choices made by Anglophone and Francophone civil servants can have a substantial impact on work related-matters such as the maintenance of effective interpersonal communication, job satisfaction, the smooth flow of cross-cultural encounters, and pride in belonging to one of Canada's official language groups.

Since the results of this study are presented elsewhere (Bourhis in press), only selected features of the investigation will be discussed here. The main goal of this presentation is to demonstrate that accommodation theory (SAT, Giles et al. 1987) is a useful framework for the study of organizational communication problems, and that its use in combination with existing organizational communication concepts can yield new insights into problems of communication in the work setting.

Ethnicity and language use

The LWE survey was conducted among bilingual Francophone and Anglophone civil servants working in the Federal Administration located in the Province of New Brunswick. As elsewhere in Anglo-Canada, the Francophone minority of New Brunswick has long occupied an economically inferior position relative to the dominant Anglophone majority (Breton, Reitz, and Valentine 1980). The New Brunswick government's adoption of the Official Languages Act of 1969, declaring English and French as having equal status, was not sufficient to alter the balance of forces that remain in favor of English as the language of social and economic advancement in the province (New Brunswick 1982). Demographically, Francophones (216,000) make up 34 percent of the New Brunswick population, whereas 411,000 mother-tongue Anglophones constitute the majority (65 percent) (New Brunswick 1982). Whereas the majority of Anglophones in the province are unilingual English speakers (more than 94 percent), slightly less than half of the Francophone population is unilingual (46 percent), and the others are bilingual (54 percent).

The structurally weak vitality position of the Francophone minority in New Brunswick helps account for the language patterns favoring English rather than French usage in communications between Francophones and Anglophones. Studies with Francophone students in New Brunswick indicate that adolescents are aware not only of the relatively weak status, power, and demographic position of their group vitality relative to the Anglophone majority, but also that such perceptions can be related to self-reports of language use in favor of English rather than French in everyday life (Allard and Landry 1986). Earlier work also showed that the acquisition of English bilingual skills by Francophone college graduates in New Brunswick was associated with a "subtractive" form of bilingualism (Lambert 1978) in which fluency in English was gained at the cost of cognitive and communicative skills in the French mother tongue (Landry 1982). Thus, Francophone minority group members in New Brunswick who have internalized the perception that their linguistic status is lower than that of the Anglophone majority may not only feel obliged to learn the language of the higher-status majority but may also feel the necessity to accommodate by converging to English when communicating with Anglophone interlocutors.

In contrast, Anglophone majority group members who perceive their own vitality position as being stronger than that of the Francophone minority may see themselves as dominant higher-status group members who need not make the effort to learn French or to accommodate by converging to the language of members of the "low status" Francophone minority. Thus dominant majority group Anglophones may be more inclined to maintain English than to converge to French when conversing with their Francophone coworkers. Hence the study was conceptualized with the general expectation that English rather than French would emerge as the more frequently used language of work among both Anglophone and Francophone civil servants of the New Brunswick Federal Administration.

The linguistic work environment LWE survey used in this study consisted of a number of sections, including respondents' self-reports of French-English language use in written and spoken communications, as well as self-reports of language use with supervisors, colleagues, and subordinates in their work setting. In addition to providing information about their ethnic background, respondents reported their recent test scores of second-language skills. The survey also included the items needed to calculate the LWE of each respondent (for details see Bourhis 1989, in press). Bilingual LWE survey forms were mailed to bilingual civil servants working in fifteen ministries of the New Brunswick Federal Administration and yielded a valid survey return rate of 81 percent. Of the respondents who completed the LWE survey, 1,495 were Francophones (65 percent) and 821 were Anglophones (35 percent). This high proportion of Francophone to Anglophone responses was in line with the actual percentage of bilingual Francophones (64 percent) present in the New Brunswick Federal Administration relative to the percentage of bilingual Anglophones (36 percent).

Self-reports of French-English language use at work, as reported by bilingual Francophone civil servants, clearly showed that Francophones spend more of their time using English (63 percent) than French (37 percent) as their language of work. Anglophone bilinguals, on the other hand, did not experience this diglossic situation, since their mother tongue was also their language of work, and they reported using mostly English (88 percent) rather than French (12 percent) at work. As regards language use in verbal encounters, results showed that whereas bilingual Anglophones tended to maintain English when communicating with Francophone colleagues (76 percent) and subordinates (78 percent), bilingual Francophones were far more accommodating, since they almost always converged to English when speaking to their Anglophone colleagues (90 percent) and subordinates (90 percent). As regards communications with supervisors, results showed that Anglophones reported using mostly English (93 percent) with their superiors, whereas Francophones were as likely to use English (52 percent) as French (48 percent) with their supervisors.

Taken together, these results showed that bilingual Francophone civil servants were more likely to converge to English with Anglophone civil servants than were bilingual Anglophones likely to converge to French with their Francophone counterparts. These New Brunswick results were in line with our expectations (Bourhis in press) and corroborated the results of previous studies of federal civil servants, which showed that Francophones were more likely than Anglophones to adapt to the language of their coworkers (Bibeau et al. 1976). Even in the Quebec work setting, where Francophones are the majority, Gendron Commission studies (Québec 1972: 93) concluded that "in inter-relationships in mixed conversation groups, English-speaking persons conceded much less to French than did French-speaking persons to English." Up to the 1970s, Quebec studies showed that more Francophone business executives accommodated by speaking English with their Anglophone counterparts than did the latter, who tended to maintain English during mixed group meetings with Francophone executives (Taylor, Simard, and Papineau 1978). The patterns of results in favor of English use obtained in both Quebec and New Brunswick may reflect the fact that, in Canada, Francophones are usually more fluent bilinguals than Anglophones.

Language skills and language use

Although much attention has been devoted to theoretical and empirical models of second-language acquisition (Gardner 1985; Hamers and Blanc 1989), it remains true that learning a second language does not guarantee the use of the second language when it comes time to communicate bilingually in cross-cultural encounters (Bourhis 1979). It is thus important to investigate the conditions in which bilinguals are likely to use their second language given the dynamic nature of language choice strategies in cross-cultural communication (Bourhis 1985; Gudykunst 1986). The LWE survey used in the present study offered a unique occasion to investigate this issue in the organizationally complex bilingual work environment of the Canadian Federal Administration.

A major aim of federal government-sponsored second official language (SOL) training programs has been to increase the number of bilingual civil servants so that both the public and government coworkers could enjoy the opportunity to work and be served in the official language of their choice. Anglophone civil servants have been bigger consumers of SOL training programs than Francophone ones, since Anglophones are less likely to be bilingual at entry into the civil service than Francophones. Given the considerable sums spent by the Canadian government on SOL training and bilingual bonuses (Canada 1988), it is important to determine if fluently bilingual civil servants are more likely to use their SOL than less fluently bilingual civil servants.

To address this issue, Anglophone and Francophone self-reports of language use were analyzed in terms of the linguistic competence of the respondents. Anglophone and Francophone respondents were categorized as "weak" or "fluent" in the SOL on the basis of their last government-administered test scores of spoken skills in the SOL (Gale and Slivinski 1988). Whereas 289 Anglophones were categorized as weak in French, 141 were labeled as fluent. Francophones categorized as weak in English numbered 358, and those who were considered fluent numbered 623. Thus these Francophone and Anglophone subgroups were closely matched in terms of their degree of competence in the SOL (weak vs. fluent). Anglophone and Francophone civil servants who were considered "very weak" bilinguals were not included in the analyses. Self-reports of language use from the four groups of respondents were analyzed and yielded the following pattern of results.

Self-reports of SOL use showed that in the case of Anglophones, fluent speakers did use the SOL more frequently at work than did those who only achieved a weak command of it. For instance, results showed that fluently bilingual Anglophones spent more time speaking in French with the public (28 percent) and with other civil servant (25%) than did Anglophone civil servants who were less competent in spoken French (French with the public 15 percent; with other civil servants, 12 percent). In contrast, results showed that less fluent bilingual Francophones had a tendency to spend almost as much time speaking in English with the public (53 percent) and with other civil servant (53 percent) as did more fluent Francophone civil servants (English with the public, 57 percent; with other civil servants, 59 percent).

Results also showed that English usage by Francophones with their Anglophone colleagues and subordinates was so extensive (88 to 91 percent) that English language competence (weak/fluent) did not distinguish Francophone respondents in their degree of convergence with Anglophone coworkers. Francophones also reported being as likely to use English with their supervisor, regardless of whether they were fluent (54 percent) or not (47 percent) in the English language. In contrast, fluently bilingual Anglophones were more likely to converge to French with their Francophone colleagues (54 percent) and subordinates (58 percent) than were less fluently bilingual Anglophones, who were much less likely to converge to French with thier Francophone colleagues (23 percent) and subordinates (23 percent). Likewise, fluently bilingual Anglophones reported being more likely to use French with their supervisors (17 percent) than those who had only a weak command of French (6 percent).

Taken together, these results demonstrate the overwhelming tendency of both fluent and nonfluent Francophones to use their SOL much more frequently than both fluent and nonfluent Anglophone civil servants. However, it is clear that for Anglophone civil servants, greater fluency in the SOL does contribute to greater use of French as the language of work in the New Brunswick Civil Administration. But the gains in French language use among fluently bilingual Anglophones remain modest considering the human and financial costs involved in training

Anglophones to speak French. Motivational factors related to the accommodation framework, along with the dominance of English as the language of work, seem best able to account for the obstinacy of even perfectly bilingual Anglophones to maintain English when conversing with Francophone coworkers (Bourhis in press).

In contrast, Francophone respondents were much more likely to accommodate linguistically with their Anglophone co-workers regardless of their level of achievement in the SOL. For Francophones, greater fluency in English seems to reinforce an already existing reality in favor of English usage as the language of work in the New Brunswick Civil Administration, a reality that all Francophone civil servants must face regardless of their level of skill in the English language. The enduring prestige of English as the language of work and economic advancement in the Canadian Federal Administration was further corroborated in the study, with results that showed that Francophones had a tendency to use English even when conversing with coworkers of their own language group. Indeed, Francophones reported using English some of the time when speaking to their Francophone colleagues (17 percent) and subordinates (21 percent). After devoting so much effort to learning English as their language of work and advancement within the Federal Administration, Francophone bilinguals may find it natural to use English even when conversing with their Francophone coworkers. In contrast, Anglophone respondents reported never using French when conversing with their Anglophone coworkers.

LWE and accommodation

Although the notion of a linguistic work environment (LWE) (Bourhis 1989) is a novel one for both the sociolinguistic and organizational communication literatures, it can be considered as one aspect of what is known as the "social network" of individuals. A social network consists of all the persons an individual comes in contact with on a regular basis in settings such as the home, the community, and the work world (Milroy 1980). In the field of organizational communication, "network analysis" is a research technique in which organization members are asked to identify with whom they have communication contact in the organization and how often they have contact with them (Kreps 1986). Such information allows the mapping of informal communication networks in the organization and leads to the identification of network role players such as opinion leaders, gatekeepers, bridges, and isolates (Monge and Eisenberg 1987).

The LWE applies aspects of social network notions to analyze organizational communications in bilingual work environments. As articulated by Bourhis (1989), a premise of the LWE is that the ethnic and linguistic backgrounds of individuals participating in organizational networks can have an impact on the language choice strategies adopted by speakers positioned within the organizational hierarchy. For instance, social networks of predominantly Francophone coworkers could contribute to an "organizational climate" (Falcione, Sussman, and Herden 1987) that produces a "French working climate" sufficiently strong to promote French rather than English use as the language of work in specific networks of the organization. One aim of the LWE survey was to explore this possibility in the New Brunswick bilingual work environment.

On a day-to-day-basis at work, individuals come in regular contact with a number of coworkers such as colleagues, subordinates, and supervisors, who constitute the social network of civil servants. The LWE of a civil servant is assessed by taking into consideration the mother tongue (English or French) and linguistic skills (unilingual or bilingual) of each civil servant making up that person's immediate work environment. A feature of the present approach is to obtain these LWE data directly through self-reports from individual respondents who themselves remain most knowledgeable about the ethnic and linguistic backgrounds of the coworkers making up their immediate work environment. In addition to ethnic and linguistic backgrounds, the status and power differentials that exist among supervisors, colleagues, and subordinates (Dansereau and Markham 1987) can be related to patterns of language use between individuals occupying these various role positions in the work setting. For instance, supervisors are often in a stronger position than subordinates to dictate which language should be used to discuss certain topics. In contrast, colleagues may negotiate more freely regarding which language should be used to conduct a particular conversation given their equal status position in the organizational hierarchy.

In the LWE survey, one calculates the intensity of Francophone presence (IFP), which is a ratio score depicting the numerical presence of Francophones relative to the total number of coworkers reported by respondents as making up their LWE [see Bourhis (1989) for details of these calculations]. The IFP can range from 1.0 to 0.0, so that a score of 1.0 indicates that all the individuals listed in a respondent's work environment are Francophone. A score of 0.5 indicates that half of the individuals in the work environment are Francophone and the other half are Anglophone. Finally, a score of 0.0 indicates that no individuals in the work environment are Francophone. An IFP score of .34 indicates that the Francophone presence in a particular LWE matches the 34 percent Francophone demographic presence in the New Brunswick population as a whole. It was proposed that an LWE in which the IFP was high should result in greater French language usage than an LWE in which the IFP was low.

The intensity of bilingualism (IB) is the ratio of coworkers identified by the respondents as being bilingual relative to the total number of coworkers present in the respondent's LWE. Like the IFP score, the IB score can range from 1.0 to 0.0, with a score of 1.0 denoting an environment in which all coworkers are bilingual and a score of 0.0 denoting an environmental made up of unilinguals only. It was expected that LWEs in which the IB was high would be associated with greater French language usage than LWEs in which the IB was low.

Separate LWE scores were calculated for the groups of Francophone ($N = 1,495$) and Anglophone ($N = 821$) respondents who took part in the LWE survey. As expected, the LWE of Francophone and Anglophone civil servants did differ. Francophone respondents reported a greater IFP (.58) and IB (.66) within their LWE than did Anglophone respondents (IFP: .31; IB: .46). Thus, the relatively weak rate of French language use reported by Francophone respondents was obtained despite very favorable IFP and IB scores that not only surpassed federal government goals for Francophone presence in the civil administration (IFP = .30, IB = .30) but also surpassed the proportion of Francophone speakers in New Brunswick (34 percent).

Thanks to the data collected during the LWE survey, additional explanations for the low rate of French language use reported by the two groups of respondents were obtained. Further analysis of LWE results (Bourhis in press) showed that the average Francophone civil servant had a total of 11.9 coworkers, of whom 1.0 (.9) was a supervisor, 8.7 were colleagues, and 2.3 were subordinates. The linguistic background of these coworkers was also quantified. The coworkers of interest listed by Francophones were *unilingual anglophones*, of whom 2.9 were colleagues, 0.7 were subordinates, and 0.3 were supervisors. Thus, the number of Anglophone unilingual coworkers reported by Francophone respondents was 3.9, or 33 percent of the Francophones' total number of coworkers (11.9). Therefore, Francophone civil servants with a LWE made up of a very imposing total IFP of .58 (and total IB of .66) must nevertheless deal with a substantial minority of coworkers who are unilingual Anglophones (33 percent). The pressure to use English with these unilingual Anglophone coworkers, including supervisors, is very great, thus accounting for the high rate of English language use reported by bilingual Francophone civil servants in the New Brunswick Civil Administration.

We can now turn to the LWE of Anglophones to account better for English language maintenance among Anglophone civil servants. Results showed that the average Anglophone civil servant had a total of 11.3 coworkers, of whom 1.0 (.9) was a supervisor, 7.1 were colleagues, and 3.3 were subordinates. However, unlike the situation for Francophone civil servants, Anglophone respondents had coworkers who were predominantly bilingual or unilingual English. Thus, Anglophone civil servants with a LWE made up of a total IFP of .31 (and a total IB of .46) were nevertheless spared the need to interact with *unilingual francophones*, who made up only 3.5 percent of the Anglophones' total coworker environment. Consequently, there would seem to be few occasions when Anglophone civil servants are forced to use French in order to communicate with unilingual Francophone co-workers. Instead, these Anglophone civil servants enjoy an LWE in which 96.5 percent of their coworkers can resort to English as the language of communication in the organizational setting.

These LWE figures help account for both the high rate of English language maintenance found among Anglophone civil servants and the high rate of English language convergence found among Francophone civil servants. It is evident that the presence of substantial numbers of Anglophone unilinguals contributes to the maintenance of English as the language of work in the New Brunswick Federal Administration. These results suggest that unilingualism can be used to force convergence to English from Francophone bilinguals who are concerned with communicative effectiveness in their work setting.

It was expected that LWEs in which the IFP was high would foster greater rates of French language use than LWEs in which the IFP was low. Results addressing this issue were analyzed in terms of both the ethnic group membership of the respondents and four ranges of IFP, which were as follow: (1) IFP: .0–.20; (2) IFP: .21–.48; (3) IFP: .49–.77; (4) IFP: .78–1. The IFP ranges chosen for these analyses were the product of a compromise between the need to use IFPs that were organizationally meaningful within the Federal Administration and the need to use IFP ranges that included respondent cell sizes appropriate for statistical analyses.

Results obtained using such analyses support the notion that for both Francophone and Anglophone respondents, high IFP scores do foster higher percentages of French language usage (reading, writing, speaking) than low IFP scores. For instance, Francophone and Anglophone civil servants taken together reported speaking French more frequently in LWEs with strong IFPs than in LWEs where the IFP was low (i.e., IFP and percentage of French use: IFP .0–.20: 14 percent French use; IFP .21–.48: 28 percent; IFP .49–.77: 44 percent; IFP .78–1: 59 percent). Results showed that higher IFPs also fostered greater use of French in conversations with superiors among both Francophone and Anglophone respondents. However, in absolute terms, Francophones used more French than Anglophones with their supervisors. For instance, whereas it took an IFP of .21–.48 to foster 25 percent French usage among Francophones, it took an IFP environment of over .78 for Anglophones to reach a similar percentage of French usage with their supervisors. Taken together, these pattern clearly supported the notion that high IFP scores in civil servants' immediate work environments did enhance the degree of French use as the language of work.

Figure 1 depicts the degree to which Anglophone and Francophone civil servants make the effort to converge to the first official language (FOL) of their colleagues, depending on the IFP in the work setting. Results show that Anglophone civil servants were more likely to converge to French with their Francophone colleagues in LWEs where the IFP was high than in LWEs where the IFP was low. For instance, whereas Anglophone respondents reported converging to French with their Francophone colleagues only 13 percent of the time in LWEs where the IFP was low (.0–.20), convergence to French with Francophone colleagues increased to 48 percent of the time in LWEs where the IFP was high (.78–1). Thus a strong numerical presence of Francophones within the Anglophones' LWE was related to increased convergence to French with Francophone colleagues.

In contrast, Fig. 1 shows that Francophone convergence to English with Anglophone colleagues was equally high (more than 90 percent) regardless of the IFP scores when the latter were in the ranges of .0 to .77. Thus, Francophone civil servants converged to English with their Anglophone colleagues (90–97 percent English use) regardless of their IFP. This pattern held, except in maximal IFP environments (.78–1), where convergence to English still prevailed but at a slightly lower rate of 81

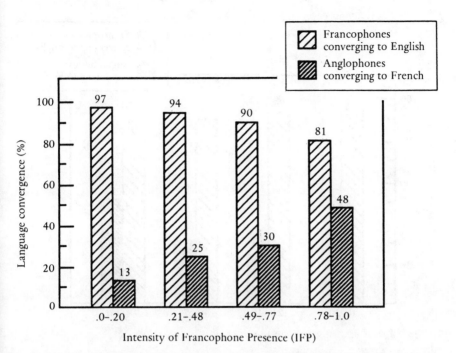

Figure 1. Intensity of Francophone presence (IFP) and convergence (in%) to language of outgroup colleagues.

percent. Regardless of their IFP within the organizational setting, it appears that Francophone civil servants are keen to attend to the communicative needs of their coworkers and do accommodate by converging to English with their Anglophone colleagues.

Although Francophone convergence to English with Anglophone colleagues was uniformly strong regardless of IFP scores, stronger IFPs were related to greater French usage in communications between Francophone colleagues. Survey results showed that whereas Francophones colleagues reported using French 74 percent of the time with each other in LWEs where the IFP was in the .0–.20 range, French usage increased to as much as 91 percent in LWEs where the IFP score was in the .78–1 range.

Figure 2 depicts the degree to which Anglophone and Francophone civil servants converged to the FOL of their subordinates in the work setting. As in the case for colleagues, results show that Anglophone civil servants were more likely to converge to French with their Francophone subordinate in LWEs where the IFP was high than in LWEs where the

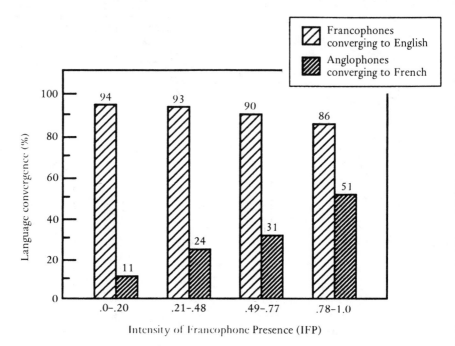

Figure 2. Intensity of Francophone presence (IFP) and convergence (in%) to language of outgroup subordinates.

IFP was low. Figure 2 also shows that Francophone civil servants reported converging to English most of the time (86–94 percent) with their Anglophone subordinates, regardless of the IFP in their LWE.

However, other survey results showed that higher IFPs were related to greater French usage on the part of Francophones with their Francophone subordinates. Results showed that whereas Francophones reported using French 64 percent of the time with Francophone subordinates in LWEs where the IFP was in the .0–.20 range, French usage increased to as much as 88 percent in LWEs where the IFP was in the .78–1 range. Taken together, Francophone and Anglophone patterns of French use with colleagues and subordinates suggest that the "organizational climate" (Falcione et al. 1987) created by a strong Francophone presence (high IFP) in the work setting may foster a "French organizational climate" that would favor greater use of French as the language of work in bilingual organizational settings (McCarrey 1988).

Contrary to expectations, a comparison of the histograms presented in Figs. 1 and 2 suggests that occupational status differentials had little effect on the accommodation strategies of Francophone and Anglophone civil servants. Indeed, the language convergence trends presented in Fig. 2 for communications between the respondents and their subordinates were virtually identical to the convergence patterns obtained for communications between Anglophone and Francophone colleagues (Fig. 1). It was expected that, among colleagues, Francophones and Anglophones would be quite likely to engage in mutual language convergence given their equal status position within the organizational structure. Conversely, it was expected that Francophone and Anglophone respondents would be less likely to converge to the language of their subordinates given the occupational status differentials that exists between such role partners in organizational structures (Dansereau and Markham 1987). Instead, the remarkably similar results in favor of English usage depicted in Figs. 1 and 2 suggest that the high status of English relative to French as the language of work seems to be more important than occupational rank in accounting for the trends.

The proportion of bilinguals (IB scores) making up the LWE of civil servants played a weaker role than IFP scores in affecting patterns of French-English language use in the work setting. Results nevertheless showed that LWEs in which the IB was high did foster greater rates of French language use than LWEs in which the IB was low (Bourhis in press).

9.5. Conclusions

The results of this study demonstrate the important role LWEs can have in determining language use in bilingual work settings. In this case, we have seen that strong IFPs contribute to enhanced French language use at work, especially among Anglophone civil servants communicating with Francophone coworkers. This pattern was not so clear in the case of Francophone civil servants who converged to English with their Anglophone coworkers even in linguistic environments where Francophones were in a clear majority. Without an LWE analysis, Francophone convergence to Anglophones may have been interpreted strictly as an interindividual phenomenon reflecting mainly motivational factors related to speech accommodation processes. However, the LWE survey results dealing with social network variables such as the IFP allowed a more complex analysis that included the role played by English as the dominant language of work in the organizational setting. These analyses attest to the utility of combining the accommodation framework with or-

300   R. Y. Bourhis

ganizational communication concepts to account better for organizational communication problems in the field.

Thanks to this combined perspective, Francophone convergence to Anglophone interlocutors can be seen as a language strategy that not only fosters the impression that Francophones are competent in the English-speaking work environment but also signals that Francophones implicitly acknowledge the high-status position of Anglophone group members in the organizational setting. The fact that Francophones converged to English with Anglophones of all occupational ranks, including subordinates, demonstrates how the status positions of ethnic group members in the intergroup structure can supplant the status achieved by individuals within the organization. Conversely, Anglophone language maintenance in the presence of Francophones of all ranks, including colleagues, can be seen as form of dissociative behavior that can be more easily sustained by dominant ethnic group members than by low-status ones. Taken together these results concur with intergroup studies showing that whereas subordinate low-status group members tend to act in ways that favor high-status, dominant outgroup members (e.g., language convergence), the latter tend to behave in ways that undermine the interests of low-status subordinate group members (e.g., language maintenance) (Bourhis 1984a; Genesee and Bourhis 1988; Sachdev and Bourhis 1985, 1987).

The present conceptualization of how the LWE framework (Bourhis 1989, in press) relates to SAT (Coupland et al. 1988) and to elements of the organizational communication literature (Jablin et al. 1987) remains tentative. Current developments in organizational communication and the social psychology of language should be useful in further developing and refining research and public policy tools such as the LWE survey. More important, the development of the LWE framework can be seen as simply one of the first steps undertaken to link accommodation theory to key elements of the organizational communication literature. This chapter has shown that this conceptual and empirical task has just begun and would seem worth pursuing.

References

Allard, R., and Landry, R. 1986. Subjective ethnolinguistic vitality viewed as a belief system. *Journal of Multilingual and Multicultural Development*, 7: 1–12.
Banks, S. P. 1987. Achieving "Unmarkedness" in organisational discourse: A praxis perspective on ethnolinguistic identity. *Journal of Language and Social Psychology*, 6: 171–90.

Bibeau, G., Mackey, W. F., Edwards, H. P., and Leblanc, R. 1976. *Rapport de l'étude indépendante sur les programmes de formation linguistique de la fonction publique du Canada*, 12 vols. Ottawa: Conseil du Trésor.

Bourdieu, P. 1982. *Ce que parler veut dire. L'économie des échanges linguistiques.* Paris: Fayard.

Bourhis, R. Y. 1979. Language and ethnic interaction: A social psychological approach. *In* H. Giles and B. Saint-Jacques (eds.), *Language and Ethnic Relations*, pp. 117–41. Oxford: Pergamon Press.

Bourhis, R. Y. 1983. Language attitudes and self-reports of French-English language usage in Quebec. *Journal of Multilingual and Multicultural Development*, 4: 163–79.

Bourhis, R. Y. 1984a. Cross-cultural communication in Montreal: Two field studies since Bill 101. *International Journal of the Socioloty of Language*, 46: 33–47.

Bourhis, R. Y. 1984b. Language policies in multilingual settings. *In* R. Y. Bourhis (ed.), *Conflict and Language Planning in Quebec*, pp. 1–28. Clevedon: Multilingual Matters.

Bourhis, R. Y. 1985. The sequential nature of language choice in cross-cultural communication. *In* R. L. Street and J. N. Cappella (eds.), *Sequence and Patterns in Communicative Behaviour*, pp. 120–41. London: Edward Arnold.

Bourhis, R. Y., 1989. Bilingual communication in organizational settings: Aspects of the Canadian Case. *In* S. Ting-Tommey and F. Korzenny (eds.), *International and Intercultural Communication Annual*, 13, pp. 244–64. Newbury Park, CA: Sage.

Bourhis, R. Y. In press. The language of work in the Canadian Federal Administratioin: The Linguistic Work Environment Survey. *International Journal of the Sociology of Language*.

Bourhis, R. Y., and Giles, H. 1977. The language of intergroup distinctiveness. *In* H. Giles (ed.), *Language Ethnicity and Intergroup Relations*, pp. 119–35. London: Academic Press.

Bourhis, R. Y., Giles, H., Leyens, J. P., and Tajfel, H. 1979. Psycholinguistic distinctiveness: Language divergence in Belgium. *In* H. Giles and R. St. Clair (eds.), *Language and Social Psychology*, pp. 158–85. Oxford: Basil Blackwell.

Breton, R., Reitz, J., and Valentine, V. 1980. *Cultural Boundaries and the Cohesion of Canada*. Montreal: Institute for Research on Public Policy.

Canada. 1988. *Commissioner of Official Languages Annual Report, 1987*. Ottawa: Ministry of Supply and Services.

Coleman, H. 1985. Talking shop: An overview of language and work. *International Journal of Sociology of Language*, 51: 105–29.

Coleman, W. 1984. *The Independence Movement in Quebec: 1945–1980*. Toronto: University of Toronto Press.

Coupland, N., Coupland, J., Giles, H., and Henwood, K. 1988. Accommodating the elderly: Invoking and extending a theory. *Language in Society*, 17: 1–41.

Coupland, N., and Giles, H. 1988. Introduction: The communicative context of accommodation. *Language and Communication*, 8: 175–82.

Coupland, N., Giles, H., and Wiemann, J. (eds.). In press. *"Miscommunication" and Problematic Talk*. Newbury Park, CA: Sage.

Daft, R. L., and Weick, K. E. 1984. Toward a model of organization as interpretation systems. *Academy of Management Review*, 9: 284–95.

Dansereau, F., and Markham, S. E. 1987. Superior–subordinate communication. *In* F. Jablin, L. Putnam, K. Roberts, and L. Porter (eds.), *Handbook of Organizational Communication*, pp. 343–88. Beverly Hills, CA: Sage.

Falcione, R., Sussman, L., and Herden, R. 1987. Communication climate in organizations. *In* F. Jablin, L. Putnam, K. Roberts, and L. Porter (eds.), *Handbook of Organizational Communication*, pp. 195–227. Beverly Hills, CA: Sage.

Fisher, B. A. 1978. *Perspectives on Human Communication*. New York: Macmillan.

Gale, C., and Slivinski, L. 1988. I/O psychology in the Canadian Federal Government: The Personnel Psychology Centre of the Public Service Commission. *Canadian Psychology*, 29: 84–93.

Gardner, R. 1985. *Social Psychology and Second Language Learning*. London: Edward Arnold.

Genesee, F., and Bourhis, R. Y. 1982. The social psychological significance of code switching in cross-cultural communication. *Journal of Language and Social Psychology*, 1: 1–27.

Genesee, F., and Bourhis, R. Y. 1988. Evaluative reactions to language choice strategies: The role of sociostructural factors. *Language and Communication*, 8: 229–50.

Giles, H. 1973. Accent mobility: A model and some data. *Anthropological Linguistics*, 15: 87–105.

Giles, H., Bourhis, R. Y., and Taylor, D. M. 1977. Towards a theory of language in ethnic group relations. *In* H. Giles (ed.), *Language, Ethnicity and Intergroup Relations*, pp. 307–48. London: Academic Press.

Giles, H., Mulac, A., Bradac, J., and Johnson, P. 1987. Speech accommodation theory: The first decade and beyond. *In* M. L. McLaughlin (ed.), *Communication Yearbook 10*, pp. 13–48, Beverly Hills, CA: Sage.

Giles, H., and Powesland, P. 1975. *Speech Styles and Social Evaluation*. London: Academic Press.

Giles, H., Taylor, D. M., and Bourhis, R. Y. 1973. Towards a theory of interpersonal accommodation: Some Canadian data. *Language in Society*, 2: 177–92.

Goldhaber, G., and Barnett, G. A. 1988. *Handbook of Organizational Communication*. Norwood, NJ: Ablex.

Gudykunst, W. 1986. Towards a theory of intergroup communication. *In* W. Gudykunst (ed.), *Intergroup Communication*, pp. 152–67. London: Basil Blackwell.

Gudykunst, W., Stewart, L., and Ting-Toomey, S. (eds.). 1985. *Communication, Culture and Organizational Processes*. Newbury Park, CA: Sage.

Hamers, J., and Blanc, M. 1989. *Bilinguality and Bilingualism*. Cambridge: Cambridge Univesity Press.

Jablin, F. 1979. Superior–subordinate communication: The state of the art. *Psychological Bulletin*, 86: 1201–22.

Jablin, F. 1982. Formal structural characteristics of organizations and superior–subordinate communication. *Human Communication Research*, 8: 338–47.

Jablin, F., Putnam, L., Roberts, K., and Porter, L. (eds.). 1987. *Handbook of Organizational Communication*. Beverly Hills, CA: Sage.

Kreps, G. 1986. *Organizational Communication*. New York: Longman.

Krone, K., Jablin, F., and Putnam, L. 1987. Communication theory and organizational communication: Multiple perspective. *In* F. Jablin, L. Putnam, K. Roberts, and L. Porter (eds.), *Handbook of Organizational Communication*, pp. 18–40. Beverly Hills, CA: Sage.

Lambert, W. E. 1978. Some cognitive and sociocultural consequences of being bilingual. *In* J. E. Alatis (ed.), *International Dimensions of Bilingual Education*, pp. 55–69. Washington, DC: Georgetown University Press.

Landry, R. 1982. Le bilinguisme additif chez les francophones minoritaires du Canada. *Revue des sciences de l'éducation*, 8: 223–44.

Mackay, W. F. 1983. U.S. language status policy and the Canadian experience. *In* J. Cobarrubias and J. A. Fishman (eds.), *Progress in Language Planning*, pp. 173–206. New York: Mouton.

McCarrey, M. 1988. Work and personal values of Canadian Anglophones and Francophones: Implications for organizational behaviour. *Canadian Psychology*, 29: 18–29.

Milroy, L. 1980. *Language and Social Network*. Oxford: Basil Blackwell.

Monge, P., and Eisenberg, E. 1987. Emergent communication networks. *In* F. Jablin, L. Putnam, K. Roberts, and L. Porter (eds.), *Handbook of Organizational Communication*, pp. 304–42. Beverly Hills, CA: Sage.

New Brunswick. 1982. *Towards Equality of Official Languages in New Brunswick*. Fredericton: Government of New Brunswick.

Québec. 1972. *La situation de la langue française au Québec: Livre 1, La langue de travail* (Commisson Gendron). Québec: Gouvernement du Québec.

Redding, W. C. 1972. *Communication within the Organization*. New York: Industrial Communication Council.

Sachdev, I., and Bourhis, R. Y. 1985. Social categorisation and power differentials in group relations. *European Journal of Social Psychology*, 15: 415–34.

Sachdev, I., and Bourhis, R. Y. 1987. Status differentials and intergroup behaviour. *European Journal of Social Psychology*, 17: 277–93.

Smircich, L., and Calas, M. 1987. Organizational culture: A critical assessment. *In* F. Jablin, L. Putnam, K. Roberts, and L. Porter (eds.), *Handbook of Organizational Communication*, pp. 228–63. Beverly Hills, CA: Sage.

Tajfel, H. (ed.). 1978. *Differentiation between Social Groups*, pp. 1–98. London: Academic Press.

Taylor, D. M., Simard, L., and Papineau, D. 1978. Perceptions of cultural differences and language use: A field study in a bilingual environment. *Canadian Journal of Behavioural Science*, 10: 181–91.

Triandis, H., and Albert, R. 1987. Cross-cultural perspectives. *In* F. Jablin, L. Putnam, K. Roberts, and L. Porter (eds.), *Handbook of Organizational Communication*, pp. 264–95. Newbury Park, CA: Sage.

Webber, R. A. 1970. Perceptions of interactions between superiors and subordinates. *Human Relations*, 23: 235–48.

Wieck, K. E. 1987. Theorizing about organizational communication. *In* F. Jablin, L. Putnam, K. Roberts, and L. Porter (eds.), *Handbook of Organizational Communication*, pp. 97–122. Newbury Park, CA: Sage.

Index

$42.50 \rightarrow 34.50$

12 Feb, 1992